Friedrich

Gersta

cker, Francis Jordan

How a bride was won

A chase across the pampas

Friedrich
Gersta
̈
cker, Francis Jordan

How a bride was won
A chase across the pampas

ISBN/EAN: 9783741144387

Manufactured in Europe, USA, Canada, Australia, Japa

Cover: Foto ©Andreas Hilbeck / pixelio.de

Manufactured and distributed by brebook publishing software (www.brebook.com)

Friedrich Gerstäcker, Francis Jordan

How a bride was won

HOW A BRIDE WAS WON;

OR,

A CHASE ACROSS THE PAMPAS.

BY

FREDERICK GERSTÄCKER.

TRANSLATED BY FRANCIS JORDAN.

WITH ILLUSTRATIONS BY GASTON FAY.

NEW YORK:
D. APPLETON AND COMPANY,
90, 92 & 94 GRAND STREET.
1869.

CONTENTS.

CHAP.		PAGE
I.	The Camp in the Thicket	5
II.	The Festival at the Hacienda	7
III.	The Messenger of the Penchuenches	14
IV.	The Surprise	22
V.	The Pursuit	28
VI.	The Bivouac	35
VII.	The Flight of the Penchuenches	41
VIII.	The Pass	45
IX.	Pedro's Adventure	51
X.	Don Enrique	56
XI.	Valdivia	62
XII.	Various Plans	67
XIII.	Afloat	78
XIV.	The Revenue-boat	82
XV.	Ashore	90
XVI.	The Cabin on the Maybee	98
XVII.	An Evening with the Cacique	104
XVIII.	The Carousal	118
XIX.	On the Morrow	125
XX.	Toward the Mountains	132
XXI.	The Gum Sands	142
XXII.	Hardships	151
XXIII.	Tchebak	158
XXIV.	Tornado	165
XXV.	Consequences	172
XXVI.	Across the Pampas	178
XXVII.	Across the Limay	183
XXVIII.	Jenkitrus	190
XXIX.	Shackered	202
XXX.	The Purchased Wife	210
XXXI.	The Hunting Excursion	218
XXXII.	The Return	230
XXXIII.	Murder	235
XXXIV.	The Cacique Mankeinw	241
XXXV.	Preparations for the Return to Chili	248
XXXVI.	On the Lagoon	253
XXXVII.	Treachery	259
XXXVIII.	Conclusion	268

HOW A BRIDE WAS WON.

CHAPTER I.

THE CAMP IN THE THICKET.

The sun shed its rays over the Cordilleras, and illuminated, high up in the mountains, a wild and picturesque scene.

In the middle of a large canebrake, extending over the whole slope, and studded with oaks and maple-trees, was encamped a number of dusky warriors around five or six fires, which had been kindled at different places, but had now nearly burned out, and were no longer fed with the dry wood everywhere lying about. The men were evidently preparing to depart at an early hour, and hardly intended to pass another night in this part of the mountains.

So dense was the thicket that it had not even been deemed necessary to secure the horses, which, without saddles and bridles, were feeding on the juicy cane-leaves. The narrow pathway, entering the canebrake, was closed by lassos drawn across it, and none of the animals would have been able to break through the bristling hedge of cane and underwood. On the western side of the clearing, where it gently sloped toward the plain, was an opening among the trees, made by the fall of one of the giants of the forest. Here was offered to the eye a wide prospect, extending to the dim, misty horizon of the Pacific; and it was directly opposite that the chief and cacique of the wild warriors lay stretched out on some guanaco-hides, close to a blazing fire.

Slender, wiry, and still youthful, was the form of this cazique, who was leaning on his left elbow, and gloomily brooding over something that had long engrossed his attention. Despite the rawness of the morning, his head (from which long, straight, and black hair hung down his shoulders), and the upper part of his body, were bare. He wore nothing but a pair of short, close-fitting blue pantaloons, and his feet were encased in *botas* made of raw horse-hide. By his side lay his party-colored poncho, large and heavy silver spurs, and bridle, and lasso, both skilfully made of thin strips of rawhide. The *bolas*, the fatal missile of the Pampas Indians, he wore, like all of them, wound round his body; a long knife was in his belt, and a *hilo* lance, nearly fourteen feet long, containing a formidable iron point, leaned against a tree, close behind him; every thing was ready for immediate use, and within his grasp.

And why were these dusky men encamped here in the neighborhood of the white settlements, and yet so carefully hidden in the almost impenetrable thicket? Where they really bent on mischief? Much blood had already been shed on both sides; and Indians, as well as Chilenos, had tried each other's strength. But as yet nothing indicated that the warriors were intent on attacking the peaceful settlements, for the sun rose higher, and the Indians still delayed their departure.

Thus hour after hour went by, and the casique did not change his place, although, evidently, a prey to extreme impatience. He had already grasped the hilt of his long knife, adorned with silver and ivory, unsheathed it, and passed his time by piercing the yellow leaves on the ground. But he was silent, and his companions chatted with each other only in a whisper. At length a shrill cry resounded in the thicket—a cry such as the gray hawk utters when hovering over a forest—and the casique started up from his reclining position. The cry was repeated a second and a third time; it was one of the scouts, who had been sent out, and was now returning to the camp. Presently there was a noise of rustling branches, and a young warrior, mounted on a neighing horse, stopped in front of the lasso drawn across the inner pathway, and which were now quickly removed in order to admit him.

The next moment the scout galloped into the camp, but not directly toward the casique, who was waiting for him with ill-concealed impatience; for he had to attend to the animal which had carried him. He jumped from the saddle, which he unfastened, tore up a handful of grass, carefully rubbed the wet back of his horse, and, drawing the bridle over its pricked ears, allowed it to trot over to the other horses. It was not until then that he went to the casique, who had risen, but uttered no syllable to accelerate the movements of the scout. Man and beast were of equal importance, and the latter often required better care and attention than the former, especially now that they were on hostile ground. The young man approached his chief. He was tall and slender, and his skin was hardly more bronzed than that of a white man exposed to the rays of a southern sun. The upper part of his body was unclothed, like that of the casique; his legs were covered with tight dark-blue pantaloons; about his thighs was wound a narrow handkerchief, checkered with blue and red stripes, and in his belt was a long knife. His body was encircled with the bolas, which contained two heavy balls covered with leather; but otherwise he was unarmed. Large iron spurs were buckled on his bare feet, and somewhat impeded his gait. All these tribes live principally in the saddle, and are at home only on horseback. On foot they are nearly always awkward and helpless.

"What news do you bring, Allumspat?" said the casique, when the youth stood before him, eyeing him gloomily. "Do you return without having effected your object, and was your foot unable to cross their trail?"

"Their trail is broad enough," replied the young Indian, while a half-defiant, half-disdainful smile was playing round his lips; "a blind man might almost follow them; large numbers of them are in the country, and their rifles are everywhere flashing in the sun."

"And our animals?" said the chief, impatiently.

"A cloud of dust indicates the route by which they are driven northward; and the Araucanians fled toward the east, and relinquished their property. Their cabins are on fire, their fields are devastated, and such of their cattle and horses as have not reached the woods have fallen into the hands of the conquerors."

"And the soldiers?" asked the cazique, frowningly,—"How many are there?"

"Who is able to count them?" was the reply. "They are to be seen on all the roads. A troop stronger than ours, and consisting only of their chiefs, are encamped down yonder in the valley at the hacienda of a Awinca,* where they are amusing themselves with music, dancing, and carousing."

"Down yonder in the valley?"

"You can see the clearing from the rock overhanging the precipice."

"I know the place," exclaimed the cazique, quickly. "The owner of the hacienda always was a friend of the Ponchuenches. It is well; he will help us. You, Allumapu, will return thither."

"Alone and unarmed?"

"The messenger of Jenkitruss, the cazique, is safe," replied the Indian, proudly; "who would dare to attack him? You will demand the restoration of our animals. We are not at war with the whites; we do not take part in their struggles. I came peaceably to this part of the country, and peaceably I intend to leave it. We spared their herds. We have never stretched out our hands for their property, and when the Araucanians asked us to assist them, the chiefs of the Peuchuenches refused to turn their lances against the breasts of the whites. Go; the sun is already high in the heavens; and, before it sets, we must start for our homes."

"And suppose they should refuse?" said the young warrior.

"Refuse?" cried the cazique, angrily. "By the wrath of Pillan! they dare not. In that case you will tell them that Jenkitruss and his men are encamped in the thicket, and will carry off their property by force. Tell them they have hitherto felt only the friendly pressure of his hand, but his lance was sharp, and his bolas never missed their aim."

"And how did they treat at Antuco the messengers who came to them as friends and with humble entreaties?" asked the scout, cautiously. "They will never see their native Pampas again?"

The cazique's eyes shot fire.

"Are you afraid, Allumapu, to convey my message to them?"

The young Indian made no reply, but drew himself up to his full height; his dark eyes beamed, and, turning, he walked over to one of the fresh horses, which he caught by the mane, and led to his saddle and bridle. In a few minutes he was ready to start; but the scout did not intend, as before, to descend to the plain. From a leathern bag, lying amidst

---

* A stranger, or white man.

the baggage, he took two strings of large sky-blue pearls, which he hung round his neck; wound a party-colored woollen ribbon about his forehead, in order to fasten with it his long black hair, and took paint and marked his cheeks and forehead with blue and red stripes; he then wrapped round his shoulders his poncho, which was adorned with yellow, red, and blue arabesques. Seizing his long lance, which was leaning against a tree, apart from the others, he looked after his lasso, and then vaulted gracefully into the saddle, almost without touching his horse's croup.

"Allumapu," cried the grave but not unkind voice of the cazique, who had looked on in silence while the young warrior was making his preparations.

He turned his horse, and stopped in front of the chief to receive his orders.

"Ride," said the cazique, nodding to him, "but—take care of yourself; our hearts are with you."

"Allumapu is not afraid of the huincas."

"I know it," said the cazique, kindly; "but he knows, too, that he need not be afraid of them, for strong arms are close at hand, and keen eyes will watch his steps."

Jenkitruss dismissed him with a wave of his hand, and the scout the next moment galloped across the clearing toward the narrow pathway, behind whose cane-hedges he speedily disappeared.

A cloud covered the face of Jenkitruss the cazique, for the suspicion which his young friend had uttered in reference to the fidelity of the huincas had made a deep impression upon him. In the valley yonder lay the cabins and haciendas of his red brethren in ruins. Hundreds of their young men had been slain; their families had been driven into the mountains, their herds taken away, their supplies for the winter stolen or burned; and, although his own tribe in the *Otra Banda* * had not taken part in this struggle, and neither threatened nor been threatened by the whites, he knew only too well the passions of men, who, after they have once drawn the sword, cannot be so soon restored to peace. But should they have dared to irritate and defy him, too? Messengers had been dispatched to him at the outbreak of hostilities, to secure his neutrality. Presents had been sent to him, in order to prove to the Penchuenches that the Chilenos did not entertain any hostile intentions toward them; that they were intent only on punishing the invasions of the Araucanians, but were desirous of living in friendship with their red brethren in the east. Was he not, therefore, justified in trusting them? And yet, how often had they deceived him—how often had the caziques of the whites sent greetings of friendship, when, nevertheless, their own men sneaked across the mountains and drove away his horses—nay, attacked and killed some of his warriors! And had he ever obtained justice, had he ever received satisfaction for such breaches of the peace? Never. "Name the criminals," said the whites, "and they shall be punished; we ourselves cannot seek for them." But whenever one of the red sons of the soil committed an offence, as the Araucanians had done now, hosts of the whites, armed with their modern engines of destruction, overran the country, and the innocent had to suffer with the guilty.

* Otra Banda is the country east of the Cordilleras.

Such gloomy thoughts flashed through his mind as he sat there, his arms folded on his breast, and his eyes fixed on the ground. But the bold, wild chief of the Peochuenches was certainly far from being indolent and irresolute under such circumstances; and, suddenly throwing back his head, he glanced searchingly toward his warriors, who, ignorant as yet of the orders which they would receive, whether to set out or to stay, were standing and conversing in a low tone.

"Saman!" cried the cazique, and from one of the groups there quickly stepped forth a little man. "You are swift and shrewd—follow Allamapu's trail, but no white man must see you. On approaching the settlements you will leave your horse in the thicket. You will return with Allamapu, or inform me what has become of him. Do you understand me?"

The Indian made no reply; he silently approached his horse, and, jumping on its bare back, the next moment disappeared in the forest. Jenkitrum, however, threw himself on the ground by the fire, and the other Indians, who saw, probably, that nothing would be undertaken for several hours, lay down and sought repose. All of them knew that they had to profit by this opportunity; for, if war should ensue, the severest fatigues and privations were in store for them.

CHAPTER II.

THE FESTIVAL AT THE HACIENDA.

THE troops of the Chilian government, after achieving their first triumph over the Araucanians, were returning from that magnificent part of the country where the tribes of the Chilian Indians have up to the present time maintained their independence, and defended their hunting-grounds against whomsoever invaded them. These wild sons of the pampas and mountains had felt so proud in their fertile valleys, and on the hills covered with sweet pastures, that they commenced harassing the white settlers on their northern frontier. Whether or not their chiefs had instigated these outrages, could not be definitely ascertained; nay, it was even improbable, for it was not to their advantage to exasperate and provoke their neighbors. Vagabonds, thirsting for plunder and spoils, were probably at the bottom of the cattle-thefts, which were constantly on the increase. Nevertheless, the chiefs had to be held responsible for them, if they could not, or would not, put a stop to such lawless deeds; and when these outrages finally became so frequent as to be intolerable, the Chilian troops invaded the land of the Araucanians, and, as they said, retaliated severely for their crimes.

It is true, they did not meet there with the whole force of the enemy; for, although several detachments of young warriors attempted to check their advance, they were unable to withstand the superior fire-arms and the murderous artillery of the troops. Thus the whole country was at the mercy of the invader, and, while the families of the Araucanians were escaping into the mountains in order to seek protection, or even into the Otra Banda, the men drove after them such of their herds as they could hastily collect, and left their haciendas and fields in the hands of the whites.

It would have been more sensible if the latter had made a moderate use of the triumph they had obtained, and contented themselves with demonstrating their power to the Indians, for, in reality, they were unable to hold the territory they had overrun. As it was, they did not behave much better than the Indians themselves would have done if they had invaded a hostile country. They destroyed the dwellings of the Araucanians, devastated their fields, pursued the poor women and children into the most inhospitable parts of the mountains, and then, gathering whatever cattle and horses they could find, drove them as rapidly as possible northward, into their own country; for they would not wait until the scattered forces of the Araucanians had united. Nor did they entirely confide in the neutrality of their neighbors, on the other side of the mountains, who might, after all, be prevailed upon to come to the assistance of their brethren, and attack the troops from the passes of the Cordilleras. In that event, the forces of the Indians would have vastly outnumbered their own, and the valor of those wild tribes was well known to them.

The Chilenos, meanwhile, reached their own frontiers, without being attacked by the Indians. The whites, however, did not seem to be overjoyed at the results, for, in *this* mode of warfare, though their friends had achieved a victory for the time, the Indians were certainly superior to them, and the settlers living on the frontier would be exposed to retaliation as soon as the troops had left that part of the country. Such considerations, however, came too late; the brave army returned, victorious, and laden with booty, and nothing remained for the haciendéros but to submit to what could not be helped, and calmly await events. On the whole, it is foreign to the nature of South Americans to look forward with fear and trepidation to the developments of the future, or to brood over the events of the past. That which *is* has a right *to be*, is the quintessence of their philosophy.

No wonder, then, that boisterous mirth reigned at the house of Señor Enrique Illinas, or Don Enrique, as he was usually called; and that the services of the military band of the last battalion of troops, who were to encamp for the night at his hacienda, were in great demand.

Don Enrique had reason to profit by this opportunity, for, this very day, his eldest daughter, Eliza, had married a wealthy haciendéro, who lived in the neighborhood, and who intended to ride over, that night, with his bride to his home. The day, therefore, was to be devoted to pleasure, and nothing more desirable could have happened to the young couple than the arrival of so many handsome and vivacious young officers, accompanied by a military band in full regimentals. The most sumptuous preparations were made for the entertainment of the guests, and the place in front of the house was crowded with gay and jubilant people.

Don Enrique's hacienda was charmingly situated on a small plateau, surrounded by hills, and so close to Concepcion, the capital of the district, that one could ride to the city and back in the course of a day, and yet so distant from it that its inmates could enjoy the delights of rural solitude. The proprietor had spared no expense, not only to bring his hacienda into a high state of cultivation, but to render it an attractive residence, in which he was highly favored by nature. In the middle of the plateau was the house, which was not high, but long, and contained two extensive wings; for Chili is a country subject to frequent earthquakes, and houses of several stories are deemed unsafe. In the rear extended a large vineyard, with numerous bowers, and crossed by shady avenues, in which were to be seen clusters of the magnificent grapes for which the district of Concepcion is famous, while the buildings containing the wine-presses lay farther back. In front were a lawn, and an orchard filled with fruit-trees; apricots, peaches, apples, pears, fig-trees of extraordinary size, pomegranates, and oranges in endless profusion. Several palm-trees had been planted in a sunny place, and, close to the house, protected from the cold winds, stood a small thicket of broad-leaved bananas, giving a tropical appearance to the whole scene. But the climate was not warm enough to ripen them, and, like the palm-trees, they were ornamental rather than useful. But the fact that they grew in the open air showed the even temperature of this part of the country throughout the year, while the fertility of the soil left nothing to be desired.

Enrique Rimas lived here with his two daughters, Eliza and Irene, the former eighteen years old, the latter scarcely sixteen. Eliza's wedding had just taken place. The only child left to him, therefore, was his younger daughter, a sweet, lovely girl, with long black ringlets, dark-brown eyes, and dimples in her cheeks and chin. Although her father's tenderness had somewhat spoiled his darling child, and, by too indulgent a treatment, rendered her somewhat self-willed and obstinate, such was her innate kind-heartedness that she shrank from offending any one, and treated her servants with the greatest gentleness. In consequence of this, there was not a *guasso** in the whole neighborhood but considered her the most welcome visitor that ever entered his cottage. There was, at the hacienda, not a peon, from the lowest stable-boy up, but who would have walked through fire for her; and when, one day, for she was too daring a rider, she had been thrown from her horse, and had to keep her bed for many weeks, it really seemed as though the people of the vicinity were intent on making a pilgrimage to Don Enrique's hacienda, so eagerly did they flock thither, every day, to inquire about the health of the general favorite.

Then Irene, who had lost her mother in her early childhood, grew up in many respects as a boy rather than a girl, and if she devoted very little of her time to needle-work, she was, in return, as well-skilled in managing a horse, throwing a lasso, and target-shooting, as any lad of her age. Nevertheless, she had preserved, in her bearing, that girlish bashfulness which sheds so irresistible a charm upon a young woman, and if her father contended that she was the pearl of all Chilian daughters, it was an assertion at which, perhaps, all Chilian mothers shrugged their shoulders, but which not

* Chilian peasant.

a young man throughout the country would have disputed.

Notwithstanding her youth, she had already had many suitors, and he who would have succeeded in winning her hand, could not have brought a more acceptable daughter-in-law to the house of his parents. But, while treating with kindness and consideration her admirers, she gave her preference to no one, and he who rejoiced most at this was her own father. For how could he have been willing to let her leave his house, since thenceforth it would have appeared to him gloomy and deserted?

On this occasion the whole neighborhood seemed to have assembled at Don Enrique's house, and all who liked to dance had arrived even from remote points in the district. Who would have missed at such a time, the sambucuca, the national dance, of which the Chilanos are so very fond? Where was to be found a more hospitable host in Chili, and where else could the guests anticipate so much pleasure?

The young Chilians found themselves as if in a paradise of angels—so many charming girls arrived at a gallop, on their neighing ponies, and the merry young folks consented reluctantly to sit down to the dinner-table, although loaded with the rarest delicacies, for all longed for the commencement of the ball.

The interior of the house, notwithstanding the large size of the dwellings of the haciendero, was not spacious enough for those who wished to take part in the dance, so that the gravel in front of the veranda had been levelled, and thus an excellent ballroom had been extemporized in the open air. The musicians were seated in the centre, and the spectators ranged on both sides, while, amid a fragrant sea of orange-blossoms, the young people were dancing, and waving their handkerchiefs in the graceful mazes of the sambucuca.

Refreshments were often handed round, and the peons and poor guassos were not forgotten. In the court-yard, on the other side of the building, a table had been set for them, and as much food and wine provided as they wished. In the middle yard, on a sort of sleigh—a vehicle much in use in this part of South America—lay a leathern bag of gigantic dimensions filled with wine—a perfect Heidelberg tun among the smaller bags. The whole hide of an ox (the usual way of preserving and forwarding wine in South America) had been taken off, every particle of fat and blood carefully removed, and the openings so closed that not a drop could escape.

This large bag was filled with excellent red wine, from the hacienda of Señor Rimas. Three of the legs were fastened with strings, but the fourth was left open, and served as a faucet. One of the peons, holding an ox-horn in his hand, stood on the sleigh by the side of the bag, in order to serve all who called for wine. Many of the guassos had brought their own horns, which, when away from home, they fasten with a string to the saddles of their horses. On crossing a rivulet, if desiring to drink, it is unnecessary for them to alight for this purpose. They only lower the horn, which they draw up filled with water, and continue their ride. Whenever one of them came to the wine-bag with a horn, or some drinking-cup found in the house, the peon

THE FESTIVAL AT THE HACIENDA. 13

standing on the sleigh turned the open keg toward him, and seated himself on the bag. By his pressure the wine was forced into the vessel held under it.

For the rest, the Chilenos, like all the other descendants of the Spanish race, are very rarely intemperate in the use of spirituous liquors, and, although the wine now added to their hilarity, not an intoxicated person was to be seen all day at the hacienda.

But they did not confine themselves to drinking, for the music passed through the open doors and windows into the court-yard. What *guerilla* could have withstood those notes! Therefore, no sooner had the ball commenced in front of the veranda, than the peons and guassos devoted themselves to the same pleasure with equal relish, and frequently with the same gracefulness as the guests of Don Enrique. Nay, the señoritas in the garden had the mortification of seeing many a young gentleman stealing away to the other side of the house, in order— although he would not dare to take part in the sambucuous there—at least to feast his eyes on the prepossessing forms of the young maidens, who also enjoyed with the utmost gayety the festivities of the day.

The main body of the Chilian army, which had passed through the hacienda at an early hour on the same day, continued its march to Concepcion, for the herds taken in the land of the Araucanians delayed its movements, and it was, therefore, not at liberty to stay too long at any point. The officers should have accompanied it, but a brief recreation was allowed them, particularly as they were no longer in the country of the Araucanians, who, dispersed as they were in all directions, and driven far into the mountains, could not have concentrated and been prepared for aggressive operations for several weeks. But, after the chastisement just received, they would never have ventured to cross the Bio-Bio River, and, in pursuit of the troops, not foot on Chilian territory. Hence, the merry youth enjoyed with all their hearts the innocent pleasures of the day.

The sun was already near the western horizon, but Don Enrique would not allow the ball to be interrupted by the approaching darkness, and torches had been piled up at the entrance of the garden to illuminate the place as soon as night had set in. Only the bride and bridegroom retired, in order to repair to the latter's hacienda; they could not do so, however, in a comfortable stage-coach, but had to ride on horseback. The animals were saddled in the court-yard, and Don Fernando (such was the name of the young haciendero) hoped to leave Don Enrique's hacienda quietly and unnoticed by the other guests, but who did not allow them to do so. Sentinels had been posted in every direction, and as the bride and bridegroom, hidden, as they thought, by a hedge of blooming orange-trees, vaulted into the saddle, the bands at a signal suddenly struck up a ringing flourish, and the friends of the newly married rushed toward them from all quarters, waved their hats and handkerchiefs, and shouted a loud, laughing farewell to them as they hastily galloped off. All then returned, and the dance commenced anew.

While the guests were hurrying toward that part of the garden whence the young couple intended to set out secretly, and, while the band was playing, a horseman halted at the garden-gate, and listened in surprise to the sudden interruption of the dancing-music. But his surprise was of short duration. The cheers and jubilant exclamations which burst forth indicated to him the harmless character of the martial notes, and, without further delay, for he had tarried there already too long, he quickly raised the wooden latch with the point of his lance, and rode slowly into the garden. The dance, however, engrossed the spectators so much that they did not notice the Indian quietly riding up to them, for Irene had just commenced dancing with a young guaso, Carlo Mara, the best and most graceful dancer in the district, and loud applause greeted the truly charming couple.

The South Americans, who are very excitable people under all circumstances, can be carried away to such an extent by the spectacle of a beautiful and graceful dance, that, for the time, they forget every thing else; and these Spanish fandangoes, sambuenecas, marimbas, and whatever their names may be, are certainly very attractive, although they bear no resemblance to the indecent pas which so-called Spanish ballet-girls often exhibit in Germany, and which we are foolish enough to applaud. The South American revels in these spectacles, and the spectators on this occasion clapped their hands with unbounded enthusiasm. The young Indian meanwhile had stopped his horse, and, resting with his right hand on his lance, gazed with admiration on the dance. Almost spellbound, he forgot his errand, and felt only that he was not at liberty to break the charm of the delightful scene. Suddenly, his horse, whose head nearly touched the hindmost spectators, neighed, and those who were standing near, startled by the sudden sound, turned toward him. They were officers, and, uttering a loud "Caramba!" looked up to the Indian, who had so unexpectedly appeared in their midst. Their first sensation was that of terror; for how could a solitary Indian have ventured to penetrate, fully armed, into the hacienda, if he had not known that his friends were at hand? Were they surrounded, betrayed?

The dancers quickly interrupted their amusement, and, on beholding the stranger, Irene hastened toward the house, as though she felt safer there. Allumapu, however, remained calm and motionless, while a sarcastic smile stole over his dusky features, when he noticed the confusion which his arrival had produced. But, in order not to alarm those to whom he had come with a friendly message, and, above all things, not to frighten the lovely girl who had fled from him so timidly, he broke off a branch of the pomegranate under which he was halting, dismounted, and, leaning his long kila lance against the tree, strode, with head erect, into the circle of the spectators.

CHAPTER III.

THE MESSENGER OF THE PENCHUENCHES.

THE officers almost involuntarily made room for the Indian warrior, who stepped so confidently into their midst and looked around to find the commander-in-chief of the troops. This, however, was a matter of some difficulty; for, as he was not familiar with the meaning of the different military emblems, and as he was misled by the profusion of gold-lace and embroidery with which South-American officers adorn their uniforms, his dark eyes passed irresolutely from one to the other, and he finally waited for somebody to address him. He thought no one but the cazique of the soldiers would venture to speak to a stranger so long as the commander-in-chief himself was present.

It is true the customs and manners of the whites differed from those of the Indians. While the warrior was standing, with the pomegranate-branch in his right hand, his left hand resting on his thigh, and his head thrown back, a proud stripling, dressed in the uniform of an officer, and displaying a pair of heavy epaulets, stepped up to him and exclaimed:

"Caramba! señor, who are you, and whence do you come? Why did you enter so suddenly into our midst and disturb the dance? What do you want?"

"Are you the cazique of these bearded men?" replied Allumapu, evidently in surprise. "And do you speak for the others?"

He propounded this question in tolerably good Spanish; at least, all understood it, and the port little lieutenant blushed slightly at the rebuke administered to him. Meanwhile the colonel commanding approached with Don Enrique, and took upon himself the examination of the new-comer, for Señor Rimas had already whispered to him that the Indian was not an Araucanian, but an inhabitant of the Otra Banda, and a member of the tribes living there. Unaccompanied warriors, however, never ventured to cross the mountains; hence, it was certain that a number of his brethren were encamped in the neighborhood, and it was of the utmost importance for them to obtain further information on this point.

"To what tribe do you belong, amigo?" said the colonel to him; "are you an Araucanian?"

"No," replied the Indian, proudly raising his head, "my home lies in the vast plain beyond the mountains. The brave Jeukitrum is my chief."

"And what brings you hither? Have you come to take part in the war? —You are too late; your red friends were too fleet-footed; we were unable to overtake them."

"The Penchuenches are not at war with their white neighbors," said the messenger, gloomily; "they are friends, and have not raised against them either their lances or their bolas."

"And what do you want, then?"

"The chief and great cazique of the Penchuenches has sent me to you."

"What does he require of us?"

The young warrior knit his brow, and looked angrily at the speaker. However, he stifled his indignation, and continued, after a short pause, in a calm voice:

"It is customary with us that a stranger must say, in front of the *toldo*" (tent or house), "who he is; but, after having done so, he is conducted into the council-tent, or a special cabin is assigned him; never do we allow him to stand longer in the open air, and exposed to the eyes of inquisitive idlers."

"You have, certainly, very singular customs," replied the colonel, smiling at the rebuke; "but, for aught I know, one of them may be that you are forbidden to disturb the peace of any house, without having announced yourself, and that you must wait outside, though the toldo were that of the most despised creature, until you are bidden to come in. I believe you forgot this, amigo, on riding so rudely into our midst. If you wish to be treated so ceremoniously, why do you, on your part, violate your own customs? Do we go to you, or do you come to us?"

Allumapu looked gloomily at the speaker; at last, pointing up to heaven, he replied:

"The sun stood there when I arrived at your gate and shouted to you, but the music, like the roar of a waterfall, drowned my voice. If you wish the doors of your houses to be kept sacred, why are they not guarded by your young men?"

"Take him into the house, señor," whispered Don Enrique to the officer, while Allumapu fixed his eyes distrustfully on the old man. What was it that the señor had said to the officer, and which he wished to conceal from the Indian? Enrique Rimas added in the same tone: "I am somewhat familiar with the peculiarities of the Indians of the Otra Banda. They are a wild, but tolerably sensible and good-natured people, and it will certainly be best for us to keep on good terms with them."

The colonel seemed not altogether of his opinion. He thought that the best course he could pursue toward these "thieving brown rascals" would be to treat them as unceremoniously as possible, and, if they should betray any hostile intentions, attack them immediately. But, in order to hear at once what the young warrior wanted of him, and, thinking that it would be prudent for him to hear his message alone, he nodded to his host, and said:

"I will act upon your suggestion and go with him into the house.—Come, amigo; and as to you others, proceed with the ball. It is entirely unnecessary for us to interrupt our pleasure on account of this fellow."

He led the way, not very well pleased with the Indian's arrival. What was it that the Penchuenches wanted on this side of the mountains, after the Araucanians had just been chastised and driven to the Otra Banda? Possibly they might ask their neighbors there to help them in their distress, and wreak revenge on their conquerors. But had they already succeeded in obtaining their assistance, and this messenger impudently come for the purpose of informing them that the Penchuenches would wage war with the Chilenos?

After beckoning to the musicians to renew the dance, he entered the hall, and, turning to the Indian, who had followed him into the house, he said, sternly:

"Well, my friend, your wish has been complied with. We are now in the toldo. Let me know, therefore, what has brought you hither."

"Pardon me," interrupted the polite old hacienderо, who, for his part at least, was not desirous of breaking with his "brown neighbors," and was intent on keeping on good terms with them, so far as he could do so by politeness, "shall we not first offer refreshments to the young man; he—"

"Pray, señor, let him first answer my questions," said the officer. "Above all, we must ascertain his intentions and the whereabouts of his comrades; he will afterward have time enough to take refreshments. We are, as it were, still in the field."

Don Enrique did not exactly agree with him. The last utterance, especially, seemed to him untenable, for the officers were certainly no longer "in the field," but were his guests, their troops having left the hacienda, and probably arrived safely at Concepcion. His politeness, however, prevented him from contradicting the colonel. These military men were accustomed to have their own way; and he, therefore, withdrew to the veranda, where he told his daughter Irene to provide cake and wine, and, perhaps, some more substantial food for the Indian, as soon as his interview with the colonel was at an end.

"And now, my friend, let me ask you if you understood the question I propounded to you?" said the colonel. "Where do you come from, what do you want, and where are your comrades?"

"You ask three questions, señor," said the Indian, smilingly, who was not at all intimidated by the colonel's frowns; "but my reply will tell you all that you need to know."

"Need to know? Carajo!" echoed the Chileno, indignantly.

Allumapu raised his hand deprecatingly, and said, quietly, "I come from the mountains; I am a messenger of the great chief Jeukitrus, the supreme cazique of the Penchuenches, who has come from his home, the immense Pampas, to the land of the Araucanians."

"Indeed!" exclaimed the officer, angrily. "Perhaps, to assist our enemies, despite all his protestations of friendship and peace?"

"To make peace between the white and red men," continued the young Indian, calmly.

"To make peace!" laughed the Chileno, incredulously.

"To make peace," repeated the Indian, nodding his head. "We do not come for the purpose of waging war, else our warriors would have invaded the country in large force, and our war-cry would not have penetrated so sweetly into the ears of the whites as the notes of the music on the veranda."

"You threaten me, then, my friend?"

"I do not threaten, but tell you merely the truth. We came hither with the most pacific and friendly intentions, but unfortunately we were too late. When we rode down to the valleys, the Araucanians had already fled like cowards; your young men were devastating the country, and driving away the herds."

"It is true, the whole campaign was very brief," laughed the colonel.

"The Chilian warriors are brave," said the Indian, evasively. "They came in large numbers, and their fire-arms carry death farther and quicker than bolas and lances do. They came at night, like the puma pouncing on his prey."

"The red thieves had long ago been warned of the retribution that would be inflicted on them; but what has all this to do with our business here? The Penchuenches saw that they were too late; very well, I will believe that they crossed the mountains, as you say, solely for the purpose of making peace; but, since we ourselves have restored it, why do they not go back to their homes, or are they desirous of settling in the land of the Araucanians?"

The sneer hidden under the colonel's words hardly escaped the Indian. A disdainful smile played round his lips, and he replied in a calm voice:

"The cabins of the Araucanians have been burned down, and their wives and children have lost their homes. The powerful whites have achieved a great victory, and the women of the Araucanians will have to dry many tears next winter. The Chilian warriors have thoroughly destroyed the property of their enemies, but in the darkness they did not distinguish that which belonged to their enemies from that which belonged to their friends; and my chief, therefore, sends me to reclaim our property, which you took unwittingly—the horses of the Penchuenches, which we brought with us from the other side of the mountains and wish to take home again."

"Ha! ha!" laughed the colonel, "that is a capital joke! As you found nothing to steal in the country, you want us to divide our spoils with you? That is a very clever idea. And Jenkitrus sent you to me for this purpose?"

"The Penchuenches do not steal," said Allumapu, proudly, bridling himself up, and knitting his brow. "Our laws say that thieves must suffer death."

"The laws are very good," said the Chileno, nodding his head, "but I suppose they are not carried into execution."

"Give us back the horses your warriors carried off, together with the herds of the Araucanians," said the Indian, who did not wish to quarrel with the colonel in a language with which he was imperfectly acquainted, "and we shall return to our native Pampas; we do not wish to be at war with the whites; we are at peace with them; we are their friends. That is what Jenkitrus says."

"And how many of your horses were taken?" asked the officer.

"Sixty-two," replied the young Penchuenche; "we had brought them with us to use when our saddle-horses were worn out."

"Sixty-two! Is that all?" laughed the Chileno. "And where do you think they are now, and who could distinguish them among the others?"

"I know them all," replied Allumapu, "every hair of them."

"Oh, I believe that you would select the best horses," said the officer, nodding his head, "I have not the least doubt of it, but you will not have a chance to do so. No one has asked you to cross the mountains and meddle with our quarrel with the Araucanians, and you have no business whatever in this part of the country. If, in coming here, you have lost horses, so much the worse for you. Look for them in the mountains of the Araucanians—I will not object to it. But of the animals which we seized in the enemy's country, you shall not get a single one, though you should stand on your heads."

"You refuse, then, to restore our property?" asked the Indian, fixing his eyes menacingly on the countenance of the Chileno.

"I do not know your property, and have nothing to do with it. Have you any other errand?"

"I have not."

"And where are your friends?"

"In the mountains," laconically replied the Indian, who wrapped himself in his poncho, and prepared to go.

"But where—in what part of the mountains? Are they far from here?"

"Who can tell where the Penchuenches are roaming?" said Allumapu, a defiant smile lighting up his features. "To-day they are here, to-morrow there. Their horses sweep, like the *pampero*, across the Pampas. They are a wild and swift people."

The colonel bit his lips, for he knew well that the Indian mocked him, but other thoughts passed at the same time through his mind.

"Is that the answer I am to convey to the cacique?" asked the Indian, turning to the door.

"It is, of course; but—you must first take some food.—Oh, Señor Enrique, Señor Enrique! Pray have some refreshments served up to our red friend. Our interview is at an end, and I believe he is hungry and thirsty."

"Certainly," exclaimed Don Enrique, eagerly. During the whole interview he had been a prey to serious misgivings, and had been impatiently pacing his veranda, for what he had heard of the conversation had made a very disagreeable impression on him. The defiant tone in which both the Indian and the colonel had spoken was by no means reassuring, and Don Enrique, frightened as he was already by the quarrel between the Chilenos and the neighboring Araucanians, was utterly averse to incurring also the hatred and enmity of the tribes of the Otra Banda. The soldiers, indeed, did not care for all this; they returned to their garrisons, and if the Indians should again invade the country,—well, they would be ordered to march once more, and wreak vengeance on them. But the settlers on the frontier suffered most by these hostilities. No matter how brilliant might be the victories of the troops, the former were subject to incessant danger, trouble, and anxiety, and therefore they did not agree at all with the manner in which the recent campaign had been conducted. By indiscriminate burning and devastation the soldiers had placed themselves on a par with the Indians, whose flying columns were, moreover, their superiors in this mode of warfare. But the opposition of the hacenderos to the orders of the government was unavailing, and nothing remained but to counteract as much as possible the mischief done by the troops. It was for this purpose that the peaceably-disposed Don Enrique resolved to win the favor of the Indian; and Irene, who had not taken part in the last dance, was quickly instructed to bring to the guest the refreshments which were already prepared for him.

Allumapu still stood irresolute in the hall, for the colonel had left him and joined the other officers outside, with whom he was whispering in an animated manner. For a moment it seemed as though Allumapu would refuse the hospitality offered him, and leave the house, to return as speedily as possible to the camp of his brethren; but his body needed nourishment, for too long the iron will of the young warrior had resisted his physical weakness. He felt that he must take food, or succumb to long-continued fatigue.

Suddenly Irene, accompanied by a servant-girl, entered the hall, and said to him in a kind tone:

"You must be hungry, señor, for you have ridden far. Eat and drink, that you may leave this house invigorated."

So saying, she poured from a bottle, which the maid had brought with her, a goblet of red wine, which she herself offered to him.

Allumapu took it; but, in doing so, so steadfastly did he gaze on the features of the lovely girl, that she dropped her eyes, blushing, and turned from him to arrange the refreshments on the table. How carefully had she selected for him the choicest delicacies, and yet how needless had been the pains she had taken! What does the Penchuenche care for delicacies, accustomed as he is to roast his horse-flesh over a fire of dry excrement, or, when in retreat from, or in pursuit of his enemies on the Pampas, to eat it raw and drink the blood? He had no time to lose, and, saying to Irene in a low voice, "*Gracias, señorita, Dios lo pague,*" he sat down and satisfied his hunger.

Irene contemplated him compassionately, and at last said kindly to him:

"I suppose you were very hungry, and yet you had to wait so long."

"The sun has risen twice," said the Indian, "without a morsel of food having touched my lips. Allumapu was very hungry."

"Poor fellow! Allumapu is your name?"

"No," said the Indian, "but the Penchuenches call me so, because I fled to them from the north in order to escape the vendetta in my own tribe."

Irene shuddered. She had heard enough of the savage customs of that tribe to be well aware that blood had stained the hands of this young man, and that, for this reason, he had been obliged to leave his tribe and family. But was he to blame for the dark deed? Poor, unfortunate beings! who grow up in their wild state, in ignorance and heathenism, and never hear of the blessings of Christianity, were they not by far more entitled to her compassion than her hatred! But the Indian did not suspect what was passing through her mind; he ate what was set before him, and emptied the glass which the servant filled and refilled with wine. Santa Maria, what an appetite! Food enough for four hungry men disappeared as if thrown into a carpet-bag. And how much wine he drank! He did not swallow it—it ran down, as it were, into a leathern sack.

The Indian finished his meal; it was not certain whether he was sated, but all the viands were consumed. He was again prepared, if need be, to eat and drink nothing for two days. He wiped his mouth with his dark-brown poncho, and dried his fingers in his waving hair; he then rose, and, holding out his hand to Irene, who took it timidly, he said:

"Thanks, señorita! many, many thanks! Allumapu is again a man, and, on returning to the Pampas, he will tell the young men at the camp-fires of the lovely flower in the land of the whites.

She shed sunshine on the pathway of a poor warrior, and will long occupy his dreams."

At these words Irene felt not a little embarrassed, and she did not know how to disengage her hand; whether the Indian noticed her confusion, or believed that he had tarried enough, he dropped her hand, and, kindly nodding to her, left the room and stepped out upon the piazza.

The scene there had undergone little or no change, and the hall had not again been interrupted. The officers, however, no longer took part in it; they were all assembled on the veranda, while the band filled the staircase leading to the garden. No one was able to leave before the musicians had opened a passage.

Allumapu advanced and glanced around. He saw the proprietor of the hacienda engaged in an animated conversation with the colonel, and that Don Enrique paused almost in dismay as soon as the Indian appeared at the door. What had the two been conversing about? And why was the staircase obstructed by the musicians, who were all the while playing? Was he to wait until they had concluded? This was impossible; time was fleeting, and he was bound to convey the unwelcome reply to the cazique; he could no longer delay. Without hesitating another moment, he approached one of the buglers, and, touching his arm, said to him:

"Let me pass, amigo."

The musician turned, without removing his instrument from his lips, and looked at him, but did not move. The Indian was about to repeat his request, when he saw the colonel coming. The officer put his hand on the Indian's arm, and said:

"Paciencia, amigo! Let the musicians play: you have plenty of time, and will stay here for a few days."

"Shall I, amigo?" replied the Indian, gloomily. "I do not wish to do so."

He again touched the bugler's shoulder. But the musicians, as if intentionally, closed their ranks, and for the first time the suspicion crossed his mind that the colonel really intended to detain him. Detain him? A defiant smile lit up his features. Yonder stood his horse, with its saddle and bridle; his lance was leaning against the tree. Did the foolish pale-faces believe that he needed a staircase to descend to the garden? The veranda was about sixteen feet high; laying his hand on the balustrade, and before any one suspected his intention, he vaulted over it with the agility of a deer, and, without accelerating his pace, walked toward his horse.

"Carajo!" shouted the colonel, on perceiving the bold leap. "Stop the spy! Do not allow him to escape! Shoot him if he should refuse to stop!"

Allumapu heard these words, and knew that his liberty was threatened; he saw several officers, to whom the musicians readily made room, rushing down the staircase. The ball was suspended; the dancers were dismayed, and the girls fled into the house; but the Indian did not lose his presence of mind for a moment. He knew the danger menacing him—he knew also that he was still able to escape. He whistled softly, and his horse sped to his side. Seizing the lance, and, with the left hand, the mane of his horse, he vaulted into the saddle. No

22   HOW A BRIDE WAS WON.

sooner did the faithful animal feel its rider than it galloped toward the gate, but the gate was closed. He lowered his lance to push back the wooden latch; the point slipped from the polished wood; he tried again, when there was a rustling noise in the bushes on the right and left, and three or four shots were fired almost at the same time. Had they missed their aim? Uninjured, he was almost inclined to charge his enemies, but he had to carry his message to Jenkitrum; the spirited pony bounded into the hedge, and his hoofs soon beat the ground in the open field. Onward he sped along the narrow pathway leading to the forest. The pursuers were not mounted—how could they have hoped to overtake him! Suddenly the horse stumbled—a bullet had hit him in a mortal place, and, rolling over, he hurled his rider into the dense underwood, from which it was impossible to disengage himself.

His enemies overtook and surrounded him. Unsheathing his long knife, he saw pistols levelled against him on all sides. He was a prisoner—further resistance was useless.

CHAPTER IV.

THE SURPRISE.

Once in the hands of his enemies, the Penchuenche submitted quietly to his fate. He had lost his game, but who knew what the next moment might bring forth? If there were no chance of escape, very well; then it would be necessary to bear patiently what could not be helped, and die like a man. The cowardly and insidious whites should not see him weak and disheartened.

Had this been the plan which the treacherous old man had whispered to the officer? for this purpose had Allumapu been invited to partake of food, and a seductive girl sent to him, that the cowardly huincas might meanwhile concert their measures and load their firearms? What would become of him?— Bah! He tossed his head defiantly, and looked disdainfully upon the numerous enemies necessary to capture him. And was it customary for them to treat in this manner the messenger of a friendly neighboring tribe, and to insult its chief? Did they really believe that Jenkitrum would quietly bear this disgrace, and not wreak a terrible vengeance upon them?

Such were also the misgivings which filled Don Enrique's mind, and, when the prisoner was conveyed to one of the outbuildings, and guarded there by several officers, the haciendero hastened in his excitement to the colonel to protest in the most energetic manner against the Indian's arrest. He said Allumapu had committed no offence whatever; he did not belong to the tribe with which they were at war, and had only brought a message to them. He added that, if he were allowed to depart without further molestation (and he himself would give him another horse in place of that which he had lost), all would be well; but if he should be detained, they would needlessly arouse the vindictiveness of the Penchuenches, and on whom would they revenge themselves but upon the hacienderos?

The colonel was quite morose and surly; he wished to use no force, but, as it had been resorted to, it was necessary to persist in the course adopted. But when he called upon some of the youths of the neighborhood to take upon themselves the safe-keeping of the prisoner, they refused. They did not care to meddle with a matter which might involve them in disastrous consequences. The settlements in this part of the country were so remote from the usual head-quarters of the troops, that they were utterly averse to unreasonable hostilities with their wild neighbors.

The colonel, dissatisfied with himself and with everybody else, had just ordered two of the musicians to guard the prisoner—he would not, perhaps, have been angry if they had suffered him to escape—and requested the others to resume their amusements, when Irene stepped into the hall, and said in a tremulous voice:

"What has the poor Indian done, señor, that your men fired at him, and captured him like a wild beast?"

"They did not fire at him, señorita," said the colonel, in a tone of embarrassment—"only at his horse, to prevent his escaping. He was not wounded at all."

"The blood ran from his forehead, when they led him into the court-yard."

"He was scratched a little in falling into the underwood; that is all. His wound will heal over-night."

"And what is to be done with him? I hope you are not going to kill him?" Asked Irene, anxiously. "Oh, so much blood has been shed already!"

"Never fear, señorita," said the Chilian officer, reassuring her; "I pledge you my word of honor that no harm shall befall him. We had only to take steps to prevent his informing his friends, who may be concealed at no great distance from your father's hacienda, since our soldiers are already close to, or at Concepcion, and here are only a few officers, whom they might easily attack with a superior force, and carry off as hostages into the mountains, in order to recover the horses they pretend to have lost."

"But the Indian does not belong to the tribe of the Araucanians, and has nothing to do with them."

"My dear child," said the officer, shrugging his shoulders, "you are not so intimately acquainted with these dusky rascals as I am; they are indescribably tricky, treacherous, and mischievous. It is quite possible that he has nothing to do with them; but it is equally possible that he only availed himself of this pretext in order to discover our strength, and afterward attack us. The plan would not have been so stupid by any means."

"And what is to be done with him now?"

"Nothing at all; we only intend to keep him in custody until we start from here, and, for safety's sake, we shall take him with us to Concepcion. Thence we will allow him to return to his mountains, and even give him another horse to ride thither. But now, dear Irene, pray do not delay the dance longer, but show again a merry face to the people outside. Your protégé is in no danger whatever."

"Father is so anxious!"

"There is no reason whatever why he should be," said the officer; "he has nothing to do with the affair. We are exclusively responsible for what has occurred; the Indians are well aware of it, and they will take good care not to undertake any thing that would at once cause us to punish them severely. But why is there no music!—Halloo, compañeros, have you fallen asleep! Let the dance begin."

The musicians played, without, however, accomplishing the wished-for object, for the violent deed which had just been perpetrated, without any reason whatever, still engrossed all minds. Moreover, night was drawing nigh, and though many guests might have intended to stay to a very late hour, and return home in the full moonlight, they seemed to have changed their minds. Especially were the young ladies anxious to leave the hacienda; the pistol-shots fired at the Indian had too forcibly recalled the stern reality to their minds. And how could they be gay, while the poor man lay bound hand and foot! No one believed that he really was a spy; in that case he would not have acted so boldly and openly, and now he was deprived of his liberty amid all these happy people! Even the guaracos and guacitas in the court-yard no longer continued their amusements, and the colonel could not prevent them from gradually leaving the hacienda.

It was late, and the colonel himself began to feel uncomfortable. The music ceased, and he gave orders to his men to get their horses, so that they might leave the place that very night. As the moon would rise at eight, they would be able to advance rapidly toward Concepcion, but some of the horses had escaped from the corral, and his men were unable to find them. Rather than leave his officers at the hacienda, he resolved to pass the night there and set out at early dawn.

Don Enrique had mats and blankets brought for his numerous guests, and the remnants of this day's dinner were served up to them for supper. There was an abundance of wine, and the young officers drank more of it than usual. They felt ill at ease at the hacienda, as neither their host nor his daughter appeared longer in their midst. The lawn in front of the veranda, which a few hours before had exhibited so merry and animated a spectacle, was now deserted and silent; they hoped that the wine would reanimate their spirits, but they were mistaken, and retired at an early hour to be on hand betimes in the morning, and start for Concepcion.

Night covered the vast forest, over which the moon shed her light, and flung gigantic shadows over the clearings. At the hacienda all were asleep; even the prisoner, exhausted by the efforts of the day, slumbered, bound as he was, hand and foot, on his mat. But he breathed heavily and uneasily, while the guard sitting by his side was dozing, or occasionally arose, paced the small room, and resumed his former place till he was relieved. The new guard had already slept several hours, and did not feel so drowsy.

It was past midnight. The guards had been relieved again, and those who had just arrived bent over the prisoner to see if he were asleep. He did not stir; his head rested on a pillow which Irene had sent him. The officer cautiously raised the poncho with which he had been covered, but the fetters were strong and secure, and, reassured on this head, the young Chileno threw himself into the corner on his own cloak, while the two buglers, who were to assist in guarding the prisoner, were pacing the small room, slowly and noiselessly, smoking their cigarettes.

Silence reigned without, for even the crickets had ceased chirping; once a dog barked, and was quiet again. Suddenly the shrill cry of a night-hawk was heard above the forest, or from the neighboring grove, for it was loud and distinct, and the prisoner involuntarily started. When the two guards, who were pacing the room, turned their backs upon him, there might have been noticed an almost convulsive motion under the poncho, but without any change of position. The dog barked again, this time louder than before, and the night-hawk's cry was repeated.

"Carajo! I wonder what sort of bird that may be!" said one of the musicians, listening. "I believe I never before heard such a note, even in the land of the Araucanians."

"You did not!" laughed the other. "I have, very often. It is a night-hawk; I once saw one that my neighbor had shot. When it commences to scream, daybreak is not far off. Thank God, this tedious night is drawing to a close!"

"I wonder what makes the dog bark and growl so much?"

"Probably one of our men has gone into the court-yard to look at the stars."

"I hope the guard outside has not been removed!"

"Of course not; there are two sentinels, one on either end of the road. It is a queer innovation, indeed, that the members of the band should stand guard; to play all day, and walk up and down, sword in hand, for several hours at night, is not very pleasant."

"I suppose you do not expect that the officers should stand guard?"

"Well, would it do them any harm? But I do not care; as soon as we get home, I shall leave the service and remove to Guillota."

"To Guillota! And what do you want to do there?"

"Marry, compañero, and settle down; for to lead such a vagabond life—"

"I wonder what is the matter with the dog outside!" interrupted the other; "he howls fearfully."

"I believe they are already stirring without," said his comrade, "I hear voices." And both stepped to the door of the low building to look out.

The prisoner raised his head cautiously and listened; he could distinctly hear the noise of galloping horses, and the bushes in the rear of the house were rustling as though somebody were breaking through them.

A signal was sounded, and the colonel, as he had jumped up from his couch, wrapped in his poncho, but bareheaded, and in his under-clothes, appeared in the door of the main building, and called out:

"Some of you will immediately look after the horses; I believe they are coming up, probably pursued by a jaguar or some other wild beast."

The horses swept up like a hurricane, the stillness of the night and the hard surface of the road causing their hoofs to be more distinctly heard. But there was a rustling noise, too, to the right, in the garden, as though a fence were breaking down.

"Caramba!" cried the colonel, in surprise. "They will break down the fence.—Whoa, whoa!" he shouted, raising his arm to drive back what he supposed to be the frightened horses.

Suddenly a wild, unearthly yell rent the air; and it seemed as though Tartarus had sent up its monsters. This outcry was responded to from all quarters, while weird horsemen with flying hair and waving ponchos appeared and rode down whatever obstructed their path.

"Halloo, Allumapu!" they cried; and as the two musicians, guarding the Indian, were about to seize their swords, they felt that some one grasped them by the neck. An irresistible power held them, as if in a vice, and before they were able to defend themselves, their heads were knocked together, and they fell senseless and motionless to the ground.

"Ho! ho!" shouted the Indian, exultingly to his friends. "Ho! Allumapu is here!" And, snatching the weapon of one of his guards from the table, he rushed out to join his brethren.

Meanwhile a scene of confusion ensued in the court-yard, and the yells and cheers, with which the Indians greeted Allumapu's appearance, added to the panic of the surprised and frightened Chilenos. They fled in all directions; only the officers, prompted by the instinct of self-preservation rather than in obedience to their sense of duty, inasmuch as they supposed that the whole attack was meant for them, rushed to their arms, and courageously confronted the enemy. But what could they accomplish against the vastly superior numbers of the Indians? The wild horsemen galloped up on all sides, and the moon shed light enough to facilitate their attack. Their lances pierced to the right and left, and the broad-hoofed horses of the Penchuenches trampled down all who opposed them. Yet only a small number of the warriors penetrated to the house, while the others were busily engaged in seizing the horses and driving them into the mountains.

The servants of the hacienda knew already how to behave under similar circumstances; and scarcely had the cry of "Los Indios! los Indios!" passed from mouth to mouth, than they quickly concealed themselves. They had not to go very far for this purpose, for such raids last only a few minutes. If the attacked succeed in hiding for a short time, they are saved. The robbers take whatever booty they find, when they leave as quickly as they come.

Completely taken by surprise were the soldiers, who suddenly saw dark, wild forms, as if risen from the ground, darting up and down in the moonlight. They were unable to hear the commands of their superiors, amid the shouts of the savages. The uncertain light seemed to add greatly to the number of the assailants; their terrible lances bristled on all sides, and the musicians, who were averse to fighting under any circumstances, glided like shadows from the road into the garden, and sought refuge under the bushes, shrubs, and vine-trellises.

During this confusion the Indians seemed to feel perfectly at home, and a cheer which rent the air burst from their lips, when Allumapu rushed into their midst, and immediately turned toward his chief, whom he had already recognized.

At this moment the colonel fled into the house for his own arms, that he might not fall defenceless into the savages' hands; but Allumapu knew him, and, brandishing the bola which hung on his belt, he hurled it at the fugitive, and hit him so powerfully in the back, that he fell senseless on the steps of the veranda.

Several officers now galloped up and discharged their pistols, but the Penohuenches left the place at once, and such of their opponents as the horses did not ride down, they drove into the bushes. Jenkitrum, however, was not satisfied with this. His messenger had been abused and taken prisoner, and this was an outrage perpetrated on himself. The cry of "*Retal! retal!*" resounded. To the right, in one of the small outbuildings, burned a lamp which the fugitive inmates had left behind. In a trice the door was burst open; a few minutes afterward the house was on fire, and the flames shed their red glare over the neighborhood. A strong east wind had arisen, driving the fire rapidly toward the main structure; and the frame-work, parched by the long-continued drought, was immediately in a blaze.

But few of the Indians, among them the cazique himself, remained in front; the others galloped out to the corral, where the horses of the officers were seized and driven off.

Don Enrique rushed from the burning building, carrying his daughter in his arms. As yet, it was, perhaps, possible for him to reach the garden from the side of the veranda; but no sooner had the savages discovered him, than one of them spurred his horse, and, with a yell, galloped up the broad staircase of the veranda. But the horse stumbled, and threw the Indian. He jumped up, laughing, and caught the dress of Irene, who fled past him, when her father perceived her danger, and, uttering a scream of terror, hastened to the assistance of his child. It is true, he compelled the Indian to quit his hold, but he himself received so violent a blow on the forehead, that he fell senseless into the burning timbers, while Irene, pursued by her enemy, scarcely knowing what she did, and frightened by the horse's fall, sped across the lawn. She heard another horse close behind her, and turned timidly aside, but immediately felt an iron arm encircling her waist, and lifting her up; she resisted, but in vain. The horse bounded forward, while she was held to his neck. "Help! help!" she screamed despairingly, and some officers, who had taken heart again and intended to rescue her, confronted her captor courageously, but they were unable to arrest him as he wildly broke through their ranks. One of them fell to the ground, another was hurled aside, a third was scarcely able to avoid the thrust which the chief levelled at him with his lance, but the movement of his horse prevented him from aiming with unerring certainty. Like an apparition, the spirited animal disappeared at the next moment in the bushes, and, with it, every trace of the Indians, to whose destructive attack only the burning buildings and a few dark bodies stretched out on the moonlit ground—a ghastly illustration of the nocturnal assault—bore witness. Some shots, however, were fired after the robbers, in the uncertain hope of bringing one of them from his horse, but a serious and immediate pursuit was not to be thought of; for the time, it was above all necessary to realize the damage done in the attack, and to ascertain the direction in which the raiders had made their escape.

At last daylight dawned upon the scene. As the first beams illuminated the horizon, the moon paled, and the flames of the hospitable residence, which up to this time had sheltered only good and happy people, lent a weird lustre to the morning. Some officers had, with infinite trouble, succeeded in saving Don Enrique, who, felled as he had been to the ground by the terrible blow dealt him, would, but for their timely assistance, have perished in the flames. They had also carried the colonel into the court-yard. But his case seemed hopeless. Though he was still alive when his friends raised him up, he could no longer speak, uttering only low wails and groans. The heavy bola (a piece of lead sewed up in leather) had broken the spine between his shoulders.

CHAPTER V.

THE PURSUIT.

THE officers, who had been fighting in various places, and now seeking to save their horses—a vain endeavor after they were once in the hands of the Indians—assembled gradually in the court-yard in the rear of the burning house. They were unable to extinguish the flames, and the fresh breeze, blowing them away from the other buildings, secured these, at least, from danger of destruction. But where were the buglers, to whose vigilance the hacienda had been intrusted last night? Not a trace of them was to be seen; in the road lay the sentinel, to whom the savages had furtively crept up and ridden down. Under the hoofs of their horses the poor man suffered severely, and expiated his deplorable lack of vigilance; he died before the officers could convey him to the court-yard.

If the musicians had disappeared, some of them had left behind their bugles, and one of the officers now sounded the signal which would call them back if they were within hearing. They slowly made their appearance, somewhat ashamed, but seemed to be entirely uninjured, and the two whose heads Allcmapo's iron hands had knocked together, appeared to have recovered, and were present with the others.

The peons and servant-girls also emerged from their places of concealment, and at sunrise even the most timid took heart again, for all knew that the savages, after an attack of this description, never returned to the scene of their ravages.

Information came that the Indians had taken all the horses, both those of the soldiers and the haciendero, and had driven them into the mountains, as well as the cattle, and this had probably been their sole object. The animals stolen from them had not been restored, and they would not recross the mountains without recovering their property, so they had simply taken the law into their own hands. If they proceeded violently on this occasion, who could blame them for it? They were rude people, and the whites had treated them in the most provoking manner.

Captain Adano took command of the small detachment, the colonel having died, despite all effort to save his life. But how were they to overtake the fugitives without being themselves mounted! Messengers were dispatched in all directions to bring horses from the neighboring haciendas, and one of the buglers was ordered to repair to Concepcion on the first horse he could obtain. He was to inform the commander-in-chief there of what had occurred, and ask him to send a squadron, in order not only to recover what had been taken by the robbers, but to inflict such punishment as would deter them from committing similar outrages in the future.

Meanwhile, none of the officers had paid any attention to the poor old man, who did not regain his consciousness until some of the servant-girls took care of him, and now he cried despairingly for his child—his Irene. Carried off! A prisoner in the hands of the savages! The idea was so dreadful that he could not endure the terrible truth; and, as soon as he was again enabled to stand on his feet, he tottered through the court-yard and garden into the vineyards and fields, calling for his lost darling in a heart-rending voice. The conflagration, the loss of his horses and cattle—he did not think of these calamities, and he would have deemed himself rich had he been able at this moment to fold his child to his heart. But in vain were all his cries and prayers. Even the soldiers looked compassionately upon the old man as he tore his white hair, and then fell on his knees and pressed his forehead into the dust. There was one hope left to him at this terrible moment: his child, perhaps, had not been carried off, but was dead and buried under the smoking ruins of his house. Oh, he wished she were dead, rather than in the hands of those merciless foes—alone, betrayed, and helpless, in the wilderness of the Pampas.

With trembling haste he rose and rushed to the ruins of his home; with his own hands he tried to remove the burning timbers to seek the remains of his "pearl," and the bystanders had forcibly to prevent him. The assurance with which they sought to console him, that his child was still alive, and that this or that officer had seen her on the horse of one of the Indians, only served to add to his despair and almost drive him mad.

Meanwhile Captain Adano did not fail to do all in his power to overtake the Penchuenches. He himself accompanied the scouts who had just returned, in order to satisfy himself of the direction which the fugitives had taken; at the outset it was very difficult to ascertain any thing about it, inasmuch as their horses had galloped in every direction to keep the cattle together. Besides, several paths led up to the pass, by which they would cross the Cordilleras. Those of whom he inquired for the shortest route gave him conflicting answers, and it soon appeared that none of them had ever been there. On advancing farther into the forest, he discovered that the trail led eastward, and the only doubt remaining was whether the Indians, in the next valley, might not have turned toward the deserted land of the Araucanians, or had taken the more direct but by far more difficult road across the mountains. They were able to cross them everywhere at this period, while the rains at a later season would render most of the passes utterly inaccessible.

The news of the nocturnal attack and the abduction by the Penohuenches of young Irene spread like wildfire. Though few of the settlers would have thought of following the savages into the mountains to take from them a few head of cattle and stolen horses, yet the calamity which had befallen the lovely girl who had won the favor of all by her amiability and modesty, excited compassion and a desire to go to her assistance. Scarcely an hour elapsed when ten or twelve young men, armed with lassos and fowling-pieces, and accompanied by horses carrying provisions, galloped up for the pursuit. Others arrived in the course of the day, and all seemed to wait impatiently for the hour to set out after the robbers. Probably they had not retreated very far, and, intoxicated with the success of their first attack, concealed themselves in one of the neighboring gorges, in order to make another raid next morning before daybreak. If this surmise should be verified, there was well-grounded hope of cutting them off from the mountains.

Horses were also brought to mount the officers, but Captain Adano still hesitated to give the signal to depart, as he wished to await the arrival of the troops for whom he had sent, and who were not expected until nightfall. This, however, did not suit the impatient guassos. If the Indians really had determined to cross the mountains, the delay would enable them to get far in advance of their pursuers, who could cut them off only by immediately following their trail. If this operation should be successful, the felling of a single tree at the right point would compel the fugitives to return and seek another pass, when they would fall into the hands of the soldiers, marching up from Conoepcion.

Four officers begged leave to accompany this expedition, and, as the captain himself was afraid lest too long a delay would frustrate the pursuit, he finally consented to let them go. The young men gladly vaulted into their saddles, and in a few minutes they were ready. But at the moment they were about to leave, Don Enrique tottered out of one of the small buildings where they had put him on a couch after he had fainted. He waved his hand, and demanded to accompany the expedition. He was deadly pale; his eyes lay deep in their sockets, and his hair floated wildly round his temples. One of the young men compassionately dismounted and led his horse to him; he himself intended to ride a pack-horse. The old man, gratefully nodding, hastened to seize the saddle with both hands, and tried to put his left foot into the stirrup; but he was unable to do so—his strength was exhausted. Sitting down on the ground, he wept bitterly, with his face in his hands.

If any thing could have added to the exasperation felt toward the robbers, it was the sight of this unfortunate father, who, the day before, was in health and prosperity, with cordial hospitality entertaining his guests, and attending to their wants, but now ruined and heart-broken. Yet he uttered no reproach—no angry word against those who had deprived him of more than his life—of his darling child. In the consciousness of his profound distress, he did not even raise his head when the pursuers, uttering cries of vengeance, spurred their horses and galloped into the open field.

Scouts sent out in advance of the column had meanwhile discovered the direction in which the Indians had fled in the morning; as the trail extended beyond the next valley, it was certain that they did not intend to turn toward the Araucanian territory. In fact, they might expect to meet there with stragglers of the Chilian army, and they had to be careful of capture by such soldiers; nothing, therefore, remained for them but to return as speedily as possible to the Otra Banda, that is to say, the extensive Pampas lying beyond the Cordilleras, whither, they were well aware, no troops would venture to follow them. What good would it have done to pursue the Indians in that part of the country? If a superior force were on their trail, they would flee across the pathless savanna, and a weak detachment of troops would soon be hemmed in and annihilated. The pursuers, therefore, hoped that they would overtake the savages in the mountains, where, either in the forests, or on the slopes of the Cordilleras, they might dare to enter upon a struggle with them.

At first the direction which the Penchuenches had taken gave rise to the belief that they would turn toward the Bio-Bio River, inasmuch as the best road extended along its banks, and as they might have driven on it most rapidly the horses and cattle taken from the whites; but it soon appeared that they had gone to the left, through the mountains, where only well-tried horsemen would venture. In this respect the Chilenos were not inferior; they were almost as much at home in the saddle as their enemies, and, without a moment's hesitation, they followed the distinct and broad track of the red men.

The ride through the dense underwood of the lower range was arduous and exhausting, and, but for the horses of the Indians, which had opened a passage, their progress would have been slow. At all events, it was evident that they were advancing more rapidly than the fugitives. It is true, the latter had moved considerably in advance, and it was all-important to make no delay in order to overtake them on ground not unfavorable to a successful attack.

The ascent into the mountains was by a path known to none of the men, often as they had been in this elevated region, nor even to their guide, an Argentine, who was well acquainted with the Otra Banda. Was this only a stratagem of the Indians to decoy their adversaries into an ambush, or to the brink of some dangerous precipice? But such a plan would have failed, for the Chilenos were well armed and numerous, and, according to the most reliable information, the Penchuenches were hardly more than forty or fifty strong, so that the former believed themselves fully able to cope with them.

The track led farther and farther into the mountains; here the party followed a gorge, where a bridle-path crossed the route, and where many deep holes obliged them to ride very slowly. There was a spring here which served as a sign, for it had filled one of the holes. The water looked muddy, hence not a long time could have elapsed since the Penchuenches had been there. If they continued the same path, they would soon fall into the hands of the avengers. But this hope proved delusive, for the trail led to the first opening on the left, and traces on the other side indicated plainly that horsemen, who seemed to have galloped in advance, had stopped there in order to direct the stolen stock into the by-path. They now ascended another steep slope, dotted with beeches, and where the luxuriant kila commenced to form the underwood; but it was already late, and in the night it would have been impossible for them to force their way through this wilderness, much less, therefore, to keep on the track of the Indians. They halted at the first water-course; it was a small brook dancing merrily over the pebbles. They would not exhaust their horses and therefore encamped for the night.

Scouts were dispatched to ascertain if the Penchuenches might not be near, but they were unable to discover anything, and thought the enemy had gone farther than they had expected. Sentinels were posted for the night, and doubled toward daybreak, in order to be entirely safe from a sudden attack, for they had to do with exceedingly wily men, familiar with all the strategy of forest warfare. Jenkitrusa, however, seemed not to contemplate an attack. The night passed without the slightest disturbance, and at early dawn the men were saddling their horses again, when the sentinel posted on the lower slope hastened up and informed them that he had heard horses neighing in the valley below.

Was it the whole force of the Penchuenches? This was hardly possible, inasmuch as they had followed the trail up to the brook and, now that day was near, it was plainly to be seen that they had ascended higher into the mountains. Who else could it be? They thought the noise had proceeded from friends. Their doubts were soon dispelled. A bugle-signal was heard in the direction in which the noise had been heard, and the exultation of the pursuers now knew no bounds.

Those who were following them were a squadron of lancers, who had come up quicker than it was deemed possible. One of the young men was immediately dispatched to the valley, to inform his friends of the right direction, and a strong detachment advanced without further delay along the track which the enemy was supposed to have taken. They knew that all they had to do was to detain him.

The troop now consisted of some forty soldiers and upward of twenty young gauchos, almost all provided with firearms, and more than able to cope with the Penchuenches, provided they were overtaken in the mountains. They had good reason to hope that such would be the case, for it is troublesome, even for Indians, to drive cattle over the mountain-paths, and frequent delays are unavoidable.

The higher they ascended, the farther they receded from the dense underbrush. Gigantic arancarias, the fruit-trees of the wild tribes, which in autumn drop large quantities of almond-like nuts, studded the flanks of the heights, and nothing grew in their shade; this enabled the party to advance with greater rapidity.

Their guide and principal scout during the whole expedition was Pedro Alfeira, an Argentine, who, about a year before, had settled in the neighborhood of Don Enrique's hacienda, and become a citizen of Chili. Not only was he familiar with the forest, but he was also acquainted with the peculiarities of the Indians and the topography of the Otra Banda. The rumor that he had spent a long time in the midst of the Penchuenches could not but be true. On this head, however, he himself was obstinately silent. But all knew that he hated the Indians bitterly, and it was for this reason that he was employed as a guide—a position for which he was exceedingly well fitted.

He had been for some time following the track, his eyes fixed on the ground, when he suddenly raised his head as if he had noticed something in front of him.

"Halloo, compañero!" whispered Captain Adano, who commanded the lancers, galloping up to his side, "what is the matter in front? The scoundrels!"

"*Quien sabe, señor!*" said Pedro, in the evasive manner of the South Americans, "*quien sabe?* But I smell smoke, and we may be near the fires of their last camp. Possibly the red brutes themselves may still be there."

"Shall we send out a scout in that direction, Pedro?" asked the officer. "I now smell the smoke myself; I am sure the breeze drives it directly into our faces."

"Caracho!" growled out Pedro, "if so, señor, I believe we need no longer send out scouts. The infernal dogs have set fire to the forest!"

"Set fire to the forest?" cried the soldiers, in dismay. "But the araucarias will not burn so quickly?"

"Forward! forward!" exclaimed Pedro, imperatively. "We must at least ascertain as speedily as possible what it is. They are hardly ahead of us, for it is certain they are hidden behind the smoke."

So saying, he spurred his horse, and, without paying any further attention to the trail, galloped toward the crest of the next hill, which was scarcely fifty yards off. Followed with equal rapidity by the other men, he soon reached it, and it turned out that his suspicion was correct.

This hill which, it was clearly seen, the Penchuenches had descended again, sloped for several hundred yards toward a deep valley, to which the main road led to the pass. In the gorge below was a dense undergrowth of kila, exceedingly luxuriant, and interwoven with innumerable creepers. From above, the valley looked like a cornfield beaten down by the storm, but the Chilenos were too well aware of the obstruction offered to their progress by these weeds, through which no horseman in the world would have been able to force his way.

It is true, the Penchuenches must have known some path, and a lancer who had been sent to reconnoitre soon returned with the information that a regular bridle-path led into the kila-thicket, and that it was trodden down; but, on the other hand, it could no longer be doubted that the grass was on fire; for from the hill they were able to discern a cloud of smoke over the thicket.

"Can we not turn to the right?" asked the officer.

"Yonder," said Pedro, "the valley grows deeper, and the kila denser. See how few the araucarias are there. No, we must if possible pass to the left, and, if we succeed in turning the place and riding along the edge of the conflagration, we shall easily find the track of the red-skinned scoundrels."

Without waiting for a reply, the guide galloped across the crest of the hill toward a spot where there was a clearing in the forest. Captain Adano rode by his side, to satisfy himself of the character of the ground. But both uttered an oath, on seeing themselves of a sudden on the brink of so precipitous a declivity, overhung with gigantic fragments of rock, that it seemed as if the slightest contact would suffice to hurl them into the depth. To ride down on this side was impossible. Men and beasts would have broken their necks. Besides, a wild mountain rivulet was foaming below, and the roar of a cascade was heard.

"Suppose we follow the path leading into the kiln-thicket," said Adano, after gazing for a few minutes upon this disheartening scene, and repeatedly shaking his head. "At all events, we must make the attempt. We can certainly turn back if farther progress be impossible."

"Do you hear that!" said Pedro, pointing his outstretched arm in the direction of the smoke.

"It sounds almost like the rattle of musketry," exclaimed the captain, quickly.

"It is the cane," said Pedro; "for every knot caught by the flames bursts with a loud report. The fire, driven by the fresh breeze, is approaching at a furious rate, and God have mercy upon us if it should overtake us in the canebrake below! You say we might turn back in the narrow pathway? Suppose one of the foremost horses should stumble, or be entangled in the creepers, and the musketry, as you say, should be all around us, amid the blaze and smoke—the buzzards would feast on our remains to-morrow! No, I have once passed through such a scene."

"What are we to do?" exclaimed the officer, looking impatiently to the right.

"The fire is turning in that direction," replied Pedro, "and, as soon as it is fully under way, you will admire the extraordinary velocity of its progress. A horse can hardly run fast enough to escape. Nothing remains for us but either to return to the place where the red rascals passed to the left, or simply to wait here until the kiln is burned down."

"But that may be for several days."

"*Quien sabe?*" replied Pedro, shrugging his shoulders. "Who knows it? And who can help it?"

"And meanwhile the poor girl is in the hands of those savages! Unfortunate father! Pedro, is it not possible for us to hew a path so that we might, at least, make an attempt to advance without running the risk of being cut off?"

Pedro shook his head emphatically, and, pointing his arm again in the same direction, he said:

"See how dense the thicket is; our knives would soon be blunted, and we could not open a passage in less than three days."

While he uttered these words, a gust of wind swept through the tops of the tall araucarias under which they were standing, and Adano exclaimed, with a deep sigh:

"This is a bad thing for us. Let a storm arise, and the whole canebrake will be a sea of fire in a short time."

"It would not be so bad if your prediction were verified," growled out Pedro,

who now for the first time looked up and perceived that the northern horizon was covered with heavy black clouds; "the sooner it is over the better for us. But for the accursed kila, we should probably have overtaken them this morning; but I believe the storm will help us, for it is coming from the northwest, which indicates rain, and if it should come the track would be again clear by noonday."

"And can we really do nothing until then! Must we remain idle?" asked Adano.

"We can let our horses rest," said Pedro; "that is all, and it is certainly desirable on an expedition which will put their mettle to the test. The less we exhaust them the fresher and stronger they will be when we need them." Acting upon his own words, he dismounted, and led his horse back to the men waiting on the summit of the hill.

He had not mistaken the signs of the weather; in less than half an hour the sky was covered by swiftly-passing clouds; the wind increased to a gale which hurled to the ground the heavy cabezas, the fruit of the araucarias, and endangered the safety of those halting under the trees. At first single heavy drops beat the ground like leaden bullets, and soon the floodgates of heaven seemed to have opened.

CHAPTER VI.

THE KILA-FIRE.

THE flames were devouring the cane with a crackling noise, and the smoke was ascending in dark clouds, emitting a strong, offensive smell. The fire, by this time, approached so near that it could be seen on the opposite slope. The sudden change in the wind, which at such a season occurs very frequently, and is often accompanied by thunder-storms, turned the conflagration more toward the south. The wet leaves became less combustible, and the dense smoke indicated the extinction of the flames.

As the place where the lancers and guassos were halting was free from underbrush and cane, they needed not to have trembled for their own safety, for the tall trees do not catch fire so easily, and when they do, it takes time to destroy them. Now that the wind was blowing in another direction, the last danger was gone, and the Chilenos sought, so far as they could, to protect themselves from the rain, which, despite their efforts, soon drenched them to the skin. But that did not trouble them much; as soon as the shower was over, they would be dry again, and, leaning against their animals, to protect with their ponchos at least the saddle from the rain, they calmly awaited the order to remount.

In the mean time Pedro alone was not idle; and no sooner had he satisfied himself that the fire in the canebrake would not be dangerous, than he descended the slope on foot as far as the point where the kila commenced, and the down-trodden cane showed the route which the Indians had taken. He had not advanced fifty yards when a path, two feet in width, led into it in an eastern direction. The tracks, it is true, were no longer to be distinguished, as the rain had effaced them; but this was of no consequence, for assuredly there was no other path in this wilderness, and, at the spot where the last vestiges of the conflagration would disappear, they would be sure to find again some traces of their enemies.

Pedro penetrated farther into the thicket until he saw plainly that there was no danger, and that his men might forthwith pass through the canebrake. The ground, however, was still hot toward the interior, and patches of fire still flickered, notwithstanding the rain, but they would not prevent the immediate resumption of the pursuit.

The rain was still pouring down with unabated violence, but this was of no importance either; the Indians were equally exposed, and the Chilenos had already been obliged to remain idle for several hours, while every minute removed the Penchuenches, who were assuredly profiting by the delay to the best of their ability.

No sooner had he emerged again from the kila than the guide gave the signal to advance, which he had agreed upon with Captain Adano. The Chilenos mounted quickly, and, taking Pedro's horse with them into the valley, they soon reached the narrow opening in the canebrake, moving in Indian file. Even this mode was fraught with difficulties, for, when the path had first been opened, the mounted men cut off a large number of strong stems in the middle, so that, being three or four feet long, they were great obstructions. They are especially dangerous for horsemen riding at full gallop, since they catch the stirrups, and rider and horse are often hurled into the sharp-pointed cane. For this reason almost all Chilenos use wooden stirrups, which, although a little clumsy, are adapted to their purpose, as no branches can entangle them, and they keep the feet warm and dry.

Fortunately the thicket was hardly half a *legua* in width and filled only the valley separating them from the next height. As soon as they had passed through it, they reached again a part of the forest comparatively open and free from underbrush; and now they lost again the track of the fugitives—a difficulty increased by the fact that the Indians, perhaps intentionally, had turned their course to the left, as if they had purposed to descend into the valley.

But here Pedro was exceedingly useful; for, perfectly familiar with the cunning of his enemies, he did not allow himself to be misled by any seeming deviation from the original course. The Penchuenches could not have crossed the mountains on the left, at least not yet, in this part of the country, owing to the precipitous character of the slopes; hence they must have turned to the right. A fresh trail was soon discovered, and followed at a gallop.

The Indians also had advanced with speed across the tolerably open ground, although now and then an undergrowth was to be met with. The dwarfed appearance of the trees, among which were many cactuses, wild apples, and myrtles, indicated that they were approaching a more elevated region.

It was discovered that the cattle of the Indians must have become accustomed to the direction of their drivers, and the whole cavalcade formed a closed column. That they had advanced more rapidly, was a matter of course, and the pursuers had to accelerate their speed if they intended to overtake the robbers on the western side of the Cordilleras. They knew full well that they must not follow them to the eastern side, where they would be exposed to the danger of being attacked by a superior force, and of having their retreat cut off.

Before them lay a bare range of heights extending in the direction of the Cordilleras and dividing the eastern and western parts of the Pampas. They had not yet reached the crest, where they would doubtless enjoy a most extensive view, when Pedro, waving his hand, signed to the horsemen following him to halt, and galloped ahead. When he had almost reached the summit, he dismounted, and crept like a serpent behind a large rock which covered his figure. Here he stood motionless for a few minutes, and gazed upon the wild, desolate landscape before his eyes.

To the right, at no great distance from him, lay the peaked cone of the volcano of Antuco, according to the belief of the Indians, the dreaded abode of their fire-spirit Pillan; thin, black smoke issued from it, swept southward by the storm still blowing with violence. The rain had ceased, but only while a layer of brighter clouds was over their heads; close behind them followed another menacing black mass, adding to the desolate aspect of the scenery.

Yonder lay the well-known pass leading to the Otra Banda; the Penchoenches, however, could not reach it from here, for a deep gorge separated these heights from the southern chain of hills, and, with the herds which they had with them, they could not venture upon crossing it; they would have been, moreover, utterly unable to break through the dense underbrush covering both slopes of the gorge. Vainly gazed Pedro's eagle-eyes to discern on one of the bare crests the moving forms of men; only a solitary condor hovered over them, and disappeared behind the crags.

"Can you not see any thing?" asked the captain, who followed him. Pedro, without turning his head, merely shook his right hand.

"Who knows where the scoundrels are?" he growled in a low voice; "they cannot yet have crossed; that is an utter impossibility, for, to do so, they must have had wings; and on these lower—" He gave a sudden start and stooped, as if afraid of being seen.

"What was that, compañero?" called out the captain, whom the sudden motion had not escaped, and who almost involuntarily seized the bridle of his horse.

"Have you your spy-glass with you, señor?" asked Pedro. "I mean the long one—bueno! Come up quickly this way—leave your horse there; it will not run away while it finds any grass."

The captain made no reply. In a trice he dismounted and hastened up to the guide, who silently pointed his arm before him, a little to the right; and the officer recognized immediately, at no great distance, figures passing across the next range. They were evidently Indians with their blue ponchos and long black hair; white men probably would not have penetrated into this part of the mountains. But they saw also that the Indians were those whom they were pursuing, for they drove before them a large herd, in which white and spotted cattle could be plainly distinguished.

"There they are! By the Holy Virgin, there are the villains!" cried the officer, angrily, handing his glass to the guide. "Look for yourself."

"H'm," said Pedro, taking the glass, but holding it in a very awkward manner; "I don't know exactly how to use such things, and prefer to rely on my own eyes. But it is certain the scoundrels are there, and they do not seem to be in a hurry."

"And they are not very far from us," exclaimed the captain, quickly. "The distance can hardly be a legua."

"Yes, if we could ride in a straight line," said Pedro, cautiously; "but in the Cordilleras, a single gorge oftentimes necessitates a circuit of three or four hours in order to reach a point which you believe to be within a stone's throw."

"And why are we hesitating still? We are losing precious time."

"*Paciencia*," said the guide, quietly. "We must first let every Indian pass the crest, for, owing to the kila-fire, they deem themselves entirely safe, and do not accelerate their steps. As soon as they are no longer able to see us, we shall start in pursuit.—There are the last of them, probably driving some exhausted beeves after the herd."

"You are right," said Adano, who laid his telescope on the stone, and looked attentively through it, "you are right; there are yet three of the red thieves driving a couple of oxen. The last of the cavalcade are now disappearing. Shall we set out now?"

"Are no more of them to be seen?" asked the guide. "Look sharp, señor, for the Penchuenches have falcon-eyes."

The officer, acting upon this suggestion, looked attentively, but he could no longer see any thing, and, jumping up impatiently, he exclaimed:

"*Afuera! compañero—afuera!* Not a trace to be seen of them any more, and if we do not spur our horses, we may just as well turn back and go home. *Afuera! Afuera!*"

Pedro gazed once more, and, slowly nodding his head, glided back, mounted his horse, and, without saying another word, resumed the pursuit. No further precautions were necessary, because the track was more distinct than in the morning; every Chilian soldier might have followed it without any difficulty whatever; and the young guascos already began to grow impatient and galloped at Pedro's side, without, however, succeeding in inducing him to hasten. They were inexperienced, knowing little of life, and inclined to rush forward with blind impetuosity. What did they consider of the necessity not to exhaust their horses too soon during an expedition of this description? They would discover it only when worn out and unable to proceed. Pedro was assuredly anxious to overtake the Penchuenches—as much so as the rest, although for a different reason; but for all that he acted in the most prudent manner in order to cover his retreat in case of failure. They would reach their destination soon enough, for he knew that the Indians would not advance with equal rapidity; after nightfall he hoped to be so near them as to discern their camp-fires, and toward morning make an attack upon the sleepers. In that event he had, of course, no doubt of complete success, for the savages, despite the precautions which they never neglected to take, could not be aware of the vicinity of their enemies.

But however near the Indians seemed to him from his former stand-point, the time seemed exceedingly long, when the day was drawing to a close and he had not yet overtaken them. There was no doubt of the right track, and yet he did not again see the Indians—another vast plateau extended in front of them, and, to his surprise, he could not perceive a living being on it. Where had the Penchuenches found a place of concealment on it?

Pedro seemed to be anxious to reconnoitre before riding out upon this plateau; but Adano had grown too impatient, and he was right in saying that not another minute ought to be lost. The water-shed was already too near, and it was a matter of indifference whether or not they were now discovered. The robbers would certainly leave no stone unturned to get away from them, whether they believed their enemy close upon their heels, or as yet far off.

The track was very distinct, and led obliquely across the plateau to a spot presenting a strange chaos of rocks of the most fantastic forms and groups. Here and there seemed to stand the ruins of ancient castles; solitary pillars loomed up, and so regular was their appearance that they seemed to be moulded by human hands, while on their tops lay detached bowlders which threatened to fall upon the heads of those daring enough to pass under them.

The Chilians paid little attention to these wonderful creations of nature. They cast scarcely a glance on the picturesque fragments, and sought only for living beings among them. As they did not discover any without, they plunged into the interior. They had no time to lose if they wished to accomplish any thing, for already the sun was sinking fast, and this region, destitute as it was of water and wood, was a bad place for them to pass the night. But they could not be very far from their enemies, and were at a loss to explain the speed with which the Penchuenches had driven the cattle over this plateau.

The rocks formed a sort of belt, or crown, on a hill running parallel to the water-shed, and scarcely a hundred yards wide. No sooner had the pursuing party passed through, than a narrow valley—in fact, only a cleft—opened beneath them, and they involuntarily uttered a cheer on beholding, almost within gun-shot range, the Indians hurriedly driving their cattle into a ravine. A part of the herd had already disappeared, but there—and another cheer rent the air—there, conducted by two men, rode a woman! Her avengers spurred their horses and sped at a furious rate down the slope separating them from the ravine.

It was no longer necessary for them to conceal their presence—nay, their appearance might serve perhaps to strike terror into the hearts of their enemies, who would be unable to concert vigorous measures for their escape. To throw them here into a panic, would be to annihilate them. There seemed to be no outlet, or only a very narrow one, from this ravine, on both sides of which steep and lofty slopes, inaccessible to mounted men, rose to an immense height. And if one of the frightened animals should turn, or refuse to move on, the cavalcade would be helpless and perish.

The space separating the Chilenos from the Indians was not so insignificant as the former had believed, for, on the mountains, in the thin, transparent air, the eye is not only deceived in regard to distances, but even overlooks obstructions in the path itself. Many a slope seems smooth and level, until you cross over it, when you meet with rents and fissures in which a horse and his rider may hide. Such proved to be the case now. There were clefts and undulations in the ground, some of which were passed over, while others were avoided. But since the ravine, in which the enemy had disappeared, was before them, it was not necessary to look for the trail. Hence, every one chose the path he deemed best, and galloped along with lightning speed. Each wished to be the first to wreak vengeance on the raiders, and bring back in triumph to her grief-stricken father the lovely flower they were bearing away.

What added to the indignation of the party was the figure of an Indian, who, leaning on his lance, stopped at the entrance of the ravine, and seemed calmly to await the pursuers galloping toward him. Did he intend to defend the pass alone?

"It is Jenkitrum—it is the chief!" shouted Pedro, as soon as they distinctly saw before them the dusky figure on the lighter background of the rock. As he stood there, the setting sun shed its last rays over him, and surrounded him with a light of magic beauty.

"He must be crazy to brave us!" exclaimed Adano, who was at Pedro's side. "If he remain where he is now, we shall capture him alive—"

"I would give two fingers of my left hand if we succeeded," cried Pedro, and an oath fell from his lips.

"Forward, compañeros!" shouted the guide. "Some of you must keep a little to the right, in order to prevent his escaping us on that side."

"He does not intend that," said one of the other officers; "but, capitano, suppose the rascals have laid a trap for us there? The ravine may be very narrow, and they may intend to roll stones on our heads as soon as we have entered it."

"And how could they get up, compañero?" laughed the guide; "the rocks are at least three hundred feet high, and almost perpendicular. No, he who is once here must pass through; but the cowards will not stand and fight."

"That fellow seems to be brave enough."

"We will pay him for it—forward, comrades!"

The lancers were about two hundred yards from the ravine, and the ground separating them from it was open and level. With a shout they sped toward the entrance, in front of which the Indian was still halting like a sentinel. Suddenly he raised his head and looked around. Had he dreamed? If so, it was with eyes open, for, taking up the bridle of his horse, he lifted his lance, as if menacingly, toward his enemies, and disappeared at the next moment.

CHAPTER VII.

THE FLIGHT OF THE PENCHUENCHES.

We must return for a short time to the Indians, who, led by Jenkitruss, had surprised the hacienda of old Don Enrique. Saman, the messenger whom the chief had sent after Allumapu, faithfully carried out his instructions, and leaving his horse in a grove of apple-trees at no great distance from the settlement, crept so cautiously through the thicket on the outskirts of the garden that he arrived prior to Allumapu, who was still waiting in front of the gate. He concealed himself there, until the officers followed the fugitive and shot his horse; he was nearly discovered, for the pursuers broke through the very bushes in which he was hidden. During the confusion which ensued for the next few minutes, however, he succeeded very easily in escaping unnoticed, and rode at a furious rate toward the mountains, where his report made a great sensation.

A plan for avenging the outrage perpetrated upon Allumapu was devised, and we have seen how it was carried into execution. The cazique of the Penchuenches, however, was not so anxious for spoils as the punishment of the whites for their perfidy. Had they not taken from him his own horses, and did he not merely retaliate upon them?

Such attacks never occur without bloodshed. For what do these tribes, risking as they do their own lives every day, care for that of a white man! Lance and bola are always loose in their hands, and their thrusts and throws are generally fatal. Thus, while Jenkitruss himself with some of his men boldly broke into the hacienda to deliver his messenger, and to engross the attention of the soldiers quartered there, the others were able to seize their horses, collect the cattle, and drive them away. On such occasions the Indians frequently intend to carry off white women, but such was not exactly Jenkitruss's purpose this time, for, as they had to escape through the forest, it was all-important for them not to be too heavily burdened, and to keep their hands free. However, the beautiful girl who so unexpectedly fell into the hands of the cazique proved too strong a temptation; and, moreover, had not the false haciendero richly deserved such a retribution?

They had burst like a hurricane into the hacienda; they killed, burned, and robbed, and disappeared as quickly as they had come. They were well versed in such undertakings, and their horses had been so well trained to it that it was almost unnecessary to direct them. Whenever a horse broke from the column, it chose its own path through the thicket so dexterously as rarely to endanger the safety of the rider.

Another woman, whom terror and anxiety seemed to have made mad, was speeding across an open meadow, outside of the hacienda. With dishevelled hair, she intended to hasten to the main building, when one of the Penchuenches—Saman, the scout—turned his horse and overtook her.

"*Misericordia!*" cried the unfortunate woman; but the wild warrior laughingly bent over her, and, while the horse rushed past her, encircled her waist, and tried to draw her up to his saddle. This proved well-nigh fatal to him, for the señora was much heavier than, deceived by her waving dress and the treacherous moonlight, he had believed her to be. He dragged her along, amid the most heart-rending screams of his victim. Suddenly another Indian came to his assistance; the new-comer sped like a shadow to his side, and, while riding at a gallop, he seized the dress of the prisoner, and with a sudden jerk threw her into the arms of his companion. Away they sped toward the thicket.

The shots fired had not been in vain. None of them, however, fell in the court-yard; however badly wounded, they clung to their saddles, but no sooner were they at some distance from the hacienda, and pursued by the Chilenos, than two of the Penchuenches reeled— one fell to the ground, and the other soon after. The former, who had been shot through the lungs, was dead; the other, whose abdomen had been pierced by a bullet, was still alive. The Indians never leave any of their dead or wounded in the hands of their enemies so long as there is any possibility of carrying them off. Hence, the injured one was quickly lifted on his horse, and supported by two of his companions. The dead was tied to his own horse and driven forward with the herd. The wounded man could not bear the rapid gallop long; he groaned and wailed aloud. One of his friends placed him on the saddle before him; the other kept by his side, and thus they followed their own party. But it was too much for a man with lacerated bowels to endure a ride over a broken path. The poor fellow hung his head; his limbs grew heavy, a violent tremor ran through his body, and he was soon quite silent and still.

"He is dead," whispered the Indian who held him. "Bring up his horse."

Not another word was spoken. The two remained a few minutes with the corpse, and then drove forward his horse, for they were not allowed to leave the dead body behind.

On they sped—not as rapidly, however, as they had hoped, for the cattle caused them infinite trouble. The horses of the officers and of the hacendero, accustomed as they already were to be driven in this manner, kept well together as soon as they were at some distance from their pasture, and single ones never tried to break loose; but not so with the oxen, which seemed more attached to the fields through which they were driven at so rapid a rate. Familiar with every by-path, one escaped here, and another there, and sought to reach a shelter in the thicket. It required the dexterity of these well-tried cattle-thieves to prevent the rest from imitating their example. Several escaped, nevertheless, and as they had run away too far, pursuit was out of the question. Moreover, the Penchuenches cared much less for the cattle than the horses, for even as food they prefer the latter, and, besides, the booty was by far larger than they expected, and twice as valuable as that which the Chilenos had stolen from them.

They were detained also by the narrow paths through the hills, and at the large thicket they escaped from their enemies, who had come up much too close to them, by setting fire to the forest, and delaying the Chilenos for several hours. Had not the rain fallen opportunely, their stratagem would have certainly enabled them to reach the Otra Banda without any further trouble on the part of their pursuers. The thunderstorm frustrated their plan, and the Chilenos were able to pass through the kila-brake much sooner than was imagined.

Irene, on being placed by the cazique upon the saddle, had fainted, and lay unconscious in his arms. He did not feel the light burden, and moved forward with the utmost rapidity; he seemed to be everywhere, in order to insure good order among his men, and to convey the spoils to a place of safety. When the unhappy girl returned to consciousness, they were already in the middle of the forest, at a considerable distance from the hacienda, and in vain were her supplications to be restored to her father. The Penchuenche did not understand what she said, and, even if he had understood her, he would have laughed at the folly of such a request. He to give up what he had once in his hands! Only if forcibly taken from him; otherwise, he had no idea of surrendering it.

Not quite so agreeable a burden carried Saman the scout, who had seized the other Chilian woman; for the señora was stout, though not tall. The horse which bore them both felt the heavy load. A change, therefore, became necessary, for Saman commenced to lag behind, and did not have the slightest desire to run the risk of being cut off. A few words exchanged with one of his comrades were sufficient for this purpose. The latter quickly brought up one of the captured animals; a poncho was buckled to its back, and the señora was told to seat herself on it. At first she did not seem to be willing to comply, but the Indians, who had no time to spare, did not treat her very ceremoniously. As a matter of course, every Chilian woman rides on horseback, but ladies' saddles were not to be had on this occasion, and the poor woman, closely followed by Saman, who was threatening her with his lance, galloped soon after into the midst of the cavalcade, hoping she would somewhere have an opportunity to flee. This, however, proved to be impossible; Saman was one of the shrewdest men in the band, and whenever she turned her head toward him to see if he were still behind her, he nodded grinningly, and indicated plainly enough that she would be unable to make her escape.

It was not until nightfall that the band stopped in their wild course; and no sooner had the cazique lowered Irene to the ground, than she hastened to her fellow-prisoner, and convulsively encircled her neck with her arms.

"Poor child," said the Chilena, feelingly; "then you have also fallen into the hands of this horde!"

"Ah, let us escape," whispered Irene to her; "it is better to wander about the forest, and die of starvation, than stay longer with these dreadful men."

"Do not despair," said her older companion; "we may succeed: do not lose heart, all may be well yet, and your father will, doubtless, try all means to deliver us."

"My poor, poor father!"

"Keep quiet, my darling—there is the chief, who had you on his horse. He is coming—do not make him distrustful, and never lose sight of me. When all are asleep, let us go; and when once away, they shall not find us again."

It was Jenkitrusa who made his dispositions for the night; but it had grown so dark that the Indians could hardly see where they were, and kindled several fires, which shed their light over the scene. Jenkitrusa, it seemed, did not intend to trouble the women, and to have intrusted Saman with the task of attending to them. He only selected the place where they were to sleep; it was under a projecting rock, where they would be protected from the heavy dew falling overnight. Saman lit a fire there, and spread his saddle-blankets on the ground; he then left the women, who saw immediately that, although they were hidden, they were so hemmed in that there seemed to be no prospect of escape. It is true, the savages were now sufficiently occupied with their booty; a few of them seemed to have received orders to prepare supper, and a young horse was quickly killed, skinned, and roasted.

The women were not forgotten; it was Allumapu—somewhat better acquainted with the habits of the whites than his wild companions—who brought them several juicy pieces of meat on a broad leaf, and arranged a flat stone as a table.

Irene recognised him—it was the prisoner.

"Oh, for the sake of the Holy Virgin, señor," she exclaimed, beseechingly, "what is to be done with us? Do not carry us too far into the mountains: my father will pay whatever ransom you may demand—oh, bring me back to him!"

"The whites are treacherous," said Allumapu, gloomily; "they would keep you and kill our messenger."

"Oh, do not believe that," cried Irene; "my father is a good and honest man; he was very angry at your being made prisoner."

"The whites are treacherous," repeated the Indian; "their tongue lies, and they hate red men. But the white flower is good; she will be the wife of a brave chief."

"Great God!" cried Irene, shuddering, and burying her face in her hands. Allumapu returned in silence to his companions.

Irene was awake all night—awake in the vain hope of being able to deceive her enemies; and often her companion, wrapped in a dark blanket, crept away to find somewhere an opening in the lines, but she was always unsuccessful. Six or seven dusky figures, holding their lances in their hands, were silently walking up and down among the fires, which were constantly kept supplied. Had she advanced another step she would have been discovered. Would she arouse the wrath of the Indians? She dared not.

Thus passed the night. It was dawning, and in a few minutes the party were in motion. Irene was placed on a horse which Jenkitrusa himself led. Even without this precaution she would have been unable to escape, for her horse was not fleet-footed, but one of those broad-backed pack-animals which are sure-footed, but clumsy and slow. Her escort, mounted as he was on a spirited steed, would soon have overtaken her.

The cavalcade galloped forward until the scouts reported that the enemy was at their heels, and would overtake them that very day. Jenkitrus knew how to meet this emergency, and, intimately familiar with the country, he did not interrupt the flight of his men until the dense thicket lay behind them. There he gave his orders, with which Allumapu was intrusted, and, while the main body hurried forward, those who remained set fire to the undergrowth.

We know how long the conflagration detained the pursuers; the delay was not sufficient to secure the escape of the Penchnenches, and the ravine was now their last hope.

It would, indeed, have been possible for them to post their men on the slopes on either side of the ravine, and, by rolling down large stones, prevent the Chilians for some time from passing through. But the whites would have quickly climbed the heights, and, by means of their fire-arms, driven the Indians from their position; nay, possibly they might have cut them off, and either made them prisoners or killed them, inasmuch as no path led thence toward the east. The cacique, however, did not wish to expose his men to needless peril, after having already fully attained his object. The only thing he had to do was to detain the enemy for a short time, and this he hoped to accomplish in another way.

When the Penchnenches reached the ravine, their scouts informed Jenkitrus that the Chilenos were galloping close behind them, and would presently come in view. So narrow was the passage that in many parts only a single horseman could force his way, but this was no objection; the attempt had to be made, and the cacique issued his orders with perfect calmness.

First the two horses to which the corpses of the slain had been tied, were sent through the ravine; they must not by any means fall into the hands of the enemies. Next came the spoils, but Jenkitrus himself caught with his lasso a white horse, and kept it by his side. The animals were slowly driven into the pass lest they should block it up at the narrow points; in that event all would have been lost. Then came the warriors, one by one, and the two women closed the procession. Already the whites appeared on the neighboring hill, and rode with wild cheers down the slope leading to the ravine.

The cacique had thrown his lasso to Allumapu, who was halting by his side, and said a few words to him. The youth disappeared with the white horse, and Jenkitrus remained alone, observing the approach of the enemy, silently and attentively, until further delay would have involved him in serious danger. It was not until then that he slowly turned away, seemingly with composure, but no sooner did the rocks conceal him from the eyes of his pursuers, than he spurred his horse and galloped after Allumapu.

CHAPTER VIII.

THE PASS.

THE sun was setting behind the wooded heights in the west, and in the ravine hung already that gray, gloomy mist which heralds nightfall. The Chilenos, on reaching the entrance of the pass, still had daylight, and concluded that the Indians were posted behind trees for the purpose of defending themselves in so advantageous a position. To their surprise, however, they did not meet with a single living being in the ravine, through which a smooth and level gravel-path seemed to lead. They stopped distrustfully and bewildered, for they took it for granted now that the Indians were lying in ambush, and had devised some trick to entice and slaughter them. Pedro himself, apparently, was by no means inclined to lead the way and reconnoitre.

"These devils cannot be trusted," he growled; "for they delight in devices of the meanest kind. You had better send your soldiers with their guns. Let them fire a few shots, and the poltroons will scamper off, for they do not like such leaden pills."

Adano made no reply, but dismounted, unfastened his carbine, and entered the pass alone. Two of his officers followed him, and the three penetrated for some distance into the ravine, which, at the entrance, was about sixteen feet wide, but gradually narrowed until they were hardly able to walk abreast. However, nothing suspicious was to be seen, but the ground showed the track. It was obvious that the Indians had sought to reach as hurriedly as possible the open country on the other side. What could they do with their arms in this narrow gorge? They could not use their weapons, as they had to swing them round their heads before throwing them, and their long and elastic cane-lances would have been powerless against men armed with pistols and carbines. To resist the whites under such circumstances would have been sheer madness, and, in order to lose no further time, Captain Adano resolved upon energetic measures. They seemed to offer the only prospect of preventing the Penchuenches from reaching the other side of the mountains.

The officers, therefore, hastened back to the entrance of the ravine, remounted their horses, and gave the signal to advance. Captain Adano, holding the bridle in his left hand, and a cocked pistol in his right, led the column at a brisk trot.

At the outset, nothing obstructed their progress. The ground, owing to the gravel with which it was covered, was smooth, and soon the pass narrowed; it was very dark, and no outlet to be seen. But the brave Chileno continued his way, for it could not be very long. Evidently some volcanic phenomena had torn the massive rocks in this part of the mountains, and, though the surface was much corroded by its long exposure to the atmosphere, it was at the same time almost destitute of vegetation. Only mosses and lichens grew here and there, and wherever a projection had been covered with a slight layer of earth, some small shrub endeavored to grow; otherwise both flanks were bare, and so precipitous that even a guanaco could not have ascended them. The Chilenos went forward as rapidly as possible, until they arrived at a point which looked as though the passage were entirely closed. A heavy fragment had fallen down from above, and blocked up almost the whole ravine, rendering the outlet so narrow that it would have been extremely difficult for a horseman to turn at this spot. But the way was of course passable; otherwise the Indians could not have been there. Captain Adano did not hesitate a moment,

NOTHING WAS SEEN SAVE SOME HUGE MOUNTAIN BIRD.

although he was well aware that this was the only place suitable for an ambush, if the Panchuenches intended to offer any resistance. It grew darker, though there was yet light enough to examine the gorge, and he believed that, farther on, it widened. There was certainly the end of the ravine, and they would presently be able to advance.—But how were they to get over the obstruction? Captain Adano urged his horse, but the animal seemed unwilling to move. It threw its head up, and snorted. The captain, who himself did not feel quite at ease, drew his pistol, and then spurred his horse again. It obeyed, but thrust its head forward, as though scenting something suspicious. It had to move in a curve, as there was at this point a bend in the pass. The captain held the bridle firmly in his left and the pistol in his uplifted right hand. Before an enemy could have reached him, he would have had time to fire. Suddenly the horse started and almost fell, pushing back those behind it. Adano spurred it violently, and, maddened by the pain, it advanced a step, but retreated immediately, snorting and rearing, and could not be forced forward.

Captain Adano made another effort, but, obedient as his horse generally was, he could not now do any thing with it.

The Chilenos meanwhile whispered to one another that they were approaching an ambush, and the guasos especially cast distrustful glances on the precipitous slopes. They were much afraid lest the Indians would hurl stones into the narrow ravine, and, unable to avoid such missiles, there would have been the most frightful havoc. Such apprehensions, however, were not verified; nothing was seen save some huge mountain-bird curiously lowering its head to discover what was stirring below.

"Caramba!" murmured the captain, "what is the matter? Some trick must be at the bottom of it."

Quickly dismounting, he drew his other pistol, and resolutely walked up to the spot where his horse had recoiled in so unaccountable a manner. He expected to discover some of the Indians posted there, who with their lances might have easily prevented any one from advancing; but they could never have withstood fire-arms. As he stepped round the stone, he saw something white—a dead horse—which obstructed the narrowest part of the ravine.

He still believed that an enemy was concealed behind the carcass, but no one was there, and the outlet was near. A glance sufficed to satisfy him that the animal had not accidentally fallen and died, but had been intentionally killed in order to arrest the progress of the Chilenos.

Their device seemed successful, for the captain, after carefully examining the place, and returning to his men, vainly conferred with them as to the steps to be taken to drive the horse past the dead animal. Moreover, the Panchuenches had selected that point with such consummate shrewdness, that the Chilenos were unable to remove the carcass. They could not convey it to the other side, for it had to be dragged by means of lassos, which would have been well-nigh impossible, as the stone formed an acute angle at this point. And, if they had gone to work, they would have stained the ravine with blood, and thus probably have frightened the horses still more. Within easy range of their wily enemies, they were compelled by such an obstruction to stop their march and remain idle! Adano bit his lips in a paroxysm of rage, but the matter could not be helped; they had to yield quietly to that which was inevitable, and to do all they could to renew the pursuit on the following morning.

The retreat from the ravine was difficult, as the horses could not be turned at some places, and had to be forced backward. The captain, meanwhile, made all his dispositions with the utmost sagacity in order to clear the way before daylight. For this purpose he ordered eight men to dismount and fasten to the dead horse lassos, by which it was removed.

The others prepared a camp outside, and Pedro, the guide, went out alone, in order, if possible, to climb the slope and survey the eastern country for the camp-fires of the Penchuenches, and to ascertain at what distance they were. His efforts were unsuccessful; nowhere in the darkness was to be seen a spark of fire. He discovered, however, at the same time, that this pass, of which he himself had hitherto been ignorant, lay almost on the highest range of the Cordilleras, and that only a sort of plateau seemed to separate him from the eastern slopes. If he had been there in the daylight, he might have had the best possible view of the boundless plain of the Pampas.

This, then, was the way through which the Indians, notwithstanding the forts established farther southward, invaded Chili again and again; and how easily might they have been prevented if it had been known! But it was not too late, and Pedro laughed scornfully at the thought of surprising and annihilating the savages should they attempt another invasion.

This, however, was an idea for the future; for the present he indulged the hope that he would, next day, in spite of the proximity of the Otra Banda, succeed in overtaking the fugitives. The cattle were exhausted, being unequal to such exertions, and, if the Penchuenches had been detained by them (for they relinquish only in an emergency any part of their spoils), they would certainly fall into the hands of the Chilenos, whose temper was by this time such as to prevent them from sparing the life of their foes.

Animated with such pleasant thoughts, Pedro returned to the camp, where he found the soldiers engaged in dragging the poor white horse out of the ravine upon the plateau in the rear, where it might be left to the buzzards and vultures.

Adano resolved this time to resume the pursuit before daybreak. His horses had fed on the juicy cane-leaves, and the sooner they could get down into the plain the better for them. If the track beyond the ravine was not to be plainly distinguished, they might wait for the appearance of daylight. All traces of blood near the stone were removed as carefully as possible, and a heavy layer of sand spread over the spot. Nevertheless, the horses still refused to proceed, and reared and snorted as before. The darkness perhaps added to their terror, for only a faint moonlight was reflected over the narrowest part of the ravine. To remove the odor of the blood, the Chileno adopted an expedient which proved quite effective. He emptied a part of the contents of his powder-horn upon the ground, and, after the excitement of the horses had abated, he exploded it with his cigarette. As soon as the smoke had risen a little he urged his own steed forward; at first it manifested some reluctance, but the repulsive smell of the blood was gone, and, pawing the earth, it obeyed and walked over the dismal place. The rest followed easily, so that in half an hour they entered a plateau, not unlike a dry lake, amid a chain of low hills. Only stunted underbrush, myrtles, and here and there scanty bunches of kila, grew here. Small, gay-colored alpine flowers were to be seen everywhere, and bridle-paths and trails of wild beasts crossed each other in every direction. But nowhere could they discover traces of the Penchuenches, nowhere did camp-fires indicate the way of their escape; and it was not until daybreak that they at last succeeded in finding again the course of the Indians, leading due east across the plateau.

The horsemen now rode with the consciousness that no more obstacles lay in their path, and that they were superior to their enemies. The plain, however, was much wider than they supposed; for the higher you rise in these mountains, the more surprising, as we have said, becomes the illusion in regard to distances. The threatening clouds of a thunderstorm rose in the southern horizon; the wind howled across the plain; it drove before it cinders and dust from the volcano, at no great distance, and covered their ponchos like a dark-gray pall. But they did not slacken their speed. On they rode, not in military order, but every rider trying to get through the underbrush as best he could. It was about ten in the forenoon, when they at last entered a narrow side-valley, where they hoped to obtain a better view of the surrounding country. Scarcely had they gone two or three hundred yards through this valley than they halted in surprise, for a vast expanse opened before them, and they gazed upon the desolate Pampas, over which the sun shed a weird light, and upon the Cordilleras, whose flanks sloped down to the treeless plain.

At first no one thought of those they were pursuing, for the scene was too unexpected and sublime. This, then, was the Otra Banda, which none of them, except Pedro, had ever seen—this was the country of the wild hordes of the Penchuenches—the region where originated all those wars and invasions which had carried havoc, not only to the shores of the Pacific, but to those of the Atlantic, and threatened both Chilenos and Argentinos.

No country could be better adapted to such warlike operations; and who could have followed those savages into the savannas, which were their homes, and extended, like an ocean, in all directions far beyond the horizon? Thither they escaped when threatened by a superior force; there they assembled again to concert measures for a new expedition as soon as the danger was past. As the tribes were constantly at variance with each other, and hostilities frequently occurred among them, so they united whenever they had to deal with a common enemy. Their messengers then speedily called together the wild auxiliaries, who might be repulsed, but could never be thoroughly vanquished and subjugated.

In the depth below, and seemingly close to the base of the mountains, whose descent is by no means so precipitous as that on the west side of the Cordilleras, meandered a river through the plain; the rich verdure nourished by it was plainly to be seen, while only here and there the water flashed as a mirror. The captain took out his telescope and opened it. What objects dotted the plain yonder? The brown tents of the Penchneches. He could distinguish forty or fifty of them, although the distance was as yet too great to discern their occupants. Or had the Araucanians, who had been driven from their homes, assembled there to wait for a return across the mountains, and vengeance for the devastation of their homes?

But where were the robbers pursued up to this time? They might be concealed in the gorges, and, if they did not ride on the crests, they could not have been seen from above. But here their path was plainly visible.

Pedro first discovered dark objects moving on one of the slopes to the left, and called the captain's attention to them. They proved to be Indians passing from one ravine to another, and then disappearing altogether. But they could not be the fugitives, for they were coming from the north toward them; from the depth to the right ascended, at the same time, a dense cloud of smoke, which could not be that of a hidden camp-fire, but evidently a signal destined for the other Indians who had come in sight. And to the right moved also several figures.

On the rugged peak was a horseman, with his poncho floating in the breeze; farther below were to be seen others, who, however, did not flee, but sought to ascend the slope on which the Chilenos were halting.

"Caracho!" said Pedro, riding up to Adano. "Beware, señor; those yonder are not escaping from us, but, on the contrary, trying to cut off our own retreat. We are here in the Otra Banda, and no one knows how many of the scoundrels may be hid in these gorges."

"But we cannot leave the poor girl in the hands of savages!" cried the captain, vehemently. "Those cowards will take to their heels as soon as we attack them. They are more afraid of fire-arms than of their Pillan."

"But not where they are on their own ground," replied Pedro. "Believe me, I have seen them make attacks upon Argentine troops which would have made your hair stand on end. And what can we do with our exhausted horses when they stop our retreat, and meet us with their united forces?"

"But who knows if the band which we have followed has any connection with those Indians!"

"Do you see the smoke yonder?" exclaimed Pedro, pointing to the right. "They answer the signal, and the fellows to the left are also moving again. You are now acting on your own responsibility, capitano; I have forewarned you, and wish to tell you that I accompanied you only to overtake the robbers, but not for the pleasure of having my throat cut. If you intend to advance into the Otra Banda, señor, I wish you joy of it, and a happy return, but I for one will ride as fast as my poor horse will carry me back through that ravine to a place of safety, for we can accomplish nothing here."

So saying, he turned, cast some distrustful glances to the right and left, where the smoke unmistakably indicated an understanding between the two parties, and then slowly led his horse up the path which they had descended a short time before.

Adano hesitated to follow his example; he was anxious to advance, and averse to returning to Chili and stating that he had fled from the enemy without being attacked. But at the same time he did not conceal from himself the danger to which they would all be exposed in case a superior force should attack him here, and obstruct his retreat to the gorge. In the mean time he calmly watched the different hordes now in full sight, but he was by no means reassured by the discovery that fires were kindled at three other places surrounding him and his men. The horde to the left could no longer be seen from the point where the whites were stationed; but, for all that, the Indians might ascend one of the gorges leading toward them, while those on the right, although quite distant yet, marched along the crest, and evidently tended to the height.

Adano could not conceal from himself that he would be in a critical position, if, entirely unacquainted as he was with the mountain-roads, and having no other way of retreat than a single ravine, which might easily be obstructed, he should be attacked by the Indians. The guassos soon put an end to his hesitation, for it had not escaped them, either, that the two hordes were coöperating, and they did not feel disposed by any means to fall into the hands of the Araucanians, who had been driven from their homes and exasperated to the utmost. It is true, they profoundly pitied Irene's fate, and had striven to the best of their ability to rescue her from the hands of the savages. That they should go still farther could not be expected, and they declared to the commander of the column, without any circumlocution whatever, that Pedro was perfectly right in demanding that they should retrace their steps, and added that they would follow his example before it was too late.

Adano, who secretly did not disapprove of what they told him, nevertheless tried to detain them until they really would be in danger; but they replied, dryly: "It would be too late then, and they would not wait longer." Moreover, a thunder-storm was at hand, and, while it would not injure the weapons of the Indians, it would wet their own fire-arms, and prevent their use. In short, they declared it was utterly impossible for them at present to recover from the Penchuenches the spoils taken from the hacienda. Possibly they might do so at a later time, but at this juncture they would return. They turned their horses and followed the track of their guide.

CHAPTER IX.

PEDRO'S ADVENTURE.

WHEREVER we may look in nature, we find a gradual, often a scarcely perceptible transition from one genus or family—from one race to another—and it is highly interesting to observe how, in the species of such genera or races one peculiarity is now more prominent, and again another. Between man and quadrupeds there are monkeys; between birds and mammals, bats; between birds and fishes, flying-fishes and those divers which really belong to the water rather than the air. In the different genera the distinctions are never very strongly marked and well defined, but there are always links closely connecting one with the other; as, for instance (between birds of prey and singing-birds), the cuckoo—which, so far as flight and appearance are concerned, strongly resembles a sparrow-hawk, but does not possess either its claws or its curved beak—manifests a strong desire to seize the property of others.

In the same manner we find in the neighborhood of all Indian frontiers men born within the borders of civilization, who, from their earliest years, have indicated far more inclination for the life of their wild neighbors than that of their own race. It is true, the occupations of their parents turn their minds that way. Stock-breeding, which is the principal business in such regions, teaches the farmer, at an early age, how to manage horses; stray cattle compel him often to cross the frontier, where he familiarizes himself with the Indians and their manners and peculiarities. At their parents' farms they have, perhaps, only a small cabin and a few acres of land, on which they raise corn and potatoes; otherwise they are not much better off than in the woods or on the prairies. They have at home the same lack of protection and comforts, and finally the mildest and most sensible laws appear burdensome, while there are no laws whatever, no judges, and no courts in the land of their roving neighbors. Their education does not restrain a vagabond spirit; for what do they know, save, at the best, to read, or write, or cipher a little? And their religion! they learn a few prayers, that is all. Almost, without exception, they become more brutal and reckless than their uncivilized friends; above all, their language is constantly interlarded with the most disgusting oaths.

Such men do not assume the good qualities of the Indians: the magnanimity which often distinguishes the character of the latter, their attachment to a native hunting-ground, nay, their national pride, inasmuch as they are never recreant to their own country and people. The frontier whites are more ready and willing to adopt Indian vices, and there are, therefore, generally no meaner and more debased beings than those "deserters of civilization," who place themselves on a par with savages, and take up their abode with those who despise them, for they are soon seen through, and who endure them only so long as they are useful, particularly in intercourse with their neighbors, expelling them as soon as they become burdensome.

According to his own statement, Pedro Alfeira had passed the larger part of his life among the Penchuenches, whose language he spoke better than his Spanish mother-tongue, and he even asserted that one of those tribes had conferred on him the rights of a chief. The Indians, however, probably were ignorant of this, for one day Pedro had suddenly disappeared from their territory. He never alluded to the motives of this sudden departure, but it was certain that something must have occurred which rendered it impossible, or at all events dangerous, for him to return. While he was formerly a devoted friend of the Penchuenches, he seemed now suddenly to have become their mortal enemy, for he never uttered their name without cursing them, and declared often that he would not rest until he saw the extermination of the whole "bloody race!"

For this reason he had willingly joined the expedition, in the hope of overtaking and chastising his former friends, impeded as they were in their progress. This expectation was disappointed by the delay which the Chilenos had at the ravine, and by the arrival of the tribes in the Otra Banda. Here the tables were turned on the whites, for it was precisely by the invasion of the land of the Araucanians that large numbers of Indians had been driven to the Pampas east of the Cordilleras, and were ready, of course, to attack any column of Chilenos that would penetrate into that region.

Pedro would not expose himself to so imminent a peril. He saw that his companions ought not to advance with their limited force any farther into the Otra Banda; that they had already gone a great deal too far, and might be momentarily cut off by the energetic and insidious enemy. Hesitation and delay, therefore, could not but add to the dangers menacing them, and, leaving to the soldiers and guasos their own decision, he trotted away. He had nothing to fear, as the Penchuenches had just been driven from this part of the mountains.

He was anxious to reach the pass before them, or the Araucanians. After he had once passed through the ravine, no Indian, owing to the late expedition and its results, would have ventured to follow him upon Chilian territory.—And the abducted girl! What did he care for her! How often had these wild men perpetrated similar outrages! They were cruel calamities for those who suffered in this manner, but he himself did not choose to put his neck into a noose because somebody else's was already in it. If the old hacendero paid a large ransom, his daughter would perhaps be restored to him; if the cazique should like the girl, he would doubtless keep her.

Engrossed with such thoughts, but keeping all the time a sharp lookout, he slowly ascended the slope, and, on reaching the summit, stopped a short time to give a breathing-spell to his horse, as well as to survey the plateau lying in front of him. But it was still silent and deserted—the low plants bent their heads before the approaching storm, while a small gray hawk hastened toward the clefts to seek a refuge.

The sky was overcast, and the dark clouds shrouded the more elevated peaks. Large rain-drops beat the ground, and suddenly a tremendous clap of thunder terrified the horse.

"Aha! my fine fellow!" laughed Pedro, firmly holding the bridle. "Did you never see any thing like that, to get frightened as a recruit at the first rattle of musketry! Forward! as soon as we reach the rocks yonder, we shall find shelter; now, we must brave it awhile," And, drawing his poncho over his knees (for a heavy shower poured down on the plateau), he spurred his horse and rode at a furious rate toward the ravine. The storm continued, but Pedro paid little attention to it. He had lain through many a long night wrapped only in his poncho, in similar weather, under a tree, or, in the open Pampas, and his health was none the worse on the following morning. He had grown up in the tempest, and his horse had never seen a stable.

Pedro himself seemed, indeed, to be well pleased with the storm which had so suddenly burst forth, for he was sure now that no Indians would cross the plateau. Those who were sheltered from the rain would surely stay where they were, and he smiled grimly on recognizing in the distance the dim outlines of the mountain through which was the road leading to Chili. Nevertheless, he fixed his eyes on the ground to see if there were any fresh tracks; but the rain, which he deemed so favorable to his escape, concealed from him that which otherwise would, doubtless, have rendered him more cautious, namely, the trail of a small band who had crossed scarcely a quarter of an hour before, riding toward the mountain.

Only once he turned to a knoll whence he was able to examine the country. He halted, looked round, and nodded, smilingly. For he saw that his companions, who had hesitated, submitted to stern necessity, and imitated his example; already they had reached the plateau and were following him. Had the Indians threatened them so suddenly? But he would not await them here, where he was exposed to the fury of the elements; in the ravine he would find shelter, and, turning again, he galloped on.

He had also glanced in other directions, but hastily and thoughtlessly. What else could he have seen than the shower beating the evergreen shrubs? Before him lay the entrance of the pass; he was only a few hundred yards from it, and, as soon as he had reached it, he would be safe. The wind was now blowing from the north, and, as the ravine ran from west to east, the rain could not enter.

Pedro was wet to the skin. The horse shook its head, hastening to reach the gorge. To the right, regardless of the storm, their long hair floating in the wind, galloped three dusky figures, mounted on foaming steeds; to the left, something was moving in the bushes, but the Argentine did not see any thing. Another flash of lightning and another roar of thunder, as though a sixty-pounder had been discharged near him!

Yonder lay the rocky gateway; it was within fifty yards of him. The rain had frozen into hailstones and rattled on the gravel.

"Caracho!" swore Pedro. "This is a serious affair. It is all owing to their foolish delay. They will have a fine time of it."

A few bounds of his horse, and Pedro would reach the entrance. He had drawn his hat over his eyes, but now raised it slightly, and glanced toward the pass. Suddenly he tried in terror to turn, but it was too late. A lasso drawn across the entrance threw Pedro and his horse. He disengaged himself immediately and sprang to his feet, but his large poncho impeded his movements. The wind rolled the wet folds around his feet, so that he stumbled and fell. He jumped up again, and tore his broad-brimmed hat from his head, but at the same moment he felt the sharp jerk of a lasso round his left arm and body. His right hand was free and grasped his knife, but a half-naked Indian galloped past him, and he was again thrown down by the tightened lasso. He was dragged across the rough ground; the knife stuck in a shrub, his face was torn by the bushes, his head struck against a stone—he fainted. The Indian dragged his defenceless victim into the thicket.

Other savages meanwhile captured the horse, and noisy, laughing Penchuenches rode by on all sides, heedless of the rain, and rejoicing at the trick by which they had captured Pedro. But their joy was of short duration; one of their scouts announced the return of the enemy, who, threatened on all sides, had been obliged to desist from the pursuit, and, in their turn, become fugitives. The small band of Indians was too weak to resist them. There were scarcely twenty, and had taken position here only to capture a few stragglers, and, if possible, detain the enemy until the main force, called up by signals, would join them. In that event, of course, the whites would have perished—and not one would have informed the Chilenos on the other side of the Cordilleras of the disastrous results of the expedition.

The red men, in fact, seemed to hesitate whether they should not at least attempt to climb the slope, and make an attack with stones; but they had no time. The Chilenos approached. Since the Penchuenches are utterly averse to leaving their horses, even for a moment, they preferred to await on horseback the approach of the enemy; and the storm lent them in this respect valuable assistance. In the saddle they move with the ease and rapidity of a bird in the air; but on foot they are awkward and clumsy, and, what is worse, lose their self-reliance and presence of mind.

The gauchos headed the column, the lancers covered the rear. The last of all was Adano, followed by a wild horde, who had suddenly arisen from all quarters.

The Penchuenches were now intent on creating a panic in the ranks of the fugitive Chilenos. Yells and cries, for this reason, resounded now on this side, and now on that; other voices responded, and kept the enemy in constant anxiety and excitement. Even the horses partook of the fears of their riders; they became frightened and unmanageable. Some of the lancers rode in among the gauchos, in whose midst they had a better chance of defending themselves against a more numerous force.

They had reached the entrance, and while two or three of the most timid dashed at the top of their speed against the lasso and were hurled back, others recoiled. At the same time the Indians, who had hitherto concealed themselves, rushed forth, and added to the confusion of their enemies by throwing their bolas into the midst of the frightened horses. Some were about to escape in terror into the forest, and would have thereby involved all in ruin, when one of the lancers unsheathed his sword and cut the lasso. This timely stroke cleared the passage, and Adano's commanding voice soon collected his men, who, while the guassos entered the ravine, and lost no time in passing through it, confronted the Indians and tried to discharge their carbines at them.

The whites saw now the disadvantage under which they would have labored in a conflict in the open plain, for nearly all the guns, being wet, missed fire. Only three or four went off, but produced hardly any injury. The report, however, badly frightened the Penchuenches, while Adano was enabled not only to cover the retreat of his friends, but to keep the enemy at bay.

Those who had discharged their carbines reloaded them under the overhanging rocks. The others put on fresh caps, and, while the captain ordered some of his men to fall back slowly and follow the guassos, he himself remained with a small force.

But the Penchuenches did not intend to advance after those who were armed with pistols and guns. Their sole purpose was to defend the frontier, drive back the white invaders, and secure the spoils; and, since they had attained these objects, they harassed the former slightly for a while, but kept carefully out of the range of the dreaded fire-arms, and did not even pursue the Chilenos after the last of them had withdrawn into the pass. They were willing to let them return to their own country.

CHAPTER X.

DON ENRIQUE.

MEANWHILE the most intense excitement reigned in the colony as the intelligence spread farther and farther that the Indians of the Otra Banda had not only dared to invade the soil of Chili, but carried off the lovely daughter of honest old Don Enrique. Of course the most exaggerated rumors were rife in reference to the attack made upon the hacienda; and, under the circumstances, this was not to be wondered at. For all had feared up to this time lest the Penchuenches, in the present war, should take sides with their neighbors, the Araucanians, in order not only to encourage them to prolonged resistance, but, in their turn, retaliate upon the settlers on the frontier.

These apprehensions were now verified; a band of that dreaded tribe had invaded a district long avoided. At the same time all refused to believe that only a small number had been concerned in the attack; that they had only fought to recover their property, and finally seized forcibly what they were unable to obtain amicably. The intelligence that Jenkitrusa, the cazique of the Otra Banda, had crossed the Cordilleras with all his tribes, and was now threatening the frontiersmen of Chili, spread like wildfire over the district. Most of the haciendaros did not wait for these rumors to be confirmed, but, lest they should hereafter have reason to deplore their foolhardiness, sent their wives and daughters either to Concepcion or farther north, into the districts remote from the seat of war, and, moreover, better protected from eastern invasions, owing to the greater height and steepness of the Cordilleras.

The men were arming everywhere to defend their property; saddled horses stood in readiness, tied to the houses, all day—nay, all night, so that messengers might be dispatched as soon as the first news of the approach of the enemy would be received. Ammunition was kept in readiness, that they might be able to offer the most obstinate resistance.

But the fears and precautions of the Chilenos proved needless, for no other attack, as had been expected, followed. Scouts, sent out in all directions, were unable to discover the presence of Indian tribes on this side of the Cordilleras, except perhaps in the southern part of Araucania. Hence, it was certain that the former attack had been made by a small band, and it seemed exceedingly strange that they should have ventured upon so hazardous an undertaking.

The greater, therefore, was the impatience with which the settlers awaited the return of the pursuers, after whom more troops had been sent. As they had to deal only with a small band, all were justified in hoping that they had overtaken the Indians in time, and seized from them what they had carried off from the hacienda. But one day passed after another, and they could only explain the delay in the return of the pursuers by attributing it to a sudden rise which was reported to have taken place in the mountain rivulets. They were said to have swollen so unexpectedly that the party would be detained until the waters had fallen. One rainy day is often sufficient to inundate the country adjoining the banks, and the same time to reduce the streams to their normal condition.

In fact, the returning troops were compelled to stay two days on the banks of a mountain torrent, and they did not pass there a very pleasant time; for, aside from the disagreeable consciousness of having been chased by the savages, they did not even feel sure whether or not they were still pursuing them. They did not know exactly which direction to take, and were not a little puzzled at the conduct of Pedro, their guide, who, to all appearance, had so perfidiously deserted them. He was more familiar with the forest than any of them, and once they had to wander about at random for half a day before finding a path.

It was on the ninth day after the attack of the Penchuenches that their pursuers returned to the settlements, with their horses exhausted to the utmost, their clothes torn to shreds, disheartened, enfeebled, and partly wounded in the last conflict, and brought with them the mournful intelligence that the spoils were conveyed to a place of safety, and the poor, unhappy girl carried away far into the inhospitable Pampas.—And Don Enrique?

The old man, to all appearance crushed both in body and mind, sat all day huddled up in one of the outbuildings of his hacienda, starting up anxiously and convulsively only when the noise outside announced the arrival of a stranger. No sooner had his daughter and his son-in-law heard of the terrible calamity than they hastened back, but he hardly took any notice of them.

"Irene!" was almost the only word

that fell from his lips. "Irene, my poor Irene, where are you?" And then he sat down again to brood over his misfortunes.

His children intended to take him to their hacienda, lest the scene of desolation should incessantly recall the terrible bereavement to his mind, but he refused to leave, for, he said, in a hoarse whisper, "Hither Irene will come when she returns." Here, and nowhere else, would he await her.

At last the men came back who had set out to deliver his child. He heard them as soon as they entered the court-yard, and rushed in trembling haste to the window; but he asked no one what intelligence had been brought. He only cast a glance on his wearied friends, who sat in gloomy silence on their horses; withdrawing without uttering a word, he threw himself upon his couch, and buried his face in his hands.

Thus he lay for two days, obstinately refusing to take food. His children intended to raise him up, but he did not allow them, and they feared lest, by persisting in their purpose, they would provoke an outburst of rage. It was not till the evening of the second day that he rose of his own accord, called for water to wash himself, and partook of the refreshments placed before him. The wild glances which he cast around the room from time to time seemed to seek for somebody that was absent.

The following morning he recovered his self-possession. He recognized his older daughter and son-in-law, embracing and kissing them. He inquired for Pedro Alfeira, who lived in the immediate vicinity of his hacienda, and who, he was aware, was familiar with the peculiarities and people of the Otra Banda, and was informed that Pedro had officiated as guide to the expedition, but had not yet returned.

Had he gone to the Indians in order to protect his child? No; on the contrary, he had fled more rapidly than the guassos and soldiers, and, to all appearance, set out alone for the settlements. Whether an accident had befallen him on the road—whether he had fallen into the hands of the Indians, or been drowned in the suddenly-swollen mountain torrent, who could tell?

Don Enrique sat a long time absorbed in his thoughts; but he struggled against this new disappointment, and ordered his horse to be saddled and brought to the door. His children remonstrated with him, for they believed that he intended to ride over to the tribes unprotected, and a prey to violent agitation, in search of his lost child, but he quickly reassured them. He knew that such an undertaking would have been utterly hopeless; and now, that he saw all had given up the unhappy girl, he resolved to act himself—not in a foolish and rash manner, but calmly and with due deliberation, in order to restore Irene.

Most of his horses had been stolen during that fatal night; at least those which happened to be near the house; but the Penchuenches had, of course, been unable to reach those which were kept in more remote pastures, and hence he had at his disposition still quite a number of excellent animals. Don Enrique also proved very soon that his mental faculties, contrary to the fears entertained for him at the outset, had not been impaired by the shock, for all the arrangements he made were clear and sensible.

The management of the hacienda he intrusted to a faithful old servant who had been born there, and who filled the same place which his father had held before him. He was instructed to rebuild the house in his master's absence, with the assistance of an architect whom he would send from Concepcion. He also ordered the servant to restore the garden, which had been shockingly devastated, to its former condition, lest traces of the attack should be visible at the time when Irene would return with him. He then closely examined all persons who knew any thing concerning the Otra Banda—and there were not very many of them—in order to discover in what part of the country Jenkitrusa, the supreme cazique of the Panchuanches, usually took up his abode. He obtained from them the following information:

The cazique had no fixed place of residence, but lived mostly between the Limal and Ouan Leufu or Black River; that is to say, considerably to the south of the pass of Antuco, and about due east of the Chilian province of Valdivia, whence also several low passes led across the Cordilleras.

One of his peons, a young man of about twenty-four, had crossed the mountains repeatedly with a merchant from Valdivia, and knew something of the language of the tribes; he was to accompany his master, who intended to have no other companion until he had arrived at Valdivia.

His son-in-law, now that he knew what the old man purposed to do, offered to go with him, but Don Enrique emphatically rejected his company.— The young man had to stay with his wife, and protect her; for in the unsettled condition of the country she could not be left alone, helpless, and without protection. And who would have taken charge of his possessions if an accident should befall him on his dangerous journey? The young man still sought to persuade him to accept his offer; but Don Enrique remained inflexible. He said he would travel alone with José, and God would protect him.

His plan was simply as follows: owing to the advanced season, he had no time to spare, or the Cordilleras would become impassable. He would, therefore, ride to Concepcion, draw from his banker as much money as he believed necessary during the journey, and then take passage on board the steamer that would start during the next few days for Valdivia. There he would mature further arrangements. He was sure of finding, in that city, guides that would take him across the mountains; and, once in the Otra Banda, he would repair to the cazique, who, it was his firm conviction, would not be able to withstand a liberal ransom.

With this hope new life seemed to have returned to the old man's heart. He no longer thought of the means of recovering his darling, but only of the moment when he would fold her once more to his heart, and could hardly await the time when he would be in the saddle, inasmuch as every hour's delay would defer the blessedness of that moment.

His friends still proposed to him to prevail upon the government to send a body of troops, and, as they had chastised the Araucanians, so they might give the Penchuenches also a proof of their power, and compel them to surrender the spoils. But Don Enrique shook his head on hearing of these fine plans, for he was too familiar with the affairs of his country, and knew too well how little he had to hope therefrom, even if the government, which would probably refuse its consent, should receive the application in a favorable manner.

A campaign against the Araucanians was something entirely different; they inhabited a narrow and well-defined territory on the western shore; while settlements had been established north and south of their country, which was bordered on the west by the Pacific, and on the east by the Cordilleras. The Araucanians, moreover, had fixed habitations, fields cultivated and fenced in, and herds on pastures belonging to them. They could be reached, therefore; and a Chilian army, as had been done already, could attack them on their own ground, and punish them for the outrages which they had committed. But they could do no such thing in regard to the hordes of the Pampas, of the real strength of which nothing definite was known, for their bands were roving everywhere, and it was utterly impossible for regular troops to overtake them. Their principal strength consisted in the rapidity with which they suddenly brought a force upon an unexpected point, and on the day following would be at a distance of many leagues. They moved with impetuosity upon small bodies, which they generally succeeded in annihilating; but before regulars they disappeared on the pathless Pampas. There the pursuers could not follow them, for none ever knew whither they would be led.

Often had the Argentine Government attempted, at least, to intimidate those savages, and confine them within their own borders, but always in vain. While heavy detachments of cavalry drove them, as it was believed, into the most inhospitable recesses of the Pampas, they were plundering once more the frontier settlements; nay, they harassed the Argentines incessantly, so that they were at last obliged to pay tribute in order to obtain peace, and release their hands for other enterprises.

Hence, Don Enrique knew too well that violent measures would not enable him to recover his daughter, since the robbers had reached the plains. They would flee, perhaps, with his child into the interior as soon as a superior force threatened them; and the only means by which he could speedily attain his object, was to turn to account the avarice of the ravagers, and offer them such a liberal ransom that they would not resist the temptation. So firmly was he convinced of the success of his plan that he almost recovered his former gayety, and did not even refuse to be accompanied by his friends as far as Concepcion.

He might have directly crossed the mountains and avoided the trip to Valdivia, but after the conflicts between the Chilenos and the Indians, and owing to the presence of hundreds of fugitive Araucanians in the mountains, he would not venture to choose this route; and even though he should apply to the government for a strong military escort, which might have accompanied him to the frontier of the land of the Penchuenches, this would, of itself, have aroused distrust. The best course for him, therefore, would be to adhere to his former plan, and cross the Cordilleras, alone and unarmed, in the southern part of Chili. There he would meet either with Jenkitruss himself, or one of the lower caziques, and then God would help him in his enterprise, that he might move the heart of the wild warrior.

As long as he was among his friends, this serene and confident mood did not depart from him. No Indian, he knew, is able to withstand a reward; their very marriages are matters of bargain and sale, the bridegroom buying his intended of the parents, who make him pay the more for their daughter, the more he is enamoured of her. Even his best horse will be sold, provided he gets an acceptable bid for it; and he sells the bolas in his belt, the lance in his hand, if he meets with a good customer.

For this purpose alone, thought Don Eurique, had the Indian carried off the delicate girl, who could not perform any of those hard labors imposed upon the wives of the Penchuenches. Was she able to take down one of their heavy tents, pack and set it up again? Could she make bridles and halters out of the tough hides of the guanaco, carry wood and water, make fires, and cook food? No, the cazique of the Penchuenches would certainly be glad to get rid of a useless woman if a good price were offered for her release.

Such were the thoughts engrossing the mind of the old man, on the deck of the steamer, as he gazed upon the sea. Often a smile would quiver round his lips when he depicted to himself the meeting with his lost daughter—how he would appear, his horses laden with valuable articles, before the cazique, whose greedy glances would devour the treasures—how the tent would open, and Irene rush exultingly into his arms, and then—but other scenes suddenly flashed through his mind: while his eyes still gleamed with joy, thoughts of death and insanity came, and he pressed his forehead between his hands, and sat for hours silent and motionless.

Although he himself revealed nothing in regard to the object of his journey, his fellow-passengers had already learned from the peon, who was not a very reticent man, the dreadful calamity befallen the old don; and the captain, a noble-hearted, though blunt and rough English sailor, did all he could to render his sojourn on board as pleasant as possible. The sad Chileno accepted with quiet gratitude the attention bestowed upon him, but it seemed almost as though he were afraid lest any one would converse with him and, violently tear open the wound which he kept closed. He held aloof from all, gloomily and timidly, listening indifferently to the remarks of others.

But as the steamer approached her destination, as the southern mountains came more and more in view, and he finally caught sight of the snow-clad cone of the volcano of Villa Rica, his eyes were henceforth fixed on the heights which separated him from his child.

The passengers on board, meanwhile,

spoke of nothing but Indian attacks, and of the outrages usually committed on such occasions. Many instances of their having carried off into the Pampas married women and girls, of whom their relatives never heard again, were related. Attempts, it was added, had been made in all cases to recover them, but in vain. No one, however, was cruel enough to repeat any of these heart-rending stories to the old man. There was something sacred in his grief, and, as all concurred in predicting that his fate would not be different from that of so many fathers before him, even the most unfeeling sailor felt compassion for him.

At length they beheld Valdivia port, and entered the magnificent bay of Corral, whence the passengers were obliged to continue their way in small boats up the river to the capital and colony.

Don Enrique even then paid no attention to his fellow-passengers. As soon as the steamer arrived at her moorings, he beckoned to one of the approaching boats; his baggage was soon transferred to it, and, while he himself took the helm, José and the two boatmen, favored by the tide, quickly rowed the frail bark up the river.

CHAPTER XI.

VALDIVIA.

On a magnificent river, but navigable only a short distance, though fully sufficient for trade and intercourse with the sea, lies the German colony of Valdivia, which is at the same time the capital of the whole district of Southern Chili, and, besides, a very singular and remarkable place.

The Chilian Government committed no blunder in choosing Germans to colonize the fertile and almost entirely unsettled south of that beautiful country, for no other nation clings with so tender an attachment to the soil which it cultivates; none is more industrious, and, above all, furnishes so good, quiet, and easily-contented citizens.

The English, French, and American immigrants, soon produce, indeed, a state of activity and enterprise in the countries in which they settle, and their colonies make even more rapid progress than those of the Germans, because they have ampler means at their disposal, and are also more reckless in their use; but soon there ensue petty wranglings and conflicts with the local authorities or the clergy, damages caused by revolutions, spoliations by officers bent on making a fortune in a short time, and the English, French, and American colonists, forthwith go to their consuls, prefer complaints, and compel the government—which, in consequence, is always involved in difficulties of this description—to pay double the amount of the losses sustained.

But the case is widely different so far as the Germans are concerned. There is no one to take any interest in the redress of their grievances. They have consuls—more than any other nation in the world—and, until recently, there were none who represented the commercial interests of their country better. Yet it is not long since the Prussian ambassador in Chili declared that the German immigrants did not concern him at all, and that, if need be, he could protect (that is to say, protest against wrongs) only such as had their Prussian passports renewed regularly every year.

Now, such immigrants are preferable for new countries. They will never involve them in difficulties, but add to the common prosperity by industry and ability. That they now and then inveigh against what they do not like, and speak against outrages perpetrated upon them, does no harm. The mouth is frequently a safety-valve for the hand.

The Germans in Valdivia were well to do, for the Chilian Government is undoubtedly the best of those of the South American republics, and did, at least, all it could to protect the interests of those settled in that country—a policy from which it derived the greatest benefit, inasmuch as the Germans soon showed that they richly deserved protection. Wherever they cultivated the soil, fertile acres and attractive chagras (small farms) were the result; the primeval forest was cleared, swamps were drained, roads constructed, and an industrial and commercial life existed such as the indolent and thriftless Spanish race never would have produced.

The only articles formerly exported from the province were raw-hides, and limited quantities of brandy from a few Chilenos in the interior of the country. This state of affairs underwent a rapid change; large quantities of cheese were made and exported; beer was brewed and shipped to the ports on the western coast of South America. The raw-hides were no longer transported to other places, but converted into leather, which was sold very profitably at Valparaiso. Wheat and flour were supplied in great abundance, and, while the industrious immigrants profited most judiciously by the extraordinary fertility, their lands rose in value from year to year, and a large quantity of goods was imported, the duties on which added considerably to the revenues of the public treasury. In short, the colony was in the most prosperous condition, and even the peaceable Indians living in the eastern part of the State, traded with the Germans, with whom they were soon on friendly terms, and small bands of them often repaired to Valdivia to barter horses and cattle for such articles as they needed. Special traders, mostly native Chilenos, bought cattle of the Germans, and drove them into the northern district of the Araucanians, or as far as Concepcion.

The town of Valdivia itself did not present a very imposing appearance, but it was evident that what prosperity it had did not owe its presence to mercantile speculation. All the houses were frame-buildings with wooden roofs; most of them were not even painted, but warm and comfortable, and furnished with tight-fitting windows, which, with their neat curtains, gave them a pleasant aspect.

The German population of the town was a motley one. Natives of all States of the fatherland had flocked to these remote shores: Prussians and Saxons, Hessians and Suabians, Bavarians and Oldenburgers, were represented in the colony. The jealousies so prevalent among the various German States had disappeared; all regarded themselves merely as Germans, and in no other colony in America ever reigned a more cordial and harmonious spirit than on the shores of Valdivia.

It is true, some had adopted the habits of the natives. They wore the variegated ponchos and broad sombreros of the Chilians, but they still spoke the language and sang the songs of their native country, wherever laborers were hewing the timber, making barrels, or roofing houses — wherever saddlers, tailors, or shoemakers, were at their work.

It was Sunday — a great holiday for the Germans of Valdivia, and, the weather being very fine, they enjoyed it. The steamer from the north had arrived, and brought letters, papers, and news, from distant homes. An immigrant-vessel from Hamburg had cast anchor in the bay of Corral, and all awaited the arrival of the fresh colonists with curiosity and suspense, for relatives or friends might be among them. No sooner had they received the news of the arrival, than three or four boats started down the river and conveyed many visitors to the ship. Most of them went for business purposes: agents, brokers, or merchants who had goods on board, and wished to land them with as little delay as possible. The rest of the colonists awaited the arrival of the new-comers at home, and most of them, dressed in their holiday clothes, were assembled near the landing.

At length one of the boats came in sight, but there were no passengers in it — was it the mail-boat? No, the man at the helm was not a post-office employé, but an old gentleman, wrapped in a dark poncho, and, to all appearance, a stranger; but at all events he would be able to give them some information concerning matters on board the ship, and the time when they might look for the arrival of the passengers. When, therefore, the boat reached the pier, all hastened toward it.

It was inconvenient that most of the Germans were not very familiar with the Spanish language, which is always the case where many immigrants huddle together in a foreign land, for it is not so necessary for them to learn the new language. But there was among them a man who spoke Spanish fluently. His name was Charles Meyer, or, as he was commonly called, Don Carlos, about whom we shall have to say a few words.

Don Carlos had not been longer in Chili than the rest of his countrymen; but he had done what none of the others did — married an *hija del pais*, a native Chilena, a year after he had arrived at Valdivia. His wedded life was not a very happy one, and it seemed that the only advantage which he derived was the rapid acquisition of the Spanish language. Meyer, or Don Carlos, had habits which utterly unfitted him for adapting himself to the manners and customs of the Chilenos; and Doña Mercedes, his wife, on the other hand, found it as impossible to become accustomed to the peculiarities of German domestic life.

Her temper, besides, was widely different from that of her husband. She was excitable, passionate, and impetuous, while Meyer, a very excellent and honest Hessian, a saddler, was the embodiment of calmness and equanimity. He was anxious to have peace at home, but Doña Mercedes converted his house into a pandemonium, and things did not grow much better on his seeking elsewhere for amusement. Meyer possessed the patience of a bear — what is still more, he possessed that of a German citizen, and bore quietly outrageous treatment at the hands of his wife; but at last he was no longer able to endure the wrongs daily inflicted on him. One evening, when he returned slightly exhilarated and belated, Doña Mercedes received him, not with a pleasant smile and a cup of tea, but with bitter invectives, and even forgot herself so far as to box the ears of her good-natured husband.

Some people thought Meyer would have submitted as usual to this demonstration of matrimonial tenderness, if he had been alone with his wife. Unfortunately, he had requested his friend Klenke, a shoemaker, to accompany him home. He suspected, perhaps, that his better Spanish half might be dissatisfied with her worse German half, and hoped to prevent an outburst of her indignation by the presence of a third person. Nevertheless, his plan failed entirely, and when Klenke, moreover, laughed at the unpleasant manner in which Meyer was received by his wife, the honest Hessian waxed exceedingly wroth.

Before his friend had an inkling of what he intended to do, Don Carlos seized Doña Mercedes, and with his cane dealt her two such well-meant blows that she fled, uttering loud screams, into the adjoining room. The mischief had been done before Klenke could interfere.

From that hour Doña Mercedes disappeared from the colony. Meyer did not care much about it; he reassured himself by believing that his wife had gone to some countrywoman of hers to complain of the "brutal *Alemano*," and to seek consolation. He went quietly to bed and fell asleep without remorse. He was sure she would return in the morning, but she did not.

Meyer worked at his trade until noon without concerning himself with his wife. Noon came, but not she; and not only was he hungry, but uneasy at her prolonged absence. At the same time he was afraid of manifesting any alarm on her account; for he had some misgivings that this might hereafter be used against him. He therefore went over to Salzer's hotel, dined, and returned to his residence. His spouse was not yet there, and nothing remained for him but to go in search of her; but in vain. At all Chilian houses, where she was acquainted, and where he inquired after her, the people had not, or pretended not to have seen her, and it was night without his having discovered her. On the following day he was certain that she had left him in earnest; for the Puerto Monte steamer, bound for Valparaiso, sailed that very morning, and several Germans, who came up from the bay in the evening, and who could not yet be aware of the flight of Doña Mercedes, assured him that his wife was a passenger, and they believed that she was on a visit to Lota or Talcahuana.

That she was gone was certain; and Meyer behaved in a very silly manner in trying to make his countrymen believe that he was mourning for the lost one. Nay, he spoke even of following her by the next steamer, and bringing her back. But he could not continue this rôle for any length of time, for he was in reality glad of having got rid of the doña, with whom he had fallen in love one day, and who was no more fit for him than he for her. Nor did he intend to follow her to Valparaiso; he did not even accept an advantageous offer to form a partnership with a countryman of his in that city, solely because he was afraid lest he should meet there with his "Spanish half," as he still called her. By the laws of that Catholic country they could not be divorced, and under the circumstances it was best for her to live in that city, and himself at Valdivia.

Henceforth Don Carlos commenced to breathe more freely, and he was very good-natured, industrious, witty, and popular among his fellow-citizens. He was one of those men, met with now and then, who seem gifted with a good deal of sense and ingenuity, but, at bottom, possess no thorough knowledge of any thing. To-day, he was to be seen busily at work in the brewery; to-morrow, he helped a saddler who had more orders than he could attend to; and the day after, he assisted a carpenter in building a frame-house, or shingling a roof. There was a great deal of restlessness in his nature; he was utterly averse to idleness, and, as he was temperate in his habits, he had no trouble in making a comfortable living.

As we have remarked, Meyer had familiarised himself with the Spanish language, and, as he was at the landing, the bystanders requested him to address the old Chileno, whose boat had just arrived, and to inquire concerning the immigrant-ship.

"*Come ata, señor,*" he said to the Chileno.

The old man cast a rapid glance on him; but as Don Carlos was an utter stranger, he was about to proceed, replying merely, "*Gracias, señor,*" when Don Carlos continued:

"One word, señor. I believe you were on board the steamer?"

"I do not know, señor," said the old man; and this reply took Meyer so much by surprise that he allowed him to pass on and walk toward the upper part of the town. At length he recovered from his astonishment, and exclaimed:

"Well, well, that is exceedingly strange! He does not know whether he was on board the steamer or the Hamburg bark!"

"How pale he looked," said another, "and how strangely he stared at me on passing by! I am afraid he is insane."

Meanwhile two merchants of Valdivia, who had gone to Valparaiso to buy a new stock of goods, arrived in another boat. They related to their fellow-citizens all that they had heard at Talcuahana (the sea-port lying close to Concepcion) concerning the outrage committed by the Penchuenches, and that Don Enrique, the unhappy father whose younger daughter had been carried off by the savages, had come on board to repair to Jenkitrusa, the cacique of the Penchuenches, in whose hands the missing girl was believed to be.

He, then, had been the old Chileno whose strange conduct had surprised them so much. Poor father! How slight a prospect of ever recovering his child! All know that the Indians had never yet voluntarily surrendered a person abducted under such circumstances; and who could compel them to do so in their Pampas, where, fleet-footed as ostriches, they gave battle only when they were vastly superior to their enemies, and dispersed whenever there was danger of a defeat? And he was going alone to the headquarters of the cazique? The merchants related that he had said he would take with him some companions from Valdivia—perhaps, Chilian soldiers.

The Germans shook their heads, but the interest they took in the stranger was soon supplanted by that in their own affairs. Letters and newspapers arrived for many of them via Panama and Valparaiso, and the landing was soon deserted.

CHAPTER XII.

VARIOUS PLANS.

NEXT day the town was full of the wildest rumors, for some Chilenos, who had arrived from Concepcion, added such terrible stories to the details regarding the outrages perpetrated by the Penchuenches, that the Valdivians began to tremble for their own safety. They spoke in earnest of preparing against an invasion, organizing the militia, erecting earthworks, and sending the women and children to Puerto Monte, a colony lying farther toward the south. The only thing which somewhat reassured the colonists was the lateness of the season; for, as soon as the regular rains, expected from day to day, set in, the Indians could not invade the province, inasmuch as the rapid rise of the rivers would probably cut off their retreat. Besides, the more cool-headed Germans soon succeeded in allaying the excitement.

They told the people that Jonkitrum, the cazique, who was said to have planned the attack upon the hacienda of Don Enrique, had always been on terms of peace and friendship with them; that several traders had already been in his dominions, and always met with the kindest treatment. It seemed improbable, therefore, that he would invade their province, particularly as the disarmed Indians on this side of the mountains would be unable to lend him any assistance. Hence, although some of the citizens had their rifles repaired, the idea of organizing a regiment was dropped, and toward evening all fear was dispelled.

The hostilities, however, prevailing between the Indians and the Chilian troops exercised an injurious influence upon the mercantile interests, intercourse with the Araucanians being suspended. As for the Otra Banda, no more business could be done with it during the present year.

For the rest, a band of Indians, men and women, who came to Valdivia during the same afternoon to make purchases, showed that the natives living on this side of the Cordilleras were averse to these quarrels. They had brought with them horses which they wished to sell, and were now sauntering through the streets, or standing still in front of the show-windows, staring at the knives, variegated handkerchiefs, and blankets, displayed therein, and discussing the value of the tempting goods.

They were of light-brown complexion, and by no means repulsive-looking people: the men were slender, but well built; the women, somewhat short and inclined to embonpoint, which, according to their opinion, adds a great deal to beauty, with handsome black eyes, and long black hair. They all were dressed in woollen garments, which they themselves wove, and died with indigo — the women wearing long blue gowns reaching to their ankles, and up to their throats, but leaving the right arms bare and free for work. A sort of mantle-collar was wrapped around the shoulders, and protected them from the cold and rain. The men wore tight pantaloons, but over them a loose gown, resembling the *sarong* of the northern Indians, and reaching far below their knees. They had no shirts; but the poncho, through which they put their heads, fell over their backs in picturesque folds. All were bareheaded, and the hair of the men hung down; but the women had arranged theirs in heavy yet tasteful braids. They were entirely destitute of shoes.

To the whites, of whose language they were ignorant, they paid no attention. On being saluted, they nodded their thanks, but the women always kept near the men, as if afraid lest the strangers should address or molest them, and yet they longed to enter the stores and get some of the fine things displayed in the windows. These tribes are, above all things, partial to colored beads, and the wife of one of the young men wore around her neck strings weighing three or four pounds.

Don Enrique, the old Chileno, came down the street, and started on meeting with the Indians. Had they come from the Otra Banda, and could they give him information concerning his child? But an attempt to inform himself proved unsuccessful. The men laughed and shook their heads; the women walked timidly behind them.

"They understand no other language than that of the Penchuenches," said Meyer, who was passing at the time, and recognized the old man he had addressed the day before; "it is a horrible tongue, señor, and breaks one's jaw to speak it."

"Did they come from the Pampas?" quickly asked the Chileno, who at first looked distrustfully even upon the German, for his foreign dialect and sunburnt face probably aroused in him the suspicion that he also belonged to one of the wild tribes.

"No," said Meyer; "they live near the Ranco Lagoon, and have nothing in common with the Penchuenches, except that they speak about the same language; nor do they ever cross the mountains."

"And did you ever cross them, señor?" asked the old man.

"I? yes, señor," replied Meyer. "I have been there twice with one of the traders, who travel almost every year as far as the Limai, and barter on the other side of the mountains. Jenkitrusa is a noble fellow, and rules with a firm hand. You are as safe in his dominions as in our own province."

"You are acquainted with Jenkitrusa?" asked the old man, in a voice tremulous with agitation.

"Of course I am," laughed Meyer; "I slept three nights in the rain in front of his tent without his ever having said to me so much as, 'Pray step in, Mr. Meyer.' Ill-mannered they are, these red rascals, but on horseback as swift as eagles; and they are not so very bad in other respects, although when we were there, some of them were drunk and cut each other's throats. They treated us Germans kindly—that is to say, I would not have advised them to steal our baggage, for the cazique would have summarily chastised them."

"And what is your occupation?"

"I have no regular occupation at present; I accept any job I can get. The less labor, the better; I can make a living without working very hard."

"Would you not like to accompany me across the mountains?"

"Well, I do not know but I would," said Meyer; "we shall talk about it some other time. We are in no hurry now. The rainy season is about to set in, and the mountains will presently be impassable."

"But I want to set out at once," cried the old man—"to-morrow—to-day, if I could. I must certainly cross the mountains."

"You must?" said Meyer, dryly. "And who will accompany you at this season, when the Indians are drinking so much apple-chicha, and are drunk all day? No one would like to risk his life in their midst."

"They will spare a father in search of his child."

"That is a pretty consolation for the rest of us," said the German. "Besides, the bad season—even though we succeed in reaching the Otra Banda, we should have to spend the whole winter with the savages, and live on horse-cutlets and peppered blood-pie. Oh, it makes me shudder to think of it!"

"And suppose I should pay you liberally for accompanying me!" said the old man, urgently. "I am rich, and I set no value on money."

"Well, I do," replied the German, "but I have only one neck, and certain it is that I shall not carry it into the mountains at this time, though you fill my pockets with gold. It would be of no avail, for we two could not go by ourselves, and you would not be able to persuade one in the whole colony to accompany you."

The old man sighed, turned, and walked silently down the street. Meyer stood and looked after him.

"Poor man!" he murmured, "I am sorry, indeed, but every one must look out for himself, and, as' for making money, there are many opportunities here in Valdivia."

So saying, he put his hands into his pockets, and went on his way. He saw the old hacendero walking toward the house of the intendant, or governor, and entering it. Don Enrique intended to apply to that official for assistance in his trouble.

Meyer himself turned in another direction, to a somewhat long but handsome building, in front of which a number of boxes and hogsheads were piled up. He passed into the cool hall, and asked to see the proprietor. He was not kept waiting a long while, for the proprietor had already noticed Don Carlos, and beckoned to him at the door of his office, which, when Meyer entered, hat in hand, was closed and locked, which did not seem at all to disquiet the German.

"You wished to see me, señor," said Meyer, in his somewhat broken Spanish, looking around the room, but discovering, to his surprise, a tall, gaunt young man reclining on a chair in the corner, and resembling an Indian rather than a white man. He wore the costume of the Chilians, and eyed the visitor with an unpleasant expression.

"Yes, señor," said the Chileno, politely, "and I am glad that you have come. It is, however, long past ten o'clock, and I was afraid lest you should miss this lucrative work."

"I was detained on the street, señor," said Meyer; "an old gentleman from Concepcion wished me to accompany him to the Otra Banda."

"It was poor Don Enrique," said the Chileno; "it is too late in the season; he will have to wait until spring."

"That is what I told him," growled the half-breed, for such he was, to all appearance; "he wished me also to go with him."

"Well, Don Carlos, you know what I want you to do?" said the Chileno, passing to business, for he did not take any interest in Don Enrique's affairs.

"I do not—at least not exactly," said Don Carlos, evasively; "do you wish me to repair any thing, or to attend to your garden? I believe we must manure the soil this year."

"But you are aware that the Hamburg bark has arrived, are you not?"

"I am, señor. We had quite a good time with the passengers, who are very jolly people, indeed."

"You know, too, what the cargo consists of?" asked the Chileno, who was familiar with Meyer's peculiarities, and did not get impatient.

"I am sorry to be unable to give you any information on this point; I have not yet seen the manifest, but can easily ascertain all about it."

"It has a mixed cargo," continued the merchant, quietly, "and will discharge half of it here, and the remainder at Valparaiso. You like to smoke good cigars, Don Carlos, do you not?"

"Well, señor," said the German, who could not but understand the allusion, glancing on the half-breed, whom he had never before seen in Valdivia, and concerning whom he did not know how far he was initiated into the peculiar business carried on at this house—"well, señor, if you have a good cigar, let me have it."

The Chileno smiled, but took one from a box near, and said:

"You need not be afraid of Señor Cruzado, who is a reliable and faithful friend of ours; he will take part in the affair. Would you like to make a little trip next Wednesday night?"

"Caramba!" said Meyer, scratching his head. He was not alarmed as to the half-breed, but the proposition itself seemed to fill him with misgivings, although he did not reject it. "It is risky business, and the last time we were near getting ourselves into serious trouble. The custom-house officers are vigilant, and, if they catch us, the deuce will be to pay. I do not aspire to be the first German that promenades at Valparaiso with a chain on his leg, and amuses himself by sweeping the streets."

"But, my dear sir," said the Chileno, "how can they catch you? You know how well every thing is arranged, so that detection is utterly impossible. We have now exceedingly dark nights; the launch is well manned, and our harbor police are so obliging and easy that they will do their duty, of course, but not an iota beyond it. As soon as the ship weighs anchor no one will give further attention to her, and the whole affair this time will be nothing but a short nocturnal pleasure-trip. The only inconvenience will be, that you will go to bed a little later than usual."

"I would I were in it already," said Don Carlos. "You talk about the business as though there were no difficulties; you seem to forget the long dark boat that darts from under the bushes on the shore. Never in my life shall I forget the anxiety I felt the last time, and I then made a solemn vow that it should remain the last."

"But, tell me, did any harm befall you? Did you not earn a handsome sum of money by the enterprise?"

"True," said the German, "no harm befell us on that occasion, for the few bullets dropped into the water or hit some boxes of cigars—but that was a mere accident, for had not the revenue-boat, in the darkness, struck a snag, it would have overtaken us in ten minutes; two of our intrepid crew, you know, jumped overboard."

"But, my dear Don Carlos, a bullet that comes within an inch of your head is as harmless as though it passed a mile from you."

"Yes, it came within an inch then, but they may take better aim; it is certain that they will be more vigilant. I should prefer to have nothing to do with the matter."

"I would not have troubled you at all," said the merchant, "but none of my men speak a word of German, and your captain, though not on his first voyage to South America, is as ignorant of Spanish."

"Very well," said Meyer, "I will go on board and settle every thing with him; it will then be unnecessary for me to enter the accursed boat."

The Chileno nodded assent. "That is more acceptable, inasmuch as it removes the principal difficulty. But you are aware that I should, in that case, be obliged to engage another man for the helm, and, aside from the difficulty of finding a reliable person for so delicate an undertaking, it would add so much to my expenses that your share of the profits would be very trifling. As you would not run any risk, you cannot look for great compensation. You must see that yourself."

Don Carlos lighted his cigar and smoked. He could not deny that the objection was well grounded, and, as he had not forgotten the money received for the last smuggling affair, he was loath to content himself with less now.

The Chileno did not disturb him in his musings, for he knew well that Don Carlos was not blind to his own interests. The German, puffing a cloud of smoke from his cigar, at last said: "You are quite right; but it is a hazardous business, after all, and it would be bad if we were caught."

"But as interpreter you will run no risk."

"Interpreter?—Bah! when I once fill my glass, I empty it. And the terms?"

"The same as before," said the Chileno, smiling. "Only the goods are more valuable, which will increase the profits, without adding to the risk."

"And when shall we start?"

"The launch is ready. Cruzado here knows the place; all you have to do is to go on board the Hamburg bark on Wednesday morning. You will find there my agent. Speak to the captain, and be informed of all to be done."

"And then?"

"You have nothing further to do than to unload the goods as soon as Cruzado arrives with the launch. You will then sail up, at all events, before daybreak, to our old landing. Are you ready, señor?"

Meyer heaved a profound sigh. He did not really like the undertaking, but the temptation to earn money with little trouble was so strong that he was unable to resist it.

"Well, I do not care," he exclaimed, "if the devil is to take me, he may just as well do so now as hereafter. I am ready, señor."

"Very well," said the Chileno, cheerfully,—"and the two gentlemen now know each other."

The half-breed had not uttered a word; he had hardly shown even by a look that he took any interest in the whole transaction. But his dark eyes were fixed searchingly on the stranger who was to assist him. He now rose from his chair, held out his hand, and said:

"Certainly, compañero, we know each other; but is the Alemano a good shot?"

"Caramba!" cried Meyer, "I trust there will be no shooting, for the customhouse officers are much better prepared for it than we."

"You are right," said Cruzado: "but a launch does not move as swiftly as a light boat, provided we have no wind for sailing, and if we are able to show them our teeth, they will always treat us with more respect than if we rely solely on our legs."

"Don Carlos is a good marksman," said the Chileno. "I often noticed his skill at the target-shooting, and I will provide guns."

Meyer shook his head, for this prospect was by no means to his liking. In a heavily-laden launch they would be unable to escape from the revenue-boat, in case they should be pursued. But further objections were of no avail, for he had already consented to take part in the business. He hated nothing so much as steady work, and had no objection to adventure, when he had an opportunity to gain a handsome sum in the course of a single night. It was severe work, and, if things went wrong, might involve him in disagreeable consequences, but yet it was soon over; and, without reflection, he put on his hat, shook hands with the Chileno and the half-breed, and left the house.

The intendant received Don Enrique with great kindness and sympathy; for he had already had from Concepcion information regarding events there, and regretted profoundly the loss which the unhappy father had sustained; but what could he do to assist Don Enrique? Was he, in accordance with the haciendaro's request, to send troops to the Otra Banda, and obtain the release of the abducted girl by negotiations, or, if they should fail, by main force? He shrugged his shoulders, for, in the first place, he was not at liberty, without the consent and order of the president, to invade the territory of the enemy; and, next, he had at Valdivia not sufficient men at his disposal to execute such a measure in the most favorable season.

There were but few troops, too few for a time when the northern Indians were at war with the state, and might easily send their bands southward, and menace the colony. How could he, then, strip the province intrusted to his care, of all means of defence? Would he not have incurred serious danger, and, in striving to help one family, exposed hundreds of others to ruin and death?—Moreover, the season was so far advanced that he could not venture to send so small a body beyond the mountains, for, if the rains should set in at the regular time, his soldiers might be cut off in the enemy's country and exposed to the attacks of the united hordes. How, in fact, could Don Enrique hope to accomplish any thing at all by force, since he was familiar with the habits and peculiarities of those tribes, which, as soon as menaced, quickly retreat to the solitudes of the Pampas, whither no troops dare pursue them? But the intendant promised to do all he could; that as soon as the steamer returned from Puerto Monte, he would write to the president, and request him not only to send a regular force to the Otra Banda in the first days of spring, as soon as the waters had fallen a little, but to order out volunteers. Energetic steps were to be taken against the savages, who had hitherto committed frequent outrages with entire impunity, and they were to be taught that there was no longer safety in their fastnesses.

However, he said to Don Enrique that nothing remained for him but to wait quietly and patiently; his misfortunes, however grievous they might be, had to be borne with resignation.

The poor father used all his eloquence to prevail upon the officer to lend him immediate assistance; he promised to defray the expense, but it was of no avail. The intendant told him that he could not risk his own responsibility, and, however anxious he might be to aid the unfortunate haciendero, he must turn a deaf ear to the appeal, for otherwise he would disregard his duty, and without prospect of success.

The only advice he could give Don Enrique, was to engage at Valdivia a few companions, interpreters, and servants, and set out at once for the Otra Banda, provided with presents for the chiefs, for which purpose he needed good packhorses. In this case he would have to make up his mind to pass the winter among the Penchuenches, but, the intendant said, it was his firm conviction that he need not fear for his own safety. Moreover, he offered to give the troubled father a letter to Jenkitruss, which might have some influence.—That was all he could do for him.

As Don Enrique had vainly tried all the morning to enlist a few men in his enterprise, the intendant's advice did not impart much comfort.

Crusado was recommended as a man perfectly familiar with the language and habits of the Indians, and the old Chileno had, therefore, already sought an interview with him; but he refused to go to the Otra Banda when the Indians were in a constant state of intoxication.

It would be too hazardous an undertaking, he said. Several Chilenos, also familiar with the peculiarities of the savages, had raised similar objections, and so had the foreigner whom he had addressed. All were unwilling to endanger their lives, except the father, who was ready and anxious for any hazard.

At first the sense of Don Enrique's loneliness weighed him down, and he sorrowfully left the intendant's house, and walked down the street; but this state of momentary hopelessness, when despair threatened to seize him, did not last long. What no one was willing to risk *with* him, could he not accomplish *alone?* Had he really need of hired assistance, when he felt himself able to execute his plans? Alas, he was ignorant of the difficulty of his undertaking, but, resolving to act by himself, he was calm and hopeful. It was not adversity that had oppressed him, but the doubt whether he was able to act or not; he had now freed himself from it, and, with head erect, and eyes gleaming with courage and determination, he walked back toward the house of a friend, where he had taken up his abode. But there he lost no time in brooding over his misfortunes and conceiving further plans, but went energetically to work to carry out his resolutions to the best of his power. He was himself quite familiar with the character of the Indians, and knew what presents to select to gain their favor. Money was not wanting; besides, he had credit to any amount in Valdivia, and, while he ordered his servant to look around for horses that could endure so long and fatiguing a journey, he went to purchase such goods as he thought necessary. He had perhaps fifty pounds of blue, white, red, and yellow glass beads, to be done up in packages, and bought all the indigo in the town. He purchased at the building of the municipality rolls of tobacco, of which the government had the monopoly, and filled two large leathern bags with them. He did not forget to buy short pipes, paper for cigarettes, Jews'-harps, brass thimbles, which the Indian women pierce and wear as ornaments around their necks, handkerchiefs of all colors, knives, spoons, and other articles, but especially red pepper, the favorite spice of the inhabitants.

These goods, together with the provisions for himself and his companion, were packed in bags of raw-hides, which withstand moisture, and may be conveniently strapped to pack-saddles. He bought also a sufficient number of good saddles, and, as his servant lost no time in looking for suitable animals, which at this season could always be purchased at moderate prices, it took him only a short time to complete his preparations for the journey.

Meanwhile the rumor of his intention spread throughout Valdivia. As there had not arrived any specially important news from Europe to engross the attention of the colonists, and, as their fears lest the Araucanians should invade the province had been dispelled, they had time to reoccupy themselves with matters of every-day interest. The plan of the old haciendero did not appear very attractive to the older inhabitants of Valdivia, since they had already heard a great deal about such expeditions; nor did they, familiar as they were with the fatigues and privations of such a journey, feel any great inclination to leave their comfortable homes, to take part in a mere adventure. But different were the feelings with which the intelligence was received by the immigrants who had just arrived from Europe, and over whom stories of Indian raids exercised an irresistible influence. One of them, a young German lawyer, named Reiwald, who was in good circumstances at home, and whom nothing but a restless spirit had induced to emigrate to America, was delighted on hearing of Don Enrique's plans, and, despite the remonstrances of most of his countrymen, who sought to dissuade him from his purpose, resolved to accompany the hacendero to the land of the Penchuenches. As he did not speak a word of Spanish, Meyer was to officiate as interpreter between him and Don Enrique, but Don Carlos could not be found, and no one was able to tell whither he had gone.

Meanwhile Dr. Pfaifel — a German physician, who had also just arrived from Europe, and who had discovered, on the second day after his disembarkation, that the colony was not by any means a promising field for the practice of his profession, as he was assured that the climate was exceedingly healthy — had also boldly resolved to join the expedition. He did not feel any inclination "to cultivate his own cabbage-garden," or to learn a trade to make a living, although he was informed that it was the best thing he could do, if he wished to prosper in the colony. Hence he thought this an excellent opportunity to make an exploring tour. Who could tell what might happen for his interest elsewhere? and books of travel, abounding in adventures and hunting excursions, had always exerted an indescribable charm upon him. Nothing, therefore, could be more agreeable than an opportunity to take part in a journey of this description; and, besides, what did he lose in the mean time? What sort of life was it that he was obliged to lead at the hotel, where he had great reason for complaint? The meat there was not well cooked; the soup was too gross; the coffee too weak; the tea too strong; in short, nothing he thought was like that to which he had been accustomed. Matters could not be much worse on the Pampas, and the sooner he departed the better.

Don Enrique had meanwhile made his preparations for the journey with so much zeal that he resolved to set out very soon. In fact, he had no time to lose; many things remained to be done, and he was obliged to attend to them in person. He did not expect to derive much benefit from the company of the two Germans, but he could not well refuse it, for, after reaching the enemy's country, it was important to have men who by turns might stand guard at night and assist him in defending his camp. The Germans would assist also in loading and unloading the pack-horses, and, if need be, lead them. The physician might render them valuable service also in case of sickness or wounds.

CHAPTER XIII.

AFLOAT.

On the day preceding Don Enrique's departure, the Hamburg bark had discharged nearly all that part of her cargo destined for Valdivia, and there were now only two launches alongside, to receive the remainder of the freight. Both belonged to a German, the one being called "Eduard," and the other "Kunigunde." Eduard lay on the starboard of the bark, and Kunigunde on the larboard. The custom-house officers on board noted down all boxes and parcels, as the duty on them was not to be paid until after they had been disembarked. The unloading of the cargo, however, did not proceed as rapidly as it might have done, and the men in the launches cursed at the slowness of the sailors, for they wished to ascend the river before nightfall, with the tide. But the delay was unavoidable; the first mate repeatedly descended into the hold to hasten the work, but so many boxes were piled upon those destined for Valdivia, that he said it was impossible for the hands to proceed faster than they did. The sun was near the horizon when the last package was hoisted on deck and lowered into the launch.

The captain had meanwhile been ashore to get his papers, and did not return until the mate gave him a signal by hoisting a flag. Preparations were thereupon made for setting sail, and the revenue officers were about to leave the ship.

The master, who had been rowed ashore by three sailors, returned with four; but the officers had forgotten this. Three of the sailors weighed the anchor and unfurled the sails; the fourth descended to the berths and did not make his appearance again until the last of the Chilenos had left the ship. They were in the captain's cabin, on whose table were bottles of wine and several glasses, which were often filled. It was growing so dark that the cabin-boy was ordered to bring the lamp, and they thought only of going on shore, and ascended to the deck.

"Caramba, capitano!" said one of them, who spoke a little English, glancing around and shaking his head, "I really do not know if it is prudent in you to leave the bay at night without the aid of a pilot. It is dark, and if you get too close to the sand-bar outside, it will be a bad business."

"Bah!" laughed the captain, "I have made the same trip four times, and the sky west is still light enough for me to perceive the land-marks. I shall have passed the bank before it is dark."

"But do not approach too close to it, capitano; it is a dangerous place," repeated the officer.

"I shall give it a wide berth, and would rather pass by the wooded shore yonder; the channel there is deep enough."

"You are mistaken, señor; there is also a shoal on which is a good deal of drift-wood. During the ebb only, the branches rise from the water."

"I know the place, and can avoid it. I should not like to remain here needlessly all night long. There is a fine breeze blowing outside, and, by to-morrow morning, I shall be a good many miles up the coast. The northern, which generally set in about this time of the year, may be expected."

"Indeed, they may," said the officer, stepping to the ladder, and looking down into his boat, lying below; "I wish you a happy voyage, capitano."

The officer and his companion shook hands with the captain, and both were soon after rowed toward the shore, where a red lantern signalized the landing-place. The town lights were burning also, and shed a lustre over the waters of the bay. At the moment the party left the bark, another fast-rowing boat passed the Hamburg ship in the direction of Corral, but changed its course somewhat on hearing the oars of the revenue-cutter, and probably seeing its shadow in the illuminated bay. Without hailing, both boats kept in the same direction, and rowed alongside a few yards before reaching the shore. The men in the small boat seemed desirous to ascertain who were in the custom-house boat. The person at the helm called out:

"Oh, Don Pablo!"

"Who is it?" was the reply.

"The revenue officer!"

"Ah, compañeros! Where do you come from?"

"From the other shore. Where do you come from?"

"From the German bark, setting sail at this moment."

"What! In the dark! What pilot is on board?"

"No pilot. The captain knows the channel."

Both boats were now scarcely a yard asunder.

"Carajo!" murmured the helmsman of the small boat. "For aught I know, the captain has half his cargo on board yet."

"It will be discharged at Valparaiso."

"There is a launch concealed among the willows on the opposite shore," said the helmsman.

"What is it there for?"

"I do not know."

"Who is on board?"

"No one. I hailed it, but no one replied. There is a house in the bushes yonder. I know the place well, for they privately sell whiskey to the sailors and boatsmen. Possibly the crew of the launch may be concealed there."

"And did you not go up to the house?"

"What for? To caution them, in case they were smugglers? The night is very dark, and I supposed they intended to board some vessel in the bay when they thought we would be in our beds."

"You may be right, but then there will be a splendid sambucuaca at Don Alfonso's to-night, and many pretty girls are said to have arrived from Valdivia."

"A plague on the rascals!"

"I wish you had ascertained more about the launch; as it is, we know nothing at all, and it may be a very inoffensive craft that has come down from Valparaiso, and stopped near the willows in order to cross over to-morrow morning and get freight."

"In that case they would have taken their sails ashore," said the other custom-house officer, who seemed to be somewhat more anxious to do his duty; "I would have remained near, but what could I have accomplished, unarmed as I am, and with only two oarsmen, in case the fellows were really smugglers? I am now on my way to the chief, in order to inform him. Let him decide what is to be done."

The officer, who had been on board the bark, muttered an oath, but he would not venture to object to the course his colleague purposed to take. The two boats thereupon passed on; one of the officers being pleased with the discovery he had made; the other exasperated at the prospect of missing the sambuqueca, and, in place of it, passing the dark and chilly night on the waters of the bay. But, however unpleasant it was for him, he had to make up his mind to do so, and to submit to what could not be helped.

Meanwhile the bark in the bay outside lost no time, and as slowly as the sailors had previously worked in the hold, as rapidly they strove now to get their ship under way. Nevertheless, it was long after nightfall before they succeeded, and on shore nothing could be discerned but the dark outlines of the mountains and the bright lights of Corral. Certain it was that their movements could not be observed.

The ebb commenced rapidly, and with it—for the breeze was exceedingly weak, and adverse rather than favorable—they drifted slowly down toward the mouth of the river.

Strange to say, the sailors did not proceed to clear the decks, and coil the ropes lying about in disorder, as is always done when a vessel sets sail. The hatchways, which had been carefully closed, were quickly opened, and arrangements made so that a considerable number of boxes in readiness might be brought up as quickly as possible. They were not very heavy, and the sailors hoisted them rapidly from the hold. Not even a lantern was permitted on deck, and the mate hung only a small blue light—which he carefully concealed under his peajacket—so close to the surface of the water that the slightest ripple might have extinguished it. This light was sufficient for their purpose, and arranged in such a manner that it could not be seen at all in the direction of Corral. The main topsail was unfurled, but the yards were not braced so as to catch what little wind there was, and the headway of the ship was impeded. Hence, the progress of the bark was not even equal to the movement of the tide, and a glance overboard would have shown the observer that the phosphorescent medusæ in the water were slowly gliding from the stern toward the bow.

The captain was pacing the quarter-deck, wrapped in his thick jacket, and had drawn his cap over his forehead. He seemed to be in no very good humor, for the business he was about to enter upon was not exactly to his liking. It is true, the darkness favored not a little the purpose of the smugglers, and on the shore toward which his ship was slowly drifting, was already to be seen the other signal, a faint-green light, which did not burn bright enough to be visible in the town opposite. Perhaps, every thing would pass off without any trouble; yet if it should arise, he would not only be punished by the Chilian authorities, but probably lose the command of his ship; the risk, therefore, outweighed the profit which he was to derive from the operation.

"Captain," said the mate, who, with another man, stepped up to his superior, "here is Mr. Meyer; you are acquainted with him, I believe; and there comes the launch which I can already see through my night-glass. Shall we heave-to, or take the launch alongside?"

"The latter would be preferable," responded the captain, without taking any notice of Mr. Meyer.

"I am only afraid," replied the mate, "we shall take her out too far."

"That is your lookout," replied the captain, shrugging his shoulders; "in a breeze such as this, you will make up for it in half an hour. At all events, I do not know in what other way we should heave-to than by bracing the top-yards as we have done. We cannot put about."

"In what time can you transfer the boxes, mate?" asked Meyer, who was perfectly at home here; "that is the most important question."

"In about half an hour."

"Then I am obliged to request you to heave-to, or, better yet, to put about," said Meyer, quietly.

"I will do no such thing," cried the captain, angrily; "I thank God the accursed hole is behind me."

"Very well, captain," nodded Meyer; "in that case, pray, mate, have the boxes lowered into the hold; I hear the launch already; it will be alongside presently, and I shall then leave the ship. Under these circumstances, I take no goods."

"And what have you to do with them?" asked the captain, turning abruptly to him.

"Nothing at all, captain, outside the bay; I do not want to be driven ashore by the breeze from the south, and to be picked up by a revenue-boat. My orders are to receive your boxes here in the mouth of the bay, and I am ready to give you a receipt for them, but not outside."

"Go away!" said the captain, and resumed his walk up and down the quarter-deck. He had not much time, however, left for reflection, for the launch was already a few yards from the larboard; it was steering with a low, dark-colored sail toward the bark.

"Well, *adios!* mate," said Meyer, shaking hands with him, "I thank you for taking me down the bay, and I will now go ashore again, for I am thirsty, and you seem to have nothing but brackish water on board."

As the captain stood near, he could not but overhear these words. He saw the launch coming alongside, and a glance satisfied him that they were already far enough from the town to have any fear of discovery. Turning and pacing the deck a few steps, he called:

"Mate!"

"Captain!"

"We cannot take with us these boxes; heave the ship to, sir, and give the man a bottle of wine."

"Very well, captain," replied the mate, who seemed fully to approve the order. "The helm alee, John! Let go there! Hans and Christian, go up and lower the topsails. Have you lead in your hands, or do you wish me to quicken your pace?—Steward!"

"Yes, sir."

"Take two bottles of wine into the cabin."

The orders followed in rapid succession; the sails caught the breeze, the bow turned slowly against the current, and ten minutes afterward it was plainly to be seen that the bark moved slowly up the river. The launch now struck gently against the larboard side of the bark, and, while some of the sailors put cushions between the two vessels, the pulley was already in motion, and one box after another was lowered.

Meanwhile two dark figures came on board: one of them was an old acquaintance of ours, the half-breed, or Señor Cruzado, as the Chilian merchant had called him; the other, a clerk of the firm. Señor Cruzado stood on deck and counted the boxes, while the clerk, without looking about him, quickly descended to the cabin, whither Meyer followed him. The steward had, meanwhile, executed the mate's order, and taken bottles and glasses into the cabin. While the captain with his two visitors were looking over several papers, and himself was counting a considerable sum of money, the boxes were transferred with rapidity to the smaller vessel. Five or six were yet on board the bark, and Señor Cruzado had already informed the German that the goods were all there, and that he might receipt for them, when the mate, who for some minutes had been peering forward, suddenly went for his night-glass, and looked into the bay.

This did not escape the half-breed; while the last boxes were lowered he approached the seaman and said, in a low voice:

"Do you see any thing suspicious, señor?"

"I do not understand what you say," growled the mate, "but if you do not take to your heels pretty soon, you will have company."

The Chileno turned from him, and, stepping quickly to Meyer, told him there was something wrong.

"Thunder and lightning!" said Meyer, in dismay, approaching the officer, "there is nothing in the wind, I hope?"

"Nothing special," replied the mate; "only a boat is coming up, and I believe it is time for us to get out of the way."

"That was what we feared," cried Meyer, in great terror.

"My dear sir," said the mate, "if you take my advice, you will get as fast as possible into your boat, else you will accompany us to Valparaiso. Where is the other señor?"

"There he comes—it would be too bad!"

"What is the matter?" asked the captain, who, at this moment, made his appearance.

"Nothing!—but we shall have visitors; I believe one of the custom-house officers has forgotten his handkerchief on board our bark.— Now, boys, to the yards, every one of you!"

"Loose the launch!" shouted the captain. "Quick! step in! Let her go!"

"Oh, I suspected this," groaned Meyer. "Why did I not keep my fingers out of the wretched affair?"

But it was too late for repentance, and the German was not the man to lose his self-possession at so critical a moment. The clerk was not yet fully alive to the danger menacing them in case the boat was really that of the officers; however, Meyer gave him no time for reflection, but seized his arm and drew him quickly to the ladder.

"But, pray tell me, señor, what is the matter?—the captain—"

"We may bid him farewell some other time," whispered Don Carlos. "It is a revenue-boat. We must leave in a hurry, or we are caught."

"Holy Mother!" exclaimed the young man, in dismay.

"Let us first get into the boat, and then you may invoke all the saints!"

In fact, it was high time. To disengage the bark from the launch, the sailors untied the rope fastening it to the bow, and it was swinging around with the current, so that the party could not descend. A sailor was about to unfasten the stern-line.

"Hold on, my friend!" cried Meyer, rushing past, "unless you wish to keep us on board."

"It is time—here she comes!" said the sailor. "Quick!"

Meyer, with catlike agility, passed down the rope and reached the launch; the clerk followed him, but, less familiar with such means of escape, he hesitated on beholding the water under him, and tried to get a foothold on the bulwarks outside.

The bark at this moment put about, and the sails filled.

"Cling to the rope, my lad," cried the sailor, "and shut your mouth!"

The Chileno did not understand what he said; but at the same moment the launch careened, forcing him from the side of the ship, and the waves closed over him. Involuntarily he complied with the advice the sailor had given him, and presently emerged from the water.

"Help!" he gasped, spirting out the water he had swallowed. "Help! I am drowning!"

A man on board grasped the line and drew it quickly; a pair of friendly arms reached out for him, and the poor fellow was taken into the boat, where, however, no one took any notice of him, for their safety now engrossed their whole attention.

Owing to the current, the bark drifted farther toward the right bank of the river; this, however, was of no consequence, as they were here in deep water, and had already passed the bank covered with trees and drift-wood. They were scarcely a hundred yards from the shore —at least from its shadow—and Meyer, who was thoroughly familiar with the peculiarities of the bay, seized the helm and turned the bow toward the shore. The breeze here was in their favor, and the boat swiftly glided away.

On the forepart stood the half-breed, wrapped up in his dark poncho, his long black hair waving round his head, as he looked into the darkness, to discover the pursuers. The bark was sailing out of the bay into the open sea. Suddenly Cruzado believed he heard human voices. He bent forward, and eagerly listened. He could distinguish some exclamation, although he did not understand it. Doubtless the same boat, which could not yet have perceived them, was hailing the bark. Time was gained, for since the current was against them, they were not able to make rapid headway, but, if they succeeded in concealing themselves for a few hours, they would be out of danger. It was unlikely that the officers would remain all night on the water; for they could not be aware of their business, else they would not have allowed the bark to set sail after nightfall.

Cruzado approached Don Carlos, who was standing at the helm, and spoke to him in a whisper. Meyer had also heard the exclamation, and admitted that nothing remained but to reach, if possible, some place of concealment. If the breeze had been favorable to them, they might have made progress, notwithstanding the tide, but, once discovered, they could not escape, and nothing would remain for them but to jump overboard, swim ashore, and allow the boat and its cargo to fall into the hands of the revenue-men.

And could they land? Might they not in the darkness strike against a snag or on a shoal? But they were already so close to the shore that the branches almost touched them.

"Strike the sail, and take out the mast!" said Meyer, in an undertone. No sooner had he given this order than it was executed, for Señor Cruzado, too, knew very well how to handle a boat.

"For Heaven's sake, no noise!"

The men lowered the mast cautiously fore and aft. The branches on the shore now touched the edge of the boat, and enabled them to draw it unseen under the underbrush, where it would have been difficult to find them in daylight. But the bow suddenly struck against something, and the boat was stopped.

"Caracho!" shouted a strange voice at this moment, in front of them. "*Ave Maria purisima!*"

"Who is there?" called the halfbreed. "Have we gone straight into the jaws of the Evil One?"

And, like a serpent, he glided forward, gazed for a moment into the darkness, and jumped overboard.

CHAPTER XIV.

THE REVENUE-BOAT.

THE crew of the launch seemed at first appalled at the new and entirely unforeseen danger. What was it? Had they run directly into a revenue-boat lying in ambush, they might as well consider themselves hopelessly lost, for out in the bay were already heard the quick and regular strokes of the oars of the returning boat, whose white sail could be seen on the smooth surface of the water. A single shout from one of the guards, and they could no longer escape discovery. Once it was thought Cruzado's voice was heard; but no other sound broke the stillness. It was only a sea-gull that was startled by the smugglers, and flew across the bay in search of a more quiet resting-place.

No one stirred in the launch; the crew scarcely ventured to breathe, for the craft outside was coming up, and, to all appearance, directly toward them. It was within a stone's throw of them.

"Caramba!" said a voice in the bay; "I am sure I saw the shadow of a small vessel at no great distance from the bark. I would you had followed me! That the bark would not allow us to detain her, we might have known beforehand, and we lost time by attempting to board her."

"Who knows what it was that you did see, amigo!" said another voice; "above all, let us row up to the place where you found the launch to-night; probably she is there yet, and we will then look around for her crew. This sort of service after nightfall does not mit me at all. I wish you had done something else than—"

The voices died away, the boat glided up the river, and soon nothing was heard but the faint sound of the oars in the rowlocks.

"Stupid fellows," murmured Meyer to himself, "not even to muffle their oars, but to make a noise which may be heard at a mile's distance! I would manage matters differently.—But I wonder what has become of Cruzado?"

He crept to the bow and looked overboard, but nothing was to be seen except an object even darker than night itself, and lying in front of the bow; but what, it was hard to say.

"Cruzado!" he whispered in a low voice.

"Are they gone?" was the reply.

"They are—at least for the present."

"Come down."

"I? Where? Into the water?"

"Here is a boat."

"But why do you not come up?"

"First examine the boat," was the reply, still uttered in a cautious voice; "I have a prisoner here."

Without saying more, Meyer lowered himself, seeking a firm foothold lest he should step into the water.

"And whom have we here?"

"He says he is a fisherman. Is this a fishing-boat? I cannot release him until we are sure that it is."

"In that case I believe you will have to hold him yet a while, compañero," growled Meyer; but he complied with Cruzado's request, without taking any notice of the prisoner, and crept past. He groped his way carefully, and when his hands touched something strange, he said, "Here is a net, and there is also a fish-tackle. Well, thank God, the man will do us no harm!"

"That is, so long as we keep our knife on his throat," said Cruzado; "I am afraid this fisherman caught himself to-night."

"Oh, señor, for mercy's sake—," cried the poor fellow, beseechingly.

"Hush!" said the half-breed. "Utter another word, and I will put my knife between your ribs. Where is the boat, Don Carlos?"

"It is already so far up the bay, that we cannot hear the oars."

"That is what I thought.—Now, compañero, climb before me into the launch. I will not let you go; you will obey me and be silent. Do you understand?"

"I do," whispered the frightened man, who had no idea into whose hands he had fallen, since he had never heard of pirates infesting the bay, nor had about him any thing worth stealing. He made his way to the bow, and looked anxiously around. The launch was filled with boxes. Had the men stolen them, and he unfortunate enough to be in the company of desperate robbers? But they had spoken of a craft passing them in the bay, and he himself had heard the movement of the oars. Police-boats rowed very seldom about the bay after nightfall. The men of the *Aduana* frequently crossed it in all directions. Those who had caught him were smugglers; he was satisfied of it. But this did not give him any comfort, for penalties were inflicted upon all who broke the revenue-laws, and if they were to make away with him, in order to silence a dangerous witness, who would ever learn of the crime, and bring them to account?

Such were probably also the thoughts of Cruzado; for, on following the prisoner, he grasped more firmly the knife which he held in his hand, and knit his brows menacingly. However, he did not feel like taking the responsibility of a bloody deed; and, besides, they were not yet driven to extremities.

"How, for Heaven's sake, did the fellow get into this thicket?" asked Meyer, when they were all on board. "Señor, what did you lie in wait for?"

"In wait for? I was asleep, for the ebb had overtaken me, and I intended to remain till the next tide, and then row home."

"In your light boat? As if you needed the tide!" said Cruzado, gloomily.

"But I have a box full of fish in tow," said the Chileno. "I could not row with it against the current."

"Is that true?"

"The line is fastened to the helm. If I falsify, you may do with me as you please."

Cruzado made no reply, but went to satisfy himself if the prisoner had told him the truth. There was really a fish-box fastened to the stern. He was one of the numerous fishermen living in the vicinity of the bay; a mere accident had caused them to fall in with him. Nevertheless, it was inconvenient to leave here a person aware of their infraction of the law, when they had yet a long way to go before reaching their destination, and, moreover, needed time, not only to stow away their freight, but to efface the traces of the crime in which they were engaged.

Nothing remained for them but to await the result of the search in which the custom-house officers were now engaged. If the transaction were kept secret, and no suspicion arose against them, they might venture slowly to work up the river under the cover of darkness; they would certainly make some headway, and might land the boxes long before daybreak; but as it was, this was not feasible, for the revenue-boat would assuredly examine the shores very carefully, and remain a long while yet in the bay. Hence, they would have to await its return, and the time thus lost might be gained after midnight, when the flood tide would enable them to sail with greater rapidity.

And what was to be done meanwhile with the fisherman? They could not leave him here, and if they took him along, they would have disclosed to him the most important part of their secret, viz., the landing-place.

Cruzado whispered something in Meyer's ear, but the German seized his arm, and exclaimed:

"No, señor. It shall not be done as long as I am on board. I do not desire murder for the sake of a few cigars. What can he do if we take from him his oars and sails?"

"He can make a noise," said the half-breed, "till the officers hear him. He will then tell him all about us, and they will pursue us. That is all."

"And what if we make him swear to keep quiet?"

"Swear?" said the half-breed, contemptuously. "Who is bound by an oath? A rope and a gag are by far better. But I don't care; let him swear, if you please, and stand the consequences. I for one can save my hide."

"And you will leave it to me?"

"I have no objection. You will then be responsible for the result."

Acting upon Meyer's suggestion, he climbed upon the boxes, unrolled the sail, wrapped himself in it, and lay down to sleep.

It is true, Meyer did not feel satisfied until he saw that his companion had really left to him the management; but, in fact, nothing further was to be done, for the fisherman could not escape, as their launch now lay between his boat and the bay, and had, moreover, driven the latter entirely into the bushes. All that could be done, was to await quietly the flood, and then, if the breeze should continue, go up with the tide. They were not very far from the landing-place, and, if nothing happened to them, they might reach it in two hours.

But what if the revenue-boat should return, and if the prisoner should attract the attention of the officers? Meyer felt that he would at least have to give him instructions, and said in a low voice:

"I wish to speak to you, señor; we have met here involuntarily, and cannot part till the tide returns. If you keep quiet until then, whether a boat pass or not, we shall afterward part as the best of friends. But if you utter the slightest sound, look at this revolver—it has six barrels. Do you understand me?"

"Perfectly, señor," said the Chileno, in a tremulous voice. "If you permit me, I will lie down and sleep."

"That is the best thing you can do, amigo," replied Don Carlos; "we shall meanwhile keep a sharp lookout. As soon as the ebb ceases, we start; but you must swear to me by the Holy Virgin, that you will follow us only two hours after we have left. Will you do so?"

"I swear it, señor," said the fisherman, solemnly.

"Very well, lie down and sleep. You have nothing to fear."

The Chileno made no reply, but took off his poncho, wrapped himself in it, and sought a place on the deck, where he might sleep. The clerk, however, was not so quiet as the fisherman; drenched by his involuntary bath, he lay on the deck, his teeth chattering, and cursing the hour when he entered upon this disagreeable affair. Meyer calmed him by throwing the other end of the sail over him. Meanwhile the German, while the the boatmen also retired, was exceedingly vigilant; he did not feel sleepy, for, whenever he listened in the direction of the bay, it seemed to him as if he heard the oars again, and as if the dreaded boat would come in sight the moment after. Thus he sat, and peered through the foliage upon the glimmering surface of the water; but hour after hour went by without a sound breaking the stillness, and gradually his eyelids grew heavy, and he fell into a fitful slumber; when he started up and listened again, no one could have made him admit that he had really slept.

He had a watch, but was unable to see the dial, and, as he drew it out from time to time, he touched the hands. The ebb would be over at midnight—perhaps a little earlier; he felt sure it could not be much longer. He took out his watch again, but started up in dismay, for the hands told him that it was already half-past one. He quickly awakened Cruzado, sleeping on the cigar-boxes as gently as though he were in his bed at home, and dreaming little of danger. The half-breed started and grasped his knife; but he was awake in a moment, and, looking up, murmured:

"What time is it, Don Carlos?"

"It is half-past one; we have slept too long; come, compañero, we must not lose another minute."

"We have plenty of time," said Cruzado, slowly raising himself up; "it will be best for us to lie still for a couple of hours; the less we shall have afterward to fear from the officers."

"Where," murmured Meyer meanwhile to himself, vainly groping on the deck for the fisherman, "where is the prisoner! He lay down here awhile ago."

"Who! The prisoner!" asked the half-breed, quickly.

"Yes. He stretched himself here, wrapped up in his poncho. The rascal has disappeared."

"Caracho!" responded Cruzado. This startling intelligence aroused him, and he ran to look after the boat. It was in its former place, ten men could not have set it afloat without getting the launch out of the way; but the Chileno had disappeared, and there was no doubt that, afraid lest his life was endangered, he had slipped overboard and escaped into the forest. And had they any thing to fear? Meyer did not think so. But Cruzado urged him to start, for who could tell if the fisherman had not a companion near? The sooner, therefore, they left the better, and if they had to lie by once more, it would certainly be preferable to choose some other hiding-place than stay longer.

The fisherman had been unable to take his boat with him, and had probably not tried to do so. Before they moved into the bay, Cruzado, as he said, "clipped his wings a little." He threw the sail, the mast, and one of the oars, into the launch, and left him only the other oar. It was then at least unnecessary for him to call for assistance, and attract the attention of the revenue-men in case they still rowed about the bay. It really was high time to move; for, as the crew were pushing their craft out of the bushes, the flood-tide had set in, and a breeze was coming up. Cruzado did not unfurl the sail immediately, but listened if he could discover any thing suspicious. Profound silence reigned over the water, on which the stars shed their light. The smugglers glided out so as to be able to catch the breeze. The mast was raised softly and cautiously, and Cruzado looked for the jib to fasten it to the spar. But this sail seemed to have disappeared, until they found the clerk, who had wrapped himself in it, and assured them that he had just fallen asleep. He would not give up his warm wrapper, for he swore, if he did, he would catch cold and die. However, the half-breed paid no attention to his refusal; he seized one of the ends, and, jerking it up, rolled out the sleeper on the boxes. He was unable to render them any service in managing the launch, which, impelled by the wind and floating with the current, was quickly passing by the bank. Scarcely a quarter of an hour elapsed when they were able to discern the lights in Corral. The red lantern at the landing was visible.

"What is going on yonder to-night?" asked Cruzado. "Generally the lanterns on the river-side are extinguished at ten, but at present they are burning after midnight; are the boats of the custom-house still prowling about?"

"That is not the reason," said Meyer, who had taken the helm, and cast a careless glance to the shore; "I was told a great ball would be given yonder to-night, and doubtless the officers of the Obilian man-of-war were invited, so that they would not extinguish the lamps at the landing."

"A ball!" murmured Cruzado to himself, chuckling. "So much the better, for the advaneros (revenue-officers) will be there. If that is so, we may venture a little farther out; we are safe enough."

"I do not know," said Meyer, without changing his course. "We had better be careful, and, at any rate, first get out of sight of those lights. The wider a berth we give them the better for us."

Nothing more was said, and Cruzado occupied himself in unfurling the sail. The good craft soon felt the breeze, and the water was heard plashing under the bow. Already the wide part of the bay was behind them, and they entered the Valdivia River.

It was not now necessary to keep near the wooded bank, and such a course, moreover, would have been highly dangerous, for the numerous tree-trunks in the water might have wrecked the boat. The mountains, which had hitherto cast their shadows upon them, now seemed to recede much farther. The party trusted to their good luck, and kept in the middle of the river, where they had the advantage of wind and tide.

On the bank lay a few scattered settlements, mostly inhabited by Germans, who had cleared the forest and tilled the soil; but no lights were seen. They had nothing to fear from these settlers. Farther above lay something dark on the water—what was it? They kept away from it, but still they had to pass. —It was a boat at anchor, which was probably waiting for the tide to reach Corral on the morrow. The crew were doubtless asleep, and they were not hailed as the launch glided by quickly and noiselessly.

In this manner they passed about half the distance to the landing below Valdivia; and Meyer, who had much anxiety, although he had not allowed his companion to notice it, began to breathe more freely. For it did not seem likely that officers, whose suspicions had really been aroused, should have come so far up the river to catch a craft of whose secret movements they were ignorant. The ball at Corral had undoubtedly favored escape, and in the course of an hour they would be beyond the reach of detection. Meyer took another oath that this would be the last boat-load that he would take up the Valdivia River under such circumstances.

"Compañero," whispered Cruzado at this moment, "what is in front there?"

"Where?" asked Meyer, in dismay.

"A little to the left of the sail—hold off some, that you may see it more distinctly."

The German now also saw a dark object, in the shadow of the trees in the river; it must be a canoe, and would certainly meet them.

"Caramba!" said Meyer, speaking to himself rather than to his companion, "it cannot be possible that we fall in with the scoundrels here in the dead of night!"

"I do not hear the oars," whispered Cruzado; "they must have muffled them."

"Well," said Meyer, "in that case I hope they are no better than we; otherwise, we shall smoke very few of our cigars."

"If they think their men will be able to take us, they are mistaken; we are well armed."

"Cruzado, amigo, that will not do; it would make matters much worse," said Meyer, beseechingly.

"Worse? I believe they are as bad as they can be. In the bay the reports of our fire-arms might have attracted the attention of the man-of-war, which would probably send a boat after us. But our pistols could not be heard here; at all events, they could not know if they were fired on the river or the banks. No, no; we must resist, and the launch must not be taken so long as I am able to fire a shot."

"The accursed custom-house—good for nothing but to make people unhappy!" wailed Meyer.

"Suppose we sail a little to the left?" suggested Cruzado. "The channel is deep enough there, and we may succeed in slipping past. The wind is so strong that they cannot overtake us."

Meyer shook his head: "There are a great many shoals on that side; we are now already too close to the left bank; if we get aground we are lost."

The suspicious boat was now so far into the river that the faint glimmer of the water enabled them to count its oars. There were four rowers, and, besides, two dark figures seated at the stern, while another stood at the bow and held a musket or a boat-hook.

After closely watching their course for a few moments, Meyer said:

"I believe I will let them come up a little closer and then run past them to the left. They will then be obliged to show their colors."

"I am afraid we shall lose the wind. There is not much of it, anyhow."

"That is on account of the trees yonder; as soon as we are farther up the river, we shall have wind enough."

The other boat, meanwhile, seemed to have paid no attention to the launch, but pursued its course. It was about ten yards in front when it suddenly turned directly toward the smugglers. Meyer profited by this unexpected movement.

"Luff a little!" he whispered to Cruzado, who stood at his side, and held the line; at the same time the bow, obeying the helm, inclined to the left, and they darted by.

"Stop! stop!" suddenly shouted one of the men sitting at the stern of the boat, and springing to his feet. "In the name of the law, what launch is that?"

"Come on board, if you want to get an answer," responded Meyer.

"Stop, or I shoot!" shouted the voice; and so close were they to each other that they could hear the man cocking his musket.

"Shoot!" growled Meyer; but, as he was nearest the enemy, he stooped as much as he could in order to have the edge of the boat between him and his pursuers, for he knew well that they would aim at the helmsman.

"Maria!" faltered the clerk, who, now awakened to a full sense of the danger, had emerged in terror from his thin poncho. "What is the matter? What do these men want?"

"A light for their cigars!" said Cruzado, dryly, when suddenly there was a flash, and a bullet struck the side, dropping into the water. But at the same moment the half-breed had taken up one of the guns, and, before his companions were able to prevent him, he discharged it at the enemy. A scream was heard, and it seemed as though there was some confusion among the officers.

These gentlemen doubtless saw that they would be unable to overtake the fugitives; and they knew that, once arrived at a place of concealment, wherever it might be, the latter would have so many accomplices, that the officers could not resist them. Long before they could obtain help from Corral or Valdivia, the smuggled goods would be out of their reach. Cruzado, therefore, on seeing that they were distancing the boat, burst into a cry of exultation. It was too soon; for the crew had only drawn in the oars for the purpose of raising the mast and unfurling the sail, which they had not needed in crossing the river. The breeze filling the sail, the boat ran at a much greater speed. Cruzado, uttering oaths, tried to draw his sail tighter, but it was of no avail. The lannah was running well, but it was built for carrying freight, and it was soon obvious that the boat, in respect of speed, was far superior.

The officers knew now that the fugitives were armed, and would not hesitate to defend themselves, for they had quickly responded to the first shot. Now, as if afraid of resistance, preferring an appeal once more in the name of the law, the officers kept at some distance, though already able to head off the smugglers. It was not until the latter were perfectly sure of this that they turned toward the middle of the river, and it was time for them to do so, for an island, a little farther above, lay in the channel; if the launch should turn there into the narrower arm of the river, which was usually deserted, the stronger crew would get the better of their adversaries, for the revenue-boat could not count upon assistance.

"Courage, compañeros!" said Meyer to the men who stood upon the deck, and seemed to be at a loss whether they should escape by swimming to the island, or defend the boat.

"They intend to board," cried Cruzado, who, gun in hand, was leaning against the mast; "but I will blow out the brains of the first man that lays his hands on our craft!"

"They are changing their course again!" exclaimed Meyer.

"That is owing to their foolish helmsman," replied Cruzado; "he knows very little of his business."

"You are right—they are coming this way again."

Meyer grasped the helm firmly. The revenue-boat was about ten yards ahead, and steered directly toward them. If both continued in the same direction for a few seconds, they would be alongside, and it was certain that the officers had greatly the advantage, for they not only had better arms, but were more skilful in using them.

"Take the handspikes, men," shouted Cruzado, "and strike the first man that shows his head on board, though you should break his skull!"

The launch turned, but not, as before, away from the revenue-boat, but toward it.

"Change your course!—put about!" cried the officers.

Whether the man at the helm did not hear, or lost his self-possession, he moved the rudder first to the right, and then to the left, so that the boat kept its course, and nearly at the same moment the launch struck it and splintered the planks.

"Hurrah!" shouted Cruzado. "Now, boys, let us rush to the bows, so that none of them may get on board! Strike at their heads!"

Two or three of the custom-house men, while their boat was breaking down, clung to the edge of the launch; but the smugglers did not care if they could swim or not. Although they did not strike them with violence sufficient to kill, they compelled them to take their hands off; and a few minutes afterward the smugglers passed swiftly up the river. Far behind floated the wreck of the revenue-boat, to which the crew clung with despairing energy.

CHAPTER XV.

ASHORE.

THE day on which Don Enrique intended to set out on his expedition to the Otra Banda dawned as bright as all the previous days had been. Not a cloud was seen, and it seemed as though Valdivia, where the weather was usually so rainy, was for once to enjoy a long and beautiful autumn.

Meanwhile, all necessary preparations had been made, and the doctor and Reiwald, the young lawyer, had bought a number of articles deemed indispensable for such a journey. Each of them needed a pack-horse of his own, and the purchases had nearly exhausted the funds which they had brought with them from the old country. This, however, did not make them uneasy, for, according to all information, their expenses would cease the moment they left the town behind them. In the country they would not require money. The Indians of the Otra Banda did not even know what it was, and in bartering would have given more for a handful of glass beads than of gold-pieces. Happy land—how long had both of them yearned to set foot on such a soil!

Don Enrique himself had six pack-horses loaded—four with presents. Besides, he took with him extra saddle-horses to be used in case the others should be worn out during the journey. He knew well, indeed, that his German companions at the outset would not be able to manage these animals with sufficient dexterity, but he could not find any one else willing to join him, or even to accompany him up to the Cordilleras, since the western slope also of those mountains is inhabited by Indians. However, the Intendant, who took a great deal of interest in the expedition, although he was unable to give Don Enrique the wished-for military escort,

THE LAUNCH STRUCK AND SHATTERED THE PLANKS.

procured for him at least assistance for the most arduous part of the journey. He had heard that there were in town three or four Indians living at the Mayhue Lagoon, which is situated on this side of the mountains; he sent for and prevailed on them to help the old señor to drive his animals to that lagoon, at the foot of the Cordilleras. The Indians, of course, were mounted, and in this manner one of the principal obstacles in the path of Don Enrique would be removed.

The packing of the horses took more time than had been expected; for not only had the loads to be equally distributed, but arranged in such a manner as to enable Don Enrique and his companions to take them off, and strap them on again, with equal ease and rapidity, which was of especial importance, considering the steep, and, in many places, almost impassable character of the mountains. Under such circumstances it was noonday before every thing was ready. Reiwald and the doctor seemed not very angry at the delay, for they were again able to dine comfortably, instead of passing the best time of the day in the saddle; they tied their horses, and, when the gong called them to dinner, they quietly entered the hotel.

Don Enrique did not imitate their example: the Indians from Mayhue had already made their appearance; the pack-horses were brought to them, and the small cavalcade, surrounded by a concourse of curious spectators, started slowly and leisurely. On all such expeditions, travellers start either about noon or late in the evening; and, though they are only able to proceed a short distance, and are obliged to pass the night almost in sight of the town, they are at least on the way, and may set out again at daybreak.

Reiwald, who saw to his dismay that the Indians had also taken the pack-horses with them, intended to call out to them to wait a moment, as they would soon finish dinner; but a doctor, whose acquaintance they had made at Valdivia, advised them to take their time in dining, and, if they wished it, a nap afterward. He himself would accompany and guide them, so that they would, at all events, overtake the party before night. Their progress on the first day would be slow, and several hours would elapse to accustom the horses to their riders and drivers.

Meanwhile the Indians left the town; at their head, Don Enrique, with no arms except a pair of holsters, each of which contained a revolver, his broad-brimmed hat over his eyes, and noticing no one. Then came the pack-horses, and then the extra ones for the saddle, hitched together in pairs; and last, José, with the small band of Indians, consisting of five men and three women, two of whom had children with them, and all mounted. The old Chileno could not have wished for persons better qualified to keep his animals in order.

The Indians rode carelessly on their slender though somewhat bony animals. Whenever a horse showed the slightest inclination to break from the line, he was soon mastered, and, by brandishing lassos, the whole line was kept in good order.

The women in the mean time were busied in a different manner, José, Don Enrique's servant, having distributed among them tobacco and paper; and, with their children before them on the pommel, they made cigarottes for their husbands and themselves. Whether their horses were galloping, trotting, or walking, it was all the same—they never interrupted their occupation a moment.

When the party passed through the last street of Valdivia, an acquaintance of ours, Don Carlos Meyer, stood at the upper window of a small and somewhat rickety house, and gazed after it as long as he could. When it had disappeared, he opened the window, and seemed so much absorbed in his thoughts, that he did not notice a man in the street, who looked up, and then entered the house. Meyer was resting on the window-edge, smoking a cigar, when a loud rapping at his door caused him to raise himself up and exclaim, "Come in!"

Meyer glanced involuntarily about the room, which really did not look fit for the reception of visitors. He had but just risen; for his poncho, which he used also as a blanket, lay on his couch, and many things were on the floor, strewed with remnants of cigars, pieces of paper, etc., indicating plainly that the room for some days had not even been swept. This was of no importance, however, for he did not receive aristocratic persons—at the best, one of his employers sometimes called on him, and frequently had to arouse him from sleep. Unconcerned in regard to the appearance of his room, but anxious at the thought of recent events, he invited the unknown visitor to enter his room.

A vague suspicion troubled him lest the police should be aware of yesterday's adventure; but, though they were, how could it be possible for them to believe that he had taken part in the affair? The smugglers had safely landed the boxes: the launch was unknown to the authorities, and he knew that a mere suspicion could not enable them to take steps against him, for they had no proofs. The appearance of the new-comer immediately allayed his fear. To all appearance, he was one of the Chillan peons, such as may be seen killing everywhere about Valdivia, and leading a life not very dissimilar to his own. They work only when their last penny has been spent, and play the señores again as soon as they have a few dollars in their pockets. But certain it was that they had no connection with the police.

"*Buenos dias, señor*," said the stranger, on entering the room, and glancing about it. He seemed, however, to take no notice of the disorder, but only to convince himself if any one else was present. "*Como esta?*"

"Thank you, tolerably well," said Meyer, who did not perceive until now that his cigar had gone out. "What do you want?"

"*Quien sabe?*" said the stranger, shrugging his shoulders after the singular fashion of the South Americans.

"Well, compañero," replied Meyer, who was not in a humor to enter upon a long conversation; "if you do not, I wonder who is to know!"

"I believe you do not recognize me, señor!" asked the peon, looking significantly at the German.

"Indeed, I don't," said Meyer.

"You don't!" continued the peon, and an almost scornful smile played round his lips. "Yes, it was very dark last night."

"Last night?"

"Or early this morning."

"This morning!" echoed Meyer, and a very unpleasant feeling stole over him. What could the peon know of last night's events? And what could he mean by alluding to them?

"It is strange," said the Chileno, "what short memories some men have! I only wished to ask what you did with my sail and my oar. Caramba! amigo. It was wrong in you to leave a poor fellow among the bushes, as you did, and I had to toil for upward of two hours until I got across the bay to my house."

Don Carlos Meyer did not blush easily, nor did he lose his self-possession very soon, but had often extricated himself with great presence of mind from unpleasant predicaments; but this time he felt the blood rushing to his face for a moment, for he was entirely unprepared for this meeting, and he did not know exactly what course to pursue, whether to deny all knowledge of the affair, or come to an understanding with the Chileno.— How could the fellow have recognized him? No one could see any thing among the bushes; it was impossible.

What added to the unhappy character of the situation was the fact that, after the collision with the revenue-boat, the sail and oar went overboard. If Meyer admitted any thing, he would have to pay for the lost articles, and who could tell if the fellow would keep silence, and not betray the whole occurrence to the police? This might involve him in very serious trouble; for a shot had been fired, and two or three men might have been drowned; nay, Meyer did not even know certainly if Cruzado, whom he thought capable of almost any atrocity, had not crushed the heads of some of those who had clung to the launch. At all events blood had been shed, human lives endangered, and the Chilian laws were very rigorous concerning such cases.

Thoughts of the most opposite character alternated through the German's head; but finally he resolved to deny every thing to the last. The Chileno could not have any proofs; he had been alone in his boat, and one might best overcome a mere surmise, by meeting it with a bold front. Hence, his first look of confusion passed into an expression of astonishment, and, after the fisherman had looked at him for a time with anxious expectation, Meyer said, quietly:

"My dear friend, are you crazy, or what do you want of me? I have just risen, and am still quite sleepy, for we had a regular carousal last night; and now you ask me what I did with your sail and your oar? You must be dreaming, or have got into the wrong house. Whom did you wish to see?"

"So," said the Chileno, who saw through Don Carlos, and, after the last words, knew what to expect of him, "then you were not in Corral last night?"

"I was not, señor."

"Nor did you afterward go up the river?"

"I did not, señor."

"You did not have with you a man named Cruzado?"

"Cruzado?"

"It is always hazardous to mention names on such occasions," said the fisherman. "You do not remember, that you called the señor, who jumped first into my boat, Cruzado?"

"You are crazy, my dear señor," said Meyer, dryly. "I know nothing about your boat, sail, or oar. Do you want any thing else of me?"

"Yes, señor, a light for my cigar," said the fisherman, calmly. "I believe yours has gone out."

"With pleasure, compañero," replied Meyer, who would have much preferred to see the fisherman insist on his assertion. His sudden silence as to the sail and oar was by no means to his liking. For the present, however, he could not help it. He had denied all knowledge of the matter.

Meanwhile the fisherman, without further allusion to the subject, lighted his cigarette with the match which Meyer handed him, and smoked a few moments with the greatest equanimity.

"Adios, compañero: I must see if I cannot find my sail elsewhere. Perhaps the revenue-boat which collided with a launch last night, or rather this morning, may have fallen in with it."

"A revenue-boat?" asked Meyer, to all appearance greatly surprised.

"You do not wish to have me tell you the story?" laughed the fisherman. "That would be asking too much. Well, then, adios! perhaps we may meet again to-night." And, without waiting for a reply, he turned, nodded over his shoulder, and left the house.

When the fisherman had gone, Meyer remained standing in the middle of the room, and, long after the Chileno had walked down the street, he gazed at the door by which his visitor had disappeared, nor did he seem surprised when it opened again immediately, and Cruzado stood on the threshold.

"Halloo!" laughed the half-breed, on seeing his companion standing, as it were, in a trance and staring at him, "what is the matter, Don Carlos? You seem to take me either for a ghost or a policeman."

"Did you meet any one on the staircase, Cruzado?" inquired Meyer.

"Not on the staircase, but in front of the house, I met a peon, who came out of the street door."

"Do you know who it was?"

"Do you think I know all the peons in town?"

"The fisherman from whom we took the sail last night," replied Meyer.

"You do not say so!" cried Cruzado. "And how did he get here?"

"He recognized me," said the German, "and he is doubtless now on his way to the magistrate."

"Caracho!" swore the Chileno.

"What are we to do now?"

"What are we to do? I do not know," exclaimed Cruzado, flinging his hat on the floor, and stroking his long hair; "such are the consequences of half-measures. If I had had my way last night, the fellow would not be running about here and instigating the police against us. What are we to do now? We shall be arrested, tried, and sentenced to twenty years' hard labor. It is sufficient to drive a man to madness!"

"But he cannot prove any thing against us," said Meyer.

"Not prove any thing? As if more proofs were necessary than that he should declare we had gone in a launch into the bushes last night at such and such a time, and had surprised him in his boat, and taken him prisoner."

"And were any of the officers killed?"

"Do you believe, compañero, that I have made inquiries on that subject?" laughed the half-breed, contemptuously. "But it makes no difference now. I for one have no desire to wait for the decision of the honorable court."

"But Don Pasquale—"

"Our respected señor is not in danger. He is the most intimate friend of the justice of the peace, and 'hawks do not pick out hawks' eyes.'"

"And suppose we should leave town for a time?" said Meyer.

"But whither?" exclaimed Cruzado. "The bark has set sail, and so has the steamer, and there are no other vessels in the bay. We are in a trap."

"Half an hour ago, there rode past my house the old Chileno, who intends to cross over to the Otra Banda," said Meyer. "I am greatly inclined to join the expedition. We would, moreover, get well paid for it."

"H'm," said the half-breed, "the idea is not so bad. But what if they should send the police after us?"

"Into the interior of the country? Never. The party passed my house. The whole town knows who joined it, and that we both refused to accompany it. Before they succeed in coming to a determination, we shall be up in the mountains."

"Of course, if the red rascals of the Otra Banda cut our throats, we shall have less trouble," growled Cruzado.

"Well," said the German, laughing disdainfully, "I prefer being chased about the Pampas, to cleaning the streets here or at Valparaiso, with a chain on my leg. I will join the expedition. You may do as you please, but I will not spend another hour in Valdivia."

Cruzado paced the room, his arms folded on his back. He had refused to accompany Don Enrique, not so much because he was afraid of the dangers of the expedition, as because the season did not suit him. But it was the best thing to be done—no one would pursue them as far as the Otra Banda; and if the police really intended to arrest them, they would not immediately seek them in the interior. Afterward, it would be too late. The German did not hesitate any longer. While the half-breed was still standing irresolute, Don Carlos drew from under his bed a pair of saddle-bags made of raw-hide, and packed into it all that he needed on the road. He did not possess much wearing apparel, and all he had scarcely filled the bags. He then cast a glance about the room, and exclaimed, laughingly:

"My old Martha may clean and arrange the house in the mean time; and now I shall go to our señor, and get money for my travelling expenses. Will you accompany me, Cruzado?"

"Grandisima!" swore the half-breed, angrily stamping the floor. "What an outrage that such a miserable villain should drive us into the mountains at this season of the year, when his throat was yesterday at our disposal!"

"And do you know of any other way of escape?"

"But what does the rascal really

know about me?—I never saw his face in my life."

"He mentioned your name," said Meyer, "and as you are the only Cruzado in the colony, the chief of police will soon find you."

"It is to you, amigo, that I am indebted for this, but it cannot be helped. Where shall we meet?"

"On the road. I do not know how far the party will ride to-night?"

The noise of horses interrupted him at this moment. Both rushed quickly to the window, but they saw only the two Germans, who had finished their dinner at the hotel, and were speeding at a gallop after their companions.

"Who are they?" asked Cruzado, in surprise. "And where are they going?"

"They are our companions," said Meyer, laughing; "but if they enter upon the journey at this rate, I suppose they will ride somewhat more slowly after a while. We have no time to lose, compañero. There is already a policeman skulking about."

"We shall meet again to-night," said Cruzado. "I do not think we are safe here. Where is your horse?"

"At Don Pasquale's pasture—no great distance from here. I need not ride through the streets of the town."

"I shall take good care not to show myself either," said Cruzado, and, putting on his hat, he quickly left.

Meyer had meanwhile made his preparations: he put his long knife into his belt, and a small pistol into one of the saddle-bags; throwing them upon his arm, he hung his poncho over his shoulder, and went as though he intended only to take an hour's ride, and not to enter upon a journey which might last over a year, provided he should ever be allowed to return to Valdivia. He then crossed the street, entered Don Pasquale's house, and was thenceforth no longer seen in the town.

His haste seemed, indeed, well grounded; for scarcely half an hour afterward a policeman rapped at his door, and, on not receiving any reply, ascended to the room. He found it in the condition above described, and stood awhile in the doorway, shaking his head. As his calls remained unanswered, he looked around without arriving at any satisfactory result. Meyer had obviously been there but a very short time before, and could not have long since risen from his bed; perhaps he was somewhere about town. The policeman departed, and sauntered slowly down the street toward the court-house.

CHAPTER XVI.

THE OATH OF THE MAYNUS.

MEANWHILE Don Carlos Meyer certainly did not tarry in Valdivia, for Don Pasquale, the Chilian merchant, whom he informed of the probable discovery of their smuggling affair, and of the events that had taken place the preceding night, fully agreed with him that he and Cruzado should leave Valdivia as soon as possible, as he himself might run the risk of having the secret exposed by means of judicial investigation. The two men—for Cruzado shortly after made his appearance at Don Pasquale's—must no longer be seen at his house, lest suspicion should arise against him. Hence, he gave without objection whatever sum they asked; filled, besides, the saddle-bags of each with tobacco and a bottle of brandy, and did not feel entirely re-assured until he had conducted them through his garden and pasture, to the road leading around the town, where he left them to saddle their horses and take the next route through the forest. Cruzado was an excellent guide for this purpose, and the two friends soon after trotted along the road leading into the interior.

At the same time they kept a sharp lookout in order to find toward nightfall the place where Don Enrique first encamped, and both believed it was at Calle Calle, where he would have more accommodation than elsewhere. But the old man, whose heart was yearning toward his child, did not care for repose as long as the sun illuminated his path, and the animals were not weary. He pressed onward to the longed-for mountains, until night set in, and he was compelled to halt at a small and wretched rancho.

Our two friends did not care to join the company immediately. For, if they were pursued, the camp would, of course, be the first place where they would be sought. Under the cover of twilight, and avoiding delay at any of the houses along the roadside, they rode on, and resolved to pass the first night in the open air. There was an excellent pasture, for a small kila-thicket extended up the rivulet. They also found fuel, and, as for provisions, they had with them enough for two days. They could take hence another, though somewhat circuitous route, generally used only in the winter-time, when the floods set in, and which was now deserted. They would then meet Don Enrique, who, owing to his numerous pack-horses, could not move very rapidly.

Meyer and his friend no longer travelled the main road, although they might have been sure that they would not be pursued so far, if they were not to be found in Don Enrique's party; but they did not wish to expose themselves to accident, and could in this part of the country continue their journey with entire security.

It is true, Meyer greatly liked to stop at several houses where he knew they would meet with good beds and a hospitable reception. He had lived a long while in the wilderness, but not long enough to wean himself from some luxuries. He was fond of a soft bed, and took his coffee in a china cup rather than a cow-horn. His companion, on the contrary, was entirely destitute of such weaknesses, and would have scarcely ever made a quarter of an hour's circuit in order to stop over night at a good hotel, provided he had with him even a scanty supply of provisions, and found a tree to protect him from the dew. In a word, he was entirely indifferent to civilized life, and, as it was now necessary for them to press onward in as stealthy a manner as possible, Meyer was obliged to submit to his directions.

Thus the two fugitives from justice passed the second night in the immediate neighborhood of the Ranco Lagoon, at no great distance from the mouth of the Lifen; and Cruzado had learned from an Indian whom they had met on the road, that Don Enrique and his men intended to encamp about two leguas from there, at the hacienda of a Chileno named Don Fernando. He had lost one of his horses, pierced on the road by a sharp lilla-stamp. This accident had detained the party. The informant had passed them at the moment they were engaged in killing the animal; two of the Indians whom Don Enrique had engaged at Valdivia, had already left him, because their progress was too slow, for they wished to return quickly to their homes. Only three Indians and their wives were with him, and it was doubtful whether they would not also leave him on the next day.

Cruzado was rather pleased with the intelligence, for he was sure now that their company could not but be welcome to the old Chileno.

"And no one else has been with him?"

"Two white caballeros with muskets," was the reply; "but they were awkward riders. One of them fell from his horse, and his musket went off."

These two were, doubtless, the Germans seen galloping past Meyer's house, and not the police of Valdivia. The Indian was dismissed with a liberal present—that is to say, with tobacco enough for a cigarette.

They soon matured a plan. At the Ranco Lagoon they had behind them the Chilian territory inhabited by white people; henceforth they would meet only with Indian ranchos, and if, at intervals, a white man had settled among them, he surely belonged to the lowest class, and had, perhaps, good reason to keep beyond the reach of his countrymen. This district, indeed, was subject to the authority of the government, and controlled by Chilian laws, but not by Chilian functionaries, for the Indians lived here under their own caziques. A so-called *capitan de amigos* held now and then some intercourse with them, and was looked upon as a delegate of the government; but, in riding occasionally through this country, his object was to report on the condition, and especially on the temper of the tribes, rather than meddle with their administration, which they would by no means permit. Add to this that persons were employed for this purpose familiar with the language of the Indians, and belonged, almost without exception, to the dregs of society—vagabonds who had adopted only the vices and bad habits of both whites and Indians. It is true, they had some knowledge of reading and writing, and rode as capitanes, telling of the heroic deeds they had performed at home. They would drink whiskey chica, returning to the settlements, where they falsified to the authorities that a seditious spirit was rife among the red inhabitants, and that they had taken infinite pains to allay their passions.

Now, Cruzado, who had himself been a capitan de amigos, was too well known to these men, to apprehend any treachery on their part, if he happened to fall in with one of them. Such persons never know in what manner they might have need of each other, and they take good care not to inform of their friends and companions more than they can help. Otherwise they might betray each other. As for the Indians, they were utterly indolent and careless. They took no interest in what the whites were doing, so long as their own persons or rights were not at stake; nay, they did not even know them. Now one came, and now another; the former to bring them goods, the latter to buy horses, or in search of stray ones, and then they left again. The names of very few of those visitors were scarcely heard, and forgotten as soon as they had disappeared.

Cruzado agreed with Don Carlos that they would not wait for the arrival of Don Enrique, but set out at once for the Mayhue Lagoon, or at the last rancho, where the road divided. Don Enrique would pass that way, and stop overnight, and there they would be able to meet with him in the easiest and most unsuspicious manner.

Hitherto the two fugitives had followed by-paths, or such roads as were little used in the summer-time; now, however, this precaution was no longer necessary, and, riding for a time along the shores of the beautiful Ranco Lagoon, they entered the highway leading to Mayhue.

The landscape extended before them in all its surpassing charms. Like a mirror, the water, whose shores were densely wooded, spread for many miles, while, at this very moment, a canoe, making a silver furrow on the lake, strove to reach the island in the centre. The background was formed by the snow-clad peaks of the Cordilleras, through which the dark pass was plainly seen. The forest bloomed with fuchsias of enormous size, and their red bells contrasted with the white flowers of the myrtle. A sweet fragrance pervaded this wild prospect, over which spread a sky of spotless azure.

All this, however, made little impression upon the two horsemen, whose eyes gazed with indifference upon this scene. Cruzado led the way and entered first into the bends which the rough path made in the neighborhood, and penetrated the underbrush, where stood here and there an apple-tree, whose knotty branches admonished them to proceed more cautiously—now into the swamp, in order to pass outside by the shore, or in the shallow water, around some dense thicket—and now galloping along the sand or turning again into the forest to reach the ford of a river emptying into the lagoons. Cruzado knew here every inch of the ground, and his companion seemed to pay as little attention to the scenery surrounding them. Wherever there was a slight clearing in the forest, or when the horses stepped slowly into the water, he made cigarettes, and, blowing the smoke into the air, pursued his way. They passed several large haciendas, but did not stop; and once only, on meeting an Indian driving a few cattle, Cruzado halted, and asked in the language of the Penchuenches:

"Halloo, compañero! what are the people of the Otra Banda doing?"

"*Tomando!*" was the laconic reply, and the Indian passed at a gallop.

The word was significant enough, for it depicted the very condition in which that tribe was always at that season—taking chicha, a fermented liquor made from apples; and, in fact, they did nothing else but drink during that month. None of the young men rode out on hunting excursions; the looms of the women stood still; not a bridle or lasso was made, and no one thought even of changing the place of encampment. Inside and outside of their cabins they lay before the barrels which white men had brought them or the skins of raw-hide made by themselves, and drank day and night, staggering to their hard conches or dropping to the floor, to sleep away their intoxication, and as soon as they were able to open their eyes again, recommencing their orgies.

"Tomando!" It is the carnival of the Indians, even their enemies are safe at such a time.

Cruzado contented himself with the word which confirmed his apprehensions, but this journey removed them from the reach of Chillan justice. There was no ship in the harbor to take them on board, nor was there communication with the south. Impassable rivers obstructed the progress of travellers in that direction. It would have been the height of imprudence for them to direct their steps to the neighboring Araucania, where, under present circumstances, certain death would have awaited them. Hence, the Otra Banda alone offered them a precarious protection, and they could not but make up their minds to rely on it. They did not feel much inclined to converse, for the road was rough and narrow, so that they were obliged to ride in single file, now up steep hills, and now down precipitous slopes. But there were no lofty mountains in their way, and as their destination drew near, the ground became more level, and covered with hard sand, where the horses were enabled to proceed with increased rapidity.

It was about three in the afternoon, when Cruzado and his friend reached a small settlement, the last on this side of the Cordilleras. Previously they had crossed the Pillan-Leufu, a river with milk-white water, and shortly after the Witchi-Leufu, a limpid stream, both of which flow into the Mayhue Lagoon. A halt was made, about a quarter of an hour afterward, in front of the cazique's cabin.

Not a man was to be seen—not even a horse. Only a few chickens were running among the apple-trees, and two small boys, naked to the waist, pursuing a lean dog, and endeavoring to throw a lasso round its neck. It was not until the dog noticed the strangers, and indicated their approach by barking, that the little fellows looked up and ran into the next cabin. As this was rather large, though its walls consisted only of rough-hewn planks, Meyer wished to stop here; but Cruzado beckoned, and said:

"Not here, compañero; this is the cazique's house, where the Chileno will doubtless stay overnight; it will be well to go to another rancho, that he may send for us. The less we force our company upon him the better."

"And what if he should not learn of our presence there?"

"Never fear," laughed Cruzado. "You must not think that a stranger can pass a night here without being talked about by the inmates of even the most distant ranchos."

"But the place seems deserted."

"Tomando!" said Cruzado, shrugging his shoulders. "Who knows in what hole they may be assembled around their barrel! But there we cannot do any thing with them, and toward nightfall they generally return to their cabins. To-morrow morning is our time."

Not waiting for a reply, Cruzado directed his horse across the clearing, past a cabin, in front of which two filthy children were seated, and up a hill, where was a somewhat larger house, with a small corn-field adjoining. The Indians probably had built it; but when Cruzado and his companion stopped before it, and an old gray dog barked, a white girl opened the door, and asked the strangers what they wanted.

"Does Don Felipe still live here, señorita?" asked Cruzado, involuntarily taking off his hat.

"He is my father, señor," replied the girl.

"We are weary travellers on our way to the Otra Banda, in search of stray horses. Can we stay here overnight?"

"I do not know, señor. My father is not at home. He and my mother have ridden to the lagoon. Was not the cazique at home?"

"The place seemed deserted, señorita."

"They have ridden over to the chicha, but they will return to-night, for to-morrow all will drink at the cazique's house. Step in, señores, until my father comes. You are welcome."

No further ceremony was needed. The two horsemen alighted, unsaddled their horses, and drove them into a corral which the young maid pointed out to them. They then carried their saddles and blankets into the house to make their own couches.

At so remote a point, where travellers usually bring with them all they want, the only thing landlords can offer them is shelter, and yet the roof is often so full of holes that it does not protect guests from cold and rain. Nevertheless, these frontiersmen are hospitable, and although they expect a small present in tobacco, or some other article of which they are in need, they are always ready and willing to share what little they have without any compensation. In return, their guests tell them about the world from which they come, and sometimes chat with them until after midnight.

Meyer, though already familiar with the customs of Chili, deemed it somewhat singular that they should be received in this courteous manner by a young lady whose parents were not at home; but he did not seem to regret it at all, for Tadea (the girl's name) was young and pretty, although her toilet was exceedingly simple. She wore a ragged cotton dress, a threadbare handkerchief of blue and red around her neck, and her feet were destitute of stockings and shoes; but her complexion was fresh and fair, though a little soap and water would have added to its charms. Thick black hair gave a peculiar attraction to her face, with its dark eyes, shaded by long silken lashes. Her hands and feet were small, and she might be—probably was—considered a belle of the Cordilleras.

But the more uncomfortable was the cabin in which she lived, as nature really seemed to have contributed as much to its furniture as art. The floor was the bare ground, trodden hard, and smoothed by long use; a block of granite, roughhewn, and rising from the ground where it had long lain imbedded, formed a table in one corner, and a few other stones and logs of wood served as chairs. He who wished to be seated had only to cover them with one of the sheepskins lying about. There were, besides, two wooden boxes in the room, and on the walls hung some dilapidated wearing-apparel for "ladies and gentlemen." Otherwise the room was empty from the floor to the roof, whose timbers, blackened by smoke, were visible everywhere. Fresh air was not wanting by any means; it is true, the walls had originally consisted of planks, whose interstices had been filled with clay, but the clay had fallen out in many places, so that the winds from every quarter, whistled through the chinks. The house formerly had a fireplace in a rude hearth in the rear wall; but it seemed to have tumbled down, and, instead of rebuilding it, the inmates had deemed it more convenient to transfer the fireplace to the middle of the house. The floor was not injured, nor did it spoil the window-curtains.

Our two fugitives were not particularly surprised at the appearance of the cabin. They would have been much more so on finding one furnished with any regard to comfort or decency. They merely hoped the roof was tight; there was a sufficient number of sheepskins; plenty of dry wood was piled up in a corner; nothing, therefore, was wanting to their comfort, at least such as they could expect in this wilderness. But the young maiden tried to do something more for them. On a pole hung a quarter of a sheep; she roasted it on the coals, and put a pot of potatoes over the fire, so that the two might expect a good supper. Cruzado, in anticipation of a meal, which he had not enjoyed for some time, had already made himself quite comfortable. Drawing half a dozen of the sheepskins into a corner, he arranged them on the floor so as to make a tolerable bed; his saddle served as a pillow; his blanket protected him from the cold night-air, and, after lighting a cigarette, he seemed to be perfectly at home.

Meyer, on his part, thought less of his comfort than of the girl, from whom he did not avert his eyes, and who engrossed his whole attention. Indeed, there was a peculiar fascination in the features of the pretty maiden, and, whenever she happened to cast a glance on the German, he felt as though an electric shock ran through his whole frame. He wished, however, she had looked a little neater and tidier. But Meyer was not so very particular in this respect, for he had had for a long time no familiar association with the better classes of Chilians. His wife, too, had been liable to serious censure, and thus it came to pass that he was willing to overlook matters of secondary importance, and did not tire of gazing into the magnificent eyes of his young hostess. He did not regain his self-possession until she put the boiled potatoes into a small wooden dish, took the roast meet with her fingers from the coals, placed it on the potatoes, and then, uttering a pleasant "*Toma*," put the dish on the floor between the two men.

"*Dios le pago!*" (may God pay you for it) murmured Cruzado, partaking with excellent appetite of the food, while Meyer, who was still timid, forgot every thing else for the present, and applied himself to the meal.

Henceforth the girl paid no further attention to her guests. Now, that she had done for them all she could, she took from a corner of the room a bag and a

"THERE EMERGED FROM THE FOREST TWENTY DUSKY FORMS" p. 102.

pickaxe, and walked across the field, leaving the cabin and its contents in the hands of the strangers.

Cruzado and Don Carlos seemed to be well pleased with the tranquillity surrounding them on all sides. After finishing their supper, they stretched themselves on their couches, and, exhausted by the long ride, soon fell into a sound slumber, which, for about two hours, was not disturbed. The sun had already sunk behind the dense wall of foliage, and the crests of the mountains were gilded by the parting rays, when there was a sudden commotion in the forest, and deafening cheers seemed to burst forth simultaneously from all quarters.

Meyer slept well, but Cruzado, more inured to such a life, which, above all things, requires a light sleep, started at the first cry, and glanced about with uneasiness. He had doubtless had a lively dream, and, at first, did not remember where he was. This lasted, however, only a few moments, when he raised himself up and listened; he was too familiar with the customs of the savages not to comprehend quickly what the noise meant. It proceeded from the Indians returning from their orgies, drunk, of course, but in good-humor, for they yelled and cheered, and now and then there responded to them cries rending the air and frightening the birds in the thickets.

And now they came up; the unshod hoofs of the horses rattled with a dull noise over the hard sand, and presently there emerged from the forest about twenty dusky forms, running down the hill at the top of their speed. The horses were covered with foam, and the long black hair of the revellers waved in the breeze, the blue ponchos fluttered around their shoulders, but their eyes sparkled with mirth, and cheer after cheer burst from their lips.

Thus they pressed onward at a gallop; in a few moments the wild cavalcade passed the cabin, and disappeared among the bushes almost before Cruzado had caught sight of them.

"What is the matter?" exclaimed Meyer, who had been also aroused, starting up from his couch. "Have the Penchoenches crossed over to this side of the mountains?"

"No, señor," laughed Cruzado; "it was a company returning from the chicha. No one knows why they start so early to-day; for generally it is not till now that the real carousal commences. They must have just finished the last barrel, and we may have arrived at the favorable time when they will be sober for a day or two."

"I should not object to it by any means," said Meyer; "for, when drunk, they are abominable. But we must have slept long, for the sun has already set. Is it not time for us to look around, and see if Don Enrique has arrived in the mean time?"

"I believe they are coming yonder this very moment," said Cruzado, jumping on a fallen tree in front of the house, and looking attentively through the bushes. "Look, Don Carlos, the road by which we came runs past the apple-tree yonder, and a party appears coming up in that direction."

"In truth," exclaimed Meyer, who quickly stood near him, "I can recognize the two white horses; Don Enrique is mounted on one of them, and one of the Germans on the other."

"White horses are of too conspicuous a color for the Pampas," said Cruzado.

"Bah! what do they know about the Pampas? I wonder where they are going to stay overnight?"

"Doubtless at the cazique's house."

"But that is full of Indians."

"Many people have room in a house," laughed Cruzado, "especially when they are drinking; they will crowd together. But I believe there comes our landlord with his señora. He is brimful! He is tottering on his horse! His wife holds him on one side."

Meyer was not much pleased with the couple now approaching. The husband—a Chileno with a fair complexion, which, at that moment, was barely discernible, owing to the dirt covering his face—was to all appearance dead drunk, and his wife was not much better, although not so helpless as her worthy lord. The husband was scarcely able to maintain himself in the saddle; an old torn poncho covered his shoulders, a dilapidated straw hat, mended in many places, adorned his head, and a pair of very short checkered pantaloons, full of holes, but half covered his limbs. And how the face of this unfortunate man looked! He was in a beastly state of intoxication, though it is wrong to use this expression, for never did beast stoop so low as this member of a race so favored by the Creator with moral perception, intellect, and will, and claiming a resemblance to Him.

Thus the besotted fellow rode up. On arriving in front of the house, he was lifted from his horse; and it was fortunate for him that Tadeo returned at this moment, and pointed out to her father the couch, to which Meyer and Cruzado carried him, while his wife cast a glance of stupid astonishment on the strangers, and thereupon reeled to her own bed in the corner.

"I believe, Don Carlos," said Cruzado, "it will be best for us to leave this amiable family for a time, and take a walk to the cabin of our old cazique."

"But, Cruzado," exclaimed Meyer, "we cannot leave the poor girl alone with these intoxicated persons?"

"We cannot?" laughed Cruzado. "And do you think, amigo, that the young lady does not pass daily, and has passed for years, through similar scenes at this season? She assuredly knows better how to deal with her parents than we do. *Vamos nos, compañero.*"

And, without waiting for a reply, he led the way down the hill, and toward the cazique's house. Don Carlos followed him.

CHAPTER XVII.

AN EVENING WITH THE CAZIQUE.

THE shades of night were hiding the forest, and only in the clearing between the huts, which Cruzado and Meyer had passed upon their arrival, and which were surrounded by a few stunted trees, were yet to be seen the last gleams of daylight. What a strange and picturesque scene was presented there to the eyes of the spectators!

Round the large cabin, which really did not look as though a family had there taken up its permanent quarters, but rather resembled the temporary stopping-place of a hunting-party, stood some twenty horses without saddles, tied with their bridles or pieces of lasso to the branches of the trees; many of the horses had not even bridles, but a piece of raw-hide had been fastened round the lower part of their heads. Amid them moved wild forms, a few entirely drunk, but all half intoxicated. Some lay on the ground, leaning on both their elbows, and talking with each other in this attitude. Others had brought along a sheep, which they killed and hung upon the branch of a tree, and cut off slices in order to feast in the cabin. Others, again, struck from a few dry old trunks, large chips to supply the fire all night long. The noise of an approaching cavalcade, turned the attention of all; even those who lay on the ground sprang to their feet in surprise, on perceiving that the new-comers were strangers. Visits in their district, especially at this season, were by no means every-day occurrences; and only in the summer-time traders from Valdivia passed through this part of the country, on their way to the Otra Banda; but they took care not to stay there too long, lest the sudden setting-in of the rainy season should prevent them from returning to Chili; and the traders who had been here last had doubtless long since gone back to their homes. To judge from the number of their pack-horses, the new-comers were traders too; no others would have crossed the mountains, and the Indians could not comprehend what had induced these whites to enter at such a season upon such a journey, when unavoidably they must pass the winter on the Pampas.

Meanwhile the horsemen came up at a brisk trot. José, Don Enrique's servant, led the way, because he was more familiar with the customs and habits of the Indians than his master, and, bestowing only careless greetings upon those who crowded curiously around him, he halted in front of the cabins, without dismounting from his horse.

Some of the pack-horses also came up, and, behind them, the Indians and their wives, who lived here, and associated at once with the others; they were immediately asked who the strangers were, and a crowd of attentive listeners surrounded them while they replied to the inquiries. Meanwhile a somewhat ragged individual emerged from the cabin. José turned toward him and asked that the members of the expedition might be permitted to stay overnight at the cazique's.

The savage listened to him very seriously without making a reply, and stepped back to inform the cazique. It was a long time before he again made his appearance, so that the two Germans were in an agony of impatience, while Don Enrique, resembling a marble statue, remained on horseback, and did not turn his head either to the right or the left. None of the others addressed them; they seemed to look upon the new-comers with indifference, until the cazique permitted them to enter his cabin.

The doctor could not endure this disagreeable delay, which began to frighten him, for they sat on their horses like proscribed outcasts. With what little

Spanish he knew, he turned at last to José, and said:

"I am sure the fellow did not inform the cazique, for no one takes any notice of us.—Shall we dismount? I am as hungry as a wolf."

"Paciencia, amigo," was the reply of the Chileno, who merely raised his hand, as if deprecatingly.

"Hear, my dear Reiwald," said the doctor; "do you know that we have doubtless been guilty of a great folly in accompanying the old gentleman on his crazy expedition?"

Reiwald shrugged his shoulders. "It was assuredly not the most prudent step that we might have taken, but by no means so foolish as our emigration to this delightful country. Since we are here, we must submit to what we cannot help."

"I do not know about that," said Dr. Pfalfel; "as yet we are able to retrace our steps; but once across the mountains—"

"We should be laughed at in Valdivia, if we left the old gentleman."

"What does he concern us?" exclaimed the doctor; "let us first look out for our own interests. If I only knew the route back to the sea-shore! It is a sorry thing not to be familiar with the language of the country, and the Choctaw these fellows talk here is a great deal worse than Spanish, of which I understand a word now and then, on account of my familiarity with the Latin."

"There comes the chamberlain of the cazique to bring us word," exclaimed Reiwald. "The fellow looks attractive! It would be a good jest if our request were politely refused."

"A very bad one indeed," replied the doctor; "for to lie in the open air all night does not long agree with my constitution."

"And with such a constitution you are going to venture into the open Pampas?"

"The Indians there possess fine tents, made of guanaco-hides. I have ascertained all about them, for I have no idea of sleeping out of doors if I can help it."

"Listen, doctor," said Reiwald. "I really believe that our request has been rejected, for the Indian is too polite. See how obsequiously he is bowing."

"In that event we shall take the old barracks by storm, and fortify ourselves," growled the doctor. "But—we are welcome—we are invited to enter."

In fact, José dismounted at this moment, and unfastened his saddle. Don Enrique also alighted, and the two Germans quickly imitated his example. The cazique had, indeed, permitted the strangers to pass the night at his house, and José now called a few Indians to assist him in unpacking the baggage, which they did with the greatest readiness. No sooner had they seen that the cazique would receive the strangers, than their whole demeanor underwent a striking change, and with particular readiness they helped the Germans, whom they knew at once to be foreigners. Not only did they assist in unbuckling the saddles and saddle-bags, but they took charge of the horses, and carried the baggage into the cabin.

But if Reiwald, who was surprised at this obliging conduct of the savages, believed that it arose from motives of disinterested hospitality, he soon discovered that he had been mistaken; for no sooner was the labor performed, than the two Germans were surrounded by a majority of the Indians, who held out their hands to them with the polite request of "*Poco tabaco, señor!*" Both, however, were anxious to be on friendly terms with these people; they, therefore, complied willingly with so modest a request, especially as the Indians were satisfied with the smallest quantity. If it just sufficed for making a cigarette, for which purpose they sent a lad to fetch cornhusks from the neighboring field, they squatted in great glee on the ground, made their cigarettes, lighted them, and blew the smoke leisurely into the air. In reality they were not so modest as they seemed, but so indolent as never to look forward to the future while they had something to gladden their hearts for the present. What did they need more tobacco for, so long as their cigarette was burning? They would not smoke two at the same time; but no sooner had they finished the first, than they would be sure to call for more tobacco.

Still another person appeared in front of the cabin before Don Enrique was able to enter. A horseman, wrapped in a very short and dirty poncho, galloped through the valley, and made his horse leap as unconcernedly over all large trunks lying in the road as though they were so many straws. To judge from appearances he was also a Chileno; but no sooner did he perceive the strangers than he stopped his horse, and carelessly leaving the animal to itself, jumped from the saddle almost the moment it halted.

He was evidently at home here, and conducted himself in an easy and unembarrassed manner, though his appearance was by no means prepossessing, and he was dressed in a soiled, yet somewhat pretentious costume. He wore yellow top-boots with very large plated spurs, a massive signet-ring on his right forefinger, and a red silk handkerchief about his neck; but his shirt was dirty, his hair uncombed and dishevelled, and, like the others, he seemed somewhat inebriated. At all events he was in a high state of excitement, and treated the strangers with a certain aristocratic *nonchalance*.

"Ah, how do you do, señores—where do you come from? From the Otra Banda? Have you brought all that baggage across the mountains?"

"We are on our way to the Otra Banda, señor," said Don Enrique, politely. "Excuse me, we are about to wait on the cazique."

"*Caramba!*" exclaimed the Chileno. "You are now going to cross the mountains? Where do you intend to pass the winter?"

"*Quien sabe?*" replied Don Enrique, evasively, and turned to the house. But he could not so easily get rid of his new acquaintance.

"In that event I must officiate as your interpreter, for my old cazique does not speak Spanish very well. I will introduce you to him. Where do you come from?"

Don Enrique hesitated to reply; the whole appearance of the man was forbidding, and he deemed it by no means desirable to be introduced by him to the chief. He had to give him an answer, however, for he did not care to exasperate him.

"From Concepcion," replied the old Chileno.

"On horseback all the way from Concepcion?" exclaimed the stranger.

"No—by way of Valdivia. I wish to stay here overnight, and, if possible, to obtain guides to accompany me to the other side."

"That will be very difficult. But let us go to the cazique, or he will grow impatient, especially as he is somewhat excited to-day."

So saying, he stepped with Don Enrique and the two Germans into the cabin. Both Reiwald and the doctor were quite anxious to witness the reception they would have by means of this distinguished person.

The cazique!—what pictures had their imagination conjured up in regard to the title! All the old stories of Cortes and Pizarro came to their minds. What added to their suspense was the delay before the chief granted them an audience. Meanwhile it had grown dark, and the entrance to the cabin did not justify any great expectations. It consisted merely of a few boards fixed perpendicularly; those who wished to enter had to push aside one of them, and afterward draw it back to its former place. This, however, did not preclude the possibility of their meeting something very different in the interior of the dwelling; at all events, they thought, the chief of a tribe must have furnished his house in a comfortable and tasteful manner, and Reiwald already looked forward with great delight to the soft guanaco-hides, on which he hoped to repose more comfortably than the preceding night. A cry of surprise—in reality, a half-suppressed oath—escaped him when inside, and he started back involuntarily on thinking of the possibility of passing the night in this stable. But they could not well withdraw, the die was cast, and the best thing they could do was to assume a cheerful look in a somewhat unpleasant predicament. For the rest, Reiwald was justified in being taken aback on beholding the interior of the cabin, blackened as it was by the smoke, and the doctor, who had his worst fears realized, groaned aloud.

The room was quite spacious; it was at least twenty by eighteen yards; its height to the inside roof was thirty feet, But this seemed to be all the convenience afforded, if any could be expected in this part of the country. In the middle of the room blazed a large fire, to which half-naked children were constantly adding billets of dry wood. The flames rose to the roof, under which a cloud of smoke floated.

The walls were destitute of hangings, the inside and outside consisting of rough-hewn planks, which, like pallisades, had been rammed into the ground, though not forming a tight enclosure. On the left side, in accordance more with utility than with beauty, there was fixed in the floor a number of poles, on which hung all sorts of saddles, bridles, trappings, and black and white sheepskins. Under them seemed to be a sort of storeroom, for there were to be seen a good many sacks, doubtless filled with provision, while the wearing-apparel was kept on the other side of the house, where hung several ponchos and blue dresses on partitions dividing the sleeping-rooms of the family. As for furniture, there was almost none; neither tables nor chairs; only some wooden boxes with lids stood on the right hand of the entrance, and it was to be seen that they were at times used as tables, for behind them lay a log, and some sheepskins spread over it indicated that it was intended to serve as a bench.

While Don Enrique seemed to think it of no consequence whether he would find here comfortable quarters or not, the two Germans observed every thing at a glance, and then directed their eyes toward the fire, where they beheld an interesting spectacle. There sat the cazique, a heavy-set, broad-shouldered man, his dark-blue poncho, striped with broad red threads, over his shoulders; his head bare, the long hair parted in the middle, and combed down on both sides; his expressive light-brown face turned toward them, and one of his hands screening his eyes that he might be able to gaze at the strangers.

His seat was raised—afterward discovered to be a barrel—and he formed the centre of a group which a painter would have desired. On his right hand stood an old, coffee-brown matron, very ugly, her eyebrows forming a continuous line, her thin lips contracted, and her small eyes glancing distrustfully at the new-comers. While, close behind him, leaning on his left shoulder, was a slender girl of prepossessing appearance, and bearing a striking resemblance to her father. Both matron and maid wore the becoming dress of the Indian women: a dark-blue wrapper, with a diadem—that is, a woollen ribbon, embroidered with white, blue, and red beads, around their forehead. It became the raven hair and light-brown complexion of the daughter.

Around these three were grouped the children; to the left of the father, in front of the sister, was a charming child of ten or eleven, with flashing black eyes; between the father's knees a naked little brown fellow, who looked as though he had just emerged from a bath of ashes; and to the right of the boy, in front of the mother, were two small children of five and seven, timidly drawing back from the strangers, at whom they glanced over their shoulders, while clinging to their mother's dress. Immediately behind the old cazique stood the crown prince—a noble, manly form, slender and vigorous, with open, good-natured features, and bearing a strong resemblance to his sister. Around were to be seen four or five others, doubtless courtiers, or perhaps poor relatives, who fill the houses of their wealthier cousins, living on their bounty. The blazing fire shed a red lustre over them. The cazique did not rise when his guests entered the room, but remained seated in a dignified attitude; his right arm on his knee, his left hand resting on the shoulder of his young scion, he waited for the strangers to address him.

Don Enrique approached, and, taking off his hat, and bowing to the Indian, he said:

"Señor Cazique, I beg of you shelter for the night: we have a long journey before us, and should like to rest here, until to-morrow morning. Permit us to do so."

The old cazique spoke some Spanish, but not enough to understand all the old haciendero said to him; he looked inquiringly at the Chileno, who had entered with Don Enrique, and, when the latter had translated the words to him, he nodded kindly and said only:

"Bueno! bueno! Donde viene?— From Valdivia, señor? Chileno?"

"Yes, señor. I am a native of Concepcion."

The cazique made no reply, but merely held out to him the fore and middle fingers of his right hand, and then beckoned him to withdraw to the opposite side of the room; for his eyes had fallen on the other two, who he saw were not natives of the soil, and he motioned to them to approach.

"*Paisano?*" he asked the doctor, who came first; and, as he did not understand the question propounded to him, the Chileno translated it, and said the cazique wished to know whether he was a Chileno, or where he was from.

"No," said the doctor, upon whom the whole ceremony made quite an impression, however ludicrous it might have seemed to him under different circumstances; "*Aleman!*" (German.)

"Aleman! eh!" exclaimed the Indian, and his face, which during his conversation with the Chileno had preserved its indifference, assumed a kind expression. "Alemanos, bueno!" and, holding out his strong hand, he shook that of the doctor so vigorously that he almost screamed with pain.—"And the other! Aleman, too!"

"Yes," replied the doctor, and Reiwald had now to put his hand into the vice. The little girl, who looked very seriously into his eyes, probably noticed that his face expressed pain, and divined the cause of it, for a scarcely-repressed smile lit up her handsome features.

"Bueno! bueno!" repeated the old cazique; and then, as if he had complied with every requirement of the ceremonial, he dismissed the two friends, and stared for a few minutes silently and thoughtfully into the flames. Whether public cares engrossed his mind, or he was pondering over the idea of concluding an alliance with foreign powers in order to renounce the supremacy of the Chilenos, to whom he did not seem very partial, who could tell? At all events his reflection was of short duration. He turned his head, beckoned to one of the ministering spirits who stood behind him, and spoke a few words in his own language. The Indian seemed to obey his order in silence, and left the house immediately. No sooner had he stepped out of the door, than a howl rent the air. It sounded as though the infernal regions had been let loose: yell after yell made the welkin ring, and, while the planks forming the door were pushed back, the Indians, who had remained outside, commenced filling the room.

"Companeros," said the young Chileno, who had officiated as interpreter to Don Enrique and his companions, "if you will follow my advice, prepare your couches for the night; there are sheepskins, and moreover you have your saddle-cloths. After the crowd is once in, you will have very little room."

"But I hope these men do not intend to sleep here," said Don Enrique, in dismay; for the cabin filled more and more with dusky forms, and the bright diadems of several women were visible among them.

"They will not sleep here," laughed the Chileno, "except a few whose heads are heavy with liquor; but they intend to drink here all night, or, at least, as long as there is any thing in the barrel on which the cazique is seated."

"And is there apple-chicha in it?"

"Chicha? No!" replied the Chileno, bursting into loud laughter. "They would empty such a barrel in five minutes, and merely stimulate their thirst thereby. It is whiskey, genuine *agua ardiente*, which the cazique received this morning from the other side of the lagoon, and, as the chicha on the Mayhue was consumed by noonday, he invited the whole crowd to drink to-night some of the whiskey. They will have a merry time, you may rely on it, and no one will go so long as there is a drop in the barrel."

The old haciendero gave a deep sigh. It was long after nightfall when the Indians had assembled; nor was there any possibility of his finding other quarters. He was therefore obliged to submit. With that mute resignation which he had shown during the whole journey, he motioned to José, who was still engaged in carrying in the leathern sacks with their baggage, to prepare couches for both of them. He communicated also to the doctor what he had heard; the German, however, did not understand all he said, but finally discovered that he was to make his bed, because so many people who would stay all night long were coming into the house.

Doctor Pfeifel was loath to believe this; it seemed to be a regular meeting, at which, probably, speeches would be made, unfortunately in the native language, and resolutions passed. But this, he thought, could not last a long time. That the multitude, for whom there would be barely room to stand, should pass the night here, was a matter of impossibility, and entirely out of the question.

Rolwald, to whom he communicated what the old haciendero had told him, burst into loud laughter, and said that the meeting would afford him by far more pleasure after the craving of his hungry stomach was appeased; until then, he could not take much interest even in the political affairs of the Penchuenches.

For the present, however, the care of the baggage engrossed their attention; for the entry of the savages, among whom there were a few degraded Chilenos, was not yet at an end; and they filled all the nooks and corners of the room in such a manner that the two Germans, who had not much confidence in the honesty of the Indians, became uneasy. If they should lose any thing, they would be unable to recover it; and if there were thieves in the crowd, they ought not render the temptation greater than it was. Hence, they took out their four leathern sacks, which they had some difficulty in finding, from among the rest, put them upon each other, placed their bridles on top of the pile, and leaned their rifles against it. After piling up their saddles and blankets, under which they had concealed revolvers and knives, they were able to look more calmly upon the noisy assembly.

Meanwhile the old cazique seemed to drop his stiff and dignified bearing. The introduction of strangers was over, every requirement of politeness, as he understood it, had been complied with, and he was again at liberty to be a "hail-fellow well met," and not the chief and representative of a tribe.

As he saw the numerous guests enter his cabin, his features brightened; he rose from his seat, threw back his poncho over his left shoulder, so that his bare right arm was free, and rolled with his own hands the barrel on which he had sat, to a pair of small blocks which had been placed close by for this very purpose, for the barrel exactly fitted in them, and, the next minute, hands which seemed to be exceedingly well versed in such occupation, began to tap it.

The cazique, however, had still remaining public affairs to attend to, for he suddenly beckoned to his chamberlain, and whispered several important words. The chamberlain nodded his head in great glee and went immediately among the Indians. Presently he made his appearance close to Don Enrique, and, beckoning to José (for he was unable to speak to the old haciendero), he said something which the servant seemed to consider a matter of course, for he went at once to his master and translated it to him.

The old Chileno listened, and slightly inclined his head; it was nothing but what he had expected—a request for tobacco, to which he responded in the most liberal manner; not, however, without committing a serious blunder, because he was not yet familiar with the manners of the Indians; for he went to one of the leathern sacks, opened it, and took from it a roll of tobacco, about two feet long, such as is sold by the Chilian Government. Instead of intrusting the distribution of the tobacco to his servant, who would have attended to the matter in the most judicious and practical manner, he went with the roll to the cazique, whose face became radiant at the prospect of so rich a present, and handed him the gift with a few kind words. Of course he supposed, in so doing, that the cazique would distribute the tobacco among his guests; but Cajnanto, the old cazique, thought otherwise, and knew how to use it to much better advantage.

In the first place, he nodded pleasantly to the Chileno, and said to him, "*Gracias, muchas gracias, señor;*" but then he paid no further attention to him, cut off a large piece, and put the remainder into a box, which he carefully locked, and the key of which he brought to his wife.

But no sooner did he commence cutting the tobacco, in order to make a cigarette from it, than all the other Indians thronged about him. He pointed out to them the stranger, who the next moment was beset by a crowd of supplicants, with whose wishes he could not but comply. He took from the sack another roll, but, as he did not care about distributing it himself, he gave it to José with the order to cut it into small pieces, and distribute it in such a manner as to let every man and woman have some. He then threw himself on his couch.

CHAPTER XVIII.

THE CAROUSAL.

It can be justly said that the Chilian Indians may claim the enviable distinction of outstripping any other human beings in the consumption of enormous quantities of intoxicating liquors. But it is not only this that excites our astonishment and disgust; what adds to it is the fact that their orgies are continued without interruption for weeks, nay, for months; in fact, they are discontinued only when there is no more liquor to be imbibed.

These carousals begin at a time when the apples ripen, of which innumerable quantities grow wild in those regions, and when many barrels have been filled with the juice, which is allowed to ferment until it produces intoxication. No Indian would think of waiting until the liquor had cleared off and been purified. The guests thereupon meet, and do not leave the place until the last drop has disappeared. Meanwhile the same sort of feast is prepared in another cabin, whither the crowd repair; and thus follows carousal after carousal, at which the drinkers partake of no solid food, and sleep only for a few hours. If it should happen, as it does sometimes, that the chicha at one cabin is exhausted before the liquor at the other is fit for drinking, the intervening day is not used for repose and recreation, but speculators keep in readiness for such chances barrels of whiskey brought up in the summer-time, and which supply the carousers. The price is fixed once for all: a horse for a barrel. There is no money, and none needed, for their whole trade consists in barter, and as the raising of animals, which find excellent pastures in the woods, is cheap, and the horses are not worth a great deal, even the poorest Indian is able to indulge at least once a year in drunken extravagance, and thereby obtain a right to take part in the general dissipation.

Even the women do not keep aloof from these orgies, although they never get drunk, which cannot be said of the Chilenos living among them. The former would consider it a disgrace, and therefore they look with contempt upon "the white trash" infesting their settlements, and usually living more by begging than honest toil.

On this night the revelry was to be held at the cazique's cabin, and the whites had arrived just in time to contribute to the feast at least the tobacco, which was usually scanty on such occasions.

While Don Enrique, after paying his tribute, had withdrawn, his two companions looked forward with great interest and suspense to the novel scene which was to transpire.—Indians! How much had the Germans heard and read of them at home; about their cunning, their sagacity and pride, their intrepidity and cruelty in war! Now they were among them, and the charm of this novel mode of life caused them to forget the discomfort and privations which they had to undergo.

They did not indeed see here anything of the famous pride of the Indians; for no one could arraign these savages for haughtiness of demeanor. No sooner did they see that Don Enrique, after giving them tobacco, drew his poncho over his head, and that, therefore, no further gifts might be looked for at his hands, than they applied with the most amiable humility to the two friends for similar presents, and left them no rest, until all, including the women, had received at least something.

Meanwhile the drinking had commenced; and it was not deemed necessary to draw the *agua ardiente* first into bottles, but it was poured into such drinking-vessels as were at the disposal of the guests. There were only two small glasses, and a few tin cups; but the others helped themselves by using cowhorns, which had been but imperfectly cleaned, and lay about everywhere.

Generally the "lady of the house" takes it upon herself to fill the glasses and horns; but the cazique's wife, that is to say, the "foremost lady in the country" would not condescend to do so, and had therefore intrusted this duty to a distant relative, who had been at her house for some time, and felt honored on being called upon to officiate. Her occupation was not difficult, but unremitting, for she stood by the side of the barrel, opening and closing the faucet, while the guests either brought the cups themselves, or had them handed to her by those who sat nearest.

The barrel was a large one, and the whiskey was strong; no wonder, therefore, that the Indians felt very comfortable, and their merriment soon became so boisterous as to "make night hideous." At the same time, the atmosphere in the room, to which was added the odor of the meat roasting on the hearth, became so close and stifling that the two Germans were repeatedly obliged to step out in order to breathe fresh air.

The cazique's wife meanwhile prepared supper—not for the Indians, who might look out for themselves, but—for the strangers; the manner, however, in which she proceeded was liable to objection. In the first place, there was not a fork in the cabin, and probably not in the whole settlement, and, in place of this useful instrument, she used her fingers, which had hardly ever been washed. Next, the old lady, who evidently was very partial to blood, had the habit of taking from the coals the pieces handed to her, after they had roasted for a few moments, and, licking them with great relish, putting them back upon the coals.

"Doctor, just look at that brown harridan," said Relwald, who was watching her. "It turns my stomach to think that any one should be compelled to eat the food she is preparing. Great Heavens, into what hands have we fallen!"

"Into those of romantic people, for whom you longed so much," laughed the doctor; "but do you not know the old rule, that you never ought to look into a kitchen? We could not eat any thing in many a first-class hotel at home, if we knew exactly how the food is prepared. I for one am exceedingly cautious in this respect, for I do not like to spoil my appetite."

"And how the children look! The word handkerchief seems to be unknown to the family. It is too late now; but to-morrow morning I will unpack and distribute some of our red woollen ones."

"As you mention the matter, I should like the old lady to have one now, for she has a very bad cold; and, if I am not much mistaken, the delicacies she is cooking are destined for us."

"It would be horrible if you were right!" cried Relwald; "but I would sooner starve than touch a morsel of that food."

"Dear friend," said the doctor, "pray bear in mind what we were told at Valdivia. These unsophisticated children of the wilderness regard as a terrible insult the refusal of what they offer to their guests, and, in the excited condition in which they are at the present time, I should not like to run the risk of exasperating them."

"No, I would die rather than eat a morsel of it," said Reiwald, resolutely.

The doctor only shrugged his shoulders, and, with a grateful bow, took an old cow-horn, filled to the brim with whiskey, which was offered him, and raised it smilingly to his lips. He was not accustomed to beverages of this description, and the few drops he tasted made him cough. When he intended to hand the horn back to the Indian who had given it him, the latter burst into loud laughter, and said to him something in his own language, which the doctor, of course, did not understand. However, he fully comprehended the gesture which the red man made; he lifted up his hand, laid it upon his lips, and threw back his head. He wanted him to empty the horn.

"My dear friend," said Reiwald, who was much amused at the expression of the doctor's face, and who now repeated the latter's own words, "pray bear in mind what we were told at Valdivia."

"Dear me!" growled the doctor. "It will not kill me." And, firmly grasping the horn, he emptied it at a draught.

"Bravo!" exclaimed Reiwald; "you have talents fitting you for this wild life."

But his laughter did not last long, for another Indian presently offered him a horn, and, to prevent his friend from deriding him, he quaffed that also.

Some Chilenos with their wives had now come in, and mingled with the company; but they looked ragged, degraded, and dirty, nor did the savages pay any attention to them, though they permitted them to take part in the festival.

And then came the supper; the cazique's wife put into a small wooden vessel the pieces of meat; took from the ashes some potatoes, and then sent the little girl with the dish to the two strangers, for the old Chileno slept, or at least feigned to sleep. The two men were exceedingly hungry; but the food, though of a savory smell, was so disgusting that they shrank from it. They, however, received the dish, with seeming thankfulness, but retired with it into the shade, and partook there only of the roasted potatoes, which they could eat without much squeamishness.

Fortunately there were in the house, among the carousing Indians, many lean dogs, which had been attracted by the smell of the roast meat; and the two Germans bestowed the cutlets upon them as soon as they could do so secretly, and thereby gained the attachment of the dirty curs to such an extent that they would not leave them during the whole evening.

But the noise in the cabin was constantly increasing. Although some of the worst inebriates seemed to have drunk themselves sober again, the agua ardiente intoxicated most of the Indians irrecoverably. What with the smoke of tobacco, the odor of the cooking, the heat, and the noise of the revellers, the stay in the room became well-nigh intolerable.

"How unfortunate that we had to

fall this very day into such an abominable hole!" groaned Reiwald, after a time, during which, seated on his saddle, and leaning his back against the sacks, he had gazed despairingly and in silence upon the scene before him. "I shall go mad if this lasts for any length of time. I wonder if these brutes will not by and by think of going home?"

"Strange people, indeed," said the doctor, who regarded the matter more philosophically. "Pray, Reiwald, notice the difference between the Indians and whites, and see how decently dressed and comparatively well bred these red-skins are, while our own race furnish the most debased among us. How dreadfully depraved those two fellows look, and how ragged and dirty the women are, compared with the neatly-dressed Indian girls and matrons! The latter have combed and braided their hair, but see the dishevelled heads of the Chilenas."

"There are more visitors!" exclaimed Reiwald. "Two Chilenos whom we have not seen yet."

The doctor turned his eyes to the door, and saw Cruzado and Meyer, who, after observing the place at a distance, had finally arrived at the resolution not to meet with the other whites, but wait until the festival would be at its height.

"One of them has a suspiciously dark complexion, and may be at home hereabouts, but the face of the other—did we not meet with him at Valdivia?"

"Indeed we did," said Reiwald. "His fat round face seems well known to me. He was among the Germans whom we met the first day after our arrival at Valdivia."

"But he wears a poncho."

"Well, I have seen many foreigners wearing this party-colored manila; they seem to have adopted it because it is fashionable here. At all events, we must speak to him."

"Wait until he has been presented to his majesty. The ceremony will take place presently. The chamberlain has already noticed, and is now hastening toward him. Probably a breach of etiquette has been committed."

"That would be dreadful," said Reiwald.

The company did not seem to observe etiquette so strictly, and Cajuanta himself was in such excellent spirits as not to allow any thing to ruffle his temper. As the barrel had been taken from him, he seated himself directly in front of the fire on a log of wood, upon which a few sheepskins had been spread; but he leaned his back against a box, which, for this purpose, had been placed behind him; on this sat his eldest daughter with another girl. He held in his hand a small glass filled with liquor. His good-natured face beamed with pleasure, and the arrival of new guests seemed to gladden rather than disturb him. Cruzado was an old acquaintance of his, who had often journeyed to the Otra Banda, and he saluted him.

"Bravo, amigo," he said, using his native language, "have you returned to the lagoons? That is right. Sit down; you will find a seat somewhere, and a horn, too; in the corner lies a pile of them, if the dogs have not carried them off.—And whom did you bring with you?"

"Do you not recognize him, cazique?" said the half-breed; "he was here already—an Aleman, Don Carlos."

"Another Aleman!" exclaimed the cacique, laughing merrily. "Yonder sit two more Germans—bueno—drink, Don Carlos, good fellow!" and with his left hand he offered him the glass, while he held out his right to shake hands, which, as well as the glass, Meyer accepted with extraordinary presence of mind.

Don Carlos, indeed, seemed to be in his proper element. First, he went to the old lady, stepping over two Indians stretched out at the fireside, and shook hands with her; next, he turned to the oldest daughter, who smiled on him, for she remembered him very well; and, after a lapse of ten minutes, he was as familiar with these persons as though he had never left them, and had passed in their midst the two years during which he had not seen any of them. Of the other strangers, neither Cruzado (who was unable to converse with them) nor Meyer took any notice. Their plan was not to solicit anything of Don Enrique, but have him make offers of his own accord. As a matter of course, this new incident did not interrupt the revelry in the least; nay, on the contrary, the Indians were intent on bringing liquor to the new-comers, which was somewhat dangerous, as they were obliged to quaff every cup proffered to them. Meyer, however, knew already how to overcome this disagreeable necessity; for he had filled his pockets with tobacco, and whenever he saw any one coming near him, he offered a handful of the noble weed, which occupied the Indian so much, that he was satisfied if the German merely raised the horn to his lips.

So constantly, however, was Meyer surrounded, that Reiwald was unable to get to him, while Cruzado had already thrown his poncho on the floor, and stretched himself on it. At last Don Carlos walked into a corner, where his countryman, profiting by this opportunity, followed him, and, putting his hand on Meyer's shoulder, he said:

"Excuse me, but I believe I heard some one say you are an Aleman, as they call the Germans here. Is it true?"

"It is," said Meyer, turning to him smilingly. "I believe I had, at Valdivia, the honor of making your acquaintance?"

"We were not mistaken, then," said Reiwald, shaking hands with him cheerfully. "And you speak Spanish?"

"I ought to, for I have been a long time in this blessed country."

"And where do you come from now?"

"From Valdivia."

"And you are going to—"

"I am on a little pleasure-trip," said Meyer, evasively. "I want to visit a few old friends, and pass some days on horseback. I am tired of the toilsome life I had to lead in Valdivia."

"Are you married?"

Meyer looked at him quickly, and with surprise.

"What makes you think so?" he asked.

"Oh, I merely asked the question," replied Reiwald, "because I was told that the Germans usually married soon after settling in a foreign country."

"Some of them are donkeys," said Meyer, thoughtfully, and after some hesitation; "but it is the most dangerous thing a man can do here, and if you will take my advice, you—"

Reiwald burst into loud laughter, and was about to make a reply, but the tobacco distributed by the whites was exhausted, and the Indians crowded on all sides, holding those ominous horns in their hands, and demanding new contributions. These demands, however, were made in so naïve a manner, and the guests conducted themselves so modestly, asking only for as much tobacco as they could hold between their fingers, that the German was unable to refuse their applications; but he could not avoid drinking from their horns, and his head began to grow heavy.

Meanwhile the old cazique fixed his eyes again upon the Germans. Perhaps he did not wish to cut off more pieces from the roll of tobacco, which he had put into the box, and what he had retained of it had been used by his family.

"Eh, Alemanos!" he cried out, lifting his head, and looking over the fire. "This way! come this way—you must drink. No one shall die of thirst at my house. You must drink!"

"What a stomach and head that old man must have!" said Reiwald, to whom Meyer translated the cazique's words, heaving a sigh; "for since I have been here he has drunk whiskey enough to make three men intoxicated. But we cannot help it, and must comply with his majesty's invitation."

"We shall take your friend with us," said Meyer.

"Certainly," replied Reiwald, laughing; "he cannot stand much, and if I am to feel wretched to-morrow morning, I wish at least to have a companion in suffering."

The cazique grew impatient, and Reiwald elbowed his way through the crowd, in order to reach Doctor Pfeifel. The doctor had just beaten a retreat, taken up a few sheepskins, and was about to make his bed. He began to grow sleepy, and was tired of the novel but disgusting scene. To gaze upon it for several hours had satisfied his curiosity, and the smoke would not incommode him so much as it had done while standing in the room. But he was not to get off so easily, for Reiwald turned a deaf ear to his excuses. The cazique had commanded, and they had to obey; hence, seizing the doctor's arm, after introducing Don Carlos to him, he drew the doctor away, and a few seconds afterward they stood before the chief, whose hilarity was growing momentarily more boisterous, and who held out to them his ever-filled glass.

"Drink!" he cried. "All Alemanos must drink—good people—Penchuenches are *parientes* (relatives). Come, Don Carlos, you must commence."

Don Carlos did not hesitate long; he himself could stand a great deal, and he knew that the old Cajuasto liked nothing so much as a hearty compliance with such an invitation. He therefore took the glass, raised it politely toward the ladies—a custom as popular among the Indians as it is in other countries—and quaffed the glass.

"Bravo!" exclaimed the old cazique. "Bravo, Don Carlos! You are a glorious fellow, and in drinking can cope with the best of the Penchnenches. And now it is your turn, amigo—what is your name?"

"Reiwald, señor."

"Reibel, what a strange name!" said the old Indian, shaking his head; "but no matter—here, Don Reibel, drink!"

The glass was soon filled—all eyes were fixed upon the stranger as it was handed to him, but Reiwald hesitated. He had taken more liquor to-night than he usually did in a month. But how could he help it? He was in the trap, and could not get out of it. So, taking the glass with a bitter-sweet expression, he looked at it irresolutely, and then attempted to drink as the others had done; but this was not an agreeable operation, for it required a certain skill of which Reiwald was entirely destitute. He was unable to swallow the draught. At first he shut his eyes, and threw up his left arm. The Indians burst into laughter, in which the cazique joined, and, wiping his face, exclaimed:

"Par Dios, amigo! you are an impetuous fellow. Give me the glass; we will see if your friend can do better."

Reiwald, a prey to the most painful confusion, sought to stammer an apology, but what language was he to use?—The Indian did not understand German; and Spanish!—With what little he had acquired of that tongue he would only have added to his ridiculous position. Besides, his cough did not permit him to utter an intelligible word, and during the pauses he heard the merriment of the red-skins. It was now the doctor's turn.

"What is your name, amigo?"

"Doctor Pfeifel."

"Are you a doctor?" exclaimed Cajuante, with eagerness; and, when the German nodded in the affirmative, he added vividly, "Bueno, muy bueno.—You must stay awhile with us; you shall have as much to drink as you want, and may cure the women and children. There, amigo, take it—take it, good doctor!" and he handed him the glass.

Reiwald's mishap was a warning to the doctor, who sipped the liquor very cautiously and succeeded in emptying the glass. He then bowed to Cajuante and was about to retire, when the cazique said to him:

"No, stay here. Sit down by my side. We shall remain together. Doctor is very good—very good—there, drink once more!"

The doctor saw that he was hopelessly committed if compelled to remain by the cazique's side; but what could he do? He evaded the invitation by declaring that it was Don Carlos's turn. The Indian acknowledged the justice of this excuse, and handed the glass to Meyer, who took it without hesitation.

"But Don Reibel cannot drink!" laughed the old chief. "Do you know what you should do, Don Reibel! Give us some music. Every Aleman can do that."

"What am I to do?" said Reiwald, who had scarcely recovered from his trial, turning to Meyer.

"Let them have some music," said Don Carlos, dryly.

"Music!" cried Reiwald, in surprise. "And on what instrument? I play the piano, but I doubt if such an instrument is to be had here."

"Tell him to give us music," said the cazique, whose utterance grew thick. Meyer translated his words, and the young German exclaimed, laughingly:

"I can whistle prettily, if that should happen to please him."

"Then, whistle a tune," said Meyer, with the greatest equanimity. "Music is music, and the red-skins are not very particular."

Reiwald looked at him in surprise; nevertheless, the request was so ludicrous that he could not resist the temptation. He was, moreover, excited by the whiskey, and in excellent humor. Besides, it was his turn to drink again. The glass had already been filled, and he felt that he could not stand any more of the "fire-water." Now, if he must whistle, he needed not to drink, and, casting a half-despairing glance on the crowd, he suddenly commenced whistling a waltz.

He was, in fact, quite a virtuoso in this art, for, though every one can whistle, few excel; and no sooner did the notes sound through the room, which was hitherto filled with deafening noise, than profound silence reigned around. It seemed almost as though the Indians held their breath, so motionless they sat and listened, and the cazique's broad face was radiant with joy. Even the glasses were no longer supplied, and every one held his empty horn or cup in his hand.

Reiwald himself was astonished at the effect he was producing. But, when he intended to stop, Cajuanto exclaimed, eagerly, "Poco mas! poco mas!" and the German now whistled a schottische, which really electrified the Indians.— Even this did not satisfy the guests: whenever he intended to conclude, all shouted, "Poco mas!" until finally he was exhausted, and he was unable to proceed. All thereupon tried to imitate the melodies they had heard, and a great uproar arose.

Reiwald tried to profit by the general tumult and withdraw; but a reward was in store for him. The cazique's eldest daughter had arisen and came to him; in her hand she held, not a laurel-wreath, with which the princesses of old rewarded skilful minstrels, but a wooden dish with boiled garden-beans, which she presented to him with a smile.

The girl was handsome, and offered him the dish with a certain grace and timidity which added to her charms. At the same time the situation was so ridiculous that Reiwald, though sober, could hardly have preserved his gravity. But as it was, his head was swimming; he was, besides, very hungry, and uttering a grateful, "Muchas gracias, señorita!"—about the only Spanish words he knew—he took the dish and retired.

On reaching the end of the room, he perceived that Don Enrique was not asleep, but sat erect upon his blankets, and was engaged in an animated conversation with the half-breed. Reiwald was utterly unable to reflect on any thing. As the doctor now rejoined him, the two partook of the beans with a good appetite, and threw themselves upon their hard couch. They still heard the noise about them, but it was indistinct, as in a dream. Reiwald also felt as though the whole cabin were whirling around him, and, to get rid of this unpleasant sensation, he had repeatedly to open his eyes and raise himself up.

Cruzado and Meyer did not stay much longer. The confusion, in fact, now knew no bounds, and then they did not wish to return too late to the house of their

Chilian host, although, to judge from the condition in which he had returned, they expected to find him fast asleep. Without bidding farewell to any one—for all come and go at such festivities as they please, and many leave the house while others enter it—they stepped out into the dark night, and Cruzado quickly raised his head as soon as they were in the open air, for there was a change in the weather. The wind had turned more toward the west, and but few stars could be seen, the sky being overcast. If the wind should shift north, rain might be looked for, which would be a serious obstacle to the expedition of Don Enrique. For the present, however, they could not arrive at any thing definite on this head. They had to wait for the morrow, and, without communicating his fears to Meyer, who was also a little under the influence of liquor, he ascended with him the clearing and the small hill which separated them from the Chileno's dwelling. Suddenly Cruzado stood and seized his companion's arm, while in front were heard loud shouts.

"What is that!" exclaimed Meyer, in surprise. "Did we get to the wrong house, then?"

"Caramba, compañero!" laughed Cruzado, "I believe Don Felipe has got sober and is beating his family. I think it is well for us not to disturb him in this pleasant occupation, and we had better return to the cazique. The Indians do not fight when drunk."

A shrill cry for help suddenly burst from the cabin, and Meyer, who had become somewhat sober, exclaimed:

"That will not do, Cruzado. There is some one in great distress—come!"

Without waiting for his companion to follow, he hastened as fast as his feet could carry him along the short distance up the hill to the cabin, from the open door of which fell a faint glimmer of light. The next moment he stood on the threshold and witnessed a singular scene.

In the middle of the room stood the old Chilian drunkard, in his shirt and pantaloons, but the former half torn from his shoulders. In his right hand he held a long knife and brandished his clinched left in the air. He foamed at the mouth, his eyes were distended, his long iron-gray hair was floating wildly about his temples, and from his lips fell the vilest and most blasphemous imprecations, such as are known only to the Spanish language, which outstrips any other in this respect. Before him, on the floor of the room, lay his wife—her dirty calico dress hanging in shreds about her—pale and bleeding, while her daughter, who had encircled her with her arms, was yelling for help.

A weird light was shed over this group, partly by the fire still burning in the middle of the room, partly by a tallow-candle which had already set fire to the paper in which it was wrapped. To judge from his attitude, the Chileno, maddened by strong drink, seemed to be intent on again attacking his wife. He had tasted blood, and, like a wild beast, panted for more, when Meyer, who had involuntarily seized a piece of wood lying outside the house, rushed with it into the room and threw it at the head of the infuriated man. Before he knew what had happened, and who had attacked him so unexpectedly, Meyer was at his throat, knocked him down, so that the knife fell from his grasp, and was hurled into a corner. Thereupon, he said, with the utmost composure:

"Good-evening, señor. You are playing well here. I believe you were about to cut the throats of your own family. Are you crazy?"

"Oh, God has sent you to me, señor!" exclaimed the maiden, clasping her hands. "Father does not know what he is doing. That accursed liquor has deprived him of his senses!"

Uttering a vile imprecation against his daughter, the Chileno sprang to his feet, and felt for his knife. Meyer, however, whom the part he had taken in the carousal rendered bold enough to enter into a fight with half a dozen demons, rushed between him and the girl, and another scuffle would have ensued had not the Chileno noticed at that moment the dark form of Cruzado standing in the doorway. Uttering a cry of anguish on recognizing his features, he staggered back, buried his face in his hands, and sank to the floor. He remained there, and no one paid any further attention to him.

Meanwhile Meyer, in conjunction with Tadea, carried her mother to the couch, where, familiar as he was with almost every thing, including even a knowledge of surgery, he examined the wound, and was soon able to announce that the mother was by no means dangerously injured. Her swoon was to be ascribed to whiskey rather than loss of blood.

"Is she dead?" asked Cruzado, with the utmost indifference.

"Oh, Santa Maria!" cried Tadea.

"Nonsense!" growled Meyer. "It is nothing but a flesh-wound, though it is very close to the carotid artery. Tie a handkerchief around it, señorita; it is of no consequence, and will heal in a few days; but, of course, she must not drink any thing until she is well again."

"Ah, thanks, señor, a thousand thanks!" said the poor girl. "Heaven sent you hither to our protection. My father was beside himself, and would have surely killed us both. Oh, I wish he would not drink another drop!"

"Reassure yourself, señorita, you are out of danger," said Meyer, comforting her, and seizing her hand, whose timid pressure electrified him; "we—shall stay with you, no harm shall befall you; and, as to your mother, she will soon recover."

The candle had burned down; it flickered and went out, filling the room with an abominable odor. The fire on the hearth still shed a dim light through the room.

"Oh, it makes me so happy to hear you say that!" said Tadea, in a low voice.

"Poor girl!" sighed Don Carlos, overcome by a strange emotion, and gazing upon the pale face of the unhappy maiden. The uncertain light effaced whatever blemishes in her appearance might have lessened his admiration by daylight; he saw only her large, lustrous eyes gazing at him; he could remark her finely-chiselled lips, and, almost without knowing what he was doing, he encircled her with his arm, and folded her gently to his heart.

The girl heaved a deep sigh, and Meyer whispered tenderly:

"My dear, poor señorita!"

"Oh! no nonsense, Don Carlos,"

growled Cruzado, whose presence had been nearly forgotten. "Come here,— help me to arrange the blankets, and throw a few billets of wood on the fire, so that we may see where we are to lie down."

Meyer had started back, and Tadeo squatted at the fire. Soon the flames leaped up again and shed a bright light over the room.

"And shall we let the old man lie there?" said Meyer, pointing to him.

"Has he his knife?"

"I threw it into the corner yonder."

"Bring it to me. Put it under the blankets, and let him sleep away the fumes of liquor."

The girl withdrew to the most distant part of the room, where her mother lay, and there arranged her bed. Cruzado, who was experienced in such matters, placed their saddles and blankets so well that they could recline on them quite comfortably. Their ponchos protected them from the cold, and soon all was silent.

CHAPTER XIX.

ON THE MORROW.

Reiwald and the doctor passed a wretched night; for the noise of the drunken Indians, although never degenerating into violent altercation, but remaining perfectly harmless, was on the increase from hour to hour, and to sleep in the midst of such an uproar was out of the question. If they became drowsy at times, some yell from a jubilant guest reawakened them, or a dog ran over them, or an Indian stumbled upon their outstretched limbs. Toward two o'clock, Cajuante, in fact, stepped over all obstructions, pulling the different sleepers to and fro, until he found Reiwald, and asked him to whistle again. The young German, who did not feel well, did not vouchsafe a reply, but wrapped himself closely in his blanket, and did not appear to awaken, however much he shook him. Cajuante was finally obliged to let him alone.

The carousal lasted till three in the morning; that is to say, the barrel was empty by that time, else the Indians would have remained all night. Some, of course, could not be removed; they had drunk immoderately, so that they had to be left on the floor, where they had fallen. Those who were still able to stand staggered out of the room, to return to their own cabins, whither the women had already withdrawn. The old cazique, who had stuck to his post to the last, had the barrel turned upside down to see if he could not squeeze out a last glass, reeled to the couch spread near his seat, wrapped himself up, and soon snored as if he would shake down the cabin.

The revelry had ceased — even the dogs had tired of their restless wandering, and lain down in the warm ashes, for no one sat near it to drive them away. The wind howled outside, through the branches of the forest-trees; presently large drops fell in quick succession, rattling on the roof—the forerunners of the rainy season; and then suddenly there came a shower, which the shingles, dried as they had been during the summer, could not prevent from penetrating into the interior. Reiwald started up in dismay, when suddenly a cold stream fell upon his forehead and drenched his face. He was so sleepy that even this did not fully arouse him, and he turned his head to and fro in order to dodge the rain; but, uttering a despairing "How dreadful!" he moved aside under another stream. He could not go anywhere else, for an Indian lay close to him, almost swimming in a pool of water. He had to remain, therefore, where he was, and, rendered insensible to the miseries of such a night by the stupor which had not yet left him, he finally drew one of the sheepskins over his face, and paid no further attention to the rain.

This night, the most hideous that Reiwald ever passed through, at length drew to a close; day dawned, and, though most of the sleepers lay stretched on the floor in varied positions, and were unable to stir, the domestic animals began their usual concert. First, the roosters announced their wakefulness, for no sooner had one of them raised his voice than his fellows responded from all quarters. This aroused the dogs, which began to scratch themselves and bite one another. A procession of ducks waddled chatteringly into the cabin, and bathed in the puddles made by the rain overnight; and they were followed by three or four turkeys, at which the dogs growled. The fowls thereupon retired over the sleepers, jumping very unceremoniously upon their breasts and shoulders. An old turkey had got into trouble with two or three dogs, and fled, pursued by them, directly across the two Germans, who started up with a cry of surprise and anger.

"This is altogether intolerable," cried Reiwald, springing to his feet; "and, oh, what a headache! I feel as if my cranium were bursting."

"A kingdom for a dish of sardines," exclaimed the doctor; "I, also, feel very ill."

"It was the most wretched liquor," groaned Reiwald, "that I ever partook of I shall not forget this night, though I live a hundred years."

"And how it looks here!" said the doctor, glancing about the room, which was now illuminated by the rising sun. "See these savages on the floor. I wish I were a draughtsman, and had a lead-pencil!"

"How comfortable the ducks seem to be! I shall have a cold, for I am wet to the skin."

"Where is your flask, Reiwald!" inquired the doctor. "As you speak of a cold, I believe it would be advisable to use a preventive."

"Do not speak of a flask," cried Reiwald; "the mere mention of spirituous liquors turns my stomach. Oh, my head!"

"Never mind," said the doctor, quietly, "I will drink alone. Where is it?"

"In the saddle-bags," said the young man, averting his face, in order not to see his friend drink.

Don Enrique was also awake. He arose, looked around, wrapped himself in his poncho, and left the cabin, without exchanging a word with his companions. They did not take umbrage at it, for they were unable to converse with him, and they knew that he never spoke to any one, unless he had to issue an order or ask a question.

The inmates of the Chilian cabin on the hill had arisen at an earlier hour. The pretty girl had kindled a fire, brought wood, and put a kettle full of water on the hearth. This aroused Crusado, who stepped out to look after the weather, which was very fine. The sky was bright, and not a cloud to be seen anywhere. Last night's shower had only been a warning of the approaching season, and possibly they might have fair weather for several days yet; if they wished to cross the mountains, they had need of it.

The young maiden now left the cabin to fetch potatoes from the neighboring field, and Meyer rose likewise. He glanced over to the corner where the drunken Chileno had fallen down the night before, and could scarcely repress a cry of surprise on seeing the fellow lying in exactly the same position on the floor. Was he dead?—No, he breathed heavily, but regularly: he was asleep; and Don Carlos, shaking his head, stepped out to attend to his toilet down at the brook, and cool his flushed face in the fresh water. He had heard nothing of the rain, and was surprised on seeing everything so wet and so many puddles in the road.

Cajuante was still asleep, and, as the day's carousal at the cabin on the shore of the lagoon was not to commence till about three in the afternoon, he had nothing to do, when an Indian, mounted on a little short-legged mare, halted in front of the cabin and asked to see him. He held a document in his hand, and said he had been instructed to deliver it only to the cazique himself.

It was, however, somewhat difficult to arouse the old man, and the whole family had to take part in the attempt; they would not have done so but for the message, which had evidently been sent by the government, and as usual struck terror into the hearts of the women. The paper *spoke!* It could utter words in black dots and lines, and the less they themselves were able to comprehend the matter, the greater was the awe with which they regarded the document, of which no one could tell beforehand what intelligence it contained.

It was a touching scene to witness the little folks shaking their father, and even calling upon their relatives to assist them. And with what wonderful composure the old cazique bore all these attacks, without giving other sign of life than drawing a deep breath now and then! These efforts were continued for upward of a quarter of an hour, when at last he opened his eyes, looked wonderingly about him, and then raised himself up. His wife knew how he had to be treated under such circumstances, and now, that he was fully conscious, she beckoned to her daughter, who presently stepped with a jar behind her father and slowly poured clear cold water over his head. Cajuante did not stir during the operation; he closed his eyes, and bent a little forward, while the water was trickling down his head. At last the jar was empty, and he rose, shook himself like a poodle, stroked his hair from his forehead, and nodded pleasantly to his anxious family.

But, before the paper brought by the messenger could be delivered to him, he had to be thoroughly dried and rubbed, which his wife did with the petticoat of her youngest daughter; and not until then could he be informed that instructions concerning public affairs had arrived for him.

He contemplated the inside and outside of the document; on the latter were written only the words, "To the Cacique Cajuaste;" he then turned it upside down, and back again; and, on finally arriving at the result that he was unable to do any thing with it—for he could not read—he said:

"Where is Cornelio?—How fortunate it is that he is here!—Send for Cornelio. He will read it to me."

The same efforts had to be made now to arouse Cornelio, the interpreter, who had the preceding night introduced Don Enrique to the Cazique, and who was a "Capitan de amigos;" for he had also taken too much whiskey, and lay in the opposite corner of the room. It was almost as difficult for them to awaken him as the cazique, and, as they had finally restored him to consciousness, he remained sitting on the floor, held his head in his hand, and uttered heart-rending groans. And he was required to read in this condition!

At length he took the paper which the cazique himself handed to him; but the letters "swam before his eyes," as he said, and he added he must first wash his head before he could do any thing. He was vexed also at having been awakened; but, as he could not help it, he put on his hat, wrapped himself up, and crept over to the brook to refresh himself.

Meanwhile Meyer had returned to the cabin on the hill, but he did not meet Tadea there. The old Chileno still lay on the floor, groaning, and his wife had also drawn her blanket over her head and did not stir; it was a mournful picture of wretchedness, and the German turned from them with an expression of utter disgust and contempt. But where was the poor girl, who, alone and unprotected, had to bear all this misery, and pass through it every day at this season of the year? He did not meet her in the neighboring field, but, on walking through a narrow grove in order to reach the water below, whither he believed she might have gone, he found her sitting, at no great distance from the cabin, at the side of a small spring running into a rough-hewn trough; she was weeping bitterly. She did not notice Meyer's approach, and it was not until he stepped near her, and put his hand on her shoulder, that she gave a start, looked timidly up to him, and, on recognising him, buried her face again in her hands.

How pretty Tadea looked on this morning! She must have risen early to wash herself and arrange her hair, which she had bound up in heavy smooth braids. How white was her complexion —and how sweetly and yet mournfully her dark eyes gazed at Don Carlos!

"My poor girl," said Meyer, profoundly moved, and as he encircled her with his arm, as if to reassure her like a child, " that was indeed a terrible night for you, and I can well imagine how disheartened you must be. Do such scenes occur very often?"

Tadea still wept, and Meyer pressed her gently to his heart; nor did he utter another word, but remained in the same attitude. At last she said in a low voice:

"It is too dreadful for me! I cannot bear it longer—I will jump into the lagoon, for father will surely kill us both."

"That abominable liquor!" cried the German, angrily. "Can he not be weaned from it?"

TADEA

"No, no, he cannot leave it alone; he drinks to excess day after day, and neglects even the necessary labors of the field. Oh, what will be the end of it!"

"But I wonder what you have a casique for!" asked Meyer. "He is your supreme judge here, and cannot permit any one's life to be endangered in so outrageous a manner. He must protect you if you apply to him."

The poor girl shook her head mournfully.

"How can he?" she said, in a low voice. "In the first place, he himself is rarely sober at this season; and, next, he does not like to interfere in the affairs of the Chilian inhabitants of this district. He would, however, exhort father to conduct himself properly; but that would be all, and father would only be more and more exasperated at mother and myself for arraigning him for maltreatment."

"But your mother seems to drink, too."

"Unfortunately she does," sighed the sorrowful girl; "and how often I have implored her to let liquor alone! but she is unable to do so, and she always irritates father by upbraiding him until he flies into a towering passion and no longer knows what he is doing."

"And have you no friend here? No one that would protect you at least from the brutality of your own parent!" asked Meyer, whose voice had grown singularly soft and tender in uttering these last words. He bent over her, and her head leaned against his breast.

"No one," she said, mournfully.—"Who would protect a poor girl here? What few countrymen of ours are here are still worse than my parents, and they are, besides, afraid of my father. None of them would dare to bid him defiance. Oh, I am very, very unhappy!"

Meyer struggled with a resolution which he was about to take. He had almost involuntarily inclined his head, and his lips touched her hair—he pressed a kiss on it, and she did not resist him. Suddenly Cruzado called out, at no great distance from him:

"Don Carlos! where in the world are you?" And there was a rustling in the bushes.

He could not have come more unseasonably. The girl gave a start and wiped away her tears; but the German, folding her once more to his heart, said in a low voice:

"Wait here for a moment, Tadea; I have something else to tell you, but must first send away that marplot; I shall be back presently;" and he hastened off in the direction in which he had heard his companion.

"Don Carlos!" again shouted Cruzado.

"Here I am! But who, for Heaven's sake, is shouting my name all over the settlement? What is the matter?"

"I could not find you anywhere," said Cruzado. "We must go. We have no time to lose. I have spoken with the old haciendero this morning; he is overjoyed at the idea that we are to accompany him, and proposes good terms. But we must set out without delay, for the wind is uncertain. It blew this morning again toward the southwest, but last night there was a regular norther, and the shower was the first warning which autumn gives. After we have crossed the

Limal, or get over to the other side, I do not care if the rainy season sets in; but if it should catch us yet on this side in the valley, where we must so often cross the accursed Witchi-Leufu, to avoid the projecting spurs, we may be cut off in the middle of the forest, and kill our horses one by one, in order not to die of starvation. I know the place; I passed through it once before, about five years since."

Meyer listened to him in silence, and looked thoughtfully. He said quietly, but firmly and resolutely:

"Let me tell you, compañero, I have changed my mind. I will not accompany you, but stay here awhile with the Indians until the affair in the colony has blown over. I do not wish to go to the Otra Banda at this season."

"You don't?" said Cruzado, slowly. "And you think, perhaps, certain persons would not find you here if they wished to arrest you? The capitan de amigos, who, by-the-way, is a scoundrel whom I have known for years, will not ride back to the white settlements to-morrow, and will not report there, I suppose, that he saw both of us here? And when he hears what has happened at Valdivia, the policemen will be immediately on your track."

"I will not be such a donkey as to wait until they are able to come up," said the German, dryly. "Before the capitan de amigos has got beyond the Ranco Lagoon, I shall be somewhere on the Rio Bueno, where I know an excellent place of concealment, and where no one will look for me. There I shall be able to discover what was the upshot of our nocturnal adventure in the bay, and if there is any fuss made about it. Maybe all our precautions are needless, and no one bestows any attention upon it."

"Listen, Don Carlos," said Cruzado, and there was a sarcastic expression in his glance, as he uttered the words—"shall I tell you why you do not desire to accompany us across the mountains?"

"Well?" asked Meyer, slightly embarrassed.

"Because you have fallen in love with the girl here, and intend to stay with her—that is the long and short of the matter; and, if you will not take it amiss, I tell you that you are about to commit a very stupid blunder."

"And why?" exclaimed Don Carlos Meyer, quickly. "I am free."

"Are you?—And what about your wife, of whom you told me on the road?"

"Bah! Did she not run away from me two years ago, and go to Valparaiso? And am I yet under any obligation to her? Did she not leave me of her own accord?"

"But I suppose you know that Catholics never divorce husband and wife, and that you are, therefore, not at liberty to marry again?"

"What do I care for your Catholic laws!" exclaimed Meyer, whose purpose, which at first had not yet been very firm, was strengthened by Cruzado's objections. "I am a Protestant, and do not care about what they permit or prohibit. For the rest, I do not intend, by any means, to remain in Chili; I am tired of living here, and our unpleasant affair in the bay has completely disgusted me with the country. Don Pasquale is looking for the speedy arrival of a ship from North America. He must allow me to embark, and you may depend upon it that I will keep out of the way until then."

"And you will take the parents of your bride with you?" inquired Cruzado, sneeringly.

"No, no," said Meyer, repressing an oath. "They are degraded beings, and the poor, unhappy girl would be irretrievably lost, if she were to stay here another month."

Cruzado made no immediate reply. Suddenly he turned his head aside, for he had heard footsteps, and saw two men coming up the pathway—Cajuante, the cacique, and the capitan — who seemed to look for them, for the old cacique beckoned as soon as he caught sight of them.

"I wonder what they want of us?" said Cruzado, gloomily.

"I am surprised at seeing the old man about already," laughed Meyer; "he was very drunk last night. I should like to know how many bottles of agua ardiente he drank."

"Something must have happened, since he has risen so early," said Cruzado, distrustfully; "generally he sleeps much longer after such orgies."

"He has a paper in his hand," said Meyer.

"Caracho!" swore Cruzado, in an undertone. "When I went with old Don Enrique into the forest this morning, I saw an Indian galloping up from below."

"Ah, Cruzado and Don Carlos—bueno!" shouted Cajuante, coming toward them smilingly, and holding out his hand to them. "I am glad to meet you. Can you read, Cruzado?"

"I?" said Cruzado, with a somewhat surly air. "Quien sabe? I do not know. Possibly I can, but I have never tried. There is your capitan, Señor Cornelio, who can surely read."

"He can, indeed," replied the Chileno, coloring slightly, "he can, amigo; yet he can read only a plain and distinct handwriting; but it is impossible to decipher if the words on this paper are Spanish or French; at least, I am unable to make them out, and, besides, my head is not very clear after last night's revelry. It seems as though it would burst but could not."

Meyer glanced at the leaf of paper, which seemed to have been torn from a book, and the capitan de amigos was right in complaining of the illegible character of the handwriting.

"And why do you not go to the old señor who arrived last night, and who is able to read any kind of writing. Give it to me; I will see him about it."

"Mercy knows where he is?" said Cajuante. "I believe he has gone to look after his horses, or down to the river, to see if it has fallen. Can you not read, Don Carlos? The Alemanes usually can do every thing."

"Let me see it," said the German. "I will try to make out what it is."

He took the leaf and glanced over it. It was illegible, indeed, but still he was able to decipher a word here and there. "Al Cacique Cajuante," he read.

"Yes, we made that out, too," growled Cornelio. "But it is a shame to trouble a man with such hieroglyphics, especially when he has a headache."

Meyer meanwhile did not avert his eyes, and his heart began to throb more rapidly, for he had discovered Cruzado's name and his own, Don Carlos, in the badly-written lines.

"It would be very strange if we should not succeed by-and-by in making out what it is. Let me keep it for a moment; I will certainly decipher it."

"A very clever man, that Don Carlos," said Cajuante, nodding cheerfully. "He might become a capitan any day."

"Yes," murmured Meyer to himself, "it would be bad if I were no longer fit for any thing else." But his thoughts were with the paper, and he cast only a fugitive glance on Cornelio. Finding that the capitan did not watch him, he looked quickly and warningly at Cruzado. This was all the hint the half-breed needed; his misgivings were confirmed. Above all, Don Carlos had to be left alone, and Cruzado soon succeeded in prevailing upon Cajuante to give the German a short time for deciphering the mysterious lines. But he had not yet got rid of the capitan, who had approached to help him.

"Oh, it occurs to me to ask you," said Cruzado, quietly, "if either of you owns a chestnut horse with white and black hind-legs and a white spot on the forehead."

"That is my horse!" exclaimed Cornelio, giving a start.

"Yours, is it?" said the half-breed, nodding. "Well, you had better look after it in time, for it started off this morning in the direction of the lagoon."

"Caracho!" cried Cornelio, starting up. "That would be a bad joke, for I intended to set out at noon. The accursed animal has played the same trick on me repeatedly.—Cajuante, may I take one of your horses in order to ride after mine?"

"You may take three of them, amigo," said the cazique, good-naturedly, "if you have need of them."

"But where are they?"

"Yes," said the old man, laughingly, "that is more than I can tell you. When we came home last night, we were very merry, and paid no attention to them, for they do not run away. But they are somewhere in the forest, you may depend on it."

The capitan paid no further regard to the letter; nay, he was glad, perhaps, to get away from it under so plausible a pretext, and now hastened down toward the cabin to get some Indian to assist him in hunting up his horse. Cruzado followed him somewhat more slowly with Cajuante, and Meyer remained alone with the letter. For the moment, the interest he took in the paper caused him to forget every thing else, even Tadeo; for he had made out enough to know that it concerned only Cruzado and himself. It is true, the letter was a mere scrawl, written with a miserable pen; but Meyer, who was a man of some education, had already gained sufficient knowledge of the peculiar handwriting of the Chilenos, so that it was not difficult for him to decipher gradually the whole document. There were some words, indeed, which he was unable at once to make out, but he soon had a clear idea of their meaning, and finally read the following startling lines:

"AL CAZIQUE CAJUANTE:

"You are informed that two Individnals, a half-breed and a German, having committed a crime in the colony, have fled into the interior of the country. One of them is named Cruzado, the other Don Carlos. They will either go to the Mayhue Lagoon, or turn toward the Rio Bueno. Policemen will be dispatched from here in both directions tomorrow morning, or perhaps to-night. If the criminals should arrive there, take them into custody and guard them well. The governor has offered a reward for their apprehension."

Meyer was unable to decipher the signature, but this was quite needless, and he trembled before the danger to which he was exposed. He did not doubt that the cazique, as soon as he heard of the order, would comply with it immediately; for he would not incur, for the sake of two strangers, the risk of getting into trouble with the Chilian Government; and especially would that blockhead, Señor Cornelio, the capitan de amigos, joyously embrace the opportunity of gaining some distinction by delivering to the authorities the prisoners, whose arrest he would, of course, attribute solely to his own energy and sagacity. And what was to be done now? Don Carlos could impossibly go to the Rio Bueno, as he had purposed doing, now that the very place where he intended to conceal himself had been mentioned in the letter.

But what if the don should destroy the letter? He might have devised some excuse for doing so, especially as no suspicion had yet been aroused against him. But what good would that do him? The writer of the letter would arrive that night, or, at any rate, the next morning, with a number of policemen; and, if really one or the other of the custom-house officers had been killed by the shot fired at them, or drowned at the capsizing of the boat, they would be in a most disagreeable predicament. Poor Tadea! He was now to leave the dear girl, who was evidently tenderly attached to him—for how could she otherwise have clung to him so affectionately—exposed to such extreme peril! But what could he do—at least for the present? One hope, and one only, remained.

He had to leave this settlement immediately; so much was certain—and moreover he had to cross the mountains with the utmost rapidity; nay, if Don Enrique was unable to complete his preparations very speedily, he and Cruzado could not wait for his departure, but had to set out in advance in order to get the Cordilleras between them and their pursuers. But the rainy season would not be all the time so inclement as to render it impossible to return when no one would be on the lookout for him. Then he could ride back without incurring any danger and bring his betrothed. His betrothed! The idea almost frightened him, for, after the bitter experience through which he had already passed, he had sworn many an oath in secret, but none the less in earnest, never to fall again into the meshes of a Chilena. But was there not an essential difference in this instance? The Chilenas on the coast had their heads full of love-adventures, finery, and no one knows what; they were, moreover, lazy in attending to household matters, and their unfortunate husbands could not do enough to satisfy their manifold wants. But this girl, who had been brought up amid privations and poverty—what luxuries did she know of? —who had ever offered her a helping hand? And would not gratitude attach her forever to the man who would deliver her from her indescribable misery? But it was impossible for him to take her now to the Pampas; and then he distrusted the Indians there too seriously to convoy so lovely a flower into their midst. No, he had to leave her for a short time yet among her dismal surroundings. He was unable to help her at present, however much he desired to do so; but he would return before long. He commenced building up in his mind all sorts of pleasing plans, and had almost forgotten the letter, when he saw Cruzado return with a hasty step. From afar he shouted to Meyer:

"Well,—what is in the letter, Don Carlos?"

"Nothing," replied the German, "but that we are to be taken into custody, wherever our friends meet us, and delivered to the policemen, who will arrive here to-night or to-morrow morning."

"That is what I was afraid of," said Cruzado. "How fortunate that that blockhead of a capitan could not read; and they make a functionary of such a fellow!"

"And what next?"

"You must tear the letter, lest it fall into any one's hands."

"That will not do; it would arouse their suspicions against us," replied Meyer; "but there is another way of rendering it illegible. There are some words in it which no one is able to make out, and if I efface a few letters here and there"—he drew his moistened fingers across several words—"I should like to see the professor that can decipher them. There," he added, obliterating other letters, "now I believe we may safely intrust the precious paper to the capitan. He will be utterly unable to discover what it is all about."

"And our names are mentioned in it?"

"No longer," laughed Meyer.

"And do you still intend to remain with your doña, Don Carlos, and wait until they take you into custody?"

"I believe not," said the German, shaking his head, "for I am almost afraid we have done mischief down in the bay."

"Very well, get your horse, then, and bring mine along. I have already put on guard an old friend of mine, for I expected that something was in the wind, and, if more uninvited guests should arrive before we are off, we shall at least get timely warning. Then you may follow me with entire confidence, for I know every inch of ground."

"And now?"

"Now I shall assist the old haciendero in getting his baggage ready, and try, if possible, to induce a few Indians to accompany us. I have frightened the old man by telling him fearful stories about the rainy season, and he and his peon went out at once to fetch the horses. I believe they are coming yonder."

"What was that you told the capitan about his horse?"

"Nothing. I only wished to get the fellow out of the way. His horse is still in the same corral where he left it last night."

"But he will be very angry on finding it out."

"What do we care for that? Now go, Don Carlos! Our horses must be saddled in a quarter of an hour."

CHAPTER XX.

TOWARD THE MOUNTAINS.

CRUZADO left and quickly went down the road, and Meyer knew well that the arrangement just made must be carried out to the letter, if they did not wish to incur the greatest danger. But he had promised Tadea to return to her immediately—he must bid her farewell, however short the parting scene might be, and no sooner had his friend disappeared behind the bushes than he glided back toward the spring.—But Tadea was not there. Had she returned to the house, for he had kept her long waiting? He looked around everywhere, and called her name, but he could not follow her to the house. He would return presently with the horses, and then go to the house for the saddles and bridles. He would yet see her once more, and speak with her, perhaps privately. At all events, he could whisper a few words, and that would be sufficient.

With this resolution he turned and hastened as fast as his feet could carry him in the direction in which he knew he would find the horses, in a small enclosed pasture, where they had grazed all night.

He easily succeeded in catching them, and was soon on his way back to the Chileno's cabin, his heart throbbing more the nearer he came to it.

"Meyer," he said to himself, " it is disgraceful that such an old fellow as you should again be head and ears in love!—No, that is not so," he went on to say, "not at all in love, or at least but a little. Shall I, however, leave the poor girl in her misery here!—such a dear, lovely creature!—But that accursed Cruzado always makes his appearance at the most unseasonable time. A bachelor's life is after all a wretched existence, and I am sick of it." He rode on for a while in silence, and other thoughts flashed through his mind. After a pause he continued: " It is a great deal of trouble indeed to take a wife from here to North America, and costs some money,—double fare, of course, but," he added, comforting himself, " I have a fine balance to my credit at Don Pasquale's; at any rate, it will defray our travelling-expenses, and, once there, I shall certainly be able to earn a livelihood. The good God forsakes no German, and has taken the Meyer family under His special protection."

His purpose became fixed, and he was so much absorbed in his thoughts that he arrived at the cabin almost without knowing how he got there. He dismounted very quickly, and, although he glanced about in order to discover Tadea somewhere outside, he did not tarry, but entered the room, which, indeed, presented a most gloomy spectacle.

The wife sat on her bed, unwashed, and with disordered hair, the traces of yesterday's dissipation still plainly visible on her coarse features. In her hand she held a bloody rag, with which she had probably stanched her wound, and, when the German crossed the threshold, she fixed her eyes upon him with a sullen expression.

The husband squatted at the fire. His face must have been prepossessing and regular in former times, for the debased life which he had been leading so long had not yet effaced all vestiges of the fine appearance with which Nature had endowed him. His long, iron-gray hair hung down over his temples, as he had risen with it from his sleep. His clothes were in shreds, and his body appeared not to have seen water for weeks; but he seemed to have sobered down, and, at the moment the German crossed the threshold, he cast a sinister glance upon his daughter, who had received the guests the day before. He had already noticed their saddles and blankets, and a vague recollection of the preceding night's closing scene arose in his mind.

"Ah, compañero," said Meyer, on entering, and glancing involuntarily at Tadea, who was just about to put her father's breakfast into a dish, "have you got over it? You had too much last night, and came near doing a good deal of mischief."

"Buenos dias, señor," said the Chileno, whose good-humor was not increased by this allusion to what had happened, "and where do you come from, if you will allow me that question?"

"From the coast," replied Meyer, laconically; "we shall not trouble you longer, for we intend to go to and return from the Otra Banda before the rainy season sets in."

"Before the rainy season sets in, eh?" said the old man, while Meyer took up his saddle and the blankets, and carried them out. When he came back for the other saddle, his host said again:

"And pray who is with you, señor?"

"An acquaintance of yours," said Meyer; "else we should not have asked hospitality of your daughter. My companion's name is Cruzado."

"Cruzado!" gasped the old Chileno, and it did not escape Meyer that the name seemed to terrify him. "I thought I dreamed of him last night."

"Here is your knife!" exclaimed Meyer, who found it on raising the saddle, and threw the weapon toward him into the ashes. "I should think you might make a better use of it than to turn it against your own wife. For shame, señor! If we had not interfered, you would, perhaps, be a murderer to-day."

"A murderer!" exclaimed the Chileno, turning pale.

"Will you not take some food, señor?" said Tadea, at this moment, carrying a small dishful of potatoes roasted in the ashes. "You cannot set out without eating any thing."

"Pray, señorita, be kind enough to put the dish in front of the door. I will put the potatoes into my saddle-bags."

The girl went out, and Meyer, who had been anxiously waiting for this opportunity, followed her. Outside, he threw down the saddle by the side of the horse, and, on taking the dish, he also took her hand, and said tenderly:

"Tadea—I wished to speak with you alone, but you did not wait for me at the spring."

"Señor!" said the girl.

"Do you believe that I have honest intentions toward you?"

Tadea looked at him gravely, and made no reply. At last she said:

"Yes—I believe it."

"Very well," replied the German, quickly, "confide in me, then. I am now on my way to the Otra Banda, but will soon return."

"And then?"

"Will you accompany me, and believe that I will do all I can to render you happy?"

"To render me happy?" said the poor girl, bitterly. "As if I could ever be happy in this world!"

"Hope and trust," whispered Moyer, in a low voice, for at this moment her father appeared. As he did not want to make a confidant of him, he took the potatoes and put them into the saddle-pocket. He proceeded now busily to prepare the horses, and was soon done. He held Cruzado's horse by the bridle; his left foot was already in the stirrup of his own, but he still hesitated. Tadea stood before him, and her dark eyes beheld him so tenderly, he longed to bid her farewell by folding her to his heart, but that was impossible; her father, with his brutal face, did not avert his eyes from him. Moyer mounted. "Adios! señor," he said. "Adios! señorita," and he once more held out his hand to her. Tadea took it, and he placed a ring upon her finger. "Many thanks, sweet maiden, for the hospitality you have bestowed on me. Farewell—we shall meet again."

A deep blush suffused Tadea's face, but she did not reject the ring, and said in a low voice:

"Farewell, señor. May God protect you on your long journey! I will pray for you."

"A thousand thanks — farewell!" And, leading Cruzado's horse by the bridle, he rode down the road.

On arriving at its bend, he turned his head once more. The girl stood in front of the house, waving her hand to him, and he felt inclined to express his happiness in an exultant cheer. But he could not long give way to those thoughts, for the present required his whole attention. On turning his head again toward the road, he saw the cazique coming to meet him, and heard him shouting:

"Pero, amigo! Where have you put the letter? Do you know what is in it? Maybe it is something important."

"Yes, cazique," replied Moyer, who had purposely crumpled the paper, and placed it into his breast-pocket. He handed it back to the Indian. "I cannot decipher it; all the writing is illegible. I have, however, made out enough to see that there is something in it about horses and a reward—"

"Pshaw!" exclaimed the cazique, extending his hand, in which he held the crumpled paper, and glancing at it disdainfully, "horses have again been stolen from the colonists, and we are to hunt them up.—Compañero, can you let me have some tobacco?"

"Certainly," answered Moyer, putting his hand into his pocket, and giving him a piece. "Here, cazique."

"Bueno," said the old man, putting the paper into his belt; and, while slowly walking back toward his house by the side of the German, he took out his knife, and cut off some tobacco. Suddenly he stood, putting the knife back into his belt, and Moyer now saw to his great joy that he produced the letter again, smoothed it on his knee, and tore from it a square piece in order to use it in making a cigarette. The letter, therefore, was no longer dangerous. The Indians, by-the-way, always use every piece of paper they can get hold of for making cigarettes, and it was to be foreseen that the remainder of the dispatch would soon be used for the same purpose.

In front of the cabin below they witnessed a bustling and lively scene, for Don Enrique, fearing Cruzado's predilections that the rainy season would set in shortly, and thereby frustrate their expedition, had not lost a moment in making his preparations. By promising a reward to the Indians, he had induced them to assist in strapping the baggage to the backs of the horses, and, as all of them desired tobacco, indigo, red pepper, or some other trifle, which could not be got in this part of the country, they went to work so energetically that scarcely a quarter of an hour elapsed when the horses were ready to start.

Meanwhile, Reiwald and the doctor, excited by the reluctant part they had taken in the carousal, and kept awake by the uproar in the room, had not fallen asleep until the Indians left; and their companions had not aroused them, for they would only have been in their way. As José had driven up their horses, their baggage was also strapped on, and the doctor and his friend were not awakened until Don Enrique proceeded to distribute the presents.

In the cabin, meanwhile, the women had made no preparations whatever for breakfast, for it is a curious fact that these tribes never take their meals at regular intervals. When it occurs to the women that they had better prepare some food, they do so; this happens some times late at night; at others, early in the morning; at others, again, toward noonday; but oftentimes they neglect this duty all day. It happens frequently that they just finish a hearty meal when some relative brings a sheep to their cabin; it is killed immediately, and half an hour afterward they are again seated round the fire, consuming fabulous quantities of meat. This morning, however, none of the women seemed to be disposed to go out so early into the field and fetch potatoes or beans; they had not even kindled a fire in the room, and two of the ugly dogs still lay curled up on the fireplace among the warm ashes.

On seeing that the sun was already high in the heavens, Reiwald raised himself up, and glanced drowsily about the room.

"Really, doctor," he said, looking wonderingly at the Indians, who had shaken him in order to arouse him, "what has happened to us," and—springing to his feet in dismay—"what has become of our baggage?"

"Halloo, countrymen," shouted Meyer, putting his head through the doorway, "it is time for us to set out; I believe you have slept enough. Every thing is in readiness, and the horses are at the door."

"Yes," said the doctor, rolling himself out of his blanket. "What do you say? We are going to set out? But where is our breakfast?"

"They have not yet kindled a fire," said Reiwald.

"No, no, that will not do," growled the doctor; "we cannot go without having at least some coffee."

"I join in the doctor's protest, sir; and you say our baggage has already been put on the horses? Our coffee-pot is in it, and we must get it out first."

Meyer remained standing, and contemplated with great pleasure the dismayed faces of his countrymen. He remembered very well how he had felt when he first arrived in the country, and missed all the comforts he had enjoyed at home. He had, however, got over such feeling long since; but these two gentlemen had yet to pass through these trials and privations. He did not wish them to delay the departure of the party, and as he saw both standing, at a loss what to do, he resolved to help them to a decision. José had also stepped in to look after the Germans, and, beckoning to him, Meyer himself took up one of the saddles and the blankets, while the peon seized the other.

"Now, gentlemen," said the former, "if you will follow my advice, you will quickly perform your ablutions, while we saddle your horses. I believe you know the bridles and trappings, José? Very well; come back speedily, or your packhorses will start, and you may have some trouble in overtaking them."

"But, sir," exclaimed Reiwald, "I have not made up my mind whether I shall accompany the old haciendero farther or not. Neither of us is able to converse with him, nor properly to drive the pack-horses."

"Would you not like to go with Don Enrique, if I accompany you as an interpreter?"

"Will you really accompany us?"

"Of course, I will; and so will my companion; we have, besides, engaged two Indians to drive our horses."

"That alters the case," exclaimed Reiwald. "But we must have coffee first."

Meyer had stepped out and given the saddle to Cruzado, who put it quickly in its place; he then went out, and returned in a few minutes with two roasted potatoes.

"There," he said, holding out a hand to each one, "now act like sensible men; there will be no coffee this morning; we cannot lose time for cooking it—take them—they are warm. They are as good as coffee, and better. At any rate, you will not see many of them for some time to come; and now make haste."

"Where is the cazique?"

"He has ridden over to the next cabin to take half a bucketful of chicha for breakfast. He will be back presently." Meyer again disappeared.

The two Germans, who had so suddenly been torn away from all the comforts to which they were accustomed, and placed in the middle of the wilderness, were almost in despair, and at a loss what to do. They would have liked to perform their ablutions, but nowhere was to be seen a washstand or even a basin, their own being among their baggage. They felt ill at ease, were hungry and thirsty, had a bad headache, and no coffee. No one seemed to bestow the slightest attention upon them; the potatoes were all they had to fall back upon, and they were quickly eaten.

"And now are we to set out?" inquired the doctor.

"Are you ready?" shouted Meyer.

"Go to the mischief!" responded Reiwald, and commenced buckling on his spurs. "What a life! I wish I had never seen this accursed country!"

Meyer had come in again and looked about everywhere to see if any thing had been forgotten.

"There," he exclaimed suddenly, "is your match-safe: it is in the midst of a puddle; you should be more cautious; and this pocket-comb probably belongs to you, too, for the Indians have no pockets. There hangs also a German halter—and the telescope yonder, do you want to leave that here?"

"We are in such a hurry," said the doctor, "that—"

"Are you ready now?"

"We have not yet washed."

"Well, you may attend to that on the road: we shall find water enough—sometimes, perhaps, a little too much of it; it was hard work to get you out: are you ready now?"

"Good heavens," said Reiwald, fretfully, "in what a hurry you are this morning! The 'train' will not start yet."

"This very minute," replied Meyer; "and if you do not mount you will be left behind."

Without bestowing further attention upon them, he hastened out of the room, vaulted into the saddle, and helped the Indians to keep the animals together. In fact, they had no time to waste. When they crossed the threshold, Don Enrique and Cruzado, who was riding by his side, disappeared among the bushes, and the last pack-horses left.

"Señor, a little tobacco," begged a few Indians, in broken Spanish, erroneously thinking this an excellent opportunity; "only a little—very little!"

"Yes," said the doctor, who understood what they wanted, "pay me a visit to-night, and I will accommodate you."

Reiwald did not know where to put his rifle, which prevented him from mounting.

"Doctor, pray hold my rifle."

"Give us some tobacco, señor," begged the Indians.

"Just hold my horse."

The Indians saw from his gesture what he wanted, and his horse was becoming restless, since it saw that the others were advancing rapidly. Obliging, as usual, they held it by the bridle, and one of them took his rifle. At last he was in the saddle, and hung the weapon over his shoulder.

"Give us some tobacco, señor."

"When I come back," said Reiwald, and sped away at a gallop. It was fortunate for him that he kept his seat, or he would have fared badly, for he could not have expected further assistance at the hands of the Indians. The next moment the cavalcade disappeared among the bushes, while the two Germans had no idea of the direction which they were to take. They were in a very bad humor, and even the sunshine, and the beautiful forest which surrounded them, did not exhilarate them. Besides, they had some difficulty in managing the horses, which, this morning, after feeding all night on the juicy pasture, seemed more spirited than ever. Reiwald had been fumbling in his saddle-bags for some time, and at last he found what he sought.

"Thank God!" he exclaimed; "I knew that I had somewhere half a cake of chocolate; it will go far to appease my appetite. Do you want a piece of it, doctor?"

"I will accept it thankfully," replied the doctor, holding out his hand. "In return I can give you a drop from my flask."

"For goodness' sake, no whiskey!" cried Reiwald. "Since last night I have a horror of it, and cannot even smell it."

"There is port-wine in it."

"That is quite another thing; port-wine is, at least, a decent beverage. Ah, that refreshes me—there, now we shall be able to stand it awhile. I would they had only given us time to wash; but these South Americans seem to be utterly insensible to the necessities of civilization.—What is that?"

A wild, piercing cry was now heard, and a little farther on they saw that they had reached a clearing, in which a few low huts had been built. There the chicha carousal was to be held on that day, and Cajuante had gone to ascertain if the beverage was drinkable or not. He came to meet the horsemen with a large earthen jugful of chicha, and Don Enrique was obliged to halt, and at least taste the liquor.

He did not drink much, but just raised the jug to his lips and returned it, with his thanks, to the cazique. Old Cajuante would have persuaded him to take more, but there was about the pale old gentleman, with the large dark eyes, something so aristocratic and reserved, that he did not venture to do so. He was more satisfied with Don Enrique's companion, Cruzado, who partook largely of the chicha.

"Bravo!" exclaimed the cazique. "I am glad to see that you like it so well. Drink, compañero, we have a great deal more."

Cruzado had good reason not to detain the party longer than was necessary, for while they were among the settlements they were not out of danger. Wiping his beard, he exclaimed, cheerfully: "No, cazique, thank you; I must be able to-day to sit securely on horseback. He then shook hands with him and galloped after the old Chileno, who had led the way.

It was now the turn of the others. No one was allowed to pass without taking a parting drink, and José and the Indians partook readily, until the Germans, accompanied by Meyer, who had rejoined them, made their appearance.

"Ah, los Alemanos!" exclaimed the cazique, chuckling, and holding up the jug. "Drink! mucho! mucho! It will do you good—it will strengthen you; and when you are over the mountains, you will get more of it."

Meyer, accustomed as he was to this chicha liquor, nodded to him, drank, and handed the jug to Reiwald. But the young lawyer looked distrustfully at the yellow-green beverage, and said to his companion:

"What is it, my friend? It looks suspicious. He does not want us to drink, does he?"

"Of course he does, sir," laughed Meyer. "It is cider, and quite pleasant."

"But it looks abominable. It is cider, you say?"

"Just taste it."

"Doctor, try it first, and tell me if it is conducive to health," said Reiwald, holding the vessel toward him.

"No, no," said the doctor, politely, "you must drink first, and then I will follow your example." Meanwhile the old cazique shook his head wonderingly, for he did not comprehend how any one could hold a jug filled with chicha so long in his hand without putting it to his lips. Meyer grew impatient and urged them to comply with the cazique's request. Reiwald, sighing, raised the liquor to his lips. But no sooner had he taken a few drops than he put it down and exclaimed:

"It is abominable! It is poison!"

"Drink! drink!" urged Cajuaato.

"Not for a million!" cried Reiwald. "This is too much! No coffee—and this disgusting beverage—there, doctor! If you ever prescribed medicine as nauseating as this stuff, may God forgive you!"

The doctor laughed, and drank a little. A shiver ran through his frame, but he overcame his squeamishness, drank a little more, and handed back the jug. All the requirements of the ceremonial having been complied with, the German shook hands with the old cazique, and galloped after the pack-horses.

They were now ascending a long and not very elevated hill, the landscape looking almost like a park, carefully and artistically laid out. Small green patches lay everywhere between groups of trees which grew in so picturesque a manner that they seemed planted by a landscape gardener. Now they reached the crest, and a beautiful scene presented itself: there was the Mayhue Lagoon, with its bright surface and densely-wooded shores, rising precipitously from the water-edge, and furrowed with deep gorges. Across the lagoon were fresh meadows and tall trees, interspersed with huts and cultivated fields. It was a singularly wild, but magnificent view, while through the valley in front was seen the distant background with the gap of the Cordilleras, by which they were to descend to the other side of the mountains.

Reiwald stopped his horse involuntarily and gazed upon the scenery, which, radiant as it was with the sunshine, presented a truly charming aspect.

"Why, doctor," he exclaimed, "this is splendid—I never before saw any thing more charming! I really did not imagine that America was so beautiful. And in such a heavenly region they drink that horrible liquor, and do not have coffee for breakfast. But even the sun has spots."

"Listen to me, Reiwald," said the doctor, while Meyer, who did not bestow much attention upon the landscape, was riding ahead, "it seems to me as though we have been guilty of great folly."

"And that did not occur to you until now?"

"We spoke previously about it. You must remember that we spent last night within the borders of civilization, and a miserable night it was. The wretched country is, so to say, the comparative of Valdivia: bad—worse; and we may be sure to meet with the superlative: worst."

"No, doctor, things cannot be worse," said Reiwald, who, on remembering recent events, no longer gazed upon the scenery, but spurred his horse to overtake the others. "That is simply impossible."

"I have a foreboding that the superlative is still in store for us," said the doctor, quietly; "yet nothing remains but to bear it as bravely as possible."

"I do not see any remedy," said Reiwald, more disheartened than before; "let us take courage, therefore, my friend. Once accustomed to camp-life, we shall be better able to provide for our comfort than heretofore; our privations hitherto were due to our lack of experience. I pledge you my word, that henceforward I will not set out in the morning until I have had my coffee, even though I should be obliged to prepare it at four o'clock. I feel ill this morning; my head aches as if a thousand wheels were working in it."

The doctor made no reply; he was in a similar condition. The rough motion of his horse, which trotted somewhat stiffly, was not calculated to restore his good-humor, and he looked down morosely on his pommel.

The road descended again into the valley, and the scenery changed in so peculiar a manner that they could not but notice it. They had lost sight of the lagoon, owing to an intervening range of hills, and the valley which they now entered was warm, and protected from the wind. Here were apple-trees covered with fruit, some of which the horsemen plucked and found very palatable. They plunged into a small grove, consisting almost exclusively of fuchsias, with myrtle-shrubs scattered here and there; towering above them were lofty maple-trees, and the flowery underbrush rose so high above the road, that the travellers were scarcely able to reach the branches.

A river foamed in front—it was the Witchi-Leufu, which they had already crossed, before reaching the cazique's cabin, and which flowed out of the same gorge through which their way led.— They would have to pass it often. Here it was a broad and rapid river, but farther on it became narrower, and finally an insignificant spring flowing from a rock. The shower during the night had produced some effect upon it, but it had not risen much. The water was yet limpid, and its depth did not inconvenience the travellers so much as the pebbles, and smooth fragments of rock lying in its bed, and admonishing the riders lest their horses should stumble.

Meyer, who was familiar with such passages, kept close to the two friends, for the doctor had been imprudent enough to draw back his horse abruptly, so that it turned, and was drifting down with the current toward a rather dangerous place at no great distance below. Meyer seized the bridle in time, and brought the animal safely to the opposite bank.

When they had got over, the doctor remarked that it was a bad place. "Have we any more rivers to pass?" he asked.

"No," said Meyer, dryly, "except this, some six times."

"You do not say so! And why do we not rather remain on this side?"

"You will see why as soon as we have proceeded a little farther. Not a goat could climb the rocks, much less a horse. But, on crossing a river, never follow the current again, for you do not know where you may bring up."

"I will not, but my horse turned, and would not obey me."

"My dear doctor, the trouble was, that you demanded too much. That does no good either in Europe or in America; it is generally best to let a horse, as well as a man, proceed as he likes."

The doctor murmured to himself, but here they were again on solid ground, and as soon as they got away from the immediate proximity of the stony bed of the river, they could allow the horses to trot. At first the road was narrow, but it soon widened, and they could journey two abreast.

"This is a strange mode of travelling," said Reiwald, breaking the silence. "No one seems to think of stopping anywhere. Yesterday morning, I believe, was the last time we took a regular meal. No dinner, no supper, no breakfast, and we are pressing on as unconcernedly as though we had no idea of stopping."

"Do you know, Reiwald," said the doctor, "to whom our old Don Enrique bears a strong resemblance? To the Wandering Jew: no rest anywhere—ever pressing onward to recover his lost child. I tell you, it sometimes frightens me to look at him."

"I am really curious to know," said Reiwald, whose attention had been engrossed by other thoughts, "in what condition we shall meet the poor young lady. This whole affair is exceedingly interesting, there is no doubt about that—piquant and romantic; and do you know that I should not wonder at all if the rich old Chilano should one day become my father-in-law?"

"You are in search of a wife, then?" replied the doctor; "permit me to wish you joy of it."

"Oh, you need not yet," said Reiwald. "The expedition begins to afford me pleasure; for, at all events, we shall see a great many novel and interesting things."

"No doubt of it, my friend," replied the doctor; "but whether they are to be always of an agreeable nature, is quite another matter. Should the maiden be really as beautiful as we were assured at Valdivia, the Indian cazique would be foolish to give her up, and what part we shall be obliged to play remains to be seen."

"Oh, don't be so gloomy," cried Reiwald. "The red rascals have no fire-arms, and a few white men can do wonders. If we arrive at his headquarters, and he refuse to give up Don Enrique's daughter, we shall attack him, and threaten to shoot him. What will he do then? He must yield."

"And the savages will afterward pierce us with their lances."

"I beg your pardon," exclaimed the young lawyer; "if we proceeded so stupidly, and released him before having reached a place of safety, we deserve to be slain. We shall keep him in our midst as a hostage, until we have secured our retreat."

"Well, well, we shall see." The doctor had read of such incidents in novels, and did not think it altogether impossible to carry his plan into execution, though he deemed success in such an enterprise decidedly doubtful. "Ah, there is the end of the forest, and we shall now, thank God, at last get out of these everlasting bushes into the open field."

"By no means," exclaimed Reiwald. "It is water—there is another river."

"Oh," cried the doctor, "this is the Witchi-Leufu again!"

It was indeed the same river, and they encountered the same difficulties as before. The doctor, forewarned by the previous danger, kept close behind, and did not even touch the bridle of his horse. Thus he succeeded in crossing the river in safety. The party did not stop on the opposite bank, but continued the journey on a better road, for about three hours, at a brisk trot, until they reached the river a third time. It seemed to them somewhat narrower, but was, on the other hand, the more rapid, as its bed was more precipitous. Meyer, who now remained abreast of them, asserted that it would be altogether impossible for them to ford at this place, if the water had risen twelve or sixteen inches higher; the horses, in that event, would be unable to withstand the violence of the current—they would be hopelessly lost.

No sooner had they crossed than they halted. A fire was quickly kindled by Cruzado. The baggage was taken from the horses, so that they could feed on the fresh grass on the river-bank, and the old Chileno had one of his provision-bags opened, containing coffee, flour, rice, and dried meat. They rested, however, only two hours, when the horses were caught and loaded again, and the travellers proceeded on their way.

"Mr. Meyer," said Reiwald, who, after partaking of a hearty meal, was in the best of spirits—"your companion's name is Cruzado, is it not?"

"It is, sir," nodded Meyer; "a queer name for a Christian, is it not?"

"And what is your Christian name?"

"Charles."

"Well, that is singular. When we stopped at the hacienda of that hospitable little Chileno, Señor Achavan, an officer from Valdivia, overtook us. He was in search of 'two criminals,' as he said, whose names were very similar to yours and your friend's."

"Were they?" asked Meyer.

"Yes, sir," answered Reiwald. "He said a conflict had taken place between them and a revenue-boat, and several custom-house officers had been shot and drowned."

"Shot and drowned?"

"Yes. A regular blood-and-thunder story."

"So? Well, and what next?" said Meyer, putting on the most innocent air. "Did he catch the criminals?"

"I believe not," responded Reiwald, laughing, for he knew by this time that he would not learn any thing by an examination.

"What a pity!" exclaimed Meyer, spurring his horse, and galloping to the front.

CHAPTER XXI.

THE OTRA BANDA.

On the same afternoon they crossed the river twice, and encamped at a very late hour. The sky, meanwhile, had undergone a change: white, feather-like stripes, spanning the firmament from the south to the north, appeared, and made Cruzado cast on them many an uneasy glance. Whence the wind came, it was difficult to determine very accurately, for it dashed against numerous projecting slopes, and blew now from one quarter, and now from another. The forest and the range of hills obstructed the view toward the north, but that there was a change in the weather could no longer be doubted, and, as the season was far enough advanced, the travellers were justified in fearing the worst. But this could not be helped; they could not proceed until daybreak, for, in the first place, the animals could not have borne the excessive fatigue, and, at every step, as they advanced in the forest, where there lay a great many fallen trees, they would have run the risk of stumbling and injuring themselves. Hence, they had to wait for daylight, especially as they had the most arduous part of the road before them.

It was a magnificent night, and Reiwald remarked he had never before seen the stars twinkling with so pure a lustre—a remark which made Meyer shake his head and wish that they could rejoice in the same way on the next night. He refused to explain himself fully, but partook with great rapidity of a dish of boiled rice and dried meat, wrapped himself up, lay down under a projecting rock, and fell asleep.

The doctor and Reiwald did not so soon get their sleeping-place in readiness, for it was the first time in their lives that they were to pass a night in the open air under a tree. They had imagined that such an event would be always attended with pleasant circumstances; among blooming shrubs, over which the foliage of gigantic forest-trees rustled, while the cloudless firmament shone above them. Add to this the mountain-stream murmuring past them, and a large fire shedding a glare over the neighborhood. It was truly enchanting. Besides, they had had an excellent supper, and, although it may be considered at least doubtful if they would not have rejected similar food, prepared in such a manner, at the dinner-table of an hotel, the physical exercise to which they were not yet accustomed, and the bracing air which they breathed, had doubtless added not a little to their appetite. They stretched their limbs comfortably on the soft forest-moss, and Reiwald began:

"Doctor, I pledge you my word, I do not remember the time when I felt as comfortable as now. I assure you, city life does not compare with this; within such narrow walls one does not become familiar with the beauties of Nature."

"Yes," replied the doctor, who had lit a cigar, and was blowing the smoke into the air; "I would not find fault with it. Formerly, when reading romantic accounts of such expeditions, I always thought them a little exaggerated—the effect of poetical license, etc. But look at this myrtle, whose branches, covered with blossoms, spread over our heads—how beautiful the little flowers look in the light of the fire—like thousands of diminutive roses! The fuchsia yonder—what do you think it would be worth at Berlin? I do not believe you could buy it there for fifty dollars."

"It is indeed beautiful," said Reiwald. "And look at the group around the camp-fire yonder—those brown faces, and the gracefulness with which they smoke their cigarettes."

"Meyer is a good fellow, too," smiled the doctor—"a regular 'everywhere and nowhere;' always busy, and yet he seems to do nothing in a hurry."

"You are right. By-the-way, do you know that I believe the two men who joined us at the Indian settlement are the same whom the police are looking for."

"What do we care for that?" replied

the doctor, who was growing drowsy; "let them settle it themselves. But I think we had better sleep, that we may be up betimes in the morning and boil our coffee."

"Never fear," said Reiwald, "I shall not set out again without it."

Their conversation ended; the others withdrew also to their different sleeping-places, and Cruzado alone sat a long while at the fire, listening to the moaning wind, and looking up now and then to the stars, which were beginning to indicate the approach of stormy weather.

On the following morning he was the first up; a glance at the sky convinced him that a change in the weather was impending. In the east only, a narrow stripe of blue was to be seen, and when the sun rose, it shed its rays upon the heights, but soon vanished behind a cloud, and the heavens were soon overcast.

The preparations for an early start were made with the greatest haste, and, while Reiwald was boiling his coffee, the doctor had to help the others to drive up the horses and strap the baggage. Even Don Enrique took part in this labor. Breakfast was soon over, for the men scarcely took time to sit down to it, and the old Chileno was quickly in the saddle again, evidently in an agony of impatience to set out.

While their route had hitherto been comparatively level, and almost destitute of obstacles, it now became far more difficult, and they were frequently obliged to cross the Witchi-Leufu, which was now often hemmed in by rocks of considerable elevation. The higher they ascended into the mountains, the narrower the river became, because it had fewer tributaries from the side gorges; but the more impetuously rushed its waters, and at times it seemed as though they would sweep away the horses. Fortunately the current was not deep, for the long-continued drought had dried up the streams.

About two o'clock in the afternoon they crossed for the last time, but had now to climb the slope of the Cordilleras, which was so steep that the pack-horses could advance but very slowly, and had often to stop to breathe. The path became so narrow that two of them could no longer walk abreast. Cruzado led the way and guided them up the mountains.

The vegetation plainly indicated the elevation of the region which they were entering. They had long since left the tall forest-trees behind, and the blooming bushes remained in the valley; only the myrtles ascended with them, although they were more stunted. But, in return, innumerable cactuses of different kinds were seen, some of which rose like tall pillars from the ground.

The path became very steep; it seemed as if they had already reached the summit, for the abrupt peaks, although towering above them to the right and left, appeared as though they could cross them in ten minutes. The travellers presently arrived at a slope so precipitous that the pack-horses were unable to ascend. All were brought to a sudden halt, and Reiwald exclaimed involuntarily, "Well, what next?"

"Well," remarked Mayer, who dismounted by his side; "we have got far enough. We may begin now."

"Begin what?"

"Carrying the baggage on our backs,"

replied the German, laughing; "yes, my dear Mr. Relwald, pray dismount; we cannot help it. All must now shoulder a leathern sack."

"You do not mean to say that we are to carry a sack?"

"Of course I do, unless you prefer leaving your baggage here; no horse or mule can carry it up for you."

"Well, that is a pretty business," exclaimed the doctor; "and afterward I suppose we shall have to carry the baggage down?"

"No," laughed Don Carlos, "we shall not; the other side is not so steep."

"Then we shall presently be on the summit of the Cordilleras?" asked Relwald. "I thought they were a great deal higher."

"You may be thankful that they are not higher at this point—Go to work, then, gentlemen, lest we should lose too much time; the weather looks ominous; you need not pay much attention to your horses in the mean time; Don Enrique will attend to them—they cannot run away."

The two Germans, shaking their heads, complied with his directions. Cruzado and the Indians had already unloaded three of the pack-horses, and were now engaged in relieving the others of their baggage. After having done so, and thereby enabled the animals to draw breath and feed on the scanty grass growing in this part of the mountains, each of the men shouldered one of the sacks, weighing between fifty and sixty pounds, and ascended slowly but steadily. Doctor Pfoifel and Relwald followed. At first they advanced briskly, but it seemed to them as if the sacks grew heavier at every step and the way more steep, so that they often stopped, drew breath, and looked up to the heights.

"Dear me," exclaimed Relwald, panting, "what are porters good for if they are not to be found where they are so needed? Do you call this 'travelling for pleasure,' doctor?"

"Pleasure! I have not had any since we set out, and matters are daily growing worse."

"How fortunate it is that we obtained reënforcements at the Indian settlement! otherwise, we would be obliged to work by ourselves."

"I would certainly have refused," growled the doctor, from whose forehead large drops of sweat were rolling down his cheeks.

"There is another sack for you below," gasped Relwald. "Ah! I am afraid I have hurt my back—I believe I am unable longer to carry any thing."

"Hurt your back? Nonsense!" cried the doctor, who saw through the stratagem, and was not willing to suffer by it. "That is what you would like, is it? Forward, my dear sir, forward! The longer we tarry here, the later we shall be."

Relwald's attempt at shirking the toilsome work was unsuccessful; he was obliged to carry his leathern sack to the summit, or at least to a certain point, and was not even allowed to breathe, or gaze upon the scenery before him, for he had to carry up his other burden.

Four hours were spent in toiling in this manner, and the two Germans, who were unaccustomed to such labors, were greatly exhausted. Arriving at length at the crest with the other baggage, they threw themselves exhausted behind a rock, regardless of the wind. They could work no more, nor did they care whether their horses followed or not. Meyer or any one else might see to them.

In this wild region is one of Nature's finest landscapes. On looking backward you behold the wooded Chill. Far below in the valley shines the mirror of the Ranco Lagoon, and in the distance towers the snowy Villa Rica, with its volcano. At this time dark clouds rested on the adjacent heights, bringing into contrast the light of the burning mountain.

"This is magnificent," said the doctor, drying his forehead; "but for this carrying of baggage, I should be in an ecstasy. Look at the scanty vegetation up here," he added; "we shall not to-night have so cosy and romantic a camp as we had yesterday."

"But I hope we shall not remain up here," cried Rolwald.

"Never fear; that wonderful fellow Cruzado, who seems to know no fatigue—for he has thrice ascended and descended, carrying up two large sacks and other articles—begins to reload one of the packhorses. For my part, I am unable to assist him, and I do not care to kill myself."

No one asked the Germans for help. Meyer was good-natured enough to lead their animals, and at the same time took along the heavy saddle-bags. He had hung their rifles over the shoulders of an Indian, and, as soon as the horses came up, the doctor and Rolwald wrapped themselves in their cloaks. The wind swept, keen and cold, from the flanks of the Villa Rica, and chilled their limbs. Lying on the ground, they were of course unable to get warm, and were glad when the order was given to mount again. But they did not doff their cloaks, hoping that the climate would grow milder as soon as they descended into the plain.

The route led up a gentle acclivity which had hitherto obstructed the view toward the east. The old Chileno stopped his horse, and the Germans galloped quickly to his side. Before them lay the Pampas, bounded by a gray and desolate horizon. Valleys lay here and there at their feet; and isolated knolls interrupted the monotonous and scantily-wooded flanks of the mountain. Beyond, commenced those terrible plains, whose immense extent made a solemn impression upon them, and no one ventured to utter a word.

Don Enrique would seek his child yonder! The doctor, who was halting at his side, glanced furtively at him. There sat the old man on his horse; the breeze played with his thin locks; both his hands rested on the pommel, and his eyes were fixed on the endless plain before him, while tears rolled into his white beard. He did not know that he was weeping, or he would doubtless have sought to overcome his emotion.

"Poor father," sighed the doctor, involuntarily, in a low voice; but these words, scarcely audible, seemed to recall the Chileno to a sense of his condition. He turned his face quickly and almost timidly to his companion, and, seizing the bridle, rode slowly toward the point where Cruzado was halting, and where the road was less steep than that by which they had ascended.

The wind howled from the north, condensed and black masses of cloud moved rapidly toward the south. High above them floated a condor, whose strong pinions struggled with the wind.

"I should like to shoot that bird, doctor," said Reiwald to his companion, seizing his rifle.

"For Heaven's sake, save your powder! we have no time."

"I have long wished to shoot a condor, and that is one. See its head."

"So have I," said the doctor; "but since these dreary Pampas are before us, and the sky so stormy, all my sporting propensities have vanished. If the rainy season should set in at this crisis, we should be in a bad predicament."

"As far as I know," said Reiwald, "the old Chileno has a tent with him. It must be in one of the sacks."

"It is doubtful if that would do us any good. We must advance as far as possible, and try to find a good place for our camp. At any rate, we have the Witchi-Leufu behind us, and it seems to me as though we shall not be much more troubled by fording rivers."

Reiwald made no reply; he was looking up to the sky. The bird, hovering over them and contemplating the strange beings below, suddenly turned and was soon out of range and sight.

The Indians during the journey had incessantly chatted and laughed with each other, but they were now silent. The gloomy weather seemed to have produced its effect upon these human hearts; they appeared serious and oppressed. The wind increased the farther down they descended into the land of the savages, and at dusk large rain-drops fell from the threatening clouds.

How desolate looked the country through which a stony path now led them! Dwarfed shrubs were to be seen here and there on the sandy soil—myrtles, cactuses, aloes, sharp-pointed grass; but there was not a tree to afford them shelter. The slopes were bare; light mists covered the path, and soon shrouded the Pampas in a dismal veil, so that it was dark before the sun had disappeared. But they pressed onward; the unhappy father was more restless than ever, and, the nearer they drew to the country where he hoped to obtain intelligence regarding his child, the more impatient he became, and urged all to advance toward the east, as long as the horses were able to see the ground.

At length the twilight passed away. It was time for them to choose a convenient place for their encampment, and it was now difficult to find the two principal necessities—wood and water. Fortunately they discovered a small spring issuing from the rocks. There was some brushwood near, with which they could make a fire, and, while the Indians proceeded to unload the horses, Cruzado dug with a pointed stick a hole in the ground, that the animals might be watered. Meyer meanwhile kindled a fire; the wood was tolerably dry, and Don Enrique himself helped to gather a supply, that they might have sufficient for the night.

As the old Chileno worked with his men, our two German friends were obliged to do so, notwithstanding their aversion to labor of this description. Cruzado meanwhile took care of their horses, for he afterward discovered, near the foot of the camp, a narrow gorge into which the spring flowed, and where was good pasture. He proposed that the fire should be lit there, lest the reflection should be seen, but the fog rendered this unnecessary. At a distance of a thousand yards the light could not be discerned, and the only precaution was, that the two Indians who had joined the expedition were to watch alternately, and keep a sharp lookout on the path by which they had come.

The travellers had to look for a sleeping place, wherever there was a convenient spot. Farther down it was more level but very stony, and the water issuing from the well rendered the ground wet, while there were only low bushes affording them any shelter against the wind. Nevertheless, the Indians, who, from their earliest youth, had been accustomed to nights of this description, managed to accommodate themselves, and were soon very comfortable. The fire burned brightly, and Reiwald noticed that the old Chileno took out his tent. But the doctor had not been mistaken; it was nothing but a low and narrow canvas roof, which, when arranged, bore some resemblance to a sentry-box upset on the ground. At any rate, there was not room enough under it for more than one person, and nothing was left for them but to shift for themselves as well as they could.

It rained so little that no one thought of it; a few large drops fell, but the wind chased away the clouds, and for a time a part of the clear sky was seen. Meanwhile supper was prepared, and a kettleful of tea boiled, although Cruzado and the Indians did not like this beverage. The latter put again over the fire a camp-kettle full of rice, which would give them more substantial food. Doctor Pfeifel and Reiwald had a little larder of their own, from which they took a box of sardines and a bottle of French brandy, which induced Meyer, who was with Cruzado, to return to them. Their arrival at the Otra Banda had to be celebrated in a becoming manner. The cognac did not last as long as might have been expected. At the same time the friends were rather dejected, for Meyer predicted they would have a bad night—the beginning of what was in store for them. The doctor tried to protest against this prediction, and asserted that weather-wise persons were often disappointed. But Meyer shrugged his shoulders, bade them good-night, and withdrew to the resting-place he had arranged for himself.

Meanwhile Cruzado collected all the leathern sacks, and with the blankets made a sort of roof; the riding-saddles were used as pillows. The Indians rolled themselves in their blankets, and a large quantity of wood was added to the fire, which was then covered with bowlders. This was all they could do, and the travellers thereupon lay down to sleep.

Doctor Pfeifel and Reiwald spread their blankets on the ground, wrapped themselves in their cloaks, and, as they were tired, soon fell asleep. Reiwald was the first to awake. Cold rain-drops pattered on his face, and he drew his hat over his eyes to protect himself.

"Oh," he suddenly heard the doctor groaning by his side, "this is horrible!"

A shower of unusual violence was pouring down.

"Doctor," said Reiwald, who was fully aroused, "this is indeed frightful."

"But I hope it is only a shower," said the doctor.

Reiwald made no reply, and sought to protect himself as well as possible; but all was of no avail. The water attacked him from below as well as above. For there were everywhere small declivities, and, not yet familiar with the precautions to be observed in selecting a sleeping-place under such circumstances, the two friends had unfortunately chosen a hollow in the ground, where the rain collected.

"Dear me!" murmured Reiwald, moving from one side to the other. "There is water under me. I can never forget this night."

"Well, Reiwald," said his friend, maliciously, "it is romantic to encamp in the forest, is it not?"

Reiwald was silent, and turned to the other side. He had to bear the first rain, and Doctor Pfeifel had not yet felt it; but now it flowed over the blankets and reached him, too, and the next moment rushed like a rivulet down the rocks, so that the two friends were almost washed away.

"Our lives are in danger!" cried the doctor, springing to his feet. "We shall catch cold here and become sick."

"My teeth are chattering as if they intended to break my jaws. I wish we had a drop of that French brandy loft!"

"Yes, but we cannot pass the night here," exclaimed the doctor, in despair.

"If you know a hotel anywhere near, doctor," remarked Reiwald, with some resignation, "I am ready to accompany you."

Pfeifel made no reply; but, drawing his cloak closely about him, he remained standing.

Reiwald groped along the next declivity, in order, if possible, to find a stone, on which he might sit down, and thus await daybreak. The storm, meanwhile, increased, and their cloaks no longer protected them. Perhaps they would not have been in so pitiable a plight but for the cold wind, which chilled them to the marrow.

"Dear me," exclaimed the doctor, suddenly thinking of their baggage; "I wonder where our rifles are? I suppose they are leaning against a rock, the barrels full of water by this time."

"Oh, you do not care to look after them now!" said Reiwald.

The doctor made no reply; he knew well that he would not have stretched out his hand for them, though they swam past him at that moment. He was engrossed only by one idea, to keep entirely still, for, at every movement he felt his drenched clothes clinging to his shivering body. He thought the storm would be but of short duration, because it had set in with such violence; he had no idea of the peculiarity of rainstorms in this country, or he would have scarcely joined Don Enrique's expedition. On this night he was to obtain full knowledge of what the words 'rain in the Cordilleras' meant. The two unfortunate Germans stood shaking with cold, wet to the skin, and greatly fatigued, cursing themselves and their fate.

CHAPTER XXII.

HARDSHIPS.

MORNING dawned, and no sooner had its first gray streaks illumined the horizon than the rain ceased. From the depths of the valley white mists ascended until they almost reached the spot occupied by the travellers, and at daylight they witnessed a truly wonderful spectacle.

The land at their feet had entirely vanished, and a vast sea, as it were, of milky waves, surging tumultuously, and enshrouding every thing as far as their eyes could reach, extended beneath them. This scene became indescribably magnificent when the sun shortly after burst from behind the ragged clouds, rose above this misty mass, and shed over it a rosy lustre. At any other time, the Germans would have been in an ecstasy; but now they scarcely vouchsafed a glance upon the sublime prospect, so much were they concerned with their own misery. At this moment Meyer approached.

"Well," he exclaimed, "it was fortunate that yesterday we advanced thus far, for after the rain we could not have crossed the Witchi-Leufu, and would probably be now hemmed in between a bend and a steep slope, on the opposite side of the river. He who is not now on this side cannot cross until spring."

"I would," said the doctor, gruffly, "that the deuce would take the Witchi-Leufu, the Otra Banda, and the whole of your Patagonia. That I was such a fool as to allow myself to be persuaded to take part in such a 'pleasure-tour' is ridiculous."

"I trust," said Meyer, with a naive air, "you did not get wet last night?"

"No," replied Reiwald, "only sprinkled. I have about four inches of water in my boots."

"Where did you sleep, then?" asked Meyer, wonderingly looking around, but seeing nothing, save the drenched saddles, while the blankets had been swept farther into the bushes. "You surely did not sleep in this natural trough, despite the signs of impending rain last night?"

"And where else, pray?"

"But, dear me, in that case the water, from both slopes, must have poured down upon you, for it is the bed of a rivulet, which will remain full until spring, and it is nothing short of a miracle that you have not been washed down into the valley."

"And where did you sleep?" asked the doctor.

"Look yonder, sir," exclaimed Meyer, "where the others lie; on the top of a mound. You may protect yourself from the rain, but not from water flowing under you."

"I am glad," said Reiwald, "that you inform us of it now. But I know one thing, and that is, that I will take my pack-horse, and retrace my steps, while I have still a sufficient supply of provisions; I do not care about travelling farther in this country."

"But, my dear sir," responded Meyer, good-naturedly, "how can you think of returning after last night's rain? Do you know that the Witchi-Leufu is this morning a broad torrent, rolling with it stony fragments as large as houses?"

"I should like never again to hear that name," cried the doctor; "but Reiwald is right—don't be obstinate, Meyer, but accompany us. You know the route; in two days we shall be again with our drunken friend Cajuanta, and in three or four days reach Valdivia."

"Unless we are drowned on the road," replied Meyer. "No, no; do not think of it—it will not do. Look at the clouds, scudding from the north—a sure sign that we shall have more rain, and, in fact, that the season has set in. We may by-and-by, perhaps, be able to comply with your wishes; but for the present we must wait patiently."

"If you knew this before, why did you join the expedition?"

"Oh, I do not care for a little rain," said Mayer, indifferently; "and as soon as we are on the Pampas, it will not inconvenience us a great deal. There are, indeed, strong winds sometimes, violent enough to blow a man from his horse, but it does not rain there as much as on the other side. People travelling now on the shores of the Mayhue Lagoon are obliged to swim."

"And are not we, too?" asked Relwald, piteously. "Look at the condition in which we are this morning."

"Yes, we must attend to that," said Meyer; "undress and wring the water from your clothes; then put them on again; they will dry speedily, and, besides, a fire is already kindled. We shall light another, that you may get dry again. I have with me some whiskey, which I obtained at the cacique's house, where I had my horn filled repeatedly, and poured the liquor into the bottle. It will warm your blood now."

He hastened to fetch the bottle, and even Relwald, who had inveighed so vehemently against whiskey, believed he had not partaken for a long time of a beverage so acceptable, and which agreed so well with him. Necessity is an excellent teacher, and the best of cooks.

But Meyer did not content himself with this; he lighted for them a special fire, and piled upon it dry brushwood, of which there was an abundance lying about; he then wrung the water from their saddle-cloths and hung them up, and also helped them to dry their cloaks, so that he finally made them in some measure comfortable. Their good rifles were in a bad condition, the water having passed over them all night. Meyer emptied the barrels, and wiped them, which was all he could do under the circumstances.

The other travellers had suffered but slightly, because they knew how to protect themselves. While the Germans, ignorant of life in the mountains, had lain down in a hole, where they could not but be inundated, the others had prudently selected places where the ground under them would remain dry. At the same time they knew how to spread their blankets in such a manner as to divert the rain.

It was a blessing to the two Germans that the storm had ceased, for they would otherwise have scarcely been able to proceed. By the time breakfast was ready, they felt tolerably recovered. Relwald, however, long after he was again in the saddle, shook his head constantly; he seemed almost as though he were unable to convince himself that he was really awake, and had passed through such scenes. The adventure appeared to him as an unpleasant dream, and now, since their retreat was cut off, the future was more gloomy than ever.

Meanwhile Cruzado, who whistled and laughed, commenced collecting and re-loading the pack-horses. In doing so he displayed the utmost caution, arranging the blankets under the saddles, lest the backs of the animals should be rubbed, when they would be unfit for further service. The Indians slowly drove the horses down the gentle slope into the mist which was waving at their feet. But the wind and the sun were already at work in it, making rents here and there, through which gray specks of the distance became visible. Finally, only a transparent film covered the plain, and suddenly revealed again the Pampas, seemingly so near that many objects could be discerned.

The travellers descended in the fog, crossed a valley, and ascended another range of mountains, whence they were able to survey the plain, as at that point they could look over the hills lying between them and the Pampas. To the left, they discerned a large lake, or lagoon, such as is to be met with everywhere at the foot of elevated ranges, and in which are gathered the waters from their declivities. Trees and shrubs studded the shores, and were to be seen also here and there on the plain, as was evident from the darker green of their foliage. Black-looking objects were among them, and the doctor, stopping his horse, and using his glass, thought he distinguished a number of houses on the meadow, near the lake. The distance, however, was as yet too great for accurate observation, and when he informed Meyer, the latter burst into laughter, and said they would find few houses there. But he himself looked through the telescope, carelessly at first, but afterward more attentively, and as his horse did not stand still enough for him to use the instrument with advantage, he dismounted, and made a long and careful survey. He called Cruzado to his side; the half-breed was now halting near, and seemed to await patiently what his companion would discover.

"Listen to me, Cruzado," said Meyer, without taking the glass from his eye. "Come here and look."

The half-breed did not comply with his invitation. He only shook his head, and said:

"What is it, Don Carlos?"

"See for yourself."

"Thank you, it would not do me much good. I can never discern any thing but mist through such instruments; my unaided eyes are better."

"Not than this telescope, my friend. Come here."

Cruzado dismounted, took the glass, and attempted to look through it, but in the most awkward manner. At last he pushed it away, and growled: "I know I cannot do any thing with this, and, therefore, you had better tell me what you see."

"Do you notice the black specks near the lagoon yonder?"

"They are apple-trees," said the half-breed.

"They are tents; there are at least thirty or forty of them," replied the German, quickly. "As yet I am unable to count all of them. A whole tribe must be encamped there."

"Tomando!" exclaimed Cruzado, nodding his head; "you may be right, so much the better; for we shall now be able to get more easily across the lagoon."

"And afterward meet no one on the Limal. How do you think we shall get across the river after last night's rain, and away yonder fresh thunder-clouds are coming up."

The half-breed shrugged his shoulders. "Quien sabe," he said, smiling. "But, amigo, what harm will ensue? The police cannot reach us from Chili; and is it not all the same whether we pass a few weeks or months on this side of the Limal, or on the other?"

"I wonder what chief is encamped down there?" said Meyer.

But Cruzado became impatient.— "Who knows!" he repeated, and, vaulting into the saddle, added, "make haste, compañero; the pack-horses are a long way ahead."

Reiwald and the doctor wanted to know now what Meyer had observed, and he soon saw that he was unable to conceal it. They had journeyed to the Pampas for the purpose of meeting the Indians, and henceforth they could not but expect to fall in with them at any moment. Neither of them was therefore frightened on hearing of Meyer's discovery; on the contrary, the doctor exclaimed, joyously:

"Thank God, we shall attain our object sooner than I thought. If we meet the savages at the foot of the mountains, the affair will be settled in a few hours. We shall then put the young lady on a horse and return as speedily as possible to the coast. I shall then have been in the Cordilleras—but a second time—"

Meyer imitated the characteristic shrug of the South Americans, returned the telescope to the doctor, took the bridle, leaped into the saddle, and followed his companion.

His prediction regarding the weather was to be fulfilled but too soon. They had not proceeded half an hour when the wind commenced blowing with redoubled violence, and, as on the last night, from the north. It chased before it enormous masses of menacing cloud, and, soon after, the first drops announced a repetition of the deluge of the preceding evening. The sky did not threaten long. The horsemen tried to protect themselves, and allowed their horses to proceed, with heads bent down. It would have done them no good to halt, for there was no shelter to be found.

They descended farther toward the plain and entered again a narrow valley, which deprived them of the view of the lagoon and the Pampas. The small rivulet they were following and obliged often to cross, swelled so rapidly that Reiwald was afraid lest it would soon become another Witchi-Leufu. But the slopes on this side contained so many clefts that a large river could not be formed: the streams remained so narrow and shallow that they did not detain the party an instant.

Don Enrique, who had heard from Cruzado that there was an Indian camp on the shore of the lagoon, which happens only at rare intervals, pressed onward, and longed to reach it that night, but it was utterly impossible, the distance being too great. Darkness surprised them sooner than they had expected, and they were obliged to halt in order to encamp.

The ground was somewhat more suit-

HARDSHIPS.

able to their purpose than the upper part of the slope had been. Stunted willows studded the banks of the rivulet which they had followed, and a little farther below were trees abounding with apples, and others with dense round tops which afforded some shelter. Meanwhile there was no intermission in the rain, and it was difficult to light a fire to prepare a cup of tea.

Both Reiwald and the doctor were silent. During the whole afternoon they had been riding abreast, or one behind the other, in gloomy silence, and as if afflicted in body and mind. They submitted despairingly to their fate, and, if a torrent had at this moment thundered by them they would have ridden into it and been drowned, with the utmost indifference, without so much as crying for help. They were so woe-begone that they no longer cared for any thing. When the doctor dismounted, and, on putting his foot on the ground, squirted a stream of water from his boot, he laughed—but so does the suicide who the next moment blows out his brains.

Meyer, who had rejoined them, wished to give his friends some good advice, but it was of no avail. Reiwald only shook his head, seated himself under a tree, drew around him his wet cloak, dropped his head on his breast, and awaited night — probably death, too; for, as he afterward related, it was his firm conviction that apoplexy would put an end to his sufferings. He did not even take the saddle from his horse; all seemed over—and why should he bestow attention on such a trifle?

The doctor seated himself on the drenched blankets, but he did not, any more than his friend, attempt to prepare a couch for the night. Meyer afterward brought him (the only food they had) a piece of dried meat; he took it, but Reiwald refused to accept any, and remarked, "It was not worth while."

The travellers, in fact, passed a dismal time on the confines of the Pampas; it was very different from the merry camp-life they had looked for on setting out from Valdivia; but such nights are by no means rare in the wilderness, and the best thing travellers can do is to bear every thing quietly and patiently.

The rain ceased early in the morning; the wind had changed at midnight toward the west, and was passing over toward the south, increasing in violence. When it veered at sunrise, it seemed as though it had swept over a snow-field, it was so cold in the valley. All slept, or, at least, sat shivering, wrapped in their cloaks. Cruzado alone had thrown off his poncho and was engaged in an effort to light a fire. At first he labored in vain, but he did not tire, and at the moment the sun rose, he had the satisfaction of seeing his extraordinary perseverance crowned with success. The flames ascended from the dry wood which he had brought in his saddle-bag for this purpose, and the unexpected sight of the fire took his companions by surprise, as, awakened by the sun, they started from their wet couches.

The scene of the preceding morning was now reënacted, but the men were more active and energetic, for all knew that they would soon fall in with the dreaded Penchuenches, and no one could forestall the reception they would meet with at their hands; for every thing depended on the decision of the chief. But would they be able to attain the object of their expedition? None of those who were familiar with the character of these independent tribes believed it—nay, the more demand might exasperate them, and, after their anger had once been aroused, how could this feeble band, whose retreat to Chili had been obstructed by the rain, have offered them the slightest resistance?

All this was perhaps to be decided in the course of a few hours; and yet, strange to say, the old Chileno did not urge his companions now with the same feverish impatience as heretofore, but gave them time enough to dry their saddles, bridles, ponchos, and blankets, and to make every provision for meeting the masters of this extensive district. Was he afraid, perhaps, of the decisive moment which was to put an end to the hopes he had so fondly cherished? He looked exceedingly pale, and his eyes beamed with a wild light. He had risen as early as any of the others except Cruzado, and took part in the preparations. He hung up his tent to dry, opened the provision-bags, and brought out what was necessary for breakfast. He looked after the pistols in the holsters, discharging and reloading them.

The doctor was aroused by the bustle surrounding him, and especially by the pleasant fire, but it was some time before he was able to move his companion, for Reiwald was so much chilled that he did not even venture to arise. The doctor however, knew an enchanting word, which had immediately the wished-for effect.

"Say, Reiwald," he said, bending over him, "coffee is ready."

"Coffee!" exclaimed the lawyer, whose teeth were chattering. "Do not jest with me in that manner."

So saying, he doffed his cloak and gazed into the sunlight. He beheld also the fire burning merrily, and his blood circulated again. He was able at least to help his friend to dry and arrange his own things. The coffee was not yet ready, but it was preparing. Meyer had attended to that, and the despairing German reawakened once more to hope and life.

The discharging of Don Enrique's pistols reminded Reiwald and his friend of their rifles, which were covered with a layer of rust, and never could have been discharged. The Doctor offered to take it upon himself to dry their clothes and blankets, if Reiwald would attend to the fire-arms—an offer accepted at once. He had brought with him every thing necessary for this purpose, and, seating himself near the fire, he went quickly to work, screwed off the pistons, removed the wet powder, put in fresh loads, and, after some vain efforts, had the satisfaction of discharging the rifles and reloading them. The revolvers occasioned him more trouble, but he finally succeeded in cleaning them also. By the time breakfast was ready the fire-arms were in good order. As for the rust, which the doctor rubbed carefully from his rifle, Reiwald paid no attention to it; he had already exerted himself too much.

Meanwhile the Indians again attended to the collecting and packing of the horses; breakfast was eaten, and half an hour afterward the travellers set out. Our German friends still cast very distrustful glances at the clouds covering

"COFFEE IS READY."

the northwestern sky, and the doctor predicted that they would have more rain in the afternoon. But so long as the wind was south, there was no reason to fear his prophecy. No rain ever came up from that quarter, except occasional thunder-storms in the summer-time.

Cruzado soon after led the way into a valley whose character indicated that they were now among the last spurs of the mountain-range, for on both sides it became lower and lower, and finally opened like a gateway. The Pampas lay before them as an ocean.

Our travellers now bestowed but little attention upon the vegetation surrounding them, for, certain as they were of the proximity of an Indian camp, they glanced often about them, only to discover on some projection, or among the rocks, the form of one of the savage warriors, who would speedily inform his friends of their arrival. But the slopes were deserted; no cattle were grazing there, for they found richer pastures in the valley; no goats suggested human habitations. No game—not even the guanacos, with which the Pampas are said to abound—were to be seen. Once a fox was noticed standing on a knoll opposite, but quickly disappeared. Several small birds of prey hovered about the mountains, but returned to the plain, where they were better fed than among the bare and desolate crags.

The travellers reached the entrance of the valley, and at their feet, at no great distance, lay the broad Noniuc Lagoon, which narrowed into a small estuary, and widened again into Lake Huetchoon. This body of water extended far toward the east, and on the northern shore could be distinctly discerned with the naked eye the dark fur-tents of the Indians, who had encamped there among the apple-trees. But on the narrow arm connecting the two lagoons with each other, there stood a substantial and rather spacious hut, which the doctor could plainly distinguish with his glass. Meyer, whom he informed of this discovery, remarked that the hut belonged to, or at least was inhabited by, the ferryman. He added that the chicha-barrels and the cider-press were kept there. At all events, there were Indians at work in the hut, for many horses were to be seen in the adjoining pasture.

"At work!" The doctor had never yet heard that the Indians ever concerned themselves with work; but, before he was able to ask further on this subject, the cavalcade, which had tarried here for an instant to survey the country, started again. As the place where they were now was rather steep, and the soil, owing to the heavy rains, soft and full of holes, the travellers had to concentrate their attention upon the path and their animals, and conversation was suspended.

They were now in full sight of the Indian camp, although as yet at a considerable distance. The Penchuenches did not seem to apprehend danger from any quarter, for nowhere had they posted sentinels, and the travellers had already descended so far as not to be seen, when suddenly there was a great commotion among the tents. Horsemen, one after another, galloped into the open prairie, and halted, doubtless in order to watch the strangers. Others were riding about at a furious rate, and driving the cattle together. It was obvious that the camp was alarmed, the savages being unable to ascertain whether or not the new-comers were preceded by a larger detachment, nearer to them than they expected.

"This is one of the advantages of white horses, Don Carlos," said Cruzado, pointing down to the plain. "If we had intended to approach stealthily, they would have certainly betrayed us, while they can never see dark-colored horses on the slopes. It will be worse on the Pampas, for it is certain that we shall be unable to avoid any prowling band. But, let us go forward; the red gentlemen are aware that we are coming, and we must see what reception we shall meet with."

CHAPTER XXIII.

TOBALUAE.

The travellers, meanwhile, descending the declivity, quickly reached the valley, and could no longer see the tents, hidden by the foliage. The plain was deserted, and not a sound was to be heard except the shrill notes of some bird of prey. The Nontue Lagoon was to their right, and they now moved along its gravelly shore. There was here a pathway leading into the Pampas.

They followed the shore scarcely half an hour when there appeared an Indian, mounted on a barebacked horse, managing it only with his legs and arms. He glided along like a shadow, and Cruzado, who was the first to notice him, waved his hand and hailed him in the language of the Penchuenches; but he disappeared, and seemed not to care about conversation with strangers.

As they advanced, they often beheld solitary Indians; but it was evident that they were only scouting, in order to ascertain the number of the party, and if others were following, some of the Penchuenches approached. Once it was thought that a messenger of the cazique was coming, for an Indian, holding a lance, and his hair floating about his temples, suddenly halted two or three hundred yards in front. But if it had been his intention to wait there, he changed his mind before the travellers arrived. They were about a hundred yards distant, when he turned his horse and galloped into the grove.

Don Enrique gazed with an anxious expression upon the wild men whose sudden appearance and disappearance, it seemed to him, did not indicate very friendly feelings. But Cruzado, now riding by his side, soon reassured him. These Indians, he informed him, had been sent out to reconnoitre and report to the cazique; they were not at liberty to hold intercourse with strangers, even though they wished to do so, because it was the duty of the chief to speak first to them, and, besides, the tribe probably did not feel secure here, since they had to cross the narrow arm of the lagoon, to reach the opposite side, and have the Pampas before them. As soon as they ascertained that they had to deal only with a small and peaceable party, they would assuredly not assume a hostile attitude. Hitherto none of the traders from Chili had ever been robbed or even molested. Jenkitrum, the cazique, maintained good order in this respect, and if sometimes horses or goods had been stolen from the whites, restitution was made as soon as the cazique had been informed of the occurrence.

The two Germans, however, looked forward with much misgiving to their first meeting with the Panchuenches.

"Well, doctor," said Reiwald, lowering his rifle and looking in his pockets for caps, "yonder is another of those rascals.—They dash through the thicket like deer, before we are able to aim at them."

"For Heaven's sake, put up your rifle, and be guilty of no folly," exclaimed the more timid doctor; "we must keep on friendly terms with those lords of the Pampas, and not commence by shooting any of them. That would be a very poor speculation, and might cost us our scalps."

"But these South-American Indians do not scalp their enemies," said Reiwald.

"Ah, yes, I remember, they only cut the throats of their captives; but I do not feel disposed to undergo even this pleasant operation."

"And shall we quietly submit to outrage on the part of the savages?" asked Reiwald, who, with the characteristic disposition of a hunter, felt an irrepressible desire to discharge the rifle at some living being.

"No one has hitherto perpetrated the least outrage upon us," replied the doctor. "That they contemplate us from afar rather than near, is, I think, very excusable, considering the sorry appearance we present after these rainy nights."

"Bah!" said Reiwald, casting a glance on his rusty rifle, "you do not wish us to appear here in black dress-coats and white cravats—there is another Indian! Keep a sharp lookout in our rear; I will protect the flank. I do not desire to be pierced by a lance from behind."

"I should like to know how I can keep a lookout. My neck is so stiff that I cannot turn it to my shoulder, much less to our rear; but you need not be afraid: the Indians seem to be peaceable, and more alarmed at us than we at them. See how unconcernedly they ride into the thicket to keep the pack-horses together.—Ah, there is a clearing!"

"It is a bend in the lagoon."

"No, I can distinguish a tent. Do not cock your rifle, lest it should go off and do mischief. Be prudent, Reiwald. Even though the Indians should design an attack, we could not seriously think of entering upon a conflict with a whole tribe of well-armed savages. We must, therefore, act with the utmost circumspection."

Reiwald was not inclined to act on these suggestions, but the exhortations of his friend, if he had ever intended to fire at the Indians, had nevertheless intimidated him. Cruzado and Don Enrique put their horses into a trot on the level ground, so that the rest of the party remained behind.

The travellers had no reason, however, to be uneasy, for most of the Indians whom they beheld were entirely unarmed, and only a few of them had hurriedly — perhaps only mechanically — taken up their lances before mounting. Larger numbers of them now made their appearance. The old Chileno and his companion were just entering the lane between the two rows of tents, when they noticed a large concourse of savages, who also had reason to wonder, for, at this season, when the rains were commencing in the Cordilleras, no one was ever known to cross the mountains, as such a trip would have led to a sojourn of five or six months on the Pampas. What now led the whites to the Otra Banda? Had their arrival any connection with the hostile expeditions which they knew were in progress on the other side? But Cruzado gave them no time for reflection, much less for questions, but, waving his arm toward them, he saluted them by shouting: "*Mari! mari!*" (the salutation of the South-American Indians), and they replied in the same words: "Whence? Whither?"

"What cazique is encamped here with his tribe?" continued Cruzado, without answering any questions.

"Tchaluak."

"And where is Jenkitruss?"

"Who knows?" laughed one of the Indians—"to-day he is on the other side of the Cordilleras, to-morrow he roams on the Pampas near the Cusu-Leufu."

"Where is the cazique's tent?" asked Cruzado, well aware that he must not look for a truthful reply, though they knew the abode of their cazique. But, above all, they had to see him; and on the relations established with him depended satisfactory information and permission to continue their journey.

No direct reply was made to this question, but a savage-looking lad, with a fresh gash across his face, which looked as if cut with a knife, turned his horse, and, with uplifted lance, galloped before Cruzado down the lane between the tents, and, doubtless, toward the dwelling of the cazique. Cruzado followed him immediately, and, accompanied by the crowd, rode at a gallop into the camp, without bestowing any attention upon their pack-horses. The drivers of the latter, however, did not lose their way, for the Indians who had come over with them from Chili had already become acquainted with the Panchuenches, or perhaps met with some old friends among them. At least they were engaged in an animated conversation, and the Penehuenches riding on each side of the cavalcade, assisted them in keeping the animals together.

The Indians desired to converse with the two Germans also, but this, of course, was impossible. Nevertheless, they nodded kindly to them, and they heard repeatedly the word "Alemanos."—The Chilian Indians no doubt had told them whence the doctor and the lawyer had come, and the Penchuenches seemed highly gratified at the intelligence.

"Say, doctor," said Relwald, who, on perceiving the kind bearing of the natives, had regained his good-humor, "is it not strange that we should enjoy here so excellent a reputation? It is doubtless because these heathens are utterly ignorant of the public affairs of the fatherland. It is my conviction that they do not read Berlin papers here."

"And, for our part," laughed the doctor, "we shall probably not expatiate on the political condition of Germany. Their language is singular. Do you understand a single word of what they say?"

"One of them," answered Relwald, "repeatedly said 'Yes,' but I cannot say whether it did not signify 'No.' Remember that we are here on the opposite side of the globe, and that autumn begins in April, and spring in November. The dog-days commence in midwinter, and people doubtless wear fur gloves on celebrating them. See these fine tents. I wish we had had one of them during the recent rains. On thinking of last night, and of passing through another like it, I feel like going mad."

"Let us drop that subject; it will be best for us to go through a course of mare's milk to prevent evil effects. Look at that large tent. Don Enrique halts there; I am sure his majesty the cazique must be at home, for the old Chileno is kept waiting."

In fact, there lay in front of them the most spacious tent they had yet seen. It was at least ten feet high, resting on poles placed obliquely, and covered with the skins of guanacos, that species of the llama celebrated for its fine fur, and which so well keeps off the rain. The tent was about twenty-four feet long and ten wide. The entrance was on the narrow side, closely covered with furs, which protect also from the winds common on the Pampas.

Similar tents were seen in different parts of the camp, but much smaller; they seemed, however, to belong to the wealthier Indians, while the poorer class were contented with a scanty frame of poles covered with dried horse-hides. There were also two huts spread over with matted reed-grass, which grows abundantly on the shores of the lagoon.

The pack-horses had now reached the open place in front of the cazique's residence, but no one seemed to think of unloading them, although there could be but little doubt that all would pass the night here. They were driven together and their bridles fastened to each other. Don Enrique, still on horseback, was at the chief's door; while Cruzado, who officiated as interpreter, entered the interior, together with the Indian who had accompanied them, in order to report at length on the character and object of the visit.

Cruzado took good care not to satisfy the Indian's curiosity in every respect, for he wished that the cazique should speak with the old Chileno himself. He therefore informed him that all he knew was, that a daughter of Don Enrique had been abducted from Chili, and he had come over the mountains to repair to the apo, or supreme cazique, in order to offer him a ransom for his child. As a matter of course, he added, that the white señor had brought with him rich presents for the chiefs who would kindly aid him in attaining his object.

The conversation within lasted a long time. The cazique had already learned, through his scouts, the number of the strangers; and the main points were to ascertain certainly who they were, and what had led them hither; whether there were any traders among them, or whether all were only companions of, and employed by, the old man. He seemed, however, to take umbrage at Don Enrique's intention to apply to Jankitrum himself—why not to him? Was he not a cazique? And what girl had been carried off? When, and where? Cruzado said he did not know. The señor had arrived, by the steamer, at Valdivia, and seemed to be in great distress at the loss of his daughter. He would certainly pay a large sum for her recovery, for he was undoubtedly very wealthy.

Tchaluak nodded gloomily. That the whites would have to pay well for the restoration of what the Indians had taken from them was to be expected; the interpreter needed not tell him that.

"Every thing else," added Cruzado, respectfully, "you may learn with all details from the old gentleman himself, if you will condescend to listen to him."

Tchaluak did not yet speak. The tribe were just about to enter upon a chicha carousal, and, in fact, the first barrel had been tapped at the moment when the approaching strangers had been descried and announced. This seemed to be an unseasonable time for the reception of a visitor; but the prospect of rich presents outweighed all objections. The cazique hesitated. He then waved his hand, and said:

"Very well, let him come in, but him only; the others may wait."

"And may we unload our animals?"

"No, I will first speak with the white-haired man; perhaps, afterward."

The order was given so peremptorily that resistance was out of the question; and Cruzado, who was perfectly familiar with the character of these people, withdrew with a bow in order to take word to Don Enrique.

Don Enrique dismounted, his heart throbbing with anxiety, and his interpreter, on helping him from his horse, whispered quickly in his ear:

"Treat the fellow inside with great kindness; he is one of the smallest, but withal wildest and most malicious caziques of the Pampas, and he is even at variance with Jenkitrum, as he asserts himself to be of nobler descent than the latter, and in consequence lays claim to the honor of being the apo, or supreme cazique of the whole country."

"What is his name?"

"Tchaluak. But you must only call him 'cazique,' and let him bear that title as often as possible. I will attend to every thing else."

So saying, he was about to conduct the old Chileno into the tent, when the doctor hailed him.

"Oh, señor, where are we to put our horses?"

Cruzado made no reply, but beckoned to Meyer:

"Don Carlos, you will see that no one dismounts. All will halt here, until Tchaluak issues his orders. Do not forget it."

While Cruzado drew back the furs covering the entrance, Don Enrique entered the tent, of which, however, he was not able to see all the interior, as there were several partitions, similar to those of a livery-stable. From above could be surveyed the whole inside, but the lower parts were closed, so that the first, which was used for the reception of visitors, was a small room by itself. A number of guanaco-skins lay on the floor and served as seats, and perhaps as couches too, for the Indians neither possessed nor needed better accommodation.

Here sat, leaning on his left elbow, Tchaluak the cazique, who, at least for the present, held in his hand the fate of the strangers who had come to him, and could do with them what he pleased. Who would have called him to account for it?

The Indian was fully aware of this. Knitting his brow, he fixed his small, half-shut eyes upon the Chileno, and a defiant, disdainful smile played round his lips, as he gazed at his bent form.

Cruzado whispered quickly and softly in his companion's ear:

"Offer him some tobacco; that will please him."

"What did you say!" cried out the cazique, suddenly and vehemently, raising himself up. "What did you whisper in my presence?"

"Cazique!" replied Cruzado, calmly, "I only told him that he was now in the presence of the most powerful and intrepid chief of the Pampas. I did not lie."

A smile illumined the cazique's stern features, and he nodded slowly. What he had just heard was nothing but what he had said of himself time and again in public meetings.

"Ask him where he comes from?" he said, in a calmer tone.

"From the north of Araucania," replied Cruzado, after exchanging a few words with Don Enrique; "from a city of the whites, called Concepcion. He is a quiet haciendero, who has never injured, but always kindly trusted, his Indian neighbors."

"And what does he now come to me for?"

"Permit us, great cazique," replied Cruzado, who had noticed that Don Enrique in the meanwhile had followed his advice and taken some tobacco from his poncho, "to offer you, before you listen to us, some of the tobacco which we have brought along as a present for you. The traders can no longer get over the mountains, and we have selected for you the best we could find at the settlements."

Tchaluak accepted the offer cheerfully; for an Indian cannot withstand presents; and the Chileno himself placed on the skins before him a large piece of tobacco, and some thin paper already cut for making cigarettes.

"Mala!" shouted the cazique, turning his head to the back part of the tent; "Ktal!" and a few seconds afterward the hides forming the partition were drawn back, and an entirely naked boy, about six years old, holding a lighted splinter of wood in his hand, glided into the room toward the cazique, to whom he held out the fire. But Tchaluak was still engaged in twisting his cigarette, in which he was quite skilled, and, having completed, he lighted it, and blew the smoke quietly through his nose. He then handed back the fire, and the boy, who meanwhile had not ventured to stir, but had been staring curiously at the strangers, disappeared in the same manner as he had come.

In the mean time not a word had been uttered, but it did not escape Cruzado that the cazique looked less sullen than previously, and, at any rate, their little stratagem had done them no harm. Their prospects, however, were not yet very favorable, for who could read on the features of an Indian what was passing in his mind, and how he would act the next moment?

"Now, speak," said the Indian, at last, "and tell the white man to seat himself on the furs yonder. He is welcome."

The old haciendero complied with the invitation, and, at Cruzado's request, gave the half-breed a brief account of what had happened, and described also the path by which the Indians had escaped from Chili. Tchaluak, although he did not understand a word of Spanish, watched him with rapt attention, but shook his head contemptuously, on being informed by Cruzado of what Don Enrique had told him, and said:

"What do I care for your conflicts with the Moluches? Fight or become reconciled; we have nothing to do with them. The Araucanians are dogs. When Tchaluak invoked their assistance in his just cause, they shrugged their shoulders, and refused to lift a lance, or saddle a horse. We have nothing in common with them, and if they have fled over the mountains into our territory, you may rest assured that they will remain there only until our young men discover them. Tchaluak hates them, and would take their spoils, but their horses are fleet, and he has hitherto seen the backs only of his enemies."

"But no Araucanian has carried off my child," cried the old man, hastily and tremulously; "it was the supreme cazique of these Pampas, it was Jenkitrusa."

"What does he say of Jenkitrusa?" asked Tchaluak, as soon as he heard the name.

"It was not the Araucanians that attacked the hacienda, great cazique, but, according to the old man's statement, Jenkitrusa came over the mountains with a detachment of his men and carried off the white girl."

"Jenkitrusa?" exclaimed Tchaluak, starting up from his seat. "Yes, I know, he was on the other side of the mountains; he loves the Moluches, and, had we followed his advice, we should have sacrificed our young warriors to assist those cowardly horse-thieves against the pale-faces. But I did not know that he took any booty there; not a word of it did he mention in council, nor did he offer to share it with the caziques. I saw, however, at his tent, a white girl—almost a child—she glided through the cabin like a timid fawn. Was it she?"

"Oh, my child! my child!" cried Don Enrique, when Cruzado translated the words to him, while his eyes filled with tears. "Thank God, she still lives! Oh, they could not crush this flower, for, after all, they are men, and have hearts in their bosoms!"

Tchaluak's eyes gleamed with a sinister fire when he divined from the old man's movements that his surmise was correct. Gazing into vacancy, he sank back upon the furs, and seemed not to hear at all, or not to take any notice of Cruzado's translation. Once it seemed as though he intended to speak again, but he quickly averted his head—was he afraid lest some eavesdropper behind the partition should hear his words? He did not break the silence for a long time, and, as he propounded no questions, Cruzado took good care not to disturb his reflection; perhaps it was favorable to them. At last he arose, and as he drew himself up to his full height before them, they beheld not a very tall, but firmly-knit and sinewy form; his bare arm, which he stretched forth from under his poncho, looked as though it were able to fell an ox to the ground. His hair hung, long and dishevelled, around his light-brown, defiant, and stern face, and his whole bearing was that of a man who knew that others had to obey when he commanded.

He looked the old Chileno full in the face, and said, in a kinder tone than he had hitherto assumed:

"It is all right. We shall speak further about it.—Malu!" he then shouted once more, and in a trice the little boy entered the room again. "Conduct the strangers to Haygoscun's tent. You will unload your animals there; I shall afterward send for the pale man, that he may present his gifts to me."

Cruzado only bowed to him, and, seizing the arm of Don Enrique, whom he led out of the tent, he told him outside what the cazique had said, and that they would pass the night in one of his tents.

"But, amigo," exclaimed the old man, "in what direction shall we seek Jenkitrusa? It is not late yet, and we might go a large part of the distance."

"Paciencia, señor," said the interpreter, reassuring him, and shaking his head; "since we have arrived among the Penchuenches, we have no longer a will of our own, but must stay here until he sends us away of his own accord."

"But what does he want of us?"

"Who knows?" replied the interpreter. "Who ever knows what these fellows want? For they never utter a word too much, and Tohaluak is one of the worst and most taciturn among them. But we shall see, for he must show his hands by-and-by; and for the present pray unpack your gifts, that we may keep him in good-humor. Be as liberal as possible. That will be the best way to deal with this cazique, and you will have at any rate plenty of gifts left for Jenkitrusa. You have with you goods enough to buy up a whole tribe, and, of course, they will be more than sufficient to ransom your child."

CHAPTER XXIV.

TOMANDO.

In front of the tent they beheld a strange scene. While the Chilian Indians, and even José, had waited with the utmost patience for the moment when further orders would be given to them, Reiwald was in great impatience, for he did not by any means like to halt, as he did, on the street, and to be impertinently stared at by some sixty Indian men and women. Notwithstanding the stringent order issued by Cruzado, he had been repeatedly about to dismount, for, besides, he felt very chilly in his scarcely half-dried clothes, and wished at least to warm himself; but whenever he made a movement to carry his purpose into effect, the Chilian Indians, who watched him anxiously, raised their arms, and Meyer entreated him urgently to wait, as it might involve them in serious difficulties, if the cazique, irritated at a breach of etiquette, should be angry with them.

"But permit me to tell you, Infante of Spain," exclaimed Reiwald, "It is worse in this respect among these coffee-colored heathens than in the fatherland, and I always thought that it was bad enough there. It is a shame that we should be pilloried here in this manner, and I am so cold that my teeth are chattering."

"You will get warm enough to-night," laughed Meyer; "I pledge you my word you will."

"I hope so; but what do you mean!"
"Did you look into the wide tent which we passed!"

"I did not. Why?"

"The Indians will drink chicha there to-night, and will doubtless invite us to take part in the carousal, provided they do not cut our throats previously. You will then have a chance to gratify your epicurean tastes."

"I am much obliged to you," said Reiwald, with a gesture of disgust; "what little I tasted of it the other night at Cajuante's cabin has fully satisfied me. Not a drop of the beverage shall ever pass my lips again, and I shall greatly prefer to drink water."

"But you will not be able to avoid it," replied Meyer. "If the Penchuenches invite us, we must drink with them, and partake of what they place before us—we cannot help it. But never fear, you will get accustomed to it, and, after we have passed three or four months in this region, we shall be so much inured to its peculiarities as even to get a red skin."

"You do not mean to say," growled Reiwald, "that we shall stay here three or four months? The mere idea is sufficient to make me crazy. But look at the doctor—what may be the matter with him?"

Doctor Pfeifel, in fact, seemed quite excited, for the Indian with the gash in his face had just come down the street again, and he stared at first at the man as though he were a ghost. It startled him to see one with a gaping wound, nearly six inches long, riding about in the open air, as though he had unwittingly drawn a black line across his face. The doctor immediately rode up to and addressed him, but, as in so doing he held his rifle in his hand, the Indian timidly retreated, and the others shouted to him not to leave his place; indeed, some Penchuenches, with uplifted lances, hurried from their tents, when Meyer noticed the danger to which the doctor had exposed himself. Without saying a word, he turned, galloped up to him, seized the bridle, and led his horse quickly back.

"Caramba, doctor! what were you doing there?" he said to him. "Did you want the Indians to pierce your body with their lances? These fellows are always ready to do so, and the arms of some of them are already itching to make a lunge at you."

"Well, I did not give them any provocation," exclaimed the doctor; "but there is a fellow riding about with a great gash in his face, and I only intended to dress the wound. If the cold should affect it, mortification might ensue."

"Bah! never mind him," laughed Meyer. "What does such an Indian care about a flesh-wound? He scarcely feels it, and it will heal as quickly as if one of us had only cut his finger a little."

"But I want to sew it up."

"If he will submit to it, you may," laughed Meyer; "but let him go now. I will just relate to the Indians what you intended to do; it will reassure them, and, on learning that you are a doctor, they will soon be friendly enough."

Such was the case, in fact, for scarcely had Meyer, with José's aid, explained to the bystanders that the stranger only meant to heal the wounded man, when the Indians commenced laughing good-naturedly, and clapped their hands. At this moment Cruzado and the old Chileno issued from the tent, and while Oruzado spoke a few words to the Chilian Indians, the little boy led the cavalcade to the designated cabin, whence the inmates were most unceremoniously ejected. Whether the tent was their own, or the common property of the tribe, they were compelled to leave it, and, moreover, not by the front entrance, but by the opening in the back part, by which they quickly withdrew, with their arms, saddles, and bridles. Tohaluak had so ordered it. The Indians who had hitherto kept aloof from the strangers now proceeded to help them very zealously.

There was a moment of confusion, for the packs had been carried into the tent in less than two minutes; then followed the saddles and bridles, but the Indians knew too well how to deal with such things, and succeeded in bringing order out of chaos. Every thing belonging to the horses was carefully put together, and while they were left to themselves, because they would speedily join the others, and seek the best pasture, the lads carried additional horse-hides and guanaco-skins into the tent, that the guests might make beds for the night.

Don Enrique, while Oruzado kept the other Indians away from the place where the old haciendero unpacked his treasures, that their covetousness might not be excited, opened one of the sacks, containing a part of the presents, and, aided by his interpreter, selected what the latter deemed most suitable to the cazique. And a strange collection they made for such a prince of the wilderness.

The first and principal gift was a very fine and long knife, with a hilt inlaid with mother of pearl, and a silver-mounted sheath; but then followed worthless colored glass-corals, which the chief could distribute among his wives; boxes of indigo, which the women used in dyeing their home-made stuffs; brass thimbles, which they pierced and hung about their necks; gayly-checkered cotton handkerchiefs; scissors; Jews'-harps, the favorite instrument of all these tribes; and, above all things, seši (red Spanish pepper), of which large quantities are raised in Chili, and of which both the whites and Indians of South America, who use it to give relish to all kinds of food, are exceedingly fond. There were still other trifles, strong rings for bridles, buckles, bells, paper for cigarettes, and last, but not least, a long roll of tobacco, of which Don Enrique had brought a large quantity, aware as he was of the partiality of the Indians to the fragrant weed. All this was tied up in a cotton handkerchief, and, while the others were preparing their sleeping-places, and José was already making a couch for his master, Oruzado and Don Enrique returned to the cazique's tent, for they knew that he was waiting with curiosity and impatience for the arrival of the promised presents. In fact, Tohaluak was already at the door, and it was only on seeing the strangers approach that he withdrew into the interior of the tent, threw himself upon the skins, and acted as though he had not risen from them at all.

At first, when Don Enrique began to display the gifts on a horse-hide before him, he feigned the utmost indifference. He nodded pleasantly on seeing the tobacco, smiled on perceiving the numerous presents for the women, and even stretched out his hand toward the achi, but withdrew it slowly and glanced over the whole, as if to say: "It is tolerably good; I am content with you." But when the Chileno produced the last and best present, he could not repress a loud, admiring. "Ah!" and seized the weapon, unsheathed it, and examined the handsomely-decorated blade.

"Cume! cume!" he exclaimed, repeatedly. "Jenkitrum has no such knife, and the blade is excellent. It is good! Ruenny, it is good! You must drink with us to-night, and to-morrow we shall speak about your plans. Tell him that. What is your name?"

"Cruzado, cazique."

"Well, tell him that, Cruzado.— Tchaluak is content."

Thus speaking, he uttered a strange guttural sound and listened, but he had to repeat the signal before it was complied with; for its object was to call into the room his wives, all three of whom made their appearance.

Two of them were very pretty and quite young. They wore the becoming costume of their country — a long blue dress, but their heads were not surmounted by such diadems as the women on the other side of the mountains wore; they were bareheaded, and their hair was arranged in two braids, hanging down over their shoulders in front. They were exceedingly bashful and reserved; remained timidly at the entrance, and waited for another sign from their lord and master, before they really dared to approach. The eldest of the three acted otherwise; without bestowing a glance or a greeting on the strangers, she glided to the presents displayed in front of the cazique, squatted down near them, and expressed her delight by clapping her hands. Her age, doubtless, entitled her to more consideration than the others, but Tchaluak seemed to think differently, for he uttered a few angry words, and beckoned to the others to approach also. But as he probably did not want the strangers to witness a family scene, he nodded to Cruzado, who interpreted it really as a sign that they were dismissed.

Meanwhile the doctor had grown very impatient in regard to the wounded man, for he could not bear the thought that any one should walk about with so large a gash in his face. He entreated Meyer again and again, until the latter promised to go in search of the patient. Now that they were the cazique's guests, they were at liberty to visit all parts of the camp, and no one could have ventured to prevent them from so doing. Meanwhile the doctor produced his surgical instruments, as well as thread and needle, and could hardly await the time when he would be allowed to sew up the wound of the "red heathen."

At length he made his appearance, though his bearing was by no means as bold as previously, for he did not trust the whites, and was perhaps afraid of some evil charm, which might injure him. But as the others laughed at him, he no longer refused to accompany Don Carlos, and entered the tent resolutely and defiantly.

José had to officiate as interpreter between him and Meyer. It was a cut which he had received from some drunken man at a chicha carousal, and he said "it would heal of itself." But Doctor

"TWO DEARS IN CONTEST."

Pfeifel differed from him; he went for water, took a sponge, and cleaned the wound. The Indian did not stir while he did so; but when the doctor laid down the sponge, dried the outside of the gash, took up thread and needle, and approached him again, he started back and looked around wildly, as if intending to run off.

"Pray tell the fool that I intend only to sew up his wound, and not his mouth."

After some protestations, by which José sought to reassure him, the Indian kept himself at last quiet, but only stretched out both his arms, and made a very wry face. After sewing up the wound, the doctor covered it with a plaster, and told him, through José, that, until the gash healed, he had to abstain from spirituous liquors; as for tobacco, he was permitted to smoke, if he had any.

The Indian seemed overjoyed when the operation was over; but, as he had complied with the request of the white man, and, as smoking had been alluded to, he did not thank the doctor for what he had done for him, but simply held out his hand, and begged for a little "tabaco," for the Indians had learned that word from the Chilenos.

Pfeifel laughed, and gave him some tobacco; but, as if this had been the signal for the rest of the Indians, all of them now thronged begging around the doctor, and it took more than half a roll to satisfy them all. The tobacco was of no consequence, provided it secured them the friendship of the Indians.

Reiwald, who could not bear to see the wounds of others, because he alleged it made him nervous, had meanwhile left the tent and strolled outside, in order to look around. The Indians had already proved that they were animated with kindly feelings, and why should he not, therefore, avail himself of the opportunity to familiarize himself, as much as possible, with the customs of these savages, in whom he took the liveliest interest?

It is strange what an influence the sky has upon us—when it is cloudy and sombre, it at once gives a gloomy cast to our mind, while, when the sun shines, we are much more inclined to preserve our good-humor even amid unpleasant surroundings. Thus the young German had long since forgotten the hardships of the preceding nights, and contemplated even with pleasure the passage of the Cordilleras. He was now sauntering down the street between the two rows of tents toward the lagoon, when his attention was attracted by several men, who had driven together a number of horses on the shore, and, lasso in hand, tried to catch one of them. The animals were mostly colts, which galloped wildly down the sandy beach, and, in their fright, sometimes stepped into the water and attempted to run into the lagoon. But it was too deep, and they returned, while the Indians laughed and cheered, and seemed to wrangle in regard to the animal which they were to catch. They pointed now to one, and now to another, and had an animated conversation. Finally they came to an agreement; the horses were surrounded, but broke through the line of the Indians, and were now speeding at a furious rate, but the pursuers, with their hair floating in the breeze, and swinging their lassos in the air, followed them at a gallop. They had scarcely advanced a hundred yards, when the horse of an Indian, who had thrown a lasso, turned on his hind-legs to withstand the accustomed jerk, and the captured animal, whose neck was in the noose, was dragged around and fell to the ground. The rest now pressed onward with redoubled speed, but the Indians halted, and while the first horseman steadily held the lasso, with which the animal had been caught, his companions drove it to a tree, standing near the shore of the lagoon, where all assembled.

Reiwald's curiosity was aroused, for he had seen that they had thrown twice into the tree, and under it lay a long and heavy piece of wood, not unlike that which butchers use to hang up slaughtered animals. His curiosity was presently satisfied. The Indian approached with the colt, a two-year old mare, and threw his rope to those who had dismounted and were waiting for him there. The others rode away and allowed their own horses to graze, while the men under the tree, by aid of the trunk, tightened the rope more and more, until the frightened animal was quite near it. Then came an operation from which Reiwald turned with a shudder of disgust, for it was a cruel way to slaughter an animal.

In a moment the lasso which had been fastened to the head of the unfortunate creature had been thrown up into the top of the tree, and several youths seized it, and drew up the colt until it sat on its hind-legs. It resisted, but a speedy end was put to its struggle by means of four nooses, with which its legs were fastened so that it could not stir; and now one of the Indians approached with his long knife, in order, as Reiwald believed, to kill it. He did not care to witness the scene longer, and returned as fast as his feet could carry him to the tent to inform the doctor of the spectacle.

"Doctor, for mercy's sake, they are killing a horse for our supper! I assure you my whole appetite is gone."

"I should much prefer their slaughtering a calf," said the doctor, who had just finished his work and distributed his tobacco, and was now packing up his instruments; "but I have made up my mind to eat among these monsters all that is offered me, even roast panther, only no human flesh. I should not even object to a decent dog, but hitherto I have seen only skeletons covered with skins. Nay, I believe, I could even eat a cat, though fortunately I have not seen such animals hereabouts."

"I believe I shall die of nausea if I am obliged to eat horse's meat," groaned Reiwald, with a woe-begone air. "I have endured every thing, lived without coffee, and consumed a piece of dried leather for breakfast, to say nothing of rain and storm, and not grumbled—but horseflesh! That would be doing violence to human nature. Let me tell you, I will build a fire and cook supper for two. When we are satisfied, we shall have no reason to eat more."

"Shall I give you a piece of good advice?" remarked Meyer, who had listened smilingly to their conversation. "You must eat, for these heathens are said to be exceedingly sensitive in this respect. Hence, the hungrier you are, the easier you will swallow what they place before you; you will have no trouble in doing justice to their hospitality."

"Well, I acknowledge the reasonableness of this trial so far as I am concerned," said Reiwald, with the resignation of despair. "At Valdivia I inveighed against the tough beef at the hotel; and now I would give a million for an old cow. Well, when I have got out of this trap, I shall thank God from my heart of hearts."

"Where are they killing the horse?" inquired Pfelfel.

"Yonder on the shore of the lagoon."

"Come with me, then, we must see it; we must not allow such an opportunity to pass without profiting by it; at all events, it will be of the highest ethnographic interest to watch the Indians engaged in this occupation."

"And our stomachs," said Reiwald, "will be afflicted with such an ethnographic squeamishness that we shall be unable to partake of a morsel of the meat."

"Never mind," replied the doctor; "science requires it, and I will go. What is the use of our journey if we refuse to see what is to be seen?"

So speaking, he wrapped himself in his cloak, for the air was rather cool, and left the tent. Reiwald struggled a while with himself; he would have liked best not to accompany his friend, but his curiosity finally got the better of him; he did not want the doctor to laugh at him, and, before the latter reached the shore, he had already overtaken him.

To their surprise they found that the horse was still alive, for its legs made several convulsive movements. An Indian held up each of its hind-hoofs lest it should jump up, and the fore-legs were also drawn asunder. In front of the unfortunate animal stood a Penchuenche, the upper part of his body naked, and, as the two Germans saw to their dismay, he had detached from the neck of the victim a large square piece of the skin, which hung down like a rag. Close by sat a couple of women who rubbed Spanish pepper on a flat bowlder and put it into a wooden dish. What was it all for?

The Indians standing before the horse, now slowly cut into the throat of the tortured animal; he was doubtless about to put an end to the sufferings of the poor creature; but no—he presently closed the wound, and said something to the woman, who immediately brought him the pulverized achi, of which he took a handful, and then—the two friends averted their heads shudderingly—pushed his clinched fist into the hole in the horse's throat.

"Great heavens!" cried the doctor, "this is horrible. I really believe, Reiwald, it would be better for us not to witness this; it has made me ill."

"And myself also," groaned Reiwald. "What do you think? Shall we remain for the dissection?"

"No, thank you, I have had enough of it. These fellows are atrocious! I wish Meyer were here to explain the object of this cruel butchery."

"Well," said Reiwald, "I think it is plain enough, and let me entreat you not to allude to it any more."

"What is that?" exclaimed the doctor, at this moment. "All are entering the large tent. Perhaps it is their church, and we shall have a chance to witness the religious service of these heathens."

"What day is this!" asked Reiwald. "I have forgotten my almanac."

"So have I; but it makes no difference, for who knows what day they are celebrating?"

"Shall we look in?"

"If we are allowed."

"There is Meyer in the crowd," exclaimed Reiwald; "come, at least they will not slaughter any horses there."

The two Germans saw now that their countryman was already beckoning, and, as they hastened to him, he exclaimed:

"Where have you been? We have been looking for you everywhere: the affair is about to commence."

"What affair? Is this the church?" inquired the doctor.

"The church? Ha! ha!" laughed Meyer. "You do not suppose these people have churches, do you? When they are allowed to have their Pillan, of whom they are dreadfully afraid, they are fully satisfied. Chicha is to be drunk here; the cazique is already in the tent, and has repeatedly inquired for you. He wants to see you, doctor."

"Me?" asked Pfeifel, in surprise.

"Yes. He heard of your having sewed up the cheek of one of the Indians, and intends, I believe, to order a pair of pantaloons of you. You will get customers here."

"Oh, nonsense! Tell me, Meyer, does the cazique really wish to see me?"

"Certainly; he has several patients whom you are to cure as speedily as possible; come, now—princes are never very patient."

They entered the tent and beheld a characteristic scene, to which even a certain solemnity was not wanting, for not a loud word was uttered, and, though there was a great concourse of people, only a few conversed, and those in a whisper. Meyer beckoned to Cruzado, who had already looked around for the doctor, and now taking him by the hand conducted him to that part of the room where Tchaluak was seated on soft guanaco-skins which had been comfortably arranged for him.

Reiwald meanwhile looked about the interior of the tent, and observed that six tolerably large barrels were placed at one end of the room, not close to the wall, however, but more toward the centre. One of them, standing closest to the cazique, had a hole in the middle, and from it flowed a stream, about half an inch thick, of that horrible yellow-green liquor, while the Indians were thronging about it and holding large cow-horns under it.

A young woman stood near. She wore her long black hair straight; like the cazique's wives, she had on both sides a narrow braid hanging down from the temples; in her ears were small pieces of copper, and about her neck a number of blue and white beads, which contrasted prettily with her good-natured and handsome face. Her dress consisted of the customary blue wrapper reaching to her knees, while the similar under-garment was fastened round her neck and fell to her ankles. The right arm was bare, and whenever a horn was filled, and no other directly ready to take its place, she put one of her fingers on the hole in the barrel, lest the liquor should run out.

The quantity of chicha which these people swallowed was astounding, and it would have afforded Reiwald great pleasure to look on, but for one of the Indians—a tall, broad-shouldered, and one-eyed fellow (his other eye had been pierced by a lance)—who approached him and offered him a hornful of the disgusting beverage. He took it, raised it to his lips, feigned to drink, and intended to return it with his thanks, but the Indian burst into a laugh, so that all turned their heads toward him, and gave Reiwald to understand that he had to drink.

"Tabaco!" asked the Indian, and held out his hand; and the German put his hand with gentle resignation in his pocket, and gave him some.

Meanwhile the doctor was introduced to Tchaluak, the cazique, but neglected to doff his cloak, which attracted the eyes of the chief. It was an old military cloak, with a scarlet collar and brass buttons, and lined with red flannel. On seeing it, Tchaluak nodded joyously, and signified that the cloak pleased him. His conversation, although he uttered the word "Aleman" in a kind tone, proved to be a matter of considerable difficulty, since he had to avail himself of the services of two interpreters, Cruzado and Meyer. Nevertheless, he asked him where he came from, if he could cure all diseases, and if he knew any magic remedies. During the interview he touched the collar, and examined the buttons of the cloak, which seemed especially to attract his attention. To all appearance, it was a warm garment, and the cazique considered it a very desirable article.

Now, Pfeifel did not like this at all; he had heard that it was customary in the Orient to offer as a present an article which a man might say he liked, and the cazique looked exactly as though he expected something of the kind. The doctor, however, would not part with the cloak; for he would have been greatly at a loss on the Pampas without it, and was thankful when the cazique, who did not wish to interrupt his libations too long, finally let him go.

The revel commenced now in a systematic manner. The Indians drank, not in haste, but with a certain earnestness and perseverance, as if they were performing a most important duty. The first barrel was emptied to the hole in the middle about as fast as the chicha would run out. Sometimes a piece of apple-peel stopped the stream, but the woman quickly removed it; when the liquor was consumed thus far, man lifted up the barrel, put it on top of another standing near, and opened a second hole, when more liquor ran out until it became thick and dark-colored. But this made no difference; they liked it for all that. The Germans had again and again to drink of the horns presented to them. Even the old Chileno was unable to avoid taking part in the carousal, and sat between the cazique and Cruzado, so as to be always ready to answer the questions of the former, and keep him well supplied with tobacco. The roll which Tchaluak had received at his tent was not used, but preserved for a later revel. About two hours had elapsed in this manner; it was in the afternoon, and already one-half of the second barrel was emptied, but the thirst of the Indians did not seem to abate in the least.

"Doctor," said Reiwald, "it is no

use talking about Bavarian beer-drinkers, with their sixteen quarts of an evening; they might come here and learn something. Never before did I see any thing like it. Look at the fellow whose cheek you sewed up; he drinks as much as any of them."

"Let him drink!" replied the doctor. "They are destitute of human nature, or they could not stand it. My stomach seems already a keg of vinegar; and how attentive these brutes are! One of them is sure to present us his horn every other minute."

"There is one good feature about this," said Reiwald. "If we should ever return to the civilized world, which, to all appearance, is problematic, we shall never again inveigh at an hotel against the claret and tough beef. We are passing now through trials which——dear me, what does the fellow carry yonder—I believe it is raspberry-jelly, my favorite dish. Why, I did not know they had raspberries here!"

The doctor looked up and observed some Indian lads, one of whom carried a large wooden dish, in which lay a red, jelly-like cake of round shape, and went with it to the cazique, in front of whom he put it down.

It was at all events a delicacy, for at the same time there were brought to the chief small pieces of bark to be used as plates. Tchaluak thereupon drew his new knife from his belt—he could not inaugurate it in a worthier manner. By-the-way, the doctor noticed that he alone wore a knife, the others probably being forbidden to do so lest fights should break out among them. The cazique cut the cake into small pieces, each of which he placed on a strip of bark, and then sent children with them to those persons on whom he wished to bestow a special proof of his esteem. The first was given to Don Enrique, who accepted it with a grateful bow, and, while Cruzado whispered a few words in his ear, disposed of it immediately.

"The old man seems to like it," said Reiwald, who had watched him attentively; "it is raspberry-jelly. How strange it is that the Penchuenches should know how to prepare it! They must have learned it from foreigners, who occasionally come over from Valdivia. Here is some of it for us."

The second dish was destined for the doctor, who owed this distinction either to his profession, or, as he almost feared, to the red lining of his cloak. He also received it thankfully, and drew out his pocket-knife.

"It must be eaten with milk, and by means of a spoon," he said; "but we must not be too particular here."

"To all appearance, I shall not get any of it," said Reiwald; "they will probably bring me a piece of horseflesh."

"What is this!" murmured the doctor. "Raspberry-jelly? bah! it burns the tongue like fire."

"How does it taste?"

"Not so bad, but it is strongly peppered."

"Well, I am also about to have some," said Reiwald. A little girl was bringing two plates, one for him, and the other for Meyer.

The latter made himself very comfortable, and acted as though he were at home. He reclined on a guanaco-skin, and, when one of the Indians handed him a horn of chicha, he quaffed it with the utmost indifference, and returned it with a gracious nod, as though he greatly relished the beverage. At this moment he cast a glance, half-curious and half-derisive, on his two countrymen, who were partaking with so much appetite of the new dish; for Reiwald had tasted it now, and seemed to like it exceedingly.

"I wish," he said, "I knew what it is; it is exceedingly pungent, and I cannot exactly say what it resembles, though it is not unknown to me."

"Yes, I cannot make it out either, it tastes almost like—" he pushed away his plate in dismay, and then examined the dish more closely. "Say, Meyer, do you know what it is?"

"Curdled horse-blood," replied Meyer, putting a piece of it with the utmost equanimity into his mouth, and he had to take pains not to burst into a fit of laughter, on perceiving the effect produced by these words.

"What!" cried Reiwald, in a tone of ineffable disgust. "What do you say it is?"

"Curdled horse-blood, with pepper," repeated Meyer, smiling; "it is nice, is it not?"

"Gracious!" exclaimed the doctor, almost paralyzed. Reiwald made no reply—he had a morsel in his mouth; but he sprang to his feet, cast a glance of horror about him, and staggered toward the entrance. The Indians looked at him in surprise, but, before he reached the fur covering, they discovered why he was hastening out of the room. They gave way to him laughingly, and the unfortunate German rushed out and hastened down the street. Nor did he return. The cazique dispatched Cruzado to look after the "sick Aleman," and the half-breed took Meyer with him. They found him, but he was in the tent assigned to them, where he lay, groaning on the floor. He probably imagined that he was worse than he really was; but nothing could prevail on him to rise. They were obliged to leave him and report to the cazique that he was too ill to appear again, and the doctor, of course, profited by this opportunity to leave the chicha-tent. The lining of his cloak, however, betrayed him. Tchaluak's eyes fell on it at the moment when he intended to leave; he told Cruzado to call him, and caused him to seat himself by his side—bestowing, thereby, a special distinction, the full value of which was hardly appreciated. But he submitted to every thing; drank chicha until two in the morning, partook of two or three horse-cutlets, and remembered but vaguely that two men had taken him "home," and put him to sleep.

CHAPTER XXV.

CONSEQUENCES.

On the following morning, the cazique sent for the doctor, but he was not up. He lay with his face buried in the furs, and groaned in the most piteous manner. By his side was Reiwald, his knees drawn up to his chin, and clasped with both hands. Meyer was the cazique's envoy, and he stood for some moments before his unhappy countrymen, who, in the depth of the wilderness, had fallen victims to the exigencies of etiquette.

"Well," he said to himself, smiling, "I am afraid the chicha did not agree with them. The doctor must have a terrible headache this morning, for he imbibed last night as much as some of the Indians, and I must arouse him.—Say, doctor!" he exclaimed, seizing his shoulder, and shaking him; but it was in vain. The doctor did not stir, and his low groans indicated that he was hardly alive.

"Dear me," exclaimed Meyer, "I did not suppose that it would be so difficult to awake him; and Mr. Reiwald has curled himself up—ah, he opens his eyes! Good-morning, Mr. Reiwald. Well, how are you, sir?"

"Gracious heavens, I am in pain," groaned the tortured German. "It seems as though my stomach were torn to pieces.—What time is it, Meyer?"

"The clock has not yet struck, nor will it, I suppose; but, according to my calculation, it is about eight. My chronometer does not go, and, when I tried to repair it the other day, I lost one of the wheels. So you have a pain in the bowels, have you?"

"It is dreadful, sir."

"If we succeed in arousing the doctor, he will prescribe for you, and I will immediately go to the drug-store," said Meyer, not at all touched; for it is well known that the best and most compassionate persons do not take pity on those who are sea-sick, or affected with a headache in consequence of dissipation. But Reiwald was not disposed to jest; he uttered an oath and turned away. Meyer now renewed his efforts to awaken the doctor, but it was of no use, and he was obliged to return and inform Cruzado of his failure.

The doctor was not needed, for the cazique was engaged in a long and animated conversation with the old Chileno; for this purpose he had gone with Don Enrique and the interpreter from his tent into the Pampas, where there was no danger of any one overhearing what they said. The conversation related exclusively to the object of Don Enrique's journey, and, to the surprise of Cruzado, who seemed to have expected the reverse, the cazique entered upon the Chileno's wishes much more readily than even Don Enrique had ventured to hope.

But Cruzado, who held intercourse with the Indians all his lifetime—nay, had grown up among them, and had their blood in his veins, soon found out that the cazique was actuated by a certain motive, though he did not make the slightest allusion to it. On the contrary, he promised to conduct Don Enrique and his companions to Jenkitrum's camp, though he said it was now on the opposite bank of the Limai, and the journey would be attended with many difficulties in crossing the swollen river with the pack-horses; still, he added that they would probably succeed in so doing: the horses would swim the stream, and the men be able to build a raft, and convey the baggage to the other bank.

"Under these circumstances, cazique," said Cruzado, "I believe you will permit us to proceed this very day, so that we may no longer trouble you and your tribe. The old man, besides, longs to embrace his child again, and he has told me that he would present to you additional gifts of high value on his return from the Limai."

"This very day?" said Tchaluak,

slowly. "Yes, certainly—but—it will be impossible for you to collect your horses so speedily."

"It will take us only an hour."

"And then we shall drink again. I cannot allow you to depart before our festivities are over."

"You have already bestowed upon us the most liberal hospitality, and we are grateful for all that we have enjoyed here."

"And then, the doctor!" continued the cazique, after a pause; "my youngest wife is ill. He must see what ails her and give her medicine."

Cruzado inclined his head; it was almost useless to raise further objections, for the cazique seemed to be determined not to let them go. These independent chiefs of the Pampas treat their guests almost as prisoners so long as they are averse to parting with them. Resistance was useless, and would have only made matters a great deal worse. Hence, he cautioned Don Enrique against betraying his impatience and entreated him to submit cheerfully to stern necessity. To-morrow, he added, they would probably be allowed to proceed, and possibly the delay might not be by any means disadvantageous, inasmuch as the Limai, owing to the late rains, would be very high, and compel them to remain on its bank for several days.

Meanwhile Meyer had returned to their tent and continued his efforts to arouse Pfeifel. It was hard work, but finally he succeeded, and the unfortunate man raised himself up. But he looked as pale as a corpse, his hair was matted, and his eyes lay wild and deep in their sockets.

"Meyer," he said, on recognising the German, "I have often drunk too much champagne, hock, beer, and punch, and I have studied the various stages of wretchedness consequent on such dissipation, and may lay claim to some experience and judgment on this point, but the indisposition following a chicha spree!—that is assuredly the most terrible that can be imagined. Sea-sickness," he added, in a more subdued tone, "is also an ailment, in which the patient would commit suicide, if he deemed his own life worth taking—but the horrors of drinking too much chicha—" He fell again upon his face, until Reiwald, who had been running up and down all the morning between the lagoon and the tent, returned and looked so piteously at Meyer that the latter burst into loud laughter.

"Well," he said, "be comforted, sir. For aught I know, we shall stay here for a day—as yet, no preparations for setting out have been made, and you may recover from the effects of the festival. What about the coffee?"

"It is ready. I take some when rushing past it."

Meyer laughed and went to the coffee-pot in order to help himself. Reiwald had had time to put something more substantial on the fire: it was a kettleful of rice and a large piece of dried meat, for he had not eaten any thing the previous day; at least not after breakfast. The doctor had likewise been aroused again by hearing coffee mentioned. He raised his head and said:

"Meyer, do me the favor of running round the corner, and getting me a herring and a bottle of soda-water."

"I am sorry," replied Meyer; "this day is Sunday, and all the stores are closed. But what is the matter with you? You look strange, indeed! What did you do with your cloak?"

"Oh, my head!" murmured Pfelfel, casting a glance on his cloak, which looked crumpled and dirty, but, wretched as he felt, he intended to clean it a little. He suddenly exclaimed:

"Those savages are infamous thieves, indeed!"

"What is the matter?" asked Meyer. "Did they steal any thing from you?"

"Steal? Pray look at this cloak. They have cut most of the buttons from it."

"Yes," laughed Don Carlos, "I might have foretold that they would take the brass buttons as soon as they had an opportunity. The women wear them in their ears, sir."

"But how am I now to button up my cloak?"

"Tie bits of packthread to the button-holes, and fasten them. You can manage that very easily. But it is time for us to go over to the big tent, for half an hour ago they recommenced drinking there."

"Chicha!" cried the doctor, in dismay.

"Of course—what else? They will soon call for us."

"Listen, Meyer. I am naturally a good, kind-hearted man; I have never yet poisoned a well, or committed highway robbery, or murder; I have never set fire to a house—nay, I have not even embezzled public money; but you may fear the worst on my part, if I should be once more compelled to raise a chicha-horn to my lips."

"Well, well," exclaimed Meyer, "if you have such an aversion to it, you may perhaps avoid it. Just remain on your couch all day and feign extreme illness. I believe the Indians will not disturb you then."

"But I confess I am not very partial to that remedy."

"The frolic will not last long," said Meyer; "they drank four barrels, and nearly the whole of the fifth. Only one barrel is left, and if you want to get any of it, you must make haste, for by noonday it will be empty."

"Thank you," replied Pfelfel, sighing; "I hope we shall not again be subjected to such temptations. Where is Don Enrique now?"

"Tomando," replied Meyer. "The old gentleman seems to have undergone a sudden change, and to have taken a liking to chicha. He drank a great deal of it."

"And does he not feel wretched this morning?"

"He is as sound as a fish—but I think our breakfast is ready. Shall I get you some horse-steak? The kitchen is just across the way."

"Meyer, you are a monster; but where is Reiwald?"

"He will be back presently," laughed Meyer, and went to the kettle, cut a piece from the meat boiling in it, putting some of the rice into the lid of the kettle, which he used as a plate, and then seated himself comfortably with his meal on one of the furs. The doctor imitated his example, bringing a tin plate from his saddle-bags, but he had no appetite. He pushed away the food, and lay down again, when Meyer exclaimed:

"There comes a messenger—now you must be ill!" And the doctor lay at once on his face, and did not stir.

It was the one-eyed Indian who had been ordered to conduct the Alemanos to the chicha-tent; Reiwald reëntered at this moment, and looked so pale, and the doctor's attitude indicated so clearly the impossibility of his complying with such an invitation, that Meyer succeeded easily in convincing the messenger, and thereupon accompanied him. The dissipation had not produced disagreeable effects upon him, and he felt able to continue it. In the tent he found the same state of affairs as on the day before; the cazique, however, who was not as talkative, sat almost motionless; some Indians came and went, and, to all appearance, brought him word; but he drank a great deal.

Cruzado had hitherto been outside; he now came in, and Tchaluak beckoned him to take again a seat by his side. The solemn silence of the previous day no longer reigned in the tent, for the Indians seemed excited by the strong drink. Women brought in dishes filled with roast meat, of which the cazique took a piece, tore it with his fingers, and devoured it, drying his hands in his hair.

"Where are the Alemanos?" he inquired at last of Cruzado.

"Sick, cazique," replied the half-breed, smiling; "the drink of the Pampas does not agree with them, and they are now very miserable in their tent."

The cazique laughed, and looked thoughtful; but his eyes had lost their usual lustre, and were dim and glassy. He asked again:

"Where are the Alemanos?"

Cruzado cast a searching glance at him, and repeated his previous answer. He saw the Indian was intoxicated, or nearly so.

The cazique burst into a laugh, and laid his hand on Cruzado's shoulder.

"And where is the old man?" he whispered to him.

"He is close by; you spoke to him a short time ago."

The Indian nodded, saying in a low voice to himself rather than his neighbor:

"A very beautiful girl — white and delicate — like a young colt. And so young — so sweet — but the women will be angry. Ha! what have they to say about it? Am I no longer the master, Cruzado?"

"Certainly, cazique," replied the half-breed, who did not yet know exactly what the intoxicated Indian was driving at, though he suspected what it was. "You are the ruler of your tribes; not only the women, but also the warriors must obey you."

"Good, Cruzado!" said the cazique, taking a horn just presented to him, and drinking it off immediately. "You are wise — you are honest. The Penchuenches are dogs," he suddenly whispered. "They are cowards, and how to a poltroon. Jenkitrus has the heart of a woman — I will tear it out and cast it to the dogs."

Cruzado was frightened, for, although the cazique had said all this in the maudlin manner of a drunkard, these confidential communications might become dangerous, and he feigned not to have heard them at all, but sat like a man who is very drowsy.

"Ha! ha! my friend," laughed the cazique, whose glances fell on him as though he wanted to read in his face his assent to what he had said, "is the chicha too strong for you, too?"

"Me? Certainly not, cazique," exclaimed Cruzado, imitating to perfection the movements of a man just aroused from his sleep.

"And what did I speak of?"

"Of a very beautiful girl—white and delicate—and you said you were the master of your tribe. Of course you are."

Tchaluak laughed disdainfully; but it was obviously difficult for him to fix his thoughts upon any thing. Led back to his first words in this manner, he suddenly moved up to Cruzado, laid his arm round the half-breed's shoulder, and whispered in a low voice:

"Cruzado—you—you are a good, honest fellow. Will you—will you help me to win the girl?"

Cruzado did not give a start—his suspicion was confirmed, and he was prepared for such a question. He only shrugged his shoulders, and replied in as low a voice:

"Yes, cazique, with all my heart, but how? Jenkitrusa has got her at present, and if he give her back to the old Chileno, of which I have serious doubt, he will take a ransom for her, and, as is customary, will cause him to be escorted back to the mountains by a strong detachment of warriors."

"And suppose—I should now give you—an escort?" said the Indian. "You can persuade him that—they are perfectly safe under my protection."

"But what if Jenkitrusa should afterward learn that his agreement was violated?" asked the half-breed.

Tchaluak bent over him and applied his lips to the interpreter's ear, but not a word fell from them—not even a whisper; he then raised himself up and said:

"Never mind—what do you care for the great Jenkitrusa's anger—so long as you live on the other side of the mountains?—How can he hurt you?—But when you come over to the Pampas ask for Tchaluak's camp—every Penahuenohe will be able to point it out to you— and you will have a friend in the plain."

At this moment, there arose wild shouts at the other end of the tent—two Indians were quarrelling and bent on attacking each other, while others prevented them. Tchaluak started up and uttered a peculiarly shrill note, which produced an almost magic effect. The two adversaries desisted immediately; profound silence ensued, and all turned their eyes toward the cazique. But, content with the obedience of his tribe, he waved his hand.

"It is good," he said; "keep peace— you know me, do you not? What! is the chicha gone? Give me another horn —my throat is dry.—Scoundrels, will you allow your cazique to die of thirst?"

He quaffed again a hornful of the liquor, and leaned back upon his couch. Probably he wished to reflect; but the effects of the preceding night's carousal, and the large quantity of liquor he had already drunk, overcame him. He shut his eyes and was still for a moment; his head drooped slowly—he was asleep!

The sixth and last chicha-barrel was exhausted, and the Indians returned to their tents to sleep away the intoxication, so that, in the afternoon, the camp seemed almost deserted. Only the women went to work as usual, and gathered wood for their camp-fires, spread out the hides of the slaughtered horses to dry them, brought water from the lagoon, washed their clothes there, and nursed the children.

Don Enrique finally met Cruzado, for whom he had already been looking a long time, while the half-breed had been on the shore of the lagoon. It was proposed to profit by the opportunity given to load their pack-horses, and set out. But Cruzado shook his head most emphatically:

"No, señor," he said, "that would be the most foolish step we could take, for Tchaluak would consider it a mortal insult. I myself would start at this moment rather than an hour later, for I no longer feel at ease here, but paciencia, amigo. We cannot help it; we must remain. By being in too great a hurry, we shall only fail to attain our object. Besides, the rest is good for our horses, which were somewhat exhausted in the mountains, and no one can tell when we may have need of all that they can do."

"Do you think we are in danger here?" asked the Chileno.

"No, not now," said Cruzado, quietly; "but they are strange people, and as unreliable as a tamed tiger; you never know when they may show their claws, and yet you may venture among them with some degree of safety, as long as you do not meddle with their hatred, their love, or their faith. But if you interfere in their customs, or arouse their jealousy, then I would as soon cross the Pillan-Leufu at high-water mark as be at their mercy."

"But we do not wish to interfere, or excite their jealousy."

"Well," said Cruzado "our object amounts to about the same thing; we come to take away a pretty young maiden whom they abducted, but regard now as their property."

"Not by force," exclaimed the old man; "I am ready to pay the cacique the highest price he asks for her; only I want to recover my child—my poor lost child! for do you think, Cruzado, that I could have an hour's rest after knowing that she is in the hands of these demons?"

"Never mind, señor; we are here to obtain her release. I did not intend to dishearten you, but only to entreat you to avoid every thing that might irritate those in whose power we are at present. Pray, follow my instructions in every respect, and do not distrust me, even though you see me hold a great deal of intercourse with the Peuchuenches."

"I was never yet distrustful of you, Cruzado," said the Chileno, mournfully. "What could you gain by deceiving an old man so terribly stricken as I am?"

"Never mind," said the interpreter. "After we have Tchaluak's tents once behind us, I believe we shall have overcome the greatest difficulties of our undertaking."

"But must we not return by the same route?"

"Who knows?" replied Cruzado, evasively; "the most circuitous route is sometimes after all the shortest; but we shall see. And now, lie down and sleep, you have more need of repose than any of us. Besides, we cannot do any thing now, and at daybreak to-morrow we will try to prevail on the cacique to let us go."

"And what if he refuses?"

"In that event, we shall stay, señor, until he consents," said the interpreter, calmly. "Paciencia!" And, nodding to the Chileno, he walked slowly down the street.

CHAPTER XXVI.

ACROSS THE PAMPAS.

ALTHOUGH Cruzado had also drunk a great deal of chicha, he did not sleep in the afternoon, but strolled about, and whenever he met an Indian, awake and sober, which was rarely the case, he entered into a conversation with him. He inquired particularly concerning the passage across the lagoon and the probable condition of the Limai, although he might perhaps have given as much information on these points as any of the Penohuenches, whom he consulted in regard to them. But at the same time he alluded to other subjects; he saw at the camp a couple of Indians who did not belong to the tribe, but to that of the Telhuets, or some other neighboring nation; and, late in the evening, there arrived on a horse, almost ridden to death, another Indian, who, bearing that the cazique was asleep, immediately dismounted, threw his saddle and blanket under a tree, and lay down. The horseman had evidently had a very long journey.

The night passed without the least disturbance. Even the wild sons of the Pampas required repose for their abused bodies. They do not, however, sleep long. No sooner do the first streaks in the east announce the approach of day, than there is a commotion in the tents; and as the women enter upon their peculiar occupations, so the men look after their horses, and prepare for hunting.

Don Enrique was one of the first to be up and doing, and he awakened Cruzado, to drive up the horses, but the interpreter shook his head.

"It will be of no avail, señor, and we shall not for all that get off an hour sooner; on the contrary, it may delay our departure, for the cazique might take umbrage at it. We must bide our time, and embrace the first good opportunity; you may depend upon it I will do so."

The morning was clear and fresh, and, while the Cordilleras were shrouded in gloomy clouds, which concealed their summits, the sun shone in the plain. Our two German friends had slept long enough, and were recovered from the injurious effects of the liquor; at least both of them looked again tolerably well, and, after taking a cup of coffee, walked out into the open air. But it was quite chilly, autumn was at hand, and from the south blew a sharp breeze which made them wrap themselves more closely in their cloaks. At this moment Cruzado came down the street; they hailed him, and asked how long they would have to remain.

"Well, señors," said the half-breed, carelessly—for he considered the two the most useless creatures under the sun—"who knows?—but let me advise you to pack up your baggage immediately, for we may get orders to start at any moment, and it would be very disagreeable then, if you kept us waiting."

The doctor understood only the words "pack up your baggage," and he exclaimed, "Bueno; adelante." Cruzado smiled and went on his way, when the cazique stepped from his tent, and at the same moment his eyes fell on the doctor's cloak.

Pfeifel, who was more afraid of the cazique's craving for his highly-prized cloak than of any thing else, turned aside in order to get out of sight among the tents, but it was too late.

"Ho!" shouted the Indian, and beckoned to Cruzado, to whom he said a few words, which immediately caused the interpreter to start in pursuit of the doctor. He soon overtook him, and turned a deaf ear to his objections and protestations. It was the cazique's order which had to be obeyed, and the doctor, in his despair, now looked around for Don Carlos, for how was he to get along without him in his interview with the Indian? But where was Meyer? He was not to be seen anywhere on the street, and nothing therefore remained for Pfeifel but to meet his fate.

He soon discovered that his misgivings were but too well-grounded, for no sooner did he approach the dreaded cazique, than the latter, without looking at him, pointed at his cloak, and spoke to the half-breed, which the doctor, of course, did not understand, but which he took for an order that he was to doff the cloak, and deliver it to the heathen. He was mistaken, however. Cruzado quickly followed the direction of Tchaluak's arm, and exclaimed then in surprise:

"*Caracho, adonde son sus botones?*"

"What!" said the doctor, who did not understand a word of what he said, and shook his head significantly. But Cruzado did not enter upon a long explanation; he seized the cloak, and pointed to the places where the buttons were wanting. He wished to know what had become of them.

"Aha," said Pfeifel, who understood now what the cazique meant. He knew a Spanish word that might perhaps explain the matter. "Ladrone" (thief); and he repeated it several times. Cruzado laughed and explained the probable cause of the disappearance of the buttons. Tchaluak, however, did not laugh, but became very angry. He quickly beckoned to an Indian, and said to him something in an angry and excited voice, whereupon the man disappeared among the tents. The doctor saw, to his surprise, that no one took any further notice of him, and that the cazique, engaged in an animated conversation with Cruzado, walked away in the direction of the lagoon.

"They are strange people, indeed," he said to Reiwald, who rejoined him as he remained standing alone in the middle of the camp. "Goodness knows what he wanted with my buttons, and no one is making any preparations for our departure. I really believe that we have rented our fur-roof by the month."

"My good knife was stolen last night," said Reiwald, angrily; "I would rather have lost ten dollars; now, when I eat, I shall have to use my fingers."

"Horse-flesh is tender, and easily eaten. For the rest, inform the cazique of your loss, and he will see that your property is restored. On hearing that my buttons had been cut off, he was greatly displeased."

"And did you get them back?"

"He has sent a policeman for them. —Halloo, what is that confounded half-breed running so fast for? The fellow is as sprightly as quicksilver, and it makes me quite nervous to see him."

"Saddle your horse! Vamos nos!" shouted Cruzado, from afar. "Oh, Don Carlos, pray explain to your countrymen, that they must pack their sacks as quick as possible."

"Are we going to set out?" asked Meyer, who made his appearance.

"This very moment, sir; I have already sent for our horses; the weather is favorable, and the Limai, it is expected, will not be very high. Make haste, or the cazique may repent of having given us leave to start."

He hastened into the tent, to see if every thing was in readiness to be placed on the horses, as soon as they arrived.

Reiwald and the doctor were rather at a loss to know whether or not to rejoice at this sudden order. They had found here an excellent tent, which, at all events, protected them from the rain, and as to horse-flesh, on penetrating farther into the Pampas, they would doubtless get more of it rather than less, and then the packing and unpacking of the baggage! The doctor, however, thought of his cloak, which he had good reason to consider endangered, and Reiwald of the raspberry-jelly, but both finally seemed reconciled. Their baggage was soon ready, for, no longer ignorant of the thievish propensities of the Indians, they had taken care to leave nothing exposed. They were occupied with their sacks, when Meyer stepped in, and, holding up his hand, exclaimed:

"Doctor, do you know what I have here?"

"How can I know? Has the cazique conferred on you the fourth class of the order of the Blue Condor, in acknowledgment of your lack of merit?"

"Your buttons!" said Meyer, holding out his well-filled hand to him. "What do you say now?"

"Indeed, I would recommend to the German police the vigilance of that of the Penchuenches, which seems to be so efficient."

"Oh, Meyer," said Reiwald, "do me the favor of informing the cazique that the Indians have stolen my knife. I will pay a suitable reward to him who brings it back; at any rate, I will let him choose between my everlasting gratitude and half a roll of tobacco."

"I will tell him of it when I see him," replied Meyer; "but I must first pack up, for we are really about to start. The cazique himself has sent out his men to collect our horses, and they have already brought in some of them. But what are you going to do, doctor? Unpack your baggage again?"

"I merely want to sew on my buttons. They are all here—not one wanting."

"But make haste."

"I shall be done long before you are ready."

Pfeifel had hardly promised too much, though the horses arrived more speedily than he had expected; however, he was not called upon to assist in loading them, for a number of Penchuenches, headed by Cruzado, entered, and the sacks and saddles were removed in an incredibly short time. Now all was in readiness. Don Enrique, in the saddle, seemed to await in impatience the time when they were to speed across the Pampas.

Tchalusk galloped down the street on

a noble black horse; he had tied a new blue ribbon around his hair, but was poorly dressed, having on a particularly mean poncho, so that even his warriors looked more decent than himself. He held his head proudly erect, glancing around in all directions, and whenever he stretched out his arm, his men hastened to obey him. He ruled by terrifying the hearts of his people, and had punished disobedience in so ferocious a manner that no one dared give him cause for dissatisfaction.

Don Enrique rode to meet him, and, holding out his hand, he requested Cruzado to tell him that he was exceedingly obliged for his hospitality, which he would never forget, and would more liberally reward him for the reception he had met with.

The cazique nodded kindly. "It is good," he said; "we were glad to be able to render you service. May Jenkitrum be as favorably disposed toward you! After attaining your object, return to our camp, and my young men shall convey you safely across the lagoon, and escort you to the frontier. Farewell."

A large number of mounted Penchuenches surrounded the party, which now passed the cazique at a brisk trot. Last of all came the three Germans among the drivers of the pack-horses. Cruzado halted by the side of the cazique.

"Ah! amigo!" exclaimed Tchaluak, and beckoned to the doctor. A few words which the cazique said to his men brought them in the way of Pfeifel's horse, which they led aside, and our friend, without knowing exactly how it happened, suddenly halted in front of the cazique.

"Ah," exclaimed Tchaluak, smiling, on fixing his eyes on the cloak, and seeing that all the buttons had been replaced, "that is right. Tell them, Cruzado, that I intend to bestow on him a special mark of honor in acknowledgment of the skill with which he healed one of my warriors. I will exchange my poncho for his cloak, and he may wear mine in commemoration of his visit to our camp."

Cruzado, who cast a glance on the cazique's garment, could hardly repress a smile, but he translated the words to Meyer, who, with a very grave air, congratulated the doctor on the distinction bestowed on him, and requested him to doff quickly his cloak and present it to the cazique. Meanwhile Tchaluak divested himself of his poncho and held it in his hand.

"Well, it is just what I expected," said Pfeifel. "I know, too, why he insisted on the buttons being returned to me. But it is better for a man to lose his cloak than his scalp. There—tell the red rogue that he had better hang himself in my cloak on the next tree."

So saying, he unbuttoned the cloak and handed it to Cruzado, who was by his side. The cazique's face meantime beamed with joy, and he stretched out his arm greedily for the coveted treasure.

"What did the Aleman say?"

"He said he wished that the poncho would protect your body and be impenetrable to the arms of your enemies," replied Cruzado, who never was at a loss for an answer.

The cazique waved his hand cheerfully, and, as Meyer at this moment whipped the doctor's horse, the animal leaped forward, and a few seconds afterward the travellers galloped along the shore toward the point where the Nontue and Huetchun Lagoons are connected, across which lies the road leading to the east.

An old Indian kept a ferry here, or rather a raft, and had also built on the north side a sort of hut, in which he could live during the winter-time, for the tribes camped there only temporarily, when the apples were ripening. In the summer-time they lived farther in the interior, where there were finer pastures and more game, such as guanacos, ostriches, and casowaries. The passage was effected with great rapidity, as all the Indians helped them with the utmost readiness. In a short time the horses were unloaded again, and the saddles and sacks laid on the raft. The ferryman had to cross the connecting arm three times before the travellers and their baggage had all been conveyed over. The Penchuenches drove the animals into the water, that they might swim to the opposite shore, and in about an hour and a half they were able to proceed.

Don Enrique rewarded the ferryman liberally, for he felt only too happy to see the Pampas before him, and he leaped with almost youthful agility into the saddle. He had had an impression that the men which the cazique had sent would accompany him only as far as the last lagoon, for it is customary for the Indians to honor a distinguished visitor by furnishing him with an imposing escort. But the Penchuenches had also taken along pack-horses with tents and poles, and seemed to be prepared for a considerable expedition. Crusado explained that they were required to go to the Limai or Jenkitruss's camp, and thence back to Tchaluak's tribe; but he took good care not to communicate the reason which had induced the cazique to adopt this course. The old man's heart was already heavy enough; he did not wish to add to his sorrows.

The party, however, were not detained by this addition to its numbers, for the Indians had fresh and excellent horses, and they are not in the habit of sparing them. From the moment they are in the saddle they continue to travel at a gallop, and when tired encamp and wait, often for weeks, until men and horses are capable of renewed efforts.

Their pack-horses were singular creatures and seemed to belong to a peculiar race, having shorter legs than the others, and any thing but prepossessing, with large square heads and protruding nostrils; they were very strong, with broad, powerful backs, and, as it were, iron limbs, resembling in their appearance the Percherons of the French, but a great deal clumsier, though certainly equal to them in speed and perseverance. The others were more slender, but all possessed broad chests and strong limbs. Beauty was of no importance on the Pampas, where only speed could be useful to the rider. The Indians have no use for fancy horses; the pony that carries him must be able to gallop for twelve, nay sixteen, hours in succession; then graze in the night, and set out at daybreak on the following morning. None but very strong horses could stand this.

A strange feeling stole over the two Germans, as, after a short ride, they left the last trees behind them, and now, surrounded by the wild Penchuenches, rode out into the Pampas.

"Doctor," said Reiwald, who was a good horseman, and already acted as though the saddle were his proper place, "I think all this is very fine; does it not seem to you like a dream?"

"I could not say that exactly," replied Doctor Pfeifel, who had not yet forgotten the loss of his cloak, and therefore did not rejoice as much as his friend did at their romantic surroundings; "if it were all a dream, I would certainly have awakened, for my ride is not very comfortable."

"But is it not beautiful here, doctor?" exclaimed Reiwald, gazing in delight upon the plain, and observing the figures on either side. "Look at those fine fellows with their waving hair—how gracefully they go! They are real Indians, and we might exhibit them for money in Germany; what do you think of engaging them for Kroll's garden at Berlin? It would be a lucrative speculation."

"But, in that event, we should also have to make a contract with the executioner of Berlin,* for furnishing them with horse-flesh."

"Do not talk so on such a morning as this; you should object to my idea less than any of us, for in your poncho you present a startling appearance, exactly like a European turned into a savage. I wish we were photographed at this moment!"

Pfeifel cast a glance of dissatisfaction

* The executioners in Germany remove dead animals, etc., from the streets.

and made no reply. The reminiscence was by no means agreeable to him.

"Well," laughed Meyer, who galloped over to them, "how do you like it this morning? The weather is very fine. On the wooded side of the Cordilleras the rainy season sets in a week earlier than here; it is generally far more inclement. I trust we shall have no rain until to-morrow, and, unless Jenkitrusa is encamped too high up the Limai, we may arrive at our destination by to-morrow evening. I wish we were already safe over the river."

"Never mind," laughed Reiwald, who, with the blue sky over him, and refreshed by the brisk ride, thought not of danger, "we shall get through—a man can do all that he earnestly intends to do.—By-the-way, Meyer, did you not speak to the cacique this morning about my knife?"

"I did," replied Meyer, nodding with a smile.

"Well—and—?"

"He said you had better go to the mischief; he had more important business to attend to than hunting up other people's knives."

"But the buttons?"

"Yes," laughed the German, "they were not 'other people's' buttons, but his own, which he did not want to be stolen from him."

"*Tout comme chez nous,*" murmured Reiwald. "But the scenery, the charm of the new wild life, soon dispelled all other thoughts from his mind. Tell me, Don Carlos, how does it happen that we see no game in the plain? I thought we should meet with plenty."

"Well, there are guanacos, though Cruzado tells me not as many as on the other side of the Limai, but there are said to be no cassowaries here at all, because too many Indians traverse this territory, surrounded as it is by rivers and lagoons. We shall see game enough on the other bank, but we have little time to spare."

"Is the flesh of the guanacos palatable?"

"Excellent."

"And what about that of the ostriches and cassowaries?"

"Still better," replied Don Carlos, laughing; "you roast the leg of an old cassowary, and you have something to while your time away with all night long; you have no idea how tough the meat is."

"Indeed!" exclaimed Reiwald.

"You will discover it by-and-by," said Meyer.

Meanwhile the cavalcade was speeding across the Pampas, where the cold breeze had long since dried the surface. Only here and there, at the bottom of slight undulations, were to be seen ponds whence rose flocks of wild ducks. Reiwald at first seized his rifle involuntarily, but it was impossible for him to halt and fire; his companions would have been out of sight before he could reload his rifle. He could not therefore indulge his sporting propensities.

Even the doctor looked sadly after the disappearing birds. "There are dainties," he said, "to which a Christian might sit down with pleasure; but these Indians never think of the appetite of their civilized guests."

The travellers pressed onward. When Reiwald once looked back, the grove of apple-trees, surrounding the lagoon, was already so remote that it looked like a meadow. Onward they sped; before them extended the vast plain, with its wave-like undulations. Whether they ascended or descended, the Indians never rode the less rapidly, and the old Chileno, mounted on his white horse, and riding with youthful grace, led the way toward his eastern destination, for which his heart yearned.

CHAPTER XXVII.

ACROSS THE LIMAI.

The travellers galloped all day without exchanging horses, in accordance with the custom of the Penchuenches; only once, toward two o'clock in the afternoon, on reaching a rivulet, they stopped, and half an hour's rest was allowed. They then resumed their journey till nightfall, when there was scarcely light left to make their camp. There were now no trees whatever; on the road, they had here and there met with a few stunted groups, and the Penchuenches had gathered some fruits, but they were hard and unpalatable, and could serve only to quench their thirst.

As they were to sleep in the open air, the Germans were again out of their element and well-nigh hopeless. In the forest they had been able to spread their blankets under a tree, to collect dry wood, plenty of which was to be found, and light and supply a fire; but here a cold wind swept by, and a heavy dew was covering the plain.

"Say, doctor," said Reiwald; "I really do not know how we are to get along; for, although we were told at Valdivia that there were no trees on the

Pampas, I never thought of fuel. I hope our friends are not such brutes as to eat raw horse-flesh."

"This will be another dreadful night," sighed Pfeifel; "I am already chilled. How fortunate it is that it does not rain!"

"That would be bad. Prescribe a cup of hot tea for me. I do not feel well."

"Gentlemen," said Meyer, approaching them, "if you wish to have supper to-night, you must help us to get fuel. After dark, we shall not be able to find any."

"Well, Don Carlos," replied Reiwald, "I believe we could not by sunlight. Show me a tree in the neighborhood."

"There are none here," laughed Meyer, "and we cannot burn wood; we must look around for different fuel. These dried chips (meaning the excrements of cattle) are as good as peat, and burn well in fair weather."

"And are we to cook our supper with them?"

"I should be glad if you had other fuel, but we must use them, and fortunately there is plenty about here."

"Well, that is not so bad," said the doctor, "but what are we to gather them in? If we had a basket—"

"A basket! That is entirely superfluous so long as you have a poncho, which will serve as well. If you find any thistle-stems bring them along—they also burn well, but do not last long; we use them for kindling."

Some of the Indians were searching for fuel, while others attended to the horses, fastening several with lassos to posts fixed in the ground, to keep the rest near them. Nothing remained for Reiwald and his friend but to follow the example set them, for they ought to render at least some assistance in order to have the right of hanging their kettle over the fire. They went therefore where the Indians had not yet been, and were quite successful. Meanwhile it had grown so dark that they could not distinguish any thing on the ground. Reiwald raised himself up and groaned, rubbing his back with his right hand; on his left arm was his poncho, which held what he had gathered.

"My spine!—I am not much accustomed to stooping."

"Reiwald," said the doctor, who stood before him with a mournful air, "suppose our friends in Berlin could see us now, and observe our occupation?"

"It is a very becoming one. We probably emigrated to engage in it. I believe we might have done better at home."

"It is a hard life, this," murmured the doctor, "If we knew all this beforehand!"

"But now that we are here, we must endure patiently what happens. Away with sentiment! I am becoming a fatalist, and believe that Fate has predestinated me."

"For this?" asked the doctor, pointing to Reiwald's load. "In that case, you ought not to have troubled yourself about jurisprudence."

"Well, at least for this wild mode of life. If I find a woman that suits me, I may settle down and become a Ponchuencha."

"Do not talk so sneeringly. Who knows what may yet be in store for us?

It seems to be very easy to get into this country, but difficult to find the way out. I do not trust that thief Tchalnak at all, and Jenkitrum still less. What are we to do if they refuse to let us return to Chili?"

A shout from the camp interrupted the conversation; it had grown very dark, and, as Meyer had lost sight of them, he believed they had lost their way. There was a faint gleam, emanating from the fire just kindled. The Germans followed it after responding to the shout; and, on their arrival at the camp, they threw down their fuel. The night passed without any extraordinary event. The sky remained moderately clear—at least, it did not rain. They started early on the following morning, mounting some of their extra horses and leading others, while those with the packs had to continue the journey with the same loads.

The Pampas presented the same monotonous spectacle; they met with a few spots covered with brushwood, at a distance having a resemblance to trees—an illusion arising from unequal refraction in the lower strata of the atmosphere. Little was to be seen, save flocks of wild ducks, and at times some horses, that fled as soon as they beheld the approach of the strangers. There was a small herd of guanacoes, which squatted in the grass as the party passed, and then, suddenly springing to their feet, made their escape. Several Indians seemed inclined to pursue them, but Don Enrique gave them no time. Onward was his only thought, and nothing could swerve him from his path.

It was about four in the afternoon when they first caught sight of the Limal. Meyer had been riding for some time at Cruzado's side, and the half-breed pointed out to him that they were close to the banks of a river. One has to be familiar with the vegetation of the Pampas to know that he approaches water, for nothing else indicates it.

"Tell me, Don Carlos," inquired Reiwald, "if we shall reach the river to-day. Cruzado said we should reach the Limal on the evening of the second day."

"There it is already!" exclaimed Meyer, stretching out his arm.

"What?"

"The Limal."

"Where? I do not see any thing but the plain."

"Do you see that patch of shrubs yonder?"

"At the ravine?"

"That is the Limal."

"And yet that half-breed asserted we should have to swim it; but I will engage to leap over it!"

"You had better try," said Meyer.

"Why, it can hardly be ten yards wide."

"Wait and see," said Meyer. "On these prairies illusions are very common, so that we never can say exactly what is before us. The Limal is a very wide river, and, as for your jumping across it, you will soon have another opinion."

"But if that is the Limal, where are the Indians? Jenkitrum, we were told, is encamped on the opposite shore, and there is nothing to be seen in that direction."

"Yes," replied Meyer, "I have also been looking for their camp, and who knows if they are farther up or down the river? At all events, it will be necessary to send messengers; we shall stop on the bank."

"I do not like the appearance of the sky; it looks again like rain," said Reiwald.

"Who can help it?" was the reply. "We must try to make the best of it."

The attention of the travellers was now engrossed by the river lying before them, for every thing depended on the condition in which they would find it. If there had been heavy rains in the Cordilleras and farther down south, they would be unable to cross; and yet it is so shallow in summer that the water reaches only up to the knees of the horses, and at many places children are able to wade it. They advanced quickly, for the mirage of the Pampas is the reverse of that of the Cordilleras, where objects seem to be near when it takes you almost a day to reach them. In the plain, we see often, seemingly at a great distance before us, an extensive forest, which we reach in half an hour, when it turns out to be but a wilderness of insignificant shrubs.

The travellers approached the river very rapidly, but the nearer they came, the more it widened, and they soon discovered that the Limai was a stream which it seemed impossible to ford at that time.

"Why do you not leap?" said Meyer to Reiwald.

"Indeed!" replied Reiwald, in surprise, "it is a great deal wider than I thought; and are we to cross it?"

"If we intend to reach the cacique; for I think he will not come over to us."

"And not a vestige of human life is to be seen on the other side! What are the Indians looking for so close to the water?"

"They have probably found the point where the river is shallowest; but never mind them; they will soon make up for it. In such things they cannot be beaten, and are worth more than a secret council of state."

The Indians were looking for some time for a ford, and one galloped up and another down the river-bank. Presently they seemed to have found the wished-for signs, for, at a yell uttered by the Indian who had galloped to the left, the rest of his companions started immediately in the same direction. To all appearances, they had discovered that Jenkitrum had encamped nearer the Ouru-Loufu or Black River, and the horsemen now started in that direction.— Scarcely had they continued this course an hour, when the man leading the way stopped again and talked excitedly, pointing over to the other side. As Oruzado told Meyer, they believed that they saw smoke, and the doctor turned his telescope in that direction. Scarcely had he done so, when he exclaimed:

"There they are! What eyes these fellows have! Even through this glass the tents look like specks."

The Indians now gathered inquisitively round the doctor to ascertain what he had seen; but no one would take the glass himself. When, indeed, the doctor offered it to any of them, they started back, as if afraid lest harm should befall them. But they wished to know what he had seen, and nodded constantly: There was a large tent surrounded by a great many smaller ones; horses or cattle, he could not distinctly make out which, were grazing on the bank; it seemed, besides, as if there were still other tents up the river.

One of the Penchuenches, who appeared to be the leader of the escort, exclaimed, confirming what he had heard from the doctor, "There are the apo's tents!" And, without listening to Don Enrique's advice, he dismounted, and ordered his men to unload the horses. The Chileno intended to protest against this, for he hoped to reach the camp on that very evening, but Cruzado shook his head and told him there was no possibility of crossing. In approaching the tent of the supreme cazique, they would have to proceed with due deliberation. He, therefore, followed the example of the others, and the old man, sighing, had to submit to what could not be helped.

The camp was made in the same manner as the day before; but they found here plenty of fuel which the flood had carried down, and now, as it was not very high, had left on the banks. But the wind was an inconvenience, for after sunrise it became so violent that they were hardly able to kindle a fire, and, in fact, did not succeed until they had erected a barrier of stones, sand, and mud, behind which the flames were protected.

At first the gale seemed to blow from the south, but afterward turned more toward the east, when it increased to a hurricane; on passing to the north, it abated somewhat, and ended in a gentle breeze from the west. It raged with such impetuosity that the travellers had to extinguish the fire, because it scattered ashes and sparks over the sleepers, and thereby threatened to burn their clothes. It was not until morning that it moderated, and by that time the sky was clear again.

From the camp of the Indians their presence had been already noticed, for the flames could not but be seen, and horsemen halted at daybreak on the opposite bank.

"Reiwald," exclaimed Pfeifel, who was the first to discover them, "look there! I never saw any thing more picturesque in my life than the figures yonder, with their waving ponchos and hair, and their long lances. What fine horses they have! See how proudly the black one in front throws back its head."

"Yes," said Reiwald, "I like them well enough so long as there is a river between us; but, in near proximity, as for instance last night, with my nose on an Indian's shoulder in order not to freeze to death, I think they are well-nigh intolerable; their perspiration is any thing but pleasant."

The Indians on the other bank shouted something, which was responded to. On each side yells were uttered, but they doubtless had a meaning well understood, for those opposite suddenly turned their horses and rode rapidly across the Pampas, becoming smaller until they disappeared in the mist covering the plain. Meanwhile breakfast was prepared, but, that no time might be wasted, the horses were loaded again. If the old Chileno had had his way, they would not have taken time to eat, for he stood with his hand leaning on the pommel, and ordered the others to mount; but Cruzado interfered.

"Patience, my friend; we must remain a long time on this side of the river, until Jenkitruss permits us to cross over. He knows that we are coming, and that is sufficient; it will be noonday at least before he concludes his deliberations with the chiefs now present at his camp. You are not yet familiar with the habits of the Penchuenches."

On setting out again, the travellers did not continue their journey, as heretofore, at a gallop, but at a moderate trot, along the bank of the rapidly-flowing Limal. The remainder of the distance to the cacique's camp was not considerable, for they had scarcely been half an hour in the saddle when they could distinguish with the naked eye tents, men, and herds.

On the other bank there was also quite a commotion; a large concourse assembled, and before long the whole population seemed to have left the tents in order to gaze at the approaching strangers. The Pampas indeed offer so few interruptions to the usual mode of life there that such a visit created a great deal of excitement. The women especially, who believed the new-comers to be traders, were highly delighted.

But how was communication with the Indians to be established? Meyer laughed on being asked by the doctor if a bridge did not cross the river. There was not even a ferry-boat, and to swim the river, which was at least one hundred and twenty yards wide, seemed impossible, or, at all events, exceedingly dangerous. But Cruzado overcame this difficulty much more rapidly than they expected, for, after exchanging a few words with the Penchuenches, who had escorted them thus far, and who seemed to be somewhat dissatisfied with him, he suddenly rode down the bank, and before the Germans fully comprehended what he intended to do, his horse plunged into the water and struggled vigorously against the current.

The half-breed, who had previously thrown off his saddle-bags in order to render it less difficult to swim, sat intrepidly in the saddle, and kept his eyes firmly fixed on the opposite shore. He reached the middle of the river, where his horse found footing on a shoal of considerable extent, which in the dry season was probably above the surface. Cruzado stopped scarcely a minute, plunging again into the water and quickly approaching the other side. The horseman dismounted, patted his animal's neck, and led it slowly up.

"Ah," exclaimed Reiwald, who with a throbbing heart had followed the movements of Cruzado; "the passage is by far easier than I thought. My white horse will swim the river as rapidly."

"It is a miserable job," said the doctor; "and the worst is, that if we are successful, we shall have to retrace our steps before long."

"Cruzado is a smart fellow," remarked Reiwald, and proceeded to unsaddle his horse, for he noticed that the Indians were again engaged in lighting a fire, and, to all appearance, contemplating a delay for some time.

The half-breed was by no means a stranger to the soil on which he had now set foot. For many a season he had lived and hunted with the natives, and Mankelaw the brother of Jenkitrusa, seemed to be partial to him, and was loath to allow him at that time to return to Chili, for Cruzado, he said, had less in common with the whites than with the Penchuenches. The Indians always had need of men familiar with the Spanish language, since they held occasional intercourse, not only with the Chilenos, but with the Argentines, at distant Fort Carmen, and often received messages from the Argentine Government. The only difficulty however was, that Cruzado could neither read nor write, and when a dispatch arrived, who was to decipher it? But he had not permitted himself to be detained, for he did not make any money on the Pampas; and, poor as he was, he desired first to accumulate a small capital to purchase the necessary horses and tents; afterward he would be of some importance among the Pehuenches, who had hitherto looked upon him as an insignificant fellow, seeking his daily bread at the hands of the different tribes. He desired to be considered by them as a free and independent man, and Mankelaw loved him only the more for this determination. On ascending the precipitous bank, he joyfully recognized his friend among the persons awaiting him.

"Ah, Cruzado," exclaimed the young chief, hastening to meet him, "you have returned to the Pampas? Well done, my friend, and I am sure you intend to stay with us, for otherwise you would have chosen a different season."

"Cazique Mankelaw, I am glad to see you," said Cruzado, while the chief embraced him after the fashion of the country; "I hardly hoped to meet you here."

"My brother is cazique—I am not," said the young man, smilingly; "bestow that title upon him—I am your friend. And now, come; our young men have just killed a mare, and our hunters have brought us this morning two guanacos. We have plenty to eat, and also warm furs and a tent for you."

"But I do not come alone."

"Whom do you bring with you? Traders from Chili? Are they eager to cross the mountains at the commencement of the rainy season? They will sell what they brought with them, and then consume what they get, before returning home."

"They are not traders."

"Not traders?" exclaimed the young chief, in surprise.

"No—the chief of the expedition is an old man from Chili, whose younger daughter your brother carried off, and he now comes to offer him a ransom for her."

"Jenkitrum—yes—I know it," he murmured to himself, after a pause, "and I wish you success with all my heart; but you could not have arrived at a more unfavorable juncture."

"Why?"

"I can tell you no more now. Come, eat and drink, and dry your clothes. Your horse is a good swimmer—you crossed the river very rapidly."

Cruzado was too much of an Indian not to know that he could no longer converse on a subject after a chief had once dismissed it. Pacioncia! He had often repeated this word to the old Chileno—he now murmured it to himself—and thereupon followed the invitation as quietly and unconcernedly as if he had swam the Limai, for the sole purpose of visiting the young chief.

CHAPTER XXVIII.

JENKITRUSS.

Mankelaw had a habitation of his own, in which he lived with his two young wives. He conducted Cruzado into the front room, which was separated from the other part of the tent by means of furs. A fire was burning, and while in another room food was prepared for the visitor, the chief gave him warm clothes, and carried his guest's away to dry them.

Cruzado had taken nothing with him across the river, except tobacco enough to last him for several days, and some to spare for his friends. He knew how welcome such a gift is in a cazique's tent. Mankelaw's face was radiant with joy when the interpreter cut him off a large piece, and handed it to him.

"And where is Jenkitruss?" asked the half-breed.

"Here. Did you not see his tent?"

"Does he intend to remain here long, or is he going over to the apple-trees? Tchaluak and his tribe are now there."

"I know it," replied Mankelaw, and his features darkened again; "Jenkitruss has already sent a messenger to call him over, but he declared that he could not force his men away from there until they had consumed all the chicha. I believe he himself is averse to leaving before that time."

Both were silent again, and slowly blew the smoke through their noses.

"Tchaluak is a powerful chief," said Cruzado, after a long pause, and Mankelaw cast a quick, distrustful glance on him.

"What do you mean?" he asked.

"He has many connections," replied the half-breed, cautiously; "his messengers have returned from the north and east."

"Ha! Did you see any of them?"

"He made no secret of it."

Mankelaw was silent; he lay stretched out on his guanaco-skin, leaning on his left elbow, and smoking in silence. A very pretty young woman brought in the food in a large wooden dish, placed it silently near the fire, and disappeared. The chief did not bestow a glance upon her.

"And he refused to believe it when I told him so," he said at last. "Day after day I have given him warning; I have often entreated him to send me over with my men; no, all was in vain, and the danger will overwhelm him before he is aware of its existence."

"And what dims his eyes?"

"A phantom—the formation of a confederacy of the tribes for the annihilation of the whites—the recovery of the territory occupied by the latter."

"But he is on friendly terms with the whites."

"He was friendly toward individuals, but the last events in Chili—the disrespectful manner in which he was treated there, the outrage perpetrated upon his envoy, who was made prisoner and bound hand and foot—have aroused his wrath, and this is the reason why I told you previously that your white friends could not have chosen a more unfavorable time to demand the restoration of what has become—perhaps to his own ruin—the property of the cazique."

"His property?"

"The white girl is his wife," said Mankelaw, gloomily.

"And, you say, to his own ruin!"

"Because it brought hatred and discord into the midst of his own family," replied the Indian. The brother of his lost young wife is one of the wealthiest and most distinguished Penchuenches; he had a quarrel with Jenkitruss, and left the camp in high dudgeon, and it was only the day before yesterday that we were informed that he had gone to the Argentines at Fort Carmen.

"But you are at peace with the Argentines?"

"A curse on the dogs!" cried the Indian, starting up. "As long as they pay us tribute, they may live; but if they dare again refuse it—" He bit his teeth and looked angry.

"The old Chileno is wealthy," said Cruzado, who had been absorbed in his thoughts; "he will give up his whole fortune to ransom his child."

"Bah! what can he offer us that we have not, and in abundance? Horses! The Pampas teem with them, and the Argentines must furnish us four hundred mares a year. Plate! Jenkitruss's horse is scarcely able to bear the silver with which its saddle and trappings are mounted. What wearing apparel we need is woven by our women—and arms! What need has a Penchuenche of what he could not take himself from his enemies?"

"But costly knives," said Cruzado. "Indigo to dye your stuffs, beautiful silk handkerchiefs, warm woollen blankets, tobacco, trinkets for your wives and daughters—in short, there are a great many things which are not to be found on the Pampas, and which are valuable to you."

"And though you were right," said Mankelaw, "you would not find my brother at this time disposed to listen to such offers, much less to grant a favor to the very pale face that wounded his pride. As he told me himself, the girl is the daughter of the man at whose house the messenger dispatched by him was attacked. Now, Jenkitruss was not at all on the war-path, but had crossed the Cordilleras with peaceable designs. The whites compelled him to assume a hostile attitude, and he might have afterward gained a great deal of booty, and carried off a number of women, but he took only one, to punish the traitor."

"I believe Don Enrique's peon reported that two women were carried off."

"Yes," smiled Mankelaw. "Saman—you remember him—a panther at which he threw his lasso jumped at him and scratched him badly—brought with him a young wife from the settlements. I believe he would not turn a deaf ear to you, but let you have her cheap."

"But Don Enrique asserts," said Cruzado, "that the Indian envoy was arrested by the Chilian soldiers, not only without his knowledge, but against his will."

"The whites have forked tongues," replied the chief, contemptuously. "Who will believe his assertion? The outrage was perpetrated at his own house, and never will he persuade Jenkitruss that he was innocent of it."

"But will he not at least listen to him?"

Mankelaw shrugged his shoulders.

"Who can tell beforehand what he will do?" he said, doubtingly. "I believe he will not even permit him to cross the river, and, though he should, he would not tolerate his presence at the camp."

"Is the girl here?"

Mankelaw made no reply, but looked thoughtfully, and Cruzado felt that he had gone too far. Quickly dropping the subject, he continued:

"There are also some Germans among us—strange people, who, to all appearances, have grown up among tall houses, and are perfectly helpless on the Pampas; at least two of them are. The third is an old friend of mine, and has been a long time in this country."

"Are they traders?"

"No; they have joined the expedition merely for the purpose of visiting this region?"

"During the rainy season?" said Mankelaw, shaking his head. "They are strange people, indeed; but the Alemanos are the best whites, peaceable and reliable, and Jenkitruss likes them; nay, he has taken them into account in laying his plans, for he hopes that they will be his allies. You know, Cruzado, that they are relatives of ours."

"I have been told," said Cruzado, "that once upon a time a ship of theirs stranded on the eastern shore."

"And the Penchnenches are descended from that shipwrecked crew," replied the Indian, proudly; "the Alemanos and Penchnenches were formerly one tribe."

"And will Jenkitruss permit the Germans to come to the camp?"

"I believe he will. But we shall see. You may speak to him yourself; he is well acquainted with you, and knows that you are a friend of mine. But what do Tchalnak's warriors want here? If they come as messengers of their cazique, why did they not cross? They are now encamped on the opposite bank."

"Tchalnak instructed them to escort us."

"To escort you! Tchalnak!"

"I will afterward tell you more about it, Mankelaw," replied Cruzado, gravely. "Tchalnak is treacherous and insidious; he is bent on mischief against all of you; beware of him. He revealed, when intoxicated, more than was prudent."

"Beware of *him*!" cried Mankelaw, laughing disdainfully. "If I were allowed to cross the Limal, you might caution him against me."

"But, I repeat it, he is bent on mischief against you."

"Let us go," said Mankelaw, pushing back the dish, from which both of them had hitherto eaten unceremoniously with their fingers. "Come, Jenkitruss heard last night of your arrival, and he is doubtless looking for us now;" and, followed by Cruzado, he walked slowly toward the dwelling of the supreme cazique, which he alone was at liberty to set foot in without having obtained permission.

Cruzado remained respectfully outside until permitted to enter; but he was kept waiting long, which, he thought, portended the failure of his mission. It seemed to him, though he kept at some distance from the entrance, as though he heard loud voices in the tent—even Mankelaw seemed to exercise no influence over his brother. The half-breed, with arms folded, was patiently pacing up and down outside.—He was unable to accelerate the matter, and he had, perhaps, lingered an hour, when the door at length opened again, and Mankelaw beckoned to his friend to come in.

The tent, or rather a house, was made of furs; its roof and walls consisted of skins skilfully sewed together, so that not the slightest breath of air could penetrate into the interior; the floor was covered with soft guanaco-skins in the most lavish manner, while the next partition consisted of trophies gained by Jenkitrum himself—the hides of beasts, whose heads and paws had not been removed. The light fell on the side protected from the wind, where the walls were arranged, so that they could be quickly opened and shut by means of strings.

Tchaluak, too, had a similar habitation, but it was by no means so richly furnished as Jenkitrum's, and doubtless large numbers of pack-horses were required to convey it from one camping-ground to another.

Jenkitrum stood in the middle of the front room, opposite his couch, which was covered with a superb American tiger-skin. He was tall and well-proportioned, with open, honest features, a Grecian nose of almost faultless regularity, a small, moist hand expressive dark eyes, to which the defiant spirit gleaming in them lent an air of singular ferocity. His complexion, like that of many Penchuenches, was not so copper-colored as that of the tribes living farther south. He had even a lighter color than many living on the western slopes of the Cordilleras, and similar to the Cayapas in Ecuador. He wore a light party-colored poncho, with arabesques skilfully woven in the stuff, but he was bareheaded, like all the rest, and had tied about his forehead a red and blue ribbon, only in order to keep his hair out of his face.

When Cruzado entered, Jenkitrum fixed his eyes long and searchingly, but not unkindly on him, and then, holding out his hand to him, he said quietly:

"You are welcome, Cruzado. It is a long time since the hoofs of your horse trod the Pampas."

"I always longed for the merry and unrestrained life on this side of the mountains, cazique," replied the half-breed, shaking hands with the Indian; "I never like to remain long in the settlements."

"You are welcome," repeated Jenkitrum, "although I regret that you have performed so long a journey in vain."

"In vain, cazique!"

"You must be hungry—"

"Mankelaw was kind enough to give me plenty of food."

"Very well—he will assign to you a tent where you may stay, for you cannot now return."

"And my companions, cazique!"

"There are a great many of them. What do Tchaluak's men want on the other side of the Limai? I did not call them."

"Nor did I request their company and protection, Jenkitrum, for I knew that I should be among friends."

"And what do they want!"

"They are waiting for us to set out for Chili."

"I will put their patience to the test," said the cazique, gloomily. "You supposed your commission a very easy one, my friend."

"The cazique Jenkitrum," said Cruzado, quietly, "has always shown himself to be a magnanimous foe, striking down his adversaries in battle, but forbearing and merciful after triumphing over them."

"Always!" exclaimed Jenkitrusa, laughing defiantly and scornfully; "did I treat my adversaries in that manner at the time we took by storm the palisaded fort of the Argentine thieves? There is not one of them alive to tell the story."

"They were men, Jenkitrusa, and—enemies."

"Very well," said the cazique, waving his hand, "we shall see about it.— What do the whites concern you? You are one of us; and what good did they do our country except clearing the forests and expelling the legitimate owners from their hunting-grounds? We are the masters here, and often we have sent them home with bloody heads when their arrogance brought them into our Pampas. May Pillan's wrath overtake them! What have we to do with them but to annihilate them whenever they throw obstacles in our way?"

"And are all the Peuchuenches animated with the same spirit?" said Cruzado, seeking for another point on which to turn his argument.

"What do you mean?" asked the cazique.

"If they all thought like you, Jenkitrusa," added Cruzado, "never could the pale-faces have obtained a footing on this soil, and even now it would be possible to drive them into the sea. But what was the reason why the Araucanians were defeated by them lately, their country traversed by white hordes, their huts burned, their herds driven off? The hatred and jealousy animating the caziques toward each other, on the other side of the mountains, as well as here on the Pampas. Was even your own arm powerful enough to cause them all to rally around the supreme leader?"

Jenkitrusa folded his arms on his breast. Cruzado was right: at the time he intended to succor the Araucanians with all his forces, many of the caziques opposed his plan, especially Tchaloak. But he resisted the thoughts which Mankelaw had also awakened in him from time to time. He was loath to brood over them, and yet they filled his heart. He beckoned to Cruzado to leave, who complied immediately.

Mankelaw accompanied him. From the time Cruzado had entered the tent, the young chief had not uttered a word. When they were again in the open air, he said:

"Well, was I right? Your Chileno will have a bad time of it during the winter, and he will be obliged to go home without accomplishing his purpose; for I know my brother. He is good and honest, but at the same time his spirit is as inflexible as iron, and all our words, so far from causing him to change his mind, will only add to his obstinacy."

"Poor Don Enrique," sighed Cruzado; "and how longingly he is now looking over to these tents, where he knows is his beloved child! How hopeful he is that he will soon fold his daughter again to his heart! I dare not meet him face to face."

"Then dispatch a messenger to him," exclaimed Mankelaw, "and send him word that the cazique refuses his presents, and will not grant his request."

"Jenkitrum did not tell me that," cried Cruzado, hastily.

"But he told me," replied Mankelaw. "He has made up his mind to keep the girl."

"And, notwithstanding my reluctance, I must return. The Chileno would consider me a traitor if I shrank from meeting him again. And how are the men yonder to pass the winter without tents and provisions? Game is very scarce on the other side of the river, and I cannot even tell whether or not they know how to hunt it. I wish the cazique had permitted them at least to cross."

"Is not the river open?" said Mankelaw. "Did any one prevent you from swimming it?"

"But how are they to convey their baggage—all the presents which they have brought along?"

"Come," said Mankelaw, without answering the question, "let me show you now your own sleeping-place. I will take you to Allumapu's tent; there is room enough for both, and you are well acquainted with him. When I was a bachelor, you stayed at my tent, but things are changed now."

While they walked toward Allumapu's tent, they met a white man, who passed them without a greeting, limping, but with a defiant air, and Cruzado involuntarily looked after him.

"You wonder at meeting here a white man?" said the young chief, laughing. "There are two of them here. This one is an Argentine, whom our warriors captured in Chili."

"An Argentine in Chili?"

"Yes; he is, moreover, an old acquaintance of ours, and lived for some time among us, until he one day disappeared with a number of our best horses. Since then he has not shown his face again, and, although we know that he had crossed the mountains, we were unable to ascertain his whereabouts, until one of Jenkitrum's men caught him and handled him roughly. He was unable to stir for two weeks, but he seems to have recovered."

"But what is to be done with him?"

"Messengers have been dispatched to Tooreopan and Palliacan, the caziques to whom belonged the horses stolen at the time. We are looking daily for their return; those caziques may then decide on his fate. He is a thief, and deserves death."

"And who is the other man?"

"A Chileno officiating as Jenkitrum's *escribano*."

"As Jenkitrum's secretary?" exclaimed Cruzado. "Jenkitrum has much writing to do, then?"

Mankelaw laughed.

"The only pen we use is our lance," he said; "but the Argentine Government sends messenger after messenger, now with presents, now with the tribute, but always with the same prayer—to-day from this, to-morrow from that white cazique of theirs, who happens to be in the ascendant—that we shall assist them in their wars."

"Well," exclaimed Cruzado, "if they sent to me a messenger ignorant of my language, I should at once send him back. What do you care for them? You do not want any thing of them."

"You are right," said Mankelaw;

"but, in that event, we should remain entirely ignorant of what is going on in the east. As it is, the case is widely different. The escribanos—for even Tooroopan, Huitallan, and PalBacan have them—are reliable men from Obili, some of them have even married Penchuenche girls, and through them we learn many things that are useful to us."

"Then there are no Argentines among them?"

"None at all. Any one may trust them, I do not."

"Escribanos among the Penchuenches!" said Cruzado, shaking his head; "I had hitherto believed that they could live only in large cities. What did Jenkeutruss formerly know of an escribano? and he would have pierced a letter contemptuously with his lance. Meanwhile the whites are advancing farther and farther, and I have been told that there is a permanent garrison at Fort Carmen, on the Cuzu-Leufu, whither their vessels make regular trips, and where they keep a great many cannon."

"Because we ourselves protect them there," said Mankelaw, haughtily; "but they dare not attempt again to occupy the upper ford; the first attempt proved a disastrous failure. Jenkitruss is right. Not one of them escaped to tell the story of their defeat, and when the next detachment came up with arms and provisions they found the place levelled with the ground, and the bones of the garrison scattered. They did not even encamp, but made their escape panic-stricken. But here we are," he suddenly interrupted himself. "This is Allumapu's tent, and until he returns you may use it," he added with a kind glance.

"And where is Allumapu?"

"He has been dispatched as messenger to the Cazique Huitallan. From what I have heard, he must be encamped on one of the smaller lagoons toward the southeast."

Mankelaw himself untied the noose of raw-hide, with which the tent had been closed, for this sufficed to keep away intruders. It was a sign betokening the owner's absence, and to set foot in such a tent would have been looked upon as a crime. The cazique alone had the right, in case visitors arrived, and had to be provided with lodging, of disposing of it, or having it taken down, if the tribe in the mean time changed their place of encampment. The owner would return and find that not only his dwelling, but the whole camp, had disappeared, when nothing remained for him but to follow the track of his brethren, which was plainly to be distinguished by the marks which the tent-poles made as they trailed along the ground.

The two men now entered together, and this entitled Cruzado to regard the tent as his own, at least till Allumapu's return. If the owner afterward disposed of it otherwise, the guest would of course be obliged to look out for another place of sojourn. A change in the weather seemed to be imminent. The wind had turned toward the west, but remained unsteady, and now it was passing again toward the northwest. In this direction heavy black clouds covered the Cordilleras, and indicated rain. The Penchuenches were not much concerned—they were well sheltered in their fur tents; but there was another bad night impending over the strangers, and the storm was to burst over them with more violence than they had expected."

At eleven o'clock at night arose a strong norther, and scarcely half an hour afterward the first drops fell, and then a deluge came, lasting till daylight, when the storm subsided with a drizzling rain; but the wind still continued to blow, and the Pampas resembled a sea rather than the land. No great effect however was made upon the waters of the Limai, for the flooded streams had not descended into it from the mountains, nor would they before nightfall. The sky was overcast and threatening; there was no doubt that there would be more rain in the course of a few hours, and it would be impossible to cross the river for many days, if not weeks.

CHAPTER XXIX.

SHELTERED.

The Germans had hardly ever passed a more wretched night. The storm prevented them even from wrapping themselves closely in their blankets, and they were soon drenched. But while they were suffering such hardships, Don Enrique was in great anxiety, for he knew too well the effect which the rain would have, and he thought it altogether improbable that he could cross the river with his baggage. Cruzado did not return, either. Had he deserted him, too! But the old man was by no means willing to let the storm keep him from his child, without at least making desperate efforts to reach her.

Don Enrique believed that Meyer was the most reliable of his companions. He determined to leave him and José in charge of his baggage, and to risk the passage of the river before it would be too late. No sooner, therefore, had daylight dawned than he awakened José, who was sleeping at his side, and ordered him to saddle the horse. As yet, all lay around wrapped in their wet blankets, as the rain did not cease all night. He remembered well enough the spot where Cruzado had crossed the day before, and, though the water had somewhat risen, it was not sufficient to render the passage more difficult or hazardous. His white horse was a noble creature, not too heavy, and full of fire and mettle. It entered the river and swam vigorously. When Don Enrique, arriving at the shoal in the middle of the current, intended to stop and rest there, the horse did not allow him. Neighing defiantly, it shook its head, plunged again into the water, and arrived safe at the opposite bank.

There stood two dusky men, who had watched with evident interest the passage of the Chileno—Mankelaw and Cruzado. Both of them knew that Jankitruss, if applied to, would never have granted him permission to cross the river; but, after he had once done so, the cazique could no longer object to it, much less be angry with the father for leaving nothing untried to recover his child.

"Bravo!" murmured Cruzado to himself, as he saw Don Enrique pressing so courageously onward through the flood; "that is a fine animal he has, and as fleet as the wind. I do not believe any of your horses, Mankelaw, would be able to overtake it on the Pampas."

"It swam the river very well," said Mankelaw, nodding; "but what next? Your German friends yet seem to be asleep."

"And Tchaluak's men will appropriate all the baggage and the gifts as soon as the river begins to rise."

"Behind the bend yonder," said Mankelaw, "lies a raft which we built on coming over here."

"Ah, good!" exclaimed Cruzado, joyously. "Jenkitrum cannot blame us for conveying the stranger's property to this side, after he himself has already crossed."

Mankelaw stood for a moment gazing thoughtfully; at last he said, resolutely:

"You may receive your friend here, and leave the rest to me. Is any man on the other bank familiar with our language?"

"Yes, the Chileno's servant, José. He has been with traders on the Pampas."

"It is well." And without paying further attention to the venerable Chileno, who was leading up his horse, he quickly disappeared among the tents. He had not much time to lose if he intended to attain his object, for he knew well how rapidly the river would rise after so violent a rain. It is true that the water, descending from the Cordilleras, would be discharged into the Naguelhuapi Lagoon, where it would increase for several hours, and then flow into the Limaî River, rushing with impetuosity and carrying with it every thing in its course.

"Did you see her?—Is she here?" was the first query which the poor father propounded to the half-breed. What did he care for the danger through which he had just passed, or for the property he had left in the hands of strangers? He inquired only for his beloved child, and, in doing so, he seized Cruzado's arm in tremulous haste.

"I do not know whether she is here or not, Don Enrique," replied Cruzado, in a calm but not disheartening tone. "I believe she is, though I did not see her."

"And Jenkitrum? Oh, when I think of that dreadful hour when he seized my poor daughter, and drew her to his saddle—and now I am to meet him again!"

"He is here—yonder is his tent."

"Ah, let us go to him!"

"We must not be in haste," said Cruzado, shaking his head. "Mankelaw, the cazique's brother, has gone to convey your baggage on a raft to this side. After last night's rain, the river will rise rapidly, and it will then be impossible to cross. We must wait until he returns. He is well disposed toward us, and if, by any one's assistance, we shall be successful, he is the man—we can never do without him."

"All right, Cruzado," said the old man, who was well-nigh in despair by the delay; "I will follow your advice—I believe you are a sincere well-wisher of mine."

"Then accompany me to the tent assigned me. We shall there kindle a fire, that you may dry your clothes—we have time enough until Mankelaw returns; afterward we can lay our plans."

So saying, he walked with the Chileno toward the tent, which was near, when the Argentine came to meet them.

"Don Enrique!" he exclaimed. "Is

It possible that you are here? I have suffered many hardships for your sake."

"Don Pedro!" cried the Chileno, almost in dismay. "Oh, you doubtless can give me some information concerning my daughter."

An Indian was galloping down, but, on seeing the prisoner conversing, he turned his horse, and, hitting the Argentine with the blunt end of his lance in the side, so that he fell to the ground, he exclaimed:

"Ah, you Argentine rascal! have you not been forbidden to hold intercourse with strangers? Do you wish to have your throat cut before it is time? Tooroopan will be here in due season. Begone into your tent, or I will amuse you with the sharp point of my lance."

The Argentine rose, and, casting a glance of deadly hatred on the Indian, merely remarked:

"This is an old friend whom I happened to meet here."

"Go!" cried the Indian, imperiously, without taking any notice of the others; and the Argentine obeyed, for he knew by experience how relentlessly the Indians punish disobedience on the part of prisoners. But Cruzado, who, above all things, was anxious not to give the Peuchuenches even the slightest cause for suspicion, seized Don Enrique's arm, as soon as the Indian had uttered his first words, and, drawing him away from Pedro, he said in a low voice:

"Come, let him alone; it is doubtful if he would tell you the truth, and besides we are not allowed to converse with him, as he is charged with having committed a crime. How do you come to know him?"

"He was the scout of the expedition which pursued Jenkitrum into the mountains. Is that his crime?"

"No, señor," replied Cruzado. "The Penchuenches were formerly acquainted with him. He stole some of their horses, and will be tried for it in the course of a few days. But here is the tent, and you may leave the rest to me."

Mankelaw had meanwhile carried his purpose into effect. Without applying to his brother for permission, he sent a messenger across the river to tell the Chileno's servants to keep the baggage in readiness, and ride down to the place where they would find the raft. This messenger was an old acquaintance of ours, Saman, who in Chili had followed Allumapu, and during the flight seized and carried off the Chilian woman. On riding down to the ford he met the Argentine whom he so unceremoniously struck and ordered back to his tent; he then trotted down and plunged as unconcernedly into the water as though it were the route he was daily accustomed to take.

There was soon quite a bustle in the camp on the other side, and the Indians there packed up their tents. Scarcely half an hour afterward they moved with the whites down to the raft, on which, under Saman's directions, they embarked their baggage without delay. Reiwald swam the Limai by José's side, but the doctor preferred the safer passage of the raft, which, owing to Meyer's intercession (for Saman strongly objected to it), was finally granted him. The raft had to make two trips before all the baggage of the whites had been conveyed to the opposite bank, and the Penchuenches of

Tahaluak's tribe hoped that it would return a third time in order to take over their tents, too, but nothing of the kind was done. The Indians were not forbidden to swim over on horseback, but their tents were not removed, and before long they themselves seemed to have given up the idea of paying a visit to Jenkitrass's camp, for they redirected their poles, and arranged every thing as if they intended to remain where they were for some time.

Jenkitrass had seen the commotion on the other side of the river, and doubtless divined the cause, but did not interfere. He allowed the strangers to come over, and it was not disagreeable to him that the Germans should visit his camp—they would bring him presents, and thereby help him to while away the long, monotonous winter. But why did the Penchuenches, who had accompanied the party, remain on the other side? Were they afraid lest their retreat would be cut off by the rising water? Their fears were not ill-grounded, for scarcely an hour elapsed since the Indians made their last trip with the raft, when suddenly a piercing yell—uttered by the Penchuenches stationed farther up—announced the waters rushing down from the mountains. Already at a distance could be seen the mud-colored waves, and the roar of the torrent was distinctly heard. All the inmates of the camp now flocked to the high bank in order to observe this interesting spectacle, and for the moment it made them forget every thing else.

While all fixed their eyes in eager suspense on the next bend, suddenly the cry burst from all lips, "There it comes! there it is!" and down surged the waters with a loud, deafening roar, drowning every other sound, and raising their foaming crests far above the level of the shore. The turbulent flood swelled the Limai two and three feet in a few seconds.

The two Germans witnessed with astonishment this exceedingly rapid rise of the river. They had hitherto deemed such a phenomenon incredible, but the Penchuenches were accustomed to it. The former knew, of course, that after a night's heavy rain, the water could not but rise, but they believed it would be by degrees. Now however they beheld, with the slightly uncomfortable impression which scenes of this description produce upon us, that it was the work of but a few moments, and that the quiet Limai was almost instantly converted into a raging torrent.

"Doctor," exclaimed Reiwald, "if this had occurred during the passage, where would we be now?"

"It is not difficult to answer that question," replied the doctor, who treated the danger very unconcernedly, since it was over. "We should be on our way to the Atlantic—perhaps better off than here, for aught I know. According to my opinion, we are now, as I had formerly the honor of suggesting to you, in a worse position than ever. Hitherto there was some possibility of retracing our steps, but now we are hopelessly caught."

"We are no worse off here than on the other side. On the contrary, there are tents enough to give us shelter; but if we pass another night such as the last one on the open plain, we might as well have our skins taken off, and he made mummies of, as examples for other travellers."

"I only wonder," said the doctor, "that the storm did not blow away the tents. What trouble we had to hold the leathern straps!—But do you see the Indians yonder, Reiwald? How skilful they are in protecting their raft!"

In fact, the Penchuenches had attended to this in time, and as soon as the first cry had warned them of the mountain overflow, they tied three strong lassos around the raft, and then awaited the effect with apparent composure. The experiment, however, did not seem to be free from danger, for they were, to all appearance, not fully convinced that their horses would be able to gain the bank, and, if they were not, all would have been lost. Additional lassos, therefore, were fastened to the rings of the saddle-straps, and held by a dozen Indians. It seemed almost as if the horses knew exactly why, for, as if to withstand a sudden jerk, they strained themselves to lighten the ropes. They succeeded in crossing, though at times it seemed as though they would be swept away. The raft was drawn up and securely fastened.

"What next!" asked Pfeifel, who had vainly looked about for Meyer. "Don Carlos is never on hand when we have need of him."

"It is fortunate, at all events, that he is here," remarked Reiwald, "for I really do not know how we should have got along on the Pampas without him."

"Somehow or other," replied the doctor.

"Probably by the aid of your '*buenos dias*,' '*buenas noches*,' '*gracias*,' and '*caramba*,' for these are the only Spanish words with which you are familiar, doctor. Your self-confidence came near playing a very bad trick upon you as well as myself. You do not even know how to beg a piece of horse-flesh."

"Oh," murmured the doctor, "hush, do not provoke me. I am still quite wet. But certain it is, that, if I am to pass another night in the rain, I shall follow the example of the frog and dive straight into the water. They are sensible animals; it is better to become wet at once than by degrees."

"Yes," said Reiwald, "if we had such water-proof coats as the frogs wear—but there comes Meyer; now we shall learn what is going to be done with us."

"Well!" said Meyer, who found the Germans quietly standing on the river-bank instead of being engaged with their baggage. "Do you wish to remain here all night?"

"Well, we do not know at all if—"

"Perhaps you are waiting for somebody to take care of your traps? That will not do! Come, gentlemen, go to work at once, or are you afraid of soiling your hands? We cannot carry the baggage on our backs to the tents.—That is right, Mr. Reiwald, take off your cloak."

His appeals were successful; the Germans, somewhat ashamed of their inactivity, proceeded to put their heavy sacks on the pack-horses, and Meyer helped to tie them, for they could not do that alone. Meanwhile José, assisted by the two Chilian Indians, had already strapped Don Enrique's baggage to the pack-saddles of the horses, and they were now able to proceed to the tents. It was high time for them to get away from here, for the sky was again overcast, and the rain commenced afresh.

Meanwhile Mankelaw had entered his brother's dwelling in order to inform him of what had happened; it could now no longer be helped. He found Jenkitruss reclining frowningly on the tigerskin covering his couch.

"Jenkitruss!" he said, "the old man in search of his daughter swam the river this morning."

"I know it," replied the cazique, briefly and gloomily; "and you took pains to convey his baggage to this side of the river."

"But I could not leave it in the hands of Tchaluak's men?"

"And what is to be done now? I hope you remember what I told you?"

"Speak yourself with him, and then make up your mind."

"But I will not see him!" cried the cazique, starting up angrily. "What can he tell me that I do not know already? Am I to sell my own wife for silver spurs and other trumpery?"

Mankelaw made no reply. Time and again he had begged him not to take the white girl for his wife, if only for the sake of that peace which he had disturbed in his own family. But his brother lent a deaf ear to his appeals. Hence, he needed no repetition of them.

"And what is to be done with the aged Chileno?" he said, after a while.

"Treat him kindly," replied Jenkitruss, quickly pacified by Mankelaw's silence, and yet conscious of having done wrong. "But I do not want to have him here in the camp. He must not come near, nor must she hear his voice, or even learn that he is on the Pampas. On the outskirts of the camp, I have a tent containing our supplies. Give him a room in it, and furs enough for a warm couch; he must not suffer from want—we have provisions enough."

"And then?"

"When the river falls, he will return to Chili. The winter will not continue as it commenced. Cruzado will stay here. I will give the Chilenos an escort to accompany them across the mountains."

"And the Germans?" asked Mankelaw. "I have taken Cruzado to Allumapu's tent. There is room enough in it; shall I quarter them there too? They do not speak our language, and Cruzado may assist them?"

"Do as you please," said the cazique, relapsing into his former attitude. "I do not wish to hear any more about the matter. As soon as the rains cease, I will leave the camp for a time. You will meanwhile remain here. On my return, I hope I shall no longer meet with any strangers."

"Are you going out hunting?"

"Yes; but I shall take my *tent* with me," he said, laying stress on the word; "when the caziques, whom I have sent for, arrive at the camp, it will not be difficult for our men to find my whereabouts. Saman knows the place which I have selected; a great many guanacos are there, and, on riding over those plains for the last time, he saw not less than three pumas in the tall grass."

Mankelaw bent his head; he knew full well that his objections would not cause his brother to change his mind, but only add to his obstinacy; hence, he left to carry out the orders, and conduct the guests to the designated quarters.

The tents among which Don Enrique was to take up his abode stood at a distance of about three hundred yards from the principal camp, and they had been erected at this somewhat higher and drier spot, because the supplies, especially salt, were better protected there than closer to the river. The so-called pamperos are storms sometimes so violent as to upset the best-fastened tents, if there were no trees to tie them to; and here was a grove of apple-trees, among which they were perfectly safe, while the rain quickly disappeared from the undulating ground.

Near the river stood some young trees, which had probably been planted by the Indians, but they did not yet afford much protection, and the main camp was established near them only because of the water, and the dry wood found on the bank.

On leaving Jenkitrum, Mankelaw met the pack-horses on their way up, and sent Saman with Don Enrique's horses to the tent destined for the old Chileno. He then requested Cruzado to take thither Don Enrique, José, and the two Chilian Indians, and tell the haciendero not to leave the place for several days to come; at all events, not until Jenkitrum would permit him.

Don Enrique asked beseechingly when he would see his daughter, but the Indian shrugged his shoulders and told him that every thing depended on the cazique's will, while Cruzado whispered to him a kind "Paciencia!" adding that that was the best thing for him. He assured him that he should have all that he desired for his comfort as long as he chose to remain.

The old gentleman submitted to every thing; he was powerless in the hands of the cazique. He could be successful only by entreaty and not by force; for the sake of his child he was obliged to endure whatever treatment he might receive.

Just as he left the place, the Germans arrived with their baggage, and were quite agreeably surprised at the accommodations provided for them. A pleasant fire was already burning, and Cruzado had told Meyer in a few words that the Germans might consider as their own so spacious and comfortable a dwelling, in which he would himself sleep. He followed the haciendero to assist in arranging Don Enrique's tent.

"Well, Don Carlos," exclaimed Relwald, as soon as they were alone, "what do you think of this? It is a parlor—elegantly furnished—four horse-skulls, probably to be used as chairs; if we had chairs, we might use them as stools. In the corner yonder is a bureau, which bears some resemblance to a sailor's chest, and I must confess that I am at a loss to know how the Penchuenches got possession of it. And these guanaco-skins! I long to make the acquaintance of an animal furnishing such useful furs."

"Well, I think you will be able to stand it here," said Meyer, glancing about cheerfully; "I really wish it would rain all night, only in order to have the agreeable feeling of being sheltered from the fury of the storm. But I know that it will not rain when *I* am in a tent; but whenever I happen to pass a night in the open air, you may wager that there will be a shower."

The doctor had no sooner entered than he went to the fire, where he warmed his hands, and, turning to his friends, said:

"I wish I could get rid of this swelling of my glands. But here we are at least able to exist, and I have a presentiment that I shall stay here long enough to recover from the hardships of the journey. What about our provisions, Meyer?"

"Who knows!" replied Meyer, who had thrown off his jacket, and hung it up on one of the poles fixed for that purpose. "I believe we have food enough for some time, but I will ask Cruzado to get us some guanaco-flesh. I saw one of these animals in a tent yonder, and I think it was killed quite recently."

"Oh, I wish we had once again a decent dinner," said the doctor, squatting down on one of the horse-skulls close to the fire. "One of my fervent wishes, however—that we might have a little room of our own—has been fulfilled."

"What about the Chileno's daughter!" asked Reiwald, who occasionally remembered the object of their journey. "Did you hear any thing of her, Meyer?"

"I inquired just now of Cruzado concerning her," replied Meyer, undressing quite unceremoniously, in order to dry his clothes, "but he put on such a mysterious air that I suspect he himself does not know much about her. She must be near by, or they would not have sent her father outside the camp. Perhaps they want to get him a little out of their way."

"A strange affair," said Reiwald, "and at the same time it is carried on, as it were, in a very business-like manner. It has lost much of its romantic character since we have been obliged to eat horse-flesh."

"Well, it might be rendered again highly romantic," said the doctor, who began to warm up, "if you, for instance, discovered the whereabouts of the girl, Reiwald, put her on your horse, plunged into the river, and swam to the opposite bank. Of course, you would have to take her back to Chili."

"Of course—and I should have behind me the whole horde of Indians, with a forest of lances, to which these Penchuenches have fixed bayonet-points, knife-blades, and Heaven knows what. Besides, I am afraid we have arrived too late, for the young lady must be married by this time, and her happy husband will doubtless, before long, cause himself to be introduced—if not in a black dress-coat, at least in a red skin—to his old father-in-law."

"They carried off at the time another Chilian girl from Concepcion or its vicinity, as Cruzado told me," said Meyer; "her parents and other relatives, however, seem not to trouble themselves much about her fate, for, as far as I know, they have not even sent by us a string of glass beads to ransom her."

"Poor thing!" said Reiwald, compassionately; "she is, perhaps, an orphan, about whom no one concerns himself. Doctor, we might act as good Christians toward her. We have brought along plenty of presents, and we may possibly be able to ransom her. We would then have accomplished something very praiseworthy by our journey, and would not be laughed at on our return. It will sound very ridiculous if we have to tell people that we merely made a pleasure-trip to the Pampas."

"And you do not count the ethnographic interest at all?" said the doctor.

"Well, that would be a tolerable subterfuge," answered Reiwald; "at all events, we must try to ferret out where the señorita is concealed, and to whom she belongs; afterward, we shall perhaps be able to make a trade with the red heathen. Meyer, you will attend to that for us, and if we succeed in ransoming her previous to our departure from the camp she may be our housekeeper here."

"I will do so with pleasure," said Meyer. "Cruzado will doubtless ascertain all about it. But if she is pretty, it will be difficult for you to procure her release, for these savages are exceedingly fond of white women. But now make yourself comfortable," he added, "for to stand here in wet clothes is surely no pleasure. We will afterward endeavor to get a boy to fetch us a kettleful of water. Wait, I will look out immediately."

"In that costume!" cried Reiwald, who believed that Don Carlos had entirely forgotten his dishabille.

"Oh, we are at home here," smiled Meyer, stepping out in his scanty costume, and soon returning with a half-grown boy. A piece of tobacco was shown to him, whereupon, uttering a loud cry of joy, he took up the kettle and hastened at the top of his speed to the river. He returned in an incredibly short time, and the Germans prepared some good coffee.

CHAPTER XXX.

THE PURCHASED WIFE.

Meyer seemed to have been mistaken; for, although he lay in an excellent tent, it rained not only all day, but all night, and next morning until noonday, and the Limai rolled its muddy waters with extraordinary rapidity through the Pampas. All communication with the Penchuenches encamped opposite had thereby been rendered impossible, nor did any one seem to care for, or feel any special desire to hold any intercourse with them. They were not seen outside the tents. Having slaughtered a young horse on the first day, it furnished them with food for some time, and that was all they needed.

All was quiet in the camp on the other side. Now and then Indian lads hastened to the river to fetch wood or water. Occasionally some Penchuenche rode about to look after the animals, perhaps to catch one, and let that on which he was mounted graze in its place on the plain. Saddles are not used by this tribe; their horses have a girth around the body, to which the lasso is fastened.

A Sabbath-like stillness reigned, and the only one who was not in good spirits, but counting in an agony the slowly-creeping hours, was the poor old Chileno. As long as he was on horseback and pressed onward through the greatest hardships and privations, he did not feel this torturing anxiety; but now that he was probably near his lost and dearly-beloved daughter, compelled to wait in inactivity, he was no longer able to overcome his impatience. Having on the first day selected a number of presents for Jenkitrum, he wrapped them up, and sent Cruzado with the package to the cazique, which Jenkitrum returned without opening. Nay, he forbade the half-breed to make any further attempts of that kind, and remarked that, if he wished to see the Chileno, he would send for him—that until then the old gentleman must remain quietly in his tent, and that he, the cazique, did not want presents. This broke off all intercourse between the two, and unless Don Enrique intended to run the risk of arousing Jenkitrum's anger, he was obliged to desist from other efforts in the same direction. Such a dreadful word as "patience" made him very irritable.

On the third morning the storm cleared off, and Meyer, who had gone to the river at daybreak, noticed to his surprise that the tents of the Ponchuenches opposite, whose fires he had seen late at night, had entirely disappeared. Not a living being was longer to be seen there; they had doubtless become tired of remaining in the rain and eating up their own horses. In Jenkitrum's camp, however, no notice was taken of their departure; it is true, some Indians stood on the bank, chatting and looking over to the other side, and the absence of Tchaluak's men was reported to the cazique; but that was all. On the other hand, Cruzado informed the Germans, on behalf of the cazique, that he would receive them on this day, and, as both had already been prepared for this since their arrival, they selected such gifts as they intended to present. At the same time Cruzado learned that Saman possessed the Chilian woman who had been abducted, and was willing to sell her if he could get a good price. This was a private affair, and did not concern Jenkitrum at all. It was necessary for the Germans to comply with the invitation, and Reiwald was cautious enough to leave his cloak behind, for, although it was not lined with red flannel, he seemed to have become distrustful of the covetousness of these lords of the Pampas, and would not rashly run the risk of losing an article so necessary to him.

Jenkitrum received Reiwald and his friend, contrary to their expectation, in the kindest manner, accepted their presents thankfully, and conversed for a time with them by the aid of the interpreter, who asked them many questions concerning their native country, and the reasons that led them to this remote quarter of the world. But he always averted at once any allusion to the abducted girl, without uttering a word, by a mere wave of his hand, and finally dismissed them as a European prince his subjects, when he wishes to terminate the audience.

When they were already at the door of the tent, he called back Cruzado and bade him ask the Germans if they would accompany him on a hunting-excursion. He added that he had been informed of their sporting proclivities, which had brought them to the country; and since they had doubtless met with very little game on their route, he would give them a chance to exercise their skill. Of course, they had to accept this invitation with many thanks, and Jenkitrum requested them to make their preparations that evening, as they would probably set out at a very early hour. He himself would furnish them pack-horses.

The audience was over, and as much as Reiwald, who was a zealous sportsman, was delighted with the opportunity thus offered him, as little seemed the doctor to like it. He would have preferred to remain in his comfortable tent, and foresaw again, and by no means unreasonably, a great many needless privations and hardships. But, as he was unable to offer any valid excuses, he had to submit to the stern necessity of accompanying the cazique; and only one consideration reassured him, viz., that in a region abounding with game they would not be obliged to eat horse-flesh.

Meanwhile Reiwald proceeded busily to unpack his hunting-apparatus; he had to discharge his rifle, clean, and reload it. The afternoon passed, they hardly knew how. It was very agreeable to them that Meyer was to take part in the expedition, and, as for their conversation with the Indians, Jenkitrum, as Cruzado told them, would take with him his escribano, who would officiate as interpreter. Cruzado was to remain at the camp.

It was about four in the afternoon when they completed all their preparations, and wearily stretched themselves on their couches. Meyer, smoking a short pipe, was lying thoughtfully by the fire, when a shout resounded outside the tent. Cruzado rose; some one asked to be admitted, and he went out to see who it was, and what he wanted. He returned presently with Saman, who immediately moved one of the horse-skulls to the fire, nodded pleasantly to all, and then, holding out his hand to the doctor, said "Tabaco!" A conversation without tobacco seemed impossible to him.

Cruzado had given Saman to understand that he would receive valuable gifts as a ransom for the abducted Chilian woman; and, instead of sitting for hours in silence, as is the habit of these Indians, before explaining what they came for, he came quickly to the point as soon as he had received the tobacco, and made himself a cigarette. He informed Cruzado that he was willing to sell to the highest bidder the woman he had brought with him from Chili, "handsome and amiable as she was." He had another wife, and as he was frequently absent from the camp, and often did not come home for weeks, the two women would quarrel and even come to blows; moreover, two wives were too expensive for him.

"And what would he take for her?"

"Well," said the Indian, thoughtfully, for this was the most important part of the transaction, "I do not know exactly what to ask for her; besides, I cannot tell what things the strangers have, or, if I need them. Let them display the goods, and we shall then the sooner come to an understanding."

Cruzado agreed to this, and requested the Germans to produce what they were willing to give as a ransom for the Chilian woman; they would then easily come to a bargain with the Indian. However, they must not offer too much at the outset, lest they should make him too avaricious.

The doctor, who had taken the goods under his charge and knew how they had been packed, brought a leathern sack and commenced unpacking it. In the first place, he exhibited a large roll of tobacco; and Saman's face, which had hitherto looked quite indifferent and careless, immediately assumed a more joyous expression. The doctor next took from a package containing cotton handkerchiefs two of the most gayly-colored, which he put with the tobacco on the hide spread out before Saman. He also brought out a small bag containing indigo, and put down two large pieces. He then added to these treasures a common butcher-knife with a wooden handle, a handful of glass beads, and last, a few Jews'-harps, of which Saman, who had just finished his cigarette, took up one and began to play.

The doctor gazed with evident pleasure on the treasures thus displayed, while Saman was not in such an ecstasy as it was expected he would be. Only the Jews'-harp met with his entire approbation, and it seemed almost as if it caused him to forget the whole transaction, for he did not cease to execute his monotonous melodies on it.

Meyer lay near on several guanaco-skins, and, to all appearance, enjoyed the scene greatly.

"Well!" said Pfelful at last, almost offended at the little attention the Indian bestowed upon the goods, "I wonder what the red caracho may want in addition."

"Fie!" exclaimed Saman, with so ludicrous an expression that Cruzado burst into loud laughter—"not caracho—ugly word!"

"Well, does he want the things, or not?" said the doctor to Meyer. "If he does not, I will put them away again, and he may go where he came from."

"Well, how is it, Saman?" asked Cruzado. "Will you trade? We are about to set out; make up your mind quickly, or you may keep the woman, and the strangers will take away their treasures."

"Yes," said Saman, putting down the Jews'-harp, and, as if absent-minded, cutting off another piece of tobacco. It is all very well—tobacco is good, glass beads are good, indigo, handkerchiefs, Jews'-harps, knife—all good; but too little. I want more of every thing—three pieces of tobacco like this" (and to render a misunderstanding impossible, he lifted up three fingers of his hand), "much indigo, many handkerchiefs, and many glass beads!"

"The fellow is impudent," said Cruzado, quietly to Meyer; "tell your countryman to repack their property."

"Ah, the trumpery is of no consequence," replied Meyer, good-naturedly; "they have brought with them more than they need, and certainly do not care to take the articles back to Chili. We cannot leave the poor girl in the hands of this fellow."

"That is not necessary," said Cruzado, who was more familiar with the peculiarities of the Indians. "Let them first act as though he had asked too much, and he will assuredly come down. They may offer him more, but should not at once yield to his demands."

Meyer translated what Cruzado had told him, and the doctor, who began to be half sorry for having entered upon the transaction, inasmuch as they could not tell what burden they might impose upon themselves by ransoming the Chilian girl, quickly proceeded to pack up.

"Stop!" exclaimed Saman, in surprise, as the doctor put the tobacco, which was most endangered, into the sack, "What is the matter? He must give more, and not take any away."

"Well, my friend," said Cruzado, carelessly, "you ask more than the strangers are willing to pay; for they are to remain for some time on the Pampas, and have afterward to make a long journey back to their homes. If you ask so exorbitantly for the woman, you must keep her."

The Indian was evidently displeased at their refusal to comply with his demand, which, if they had accepted, he would then have immediately increased. Besides, he was loath to let the strangers discover that he was more anxious to make the trade than to keep the woman, for, at the best, he would not have obtained from his brethren so much as an old horse for her. If Saman could not get along with her, others were not inclined to try. However, he finished his cigarette before speaking another word. At last, when the doctor had put away the sack, and, considering the matter at an end, resumed his seat by the fire, Saman rose slowly, murmured something to himself, and left the tent.

Meyer now became uneasy. "Amigo," he exclaimed, "if you make him angry, the affair is settled. If another roll of tobacco will satisfy him, I am quite ready to give it.—Mr. Reiwald, do not forsake the poor woman. It is dreadful for her to live among these savages."

"I am of your opinion, too," exclaimed Reiwald, springing to his feet. "I will call him back; a handful of trinkets more or less is of no consequence."

Cruzado beckoned to him. "The Indian, I affirm, shall not keep her, nor, in fact, does he wish to do so, for what he has seen has already awakened his covetousness; but let him return of his own accord. Meyer, tell your friend to sit down again. I will stake my head against a glass bead that he will be back in less than a quarter of an hour."

The prediction was verified, for scarcely had Reiwald resumed his seat, when the door opened, and Saman returned as quietly and unconcernedly as though he had stepped out only to look after the weather. He asked Cruzado immediately to have the goods displayed once more, and, after the doctor had complied with his request, he repeated his former demand. But Cruzado knew now that he was anxious to get rid of the woman, and, after a short time, Saman consented to make the trade, provided another roll of tobacco and two handfuls of red pepper were added. The Germans readily complied with this demand, and, when Saman wrapped every thing carefully in his poncho, he asked for an additional roll of tobacco, more achi, and two red handkerchiefs.

Cruzado laughed, and suggested the departure of the Indian to a very hot place; but the fellow begged so earnestly, that Reiwald finally gave him more tobacco, a pair of scissors, and a handful of brass thimbles, which seemed to satisfy him, although he asked for paper for his cigarettes. He received that too, but still remained standing, as if he had forgotten something. He did not remember, however, what else to beg for, and finally left the tent, in order to introduce the woman, and deliver her to her new master, the doctor—for it was Pfeifel who had paid the ransom.

THE PURCHASED WIFE. 215

"There," laughed Reiwald, after Saman had withdrawn, "the sale is over, and I can tell you now, doctor, that I am quite anxious to see our Chilian belle. Of course, she will throw herself at our feet, and thank us for having released her. You may rely on it, there will be a touching scene."

Meyer, who had made for himself a sort of sofa from some pack-saddles and guanaco-skins, which he spread over them, was reclining on his elbow and smoking his cigarette.

"Really," he said, chuckling, "we ought to draw lots for her, for one of us must be her caballero on the road; the doctor, however, will take that upon himself."

"Let me tell you, Don Carlos," replied Pfeifel, "I have so much to attend to that I have no time to spare. For the rest, I hope the lady will be independent and self-reliant enough to take care of herself, for I have been told that all Chilenas are skilful riders."

"I do not think she is very pretty," remarked Reiwald, "to judge from the low price paid to her worthy owner. I believe the whole amount we gave falls short of five dollars. What can you expect for that?"

"At all events, this is a brilliant adventure, Reiwald," said the doctor, "one of those which you have so desired—a helpless woman, carried off from her home by barbarians, and we, a couple of Don Quixotes, swimming on our chargers a foaming torrent—"

"But you did not swim it at all, doctor; you and the other sacks were conveyed on the raft."

"That makes no difference, for, at all events, I felt as much anxiety as though I had encountered it, for the raft came near being swept away.—So we swam a mountain-torrent, and hunted up an Indian tribe to release the unfortunate señorita, whose name possibly may be Dulcinea. Even Don Carlos joined the expedition, or was compelled to. The matter is as yet enshrouded in mystery," he added, glancing at Meyer.

"But the adventure terminates in a prosaic manner," interrupted Reiwald, "for instead of releasing the unfortunate princess, guarded by a giant, and spilling our blood for her, we obtain her deliverance by paying five dollars' worth of goods, after higgling a long while with a very dirty Indian."

"Bah!" replied the doctor, "he is at least a genuine red-skin, that lives on horse-flesh and blood-pies; and can you wish for more romantic scenery than this guanaco-skin tent — we seated here on horse-skulls, Meyer yonder reclining on his couch and smoking? I am fully satisfied, and confess to you that I am waiting impatiently for the appearance of the wild warrior who is to bring to us his fair captive, that, like knight-errants of yore, we may break her fetters, when she will throw herself at our feet, thanking us and the gods."

"The doctor talks poetically," laughed Meyer, in great glee. "I wish the old Chileno success in ransoming his daughter, but I am doubtful, for, if the cacique now sets out upon a hunting excursion, to which he will hardly invite Don Enrique, the latter may wait here a long time, unless meanwhile he has a chance to rescue the girl. It is certain that Saman parted very willingly with his wife, and I am afraid he has good reason. Did you not see her, Cruzado?"

"Who?" asked the interpreter, who understood only the last words addressed to him.

"The Chilian woman whom Saman has just sold to us."

"No," said Cruzado, shaking his head; "since we are here he has kept her all the time in his tent, and not even allowed her to fetch water and wood. But, I believe, there he is coming! He has made haste to bring her."

"How unfortunate," said Relwald, "that we have not even a chair for the lady! I believe I shall have to offer her my horse-skull."

The conversation was interrupted, for at this moment the door opened, and the Chilian woman, followed by Saman, entered the tent. Of course, all fixed their eyes attentively on her; and both Relwald and the doctor had just time to see that she was still young, and even good-looking, though she wore a ragged and dirty dress, when Meyer uttered a loud cry.

"O heavens!" he said, as he raised himself up, with an air of astonishment. His cigarette dropped from his mouth, and he stared at her as though she had risen from the dead.

The captive now turned her eyes involuntarily toward Meyer, and, strange to say, the sight of him seemed equally to surprise her. While he remained in his half-reclining attitude, like a marble statue, she quickly regained her self-possession, and, hastening to him, encircled his neck with her arms, exclaiming:

"Don Carlos! My Carlos! Oh, you have saved me, have you not?"

"My wife!" gasped Meyer. "'Tis she, as sure as I live!"

But he seemed more surprised than delighted, and would certainly have sunk to the floor if she had not held him in her embrace. The spectators were confounded, except Saman, who probably considered it a matter of course that the white woman was glad of escaping from him, and recognizing one of the strangers.

"Forsooth, Meyer," exclaimed the doctor, "an exceedingly fortunate coincidence! I shall henceforth believe in miracles. Why, this is the most romantic affair I ever heard of."

"Indeed, we may congratulate you," exclaimed Relwald.

Cruzado alone stood with arms folded, and looking as if he endeavored to avoid bursting into a fit of laughter; for Meyer had told him on the road the history of his life, and he knew well under what circumstances Meyer's wife had left him.

"Pray," said Meyer, in a piteous tone, "do not trouble yourself. This lady—" But the lady did not allow him to continue, for she folded him with gushing tenderness to her heart, regardless of the presence of his friends, exclaiming:

"Ah, I did not deserve, Carlos, that you should expose yourself to such dangers for my sake. Oh, if you knew how happy this makes me!—And how did you ascertain my whereabouts and my misfortune? But I will no longer call it a misfortune. Ah, how happy I am that I am with you again! All is well now, and for the sake of this blissful moment I would willingly bear ten times as many hardships as I have undergone."

Meyer heaved a deep sigh; so completely was he taken by surprise, and so much was he afraid lest the others, if they were aware of his feelings, would deride him, that he finally submitted to necessity. He rose, embraced his wife, but with much less tenderness than she had manifested, and then, turning to the two Germans, he said:

"Gentlemen, I have the pleasure of introducing you to my wife, Señora Mercedes Meyer."

"I am ashamed," said Mercedes, "of appearing in such a costume before the gentlemen; but if you knew what I have suffered during the last few weeks—" So saying, she covered her face with her mantilla. Meyer meanwhile thought of other things. He was pacing the tent with a quick step, when Saman approached him, and, holding out his hand, said, smilingly:

"Tobacco, amigo! You have recovered your wife."

Moyer did not understand immediately what he wanted of him; but Cruzado was no longer able to repress his mirth, and burst into a peal of laughter. Moyer, however, was not in a mood to treat the Indian very ceremoniously; he seized him by the arm, turned him about, and put him out. Saman seemed to consider this all right; at least he did not offer any resistance, but returned, to all appearance well satisfied with his bargain, to his own tent.

"Well," said Meyer to Cruzado, after the Indian had left, "what are we to do now? My wife has been restored to me, and to-morrow I am to take part in the hunting excursion of the cazique, who will take no excuse for my absence."

"Be comforted, Don Carlos," replied Cruzado, "for to-day we shall make a partition in the tent; there are furs enough, and in the back part is already a sort of 'bunk,' which Allamapu used. When you are away, your wife may live alone there. I will go to Don Enrique, because Jenkitrum has no need of me in the mean time."

"And you intend to leave me so soon?" asked Mercedes, with the most tender solicitude. Meyer made no reply, and, evidently well satisfied with Cruzado's suggestion, proceeded immediately to make the partition. After completing it, he threw himself again upon his couch, without taking further notice of the señora, and smoked more vigorously than ever; but the good-natured smile had disappeared, and he really did not look like a man who, by a happy play of fortune, had just recovered his beloved wife.

The señora, who knew well how guilty she was, took good care not to remind him of her shortcomings, or incommode him by too many caresses. Time heals all wounds, and she herself went gladly to work to prepare her couch for the night. She was overjoyed at her escape from the hands of the Indians, and at the prospect of returning to her beloved Chili. She would, by-and-by, explain every thing to her husband and pacify him.

Meanwhile evening had come, and it was time for making supper, which Cruzado had to do by himself on this day, for Meyer did not stir; nay, when supper was ready, he hardly moved to partake of the meal. He bestowed no attention on his wife. Cruzado had to bring her supper, while Don Carlos, after drinking a cup of tea, and eating a few morsels, lay down on his furs and fell asleep. Pfeiffel retired very late, for, as he did not know how early Jenkitross intended to set out, a great many things had to be arranged. He had scarcely shut his eyes, when somebody seized his shoulder and shook him.

"Ah!" he exclaimed, starting up in dismay. "Who is there?"

"It is I," said Meyer, "Cruzado has just awakened me. Where is your candle?"

"What do you want it for? Let me sleep at least an hour."

"A messenger from Jenkitross was here just now," continued Meyer; "the horses are saddled. We must set out."

"Set out? At ten o'clock at night?" exclaimed the doctor, who thought he was to be deprived of his night's rest.

"Ten o'clock?" said Meyer. "It is three in the morning. You have slept as soundly as a rat. Where is your candle?"

The doctor was so drowsy as to be unable to realize that it was so late, but he groped for the candle, which was standing by his side; and Meyer, stirring up the embers, lighted it quickly.—Voices resounded from without, and horses were stamping at the door. Reiwald also had meanwhile been aroused, and while Cruzado proceeded to carry out the saddle-bags, and fasten them, the Germans took up their hunting-utensils and stepped out. The fresh night air soon revived them, and scarcely ten minutes afterward they trotted briskly toward the rendezvous, whence they were to start with the cazique

CHAPTER XXXI.

THE HUNTING EXCURSION.

Reiwald and his companion were greatly surprised on finding vacant the place on which the cazique's tent had stood. Not a vestige was longer to be seen there, but some forty horses, loaded with baggage, or mounted by Indians, were ready to start. It seemed strange to Reiwald that a solemn silence prevailed, and that, among so many, not a word was spoken.

This did not look like a merry hunting cavalcade about to speed across the Pampas; on the contrary, a band of demons preparing for an ambuscade, or some stealthy attack. Even the horses seemed to observe the same caution as their masters, for none of them neighed or snorted, and only stamped the ground impatiently, as if tired of the delay. When the Germans, for whom the others had apparently been waiting, were there scarcely ten minutes, the signal to start seemed given; but no command was heard—the foremost animals led the way, and the others followed slowly, passing by the tents, which remained standing, and out into the open plains. The ground was still so soft that even the footsteps of the horses could not be heard, nor was any thing to be seen, except that detached group of tents, where Don Enrique had taken up his abode, and which the Indians shunned, as they advanced, looking, as it were, like a squadron of spectres.

"Forsooth, Reiwald," said the doctor to his friend, who was riding by his side, involuntarily speaking in a whisper,

"This is a very strange affair, and we are here under the cover of darkness, as if we owed somebody money, and were endeavoring to avoid him."

"How many men and horses there are here!" exclaimed Relwald; "I really believe they intend to kill all the game on the Pampas. It will be, however, an interesting excursion, for we shall certainly have great success."

"But I wonder why they are proceeding on such an occasion with so much solemnity?"

"Well, you do not wish us to make a noise and scare away the game?" said his friend. "In the camp it was unnecessary to keep silence; but good hunters never make any unnecessary outcry. They always pursue their course as noiselessly as possible, so that if any bird or beast is near, they do not frighten it."

"I do not know," replied the doctor, "but this seems to me not very like a hunting party, but rather an expedition for the purpose of taking us out into the Pampas, and deserting us at some lonely spot. We do not even know in what direction we are moving—for the sky is overcast, and, for my part, I should be altogether unable to retrace my steps."

"Never fear," said Relwald; "so large a number of horses cannot but leave a broad track. Your apprehensions are not well grounded, and I only wonder why we are riding so slowly. Can you tell me the reason, Meyer?"

Meyer had not yet spoken a word all the morning, for he still felt yesterday's unpleasant surprise, and thoughts of a different character engrossed his attention. On the other side of the Cordilleras lay a small cabin, where a poor, unfortunate girl was waiting with a throbbing heart for his longed-for return.

"I feel like blowing out my brains," he murmured to himself.

"What do you say?" asked Relwald, who had not quite understood him.

"This is a fine morning!" growled out Meyer. "All that is wanting is a little shower to lay the dust."

"You must be crazy," said the doctor; "the ground is still so wet that the horses move very slowly; but I believe it is daylight—look at that bright streak yonder, Relwald."

"I believe you are right," replied Relwald. All rode in silence, absorbed in their reflections. It was dawning. A light breeze swept the Pampas from the east, where the sky grew brighter and brighter. Suddenly a rosy lustre was shed over the horizon, and in a few minutes the sun rose. But our two friends took hardly any notice of the surpassingly beautiful morning, for their surroundings engrossed their attention at this moment. It was not until then that they recognized their companions, and in truth nothing more picturesque could be imagined than this cavalcade. They turned their horses a little aside to be better able to survey and admire the scene.

At the head rode Jenkitrnas, bareheaded, as usual, with his long hair upon his shoulders, holding his lance in his hand, and his horse tricked off with many silver ornaments on its saddle and trappings. Close behind him rode three beautiful young women, clad alike in a tasteful blue costume, but differing from one another in appearance.

Two of them seemed to be Indians; their color, if not very dark, was at least a light bronze. They wore ornaments of glass beads about their necks, and in their ears. The third presented a striking contrast; for her complexion was of dazzling whiteness, and her black hair was not straight, like that of the Indian women, but surrounded her temples, and fell about her neck in ringlets. She looked pale and careworn, while the other two were gayly chatting and laughing with each other.

The Indian women know nothing of course of saddles, and mount their horses astraddle, though this lady was evidently not yet accustomed to such a mode of travelling; her two companions sat boldly and confidently, regardless of the fact that they somewhat exposed their plump brown limbs. The young white woman had wrapped about her body an additional garment, which, on either side, almost touched the ground; and, hanging her pretty head, she rode in mournful silence at the side of her companions.

"Heavens!" whispered Reiwald to the doctor, "that is old Enrique's daughter. Oh, what a sweet girl!"

"Now I know why we stole away so mysteriously, like thieves in the night," said the doctor. "Look at the multitude of pack-horses. In order not to meet the old Chileno, Jenkitrus has changed his place of encampment, and will now stay somewhere else on the Pampas, where, when the next shower obliterates his tracks, no one will be able to find him. It is certain that our expedition, so far as the poor girl is concerned, has been in vain, for you may depend on it that the rascal will not give her up, and, to tell the truth, if I were in his stead, I would not."

"Poor child!" sighed Reiwald, "I wonder if she suspects that her father for several days has been so near her!"

"I do not think she does, or she would not sit with so calm and resigned an air on her horse; and what good would it do her? She would be unable to hold any intercourse with her father; it would have only added to her grief—perhaps have driven her to despair."

"How surpassingly beautiful she is, and how pale!—Merciful Heavens, I would not like to shed the blood of any human being, but I believe it would give me no remorse to put to death that copper-colored cazique."

"Whereupon his men would simply cut your throat—that would be the result of your heroic deed," said the doctor. "No, since the neighboring governments are unable to put a stop to the outrages committed by these savages, I am pretty confident that we two shall not bring about a change in that respect. I wish the mischief would take them all.—But see, Jenkitrass commences galloping, and I think matters will become somewhat livelier."

He was right. It was now daylight, and the morning rays pierced the fog, scattering it in thin masses over the plain. The men, however, were able to see the ground, over which they had to lead their horses; and though, on account of the numerous holes, it was not advisable to ride fast in the darkness, they were now enabled to avoid every thing dangerous to the safety of the animals.

The slow pace at which they had ridden, had long since been irksome to the

Indians; they were not accustomed to it, and even the horses at the outset could hardly be restrained from quickening their pace, for they scarcely ever moved otherwise than at a gallop. Now there was a sudden change. The cazique pressed his heavy silver spurs into the flanks of his black steed, so that it darted forward, and the women followed their lord and master. The other Indians, about twenty of them, kept near their chief, having their lassos coiled up behind them on their saddles, their bolas tied about their waists, and their lances ready. Even the pack-horses, of which there were perhaps fifty, carrying the tent bundles on their backs, and trailing the light poles on the ground, kept pace with the others.

Jenkitrus in the meanwhile repeatedly looked back, and, to all appearance, sought for the Germans. One of his Indian wives galloped ahead and led the way, while the cazique turned aside and stopped until the Germans were by his side.

"Ah, the Germans," he said, nodding to them kindly, and speaking a mixture of Spanish and Indian, which the two friends did not understand, except the word "Alemanos," which they had already heard so often. "Did you really comply with my invitation? Well, I am glad of it. Let us see now what you can do with your rifles, and whether you can kill with them more game than I with my bola."

"Yes," said the doctor, who was at a loss to know what the cazique said to them, "fine morning to-day, only a little fresh."

The cazique, smiling, shook his head, and beckoned to his escribano, who had meanwhile been conversing with Meyer, and inquiring of him about Chili, but especially about the cazique Cajuante's village, where he seemed to be acquainted. The escribano was to officiate as interpreter between them, but even this was insufficient; for Doctor Pfeifel, mounted as he was on a particularly restless horse, did not get along very well with his Spanish. Meyer had to be called up, and Jenkitrus then explained to them that he intended to encamp for several months at the place whither they were moving, and that afterward he would perhaps go still further east. The Alemanos, he said, might remain with him as long as they pleased, and hunt guanacos, ostriches and pumas, to their heart's content.

"But I should like to know whither we are going," inquired the doctor, somewhat imprudently, for, if any strange name had been mentioned to him, he would have had no idea of the situation of the place. The cazique, however, laughed, and, stretching forth his arm—(they were now taking a southeastern direction)—he said, "Thither." So saying, he spurred his horse, and galloped to his wives at the head of the column.

They proceeded at a rapid rate for a time, when suddenly one of the Indians rode up to the doctor, seized his arm with his left hand, and pointed with his lance. Pfeifel looked in the direction indicated, and noticed immediately in the plain a number of strange creatures, which looked like men carrying bundles on their backs, and tottering under their burden.

"What are they?" exclaimed the doctor, in surprise.

"*Choique*," replied the Indian, laughing.

"What is that?" asked the doctor. "I know no more now than before."

The Indian smiled, but, as if believing the doctor had not understood him, because he had spoken in too low a tone, he bent over him and shouted, "Choique!" so loud that not only the doctor started, but his horse made a bound forward. Pfeifel, however, learned by Meyer's aid, that the animals were ostriches, or cassowaries, which, pressing awkwardly onward by means of their legs and wings, were avoiding the hunters. It was really ludicrous to see them throw up their long, thin legs, and try to balance themselves with their wings, which are unfit for flying, and beating the air like windmills. Reiwald, delighted with the spectacle, asked why they did not stop and shoot the birds. But the Chilian interpreter, whom Jenkitrusa called Tymaco, assured him that no one would dare to detain the party for the sake of a miserable *avestrus*. They would meet with plenty of them, the more as they advanced into the Pampas, and, moreover, they could not do any thing with them, for only their feathers were valuable.

"Ha, guanaco!" suddenly exclaimed Jenkitrusa, whose eagle eye constantly swept the plain, though he did not seem to take any notice of the flying cassowaries. At the same moment his horse felt the pressure of his thighs, and it was a fine spectacle to see the chief darting across the plain. Without turning his head, he threw his lance to the next hunter, and while his steed scarcely appeared to touch the ground, he raised himself up in the saddle, and unfastened the bola, which, like his men, he wore around the body.

The others did not take part in the pursuit, for they did not yet need provisions, and must not tarry too long lest they should reach the new place of encampment at too late an hour. This was only a little private recreation of the cazique, and they knew full well that he did not need assistance on this occasion. Only two Indians galloped behind him, holding their lances.

Young Reiwald, meanwhile, watched the movements of the cazique with the greatest suspense, for in the distance he beheld a number of long-necked animals, which, on account of their thick wool, seemed much larger and stronger than they really were. The cazique did not exactly direct his course toward the spot where they were standing, with their heads raised suspiciously, and gazing upon the intruders. He rode in an oblique direction, as though he intended to gallop past them; but, in adopting this stratagem, he came close up before they became fully aware of the danger menacing them. Not until then, when he knew that he was within range of the game, did he suddenly change his course, and, like an arrow from the bow, darted straight at them. All this occurred so rapidly, that the frightened creatures for a moment did not know in what direction to escape; they dispersed to the right and left, and stopped again until one of them took the lead, when, followed by the rest, it sped at a furious rate across the Pampas. But it was too late, at least for the hindmost. The Indian was after them, and, standing in his stirrups, his right arm uplifted, and brandishing the bola round his head, he kept close on their track.

Seeing that the pursuer was gaining upon them, the animals turned to the left, so that they fled back in the path travelled by the excursionists, and this enabled the Germans to enjoy the scene in all its details. The cazique was, perhaps, a hundred yards from the game, when he suddenly drew himself up. The bola was whirled once more around his head, and almost at the same moment one of the guanacos fell heavily to the ground. Jenkitrusa, however, bestowed no further attention upon it. He turned and galloped slowly back to his party, while the two Indians sped toward the dying animal, but did not dismount. Both of them threw their lassos around the head of the fallen creature, and soon returned, dragging it still living after them, as fast as their horses could go. On their arrival, the guanaco's neck was broken, and it was strapped to the back of one of the pack-horses. The doctor and Reiwald had halted and saw now to their surprise that the bola, consisting of three balls and thongs, had so firmly encircled the legs of the guanaco that they could hardly be removed. But while one of the Indians was engaged in so doing, the other skinned one of the hams and cut from it in a most skilful manner thin pieces, about a foot wide, which would certainly furnish excellent steaks.

"Doctor," exclaimed Reiwald, in great glee, "we shall have fresh meat tonight. That was a good idea on the part of the cazique. I hope the heathens will not now kill another horse."

"Look at the number of colts they have taken along," said the doctor; "I believe they are all destined for the table. But let us make haste. Our friends are already almost out of sight."

"I wonder what he is doing now with the steaks!"

"Oh, never mind him. He will take care of them."

Turning their horses, they followed the party which was galloping at a considerable distance in front. Nothing remarkable transpired until evening. They met repeatedly with ostriches and guanacos, and twice with a small and exceedingly graceful kind of deer, but the Indians did not stop to pursue them. They always replied that they would meet with a great deal of game of the same description, and so there was no halt until the sun was near setting, when they made preparations for encamping.

The large tent of the cazique, which they had brought with them, was not erected, but they put up a number of small ones in an incredibly short space of time. Two of them were destined for Jenkitrusa and his wives, one for the Germans and the interpreter, and, as for the rest, they might get along as well as they could. There was not room enough for all of them, but this was no great misfortune, as the sky was not overcast, and, so long as the weather was dry, they did not object to sleeping in the open air. Several fires had already been kindled. An abundance of very hard thistles grew in the vicinity; besides, there were to be seen here and there a few myrtle shrubs with very thick and brittle roots, protruding from the ground, so that they had plenty of fuel.

The baggage had arrived in the meantime, and Reiwald, who was quite an epicure, looked with suspense for the steaks which, by anticipation, he had enjoyed the whole afternoon. The last horse, on which the guanaco had been placed, came somewhat later than the others, and four or five Indians accompanied it. The guanaco, to Reiwald's surprise, was delivered to the men, each of whom cut a piece from it and disappeared, while the German made at the same time a discovery which filled him with dismay. No sooner had the Indians, who had accompanied the guanaco arrived, than they dismounted, and, removing the sheepskins from their saddles, produced the steaks, which they had previously cut off. They had sat upon them during their ride of four or five leagues, and thereby rendered the meat exceedingly tender.

"Great Heavens," exclaimed Reiwald, as a vague suspicion of what this meant dawned upon his mind, "I hope they do not want us to eat this meat!"

"Let me tell you," said Meyer, "it is a real delicacy; they prepare it in Chili after the same fashion. It will melt on your tongue."

"Gracious," exclaimed Reiwald, "is it impossible, then, to find in this accursed country a single dish that does not turn one's stomach. What an appetite I had, and now it has gone again!"

"Bah!" said the doctor, who was standing by his side, "you must not be so particular; you must bear in mind that we eat every thing with great relish at the hotels without knowing how it is prepared. Why do you examine into every thing? Pray do not trouble yourself about things that do not concern you."

"But those fellows have been seated the whole afternoon on the meat," cried Reiwald, in despair.

"Well, what of it?" replied the doctor, shaking his head. "It lay at least under a sheepskin, and the fire will purify the meat. Come and let us prepare our sleeping-place."

Reiwald, however, was unable to eat anything on that evening, and, as they had not taken any provisions with them save some coffee, he had to go to bed hungry. The doctor, on the other hand, ate a large piece of the meat, which was destined only for them and the cazique. He declared afterward, perhaps only to tease Reiwald, that he had never before eaten a more delicate dish of venison.

The next day's journey was a very short one, for by ten o'clock they had reached the place where Jenkitruss intended to stay for a time and engage in hunting. In fact, a more pleasant location could not have been found anywhere on the Pampas, and it would have delighted a painter's eye. A rivulet, that flowed only in the winter-time, passed here into a lagoon about two hundred yards wide, which, although not surrounded by mountains, had its shores somewhat higher than the country around, so that the water was well protected from the wind. A group of trees stood in such a manner at the mouth of the stream that the tents could be erected among them, while the sloping southern shore was covered with dense shrubs, yielding an abundance of good firewood.

Almost in a moment the whole camp was prepared, and even the cazique's large tent was put up as quickly as it had been taken down.

"There," said Meyer, when their own tent was finished and appeared to them quite comfortable; "if you will now follow my advice, one of you—I mean the best marksman—will go out and kill for our kitchen either a guanaco or a deer; otherwise we shall again have to subsist on horse-flesh. I will meanwhile put things in order and make coffee."

"Well, I will go," said Reiwald. "I should like best to try it on foot, if I knew that there was any game near."

"Oh, there is plenty," replied Meyer, "but can you carry it home on your back? Wait; I wonder what the Indians want to do? They have not even unsaddled their horses yet.—Tymaco, what is the matter? Why does not the cazique dismount?"

"There is to be a grand hunt," said the interpreter. "The Indians that were sent out ahead have seen large numbers of guanacos and deer beyond the hill yonder, at no great distance, and we are going to surround them. Tell the Germans to be ready as soon as possible. When the tents are all up, we intend to start."

"Well," said Meyer, "we shall certainly have plenty of meat, and may defer preparing coffee."

The doctor was not altogether pleased with the intelligence; he would have preferred recreating himself a little after the hardships of the journey; but as a large piece of ground was to be surrounded, no one was allowed to remain at the camp. Even the women were to take part, and Reiwald noticed that the two Indian wives of the cazique burst into loud exultation and cantered up and down gayly. Irene sat silent and resigned on her horse, a small, but excellent trotter, which had already excited Reiwald's admiration, as, without changing its place, it kept with the others at a gallop, and had to be restrained in order not to outstrip them.

Not even a guard remained at the camp, and no fires had been kindled yet. The warriors put down their lances, and doffed their ponchos so as not to be impeded in their movements. The cazique assumed command of the hunters and arranged their plan of operations. He knew exactly where the game was, for he was familiar with every inch of the ground, and was aware of the direction the animals generally took when startled by the approach of hunters. He therefore divided his men into two equal detachments. He himself, accompanied by the women and the Germans, his escribano, and five or six Indians; the other party turned to the left, rode at first at a slow trot up the hill, and passed the crest at a still slower pace, for they caught sight already of a number of guanacos. They moved on at the same rate until another undulation was reached, when they began to gallop as fast as their horses could carry them, in a curved line, one of them remaining behind and halting at certain intervals.

Jenkitrum, on his part, observed the same precautions, and in an exceedingly short time the wild animals were surrounded, so as to be now hardly able to escape without coming within range of the bolas or lassos of the hunters. At the same time steps were taken with a circumspection which delighted Reiwald, who was a great sportsman. No sooner had they reached the next elevation than the game became uneasy. A flock of long-legged cassowaries gave the first alarm and tried to break through the line toward the south. In so doing, they took the very course in which the doctor was slowly jogging along. On getting sight of him, they started, and were turning, when they beheld the approaching forms of new enemies, and fled at the top of their speed. The doctor became so highly excited that he was at a loss to know at which of the birds to aim first. In his agitation he did not notice that one of the young Indian women had also turned her horse and was speeding straight toward him. At this moment a large cassowary passed close to him, pressing onward with legs and wings. Was he to fire shot or a bullet at him? He thought he would try the bullet first; if he missed with that he would certainly hit it with shot. The cassowary escaped uninjured, but his own horse, unaccustomed as it was to the reports of fire-arms, reared and plunged, while the rider had to take great pains to keep himself in the saddle. It was fortunate for him that he did not hear the laughter of the young huntress who flew past him twirling the bola around her head as dexterously as a warrior. She threw the next moment, and entangled the legs of the bird, which fell to the ground and vainly struggled to disengage itself from the fatal coil.

Jenkitrusz, who had witnessed this skill, uttered a cry of exultation, but the hunt engrossed his attention so much that he did not take further notice of this little incident.

Some smaller Pampas deer, with short antlers, seemed inclined to move toward the east, but were intimidated by the appearance of their enemies, and, on turning south, found the road there also obstructed. They retreated again, and gathered in the centre of the circle formed by the hunters, where they were joined by a number of guanacos, which, frightened and bewildered, stopped in the midst of the deer. Several cassowaries had broken through the line above; one of the Indians caught the last of them with his lasso, and without deeming it worth while to stop on that account was dragging the bird after him.

The Penchuenches approached nearer the game, until within rifle range of some of them huddling together, trembling and panic-struck. Reiwald knew that if he fired into their midst, one bullet might kill three or four; but he hesitated, although in their flight he was never certain of hitting one. At the same time, his horse became so restless that he could hardly master it. Suddenly the cazique gave a signal, and the Indians rushed in from all quarters.

A short time previously Reiwald thought he had noticed an animal creeping slowly, like a snake, through the tall grass, in a straight line, and across the interval lying between the German and his neighbor, the young white woman. What was it? He cast a glance toward Irene, and saw that she also had been unable to resist the pleasure of the chase. She sat no longer gloomy and abstracted on her little horse, which pranced and cantered in the sprightliest manner, but she was flushed with excitement, and, having recognized what was in the grass before her, turned her head toward the cazique, and stretched out her arm.

Jenkitrusz, who hardly ever lost sight

of her, noticed immediately the gesture she made and followed with his eyes the direction she indicated. At the same moment he transferred the bola to his left hand, with which he held the bridle; then, leaning back in his saddle, he quickly unfastened the lasso. He held it in a moment ready for use, between his fingers, and uttered a yell, whereupon his horse darted toward the animal half-concealed in the grass.

The latter seemed to perceive the movement directed against it, and lay still and motionless, but the horse was already close upon it: the lasso was whirling around the cazique's head, and it was not till then that, suddenly starting up from the ground, a large puma darted at a furious rate past Irene and broke through the line of the hunters.

"A lion!" shouted those who were near to it; but Jenkitrum was already on its track, and the deer again engrossed their attention. The game dispersed in a panic, and the Indians pursued them with bolas and lassos. Here fell a guanaco, struck by the bolas; there a deer, hopelessly entangled in the lasso, vainly struggled along the ground. Relwald, warned by the doctor's experience, and unwilling to shoot in the saddle, dismounted, missed a guanaco, but brought down a deer with a load of shot.

Greatly as he rejoiced over this achievement, Relwald hardly vouchsafed a glance upon the animal he had killed, for, at no great distance from him, the cazique hurled his lasso at the puma, which was caught in it, and the next moment jerked aside. Jenkitrum, familiar as he was with the nature of these formidable beasts of prey, spurred his horse to its utmost speed, lest the lion should succeed in regaining his feet. But the puma was more agile and quick than the horse, which was unable to obey immediately the cazique's orders. With a violent effort the puma sprang up, and its sharp teeth attempted to tear the rope, but in vain : the tough leather withstood its bite, so that the beast soon desisted from the attempt and rushed straight upon its enemy,

Jenkitrum had not lost sight of the puma for a second, and seemed by no means willing to engage in so dangerous a conflict. Two Indians were galloping up at this moment, but he wished to dispatch the puma before they came to his assistance. The horse by this time probably anticipated what was to be done, for it broke away at the top of its speed. The puma followed, but the lasso prevented it from leaping; the fore-paw got entangled, and it was down again. The cazique bestowed no further attention upon the lasso, which was well fastened to the saddle-girth. He took the bola which he had held in his left hand, turned his horse and stopped, facing his terrible adversary. The puma, dragged as it was along the ground, had hitherto been unable to regain a firm foothold, but no sooner did the rope slacken, than the beast, with unabated fury, sprang to its feet again, and looked its adversary full in the face, but did not leap.

"Aha!" laughed the Indian. "You think I have released you, my fine fellow!" And, without ceasing to whirl the bola, he seized the lasso, which now lay straining on his knee, and jerked it. No sooner did the puma feel the movement than its fury redoubled, and, uttering a hoarse noise, rushed toward the horse. The latter attempted to turn aside, but the cazique held the bridle firmly, and, at the same moment, threw his missile at the puma, whose forehead it struck, so that it fell dead without uttering a sound.

This scene passed with great rapidity, but Reiwald stated afterward that he had never before seen any thing more interesting than this vigorous Indian catching the lion of the Pampas—not dragging it to death in a cowardly manner, but bravely facing and killing it. Irene, forgetting every thing else for the moment, fixed her eyes in trembling suspense on the cazique's noble form, and a smile overspread her pale features as the dangerous animal fell dead. Wild, deafening cheers rent the air; here and there several Indians galloped after the escaped game, and attempted to overtake some of the guanacos, which are by no means so swift-footed as the deer. Others assembled at no great distance from the cazique, and gathered the game that had been killed. There was a great deal of it. Seven guanacos, four deer, three cassowaries, and the puma, lay on the ground. The hunters had now provisions to last them for some time, though nothing more should be killed for the next few days.

The scene was quite animated at the moment when the game was loaded upon the horses; the Indians stood about laughing and chatting, and telling one another what they had seen, and how they had secured their prey. They laughed at the "four-eyed Aleman" (the doctor wore spectacles), who had missed his aim, and, at the same time, barely escaped falling from his horse, while Entanjal, the cazique's second wife, had so quickly killed the cassowary with her light bola. It was fortunate for the doctor that he did not understand the stories told about him, and how they were making merry at his awkwardness and mishap.

On the whole, the Germans did not distinguish themselves in this chase; at least, they did not convince the Ponchuenches of the formidable character of their fire-arms, since with the three shots they had fired they killed only a single animal. But Jenkitrum, whose face was radiant with joy, rode up and made his interpreter tell them that he was glad they had assisted at so fine a hunt; that they might ride out with their guns the next day by themselves, in order to see how much game they were able to kill, for rifles were not suitable, while lassos and bolas were by far more effective.

The loading of the horses did not last so long as the Germans expected, and the doctor was still busily engaged in examining the puma when some Indians came to carry it away. They had not brought pack-animals with them, but, as the distance was short, their saddle-horses were able to bear the double weight of the Indians and the booty. One of them therefore mounted, and the others handed to him pieces of venison, which he held before him on the saddle; the others followed his example, and, while the sun was yet high, the excursionists returned to their tents.

CHAPTER XXXII.

THE RETURN.

THE Germans liked their abode on the shore of the small lagoon far better than that at their other stopping-places during their present journey. They had food enough, though consisting only of meat, but at least they were at liberty to prepare it after their own cleanly fashion; and when the Indians, after a few days, killed a young mare, no one compelled them to partake of it. Some indeed was offered to them, but the Penchuenches laughed good-naturedly at their refusal to accept it. The Alemanos, they thought, did not know better, and henceforth they were not any more troubled. Both of them afterward went out hunting on their own account, and as they were quite successful—on foot, too, which seemed incomprehensible to the Indians—they recovered some of the respect which they seemed to have lost.

Reiwald and his friend did not see the young white woman very often, and, as they did not even speak her language, they were unable to hold intercourse with her. It seemed as though Jenkitrusa did not intend ever to return to his former place of encampment on the Limai; at least, he once asked the Germans if they purposed passing the winter on the Pampas. In that event, they might shortly accompany him to the eastern part of the plains and visit some caciques living there. He always treated them very kindly, and differed from all the Indians whom they had hitherto met, in never asking for any thing—not even for a piece of tobacco. If they gave him any—for they had brought with them most of their supply—he accepted it with cordial thanks, and smoked it with great relish. It was observable, too, that he was delighted with some strings of red and blue corals which they presented him; but he never asked, as others had done, for this and that, nor did he manifest any desire for Reiwald's cloak or any thing else which the Germans possessed.

Thus pleasantly passed here three weeks. Heavy showers had occurred repeatedly, particularly in the beginning of their sojourn on the shore of the small lagoon, and there had been also several storms of such violence that, when they were surprised by them on the Pampas, they were hardly able to remain on horseback. But their camp was so well protected from the wind, that they felt little or nothing of it. At the close of the three weeks calmer and drier weather set in, and the sun quickly evaporated the moisture of the soil.

Meyer seemed to be exceedingly comfortable, and, strange to say, he did not express the slightest inclination for his wife. He once spoke of even accompanying the cacique to Fort Carmen, whence it was said, it was easy for travellers to reach the Argentine Republic. Reiwald was, perhaps, quite justified in suspecting him of laying plans to run away, in his turn, from his just-recovered wife, especially as he surmised that almost insurmountable difficulties prevented him from revisiting Chili. It is true he could not meet with a better opportunity for carrying his schemes into effect than was now offered him; but he seemed to regret already having hinted that his attention was engrossed in this way. At all events, he skilfully evaded further queries and allusions, and never lost his temper.

They were surprised one day by a request from the cazique, to accompany him for a few days to the old camp. At an advanced hour of the preceding night, a messenger had arrived thence, and, to all appearance, brought important news, for Jenkitrusa looked gloomy and reserved. The Germans would have preferred to stay, and especially did Meyer, by means of all sorts of subterfuges, attempt to avoid returning to the camp, but in vain. Tymaco told him at once that he would never receive permission to remain, as the cazique would leave his tent and his wives under the protection and surveillance of an old chief. The other Penchuenches did not leave, as Jenkitrusa would return in the course of three or four days.

The preparations for the trip were rapidly made; and, as they did not take any baggage or pack-horses with them, and as their horses were in excellent condition, they could travel the whole distance at a gallop. Nevertheless, they did not reach the Limay until late at night, and, as the Germans had surrendered their tent to Doña Mercedes, and did not wish to disturb the lady in the dead of night, they kindled a fire on the river-bank, and encamped in the open air. It was a clear and calm night, and they were getting more accustomed to the inconveniences of Indian life.

Reiwald meanwhile thought of the beautiful but unhappy white woman.— Were they to conceal from her father that they had seen his daughter, and that she was alive and well? This would at least afford some consolation to him. But Meyer, whom he consulted on this point, exclaimed in dismay:

"For mercy's sake, do not meddle with female affairs among the Indians. The cazique knows that her father is here to ransom her, but he refuses to enter upon any negotiations on this point, and declines even to see the Chileno. Do you wish to interfere in a matter so delicate, and play the mediator?—In that event, permit me to congratulate you; but, if you should be badly treated, pray remember what I tell you."

"And what if he should afterward discover that we knew of it?"

"But what does it concern you?" said Meyer. "Do you not know that it is exceedingly foolish to meddle with other people's business? And if I had been shrewd—" It occurred to him, probably at this moment, that it would not be prudent for him to say more; and, breaking off in the middle of his sentence, he turned to the other side and fell asleep. On the following morning, there was quite a commotion at the camp; horsemen were galloping up and down among the tents, and the whole population seemed to be excited. Something extraordinary was about to transpire, for when Cruzado at sunrise repaired to the place where the friends were encamped, he told them that the trial of the Argentine prisoner was to take place on that day, and that some of the most powerful chiefs had been summoned for this purpose from their remote winter quarters.

For all that, the prisoner was meanwhile allowed to go freely about the camp, and it was scarcely deemed necessary to keep him under surveillance. At first, indeed, owing to the rough treatment he received at the hands of the Indian who had dragged him on the ground, he was so lame and bruised, that he was barely able to walk from one tent to the other. During the last week, however, his health had much improved. His leg had healed, and, as his enemies in general treated him—if not very kindly—at least indifferently, he no longer seemed to apprehend any danger. He himself knew of many instances of prisoners whom the Indians had at first intended to execute, and whom they had kept for a long time at their camp, and finally treated as regular members of their tribe. He thought a similar fate awaited him, too, and he would sooner or later find an opportunity to make his escape; he only needed to bide his time.

But this morning he was startled on meeting in the camp with the cazique Tureopan, who rode past him, not only disdainfully, but with a most scornful and malicious smile. He knew that this cazique hated him above all, and he had good reason for so doing. What could have led him from his remote winter quarters to this camp? An expedition? But in that event Jenkitrus would not have divided his tribe into halves. All doubt was soon to be dispelled, for additional visitors arrived at ten o'clock in the morning—the cazique Pallisaen, by whose side Allumapu was riding. How intensely that Indian hated him, he knew very well.

They assembled in one of the larger tents, and the Argentine was just thinking if it would not be best for him to keep out of the way, and take a walk up the river, when Saman, who had caught a horse, and was holding his lasso in his right hand, rode up to him and said:

"Follow me, my friend; the caziques want to see you. They would like to know what you did with all our horses."

"What do I know about them?" replied the Argentine, sullenly. "Did you appoint me their custodian?"

He was about to pass Saman and go on his way, but the Indian stopped him, and, bursting into laughter, exclaimed:

"That will not do you any good, my friend; Jenkitrus wants to see you, and you must obey."

The Argentine started; his worst fears seemed about to be realized. But what could he do? Flee? Whither? And at this moment he was not even mounted, while the Indian was before him, lasso in hand. Nothing remained for him but to obey. Feigning the utmost indifference, and throwing back his head, he asked:

"What does the cazique want of me? No matter, I will go to him."

He turned, and, slowly followed by Saman, walked to the council-tent, which the Indian pointed out to him.

Meanwhile Cruzado had informed Doña Mercedes that the owners of the tent had returned, and the lady, therefore, moved into the room destined for her. The doctor was busily engaged in stirring up the fire and preparing coffee, while Reiwald sat quietly on a horse-skull by the fire, and smoked his pipe.

Cruzado left the place in order to ascertain what would be the result of the meeting, as Jenkitrus himself had told him that the prisoner was to be tried. Meyer lay again in his favorite recumbent attitude, with his cigarette, but looking by no means so unconcerned as usual, and glancing now and then timidly at the small fur partition, behind which he knew his wife was making her toilet. Suddenly the door of the tent opened, and an Indian appeared on the threshold, who gazed upon the group with a peculiar smile; he did not, however, advance, but waited for an invitation.

He was a tall young man, with open, good-natured features, but a much darker complexion than that of the Penchuenches. The doctor looked at him in surprise, for up to this time every Indian that wished to enter the tent had announced himself by a shout. Reiwald took the pipe from his mouth, and contemplated the new-comer, whom he did not remember having ever seen before. The visitor, nodding to them kindly, said:

"Mari! Mari! Alemanes."

"Pray," said Reiwald, "explain yourself. Perhaps, you are a new neighbor of ours and wish to give us your compliments?"

The young man shook his head smilingly, for he did not understand the words. He remained standing in the entrance, and Reiwald continued with a corresponding gesture:

"Step in, señor. Be seated; I will get you a chair."

The Indian complied with the invitation, but still stood glancing about the tent.

"He is obviously in search of some one," said the doctor. "We cannot converse with such rascals. Put the fellow out.—Reiwald, coffee is ready. Tell him to visit us some other time, when we are not at home."

The young man, who seemed also to give up all thought of entering upon a conversation with the strangers, now walked unceremoniously into one of the corners of the tent, where there were additional guanaco-skins. He spread them out, and threw himself upon them.

"In truth," remarked the doctor, "he acts as though he were at home here."

"And I believe he is," replied Meyer, who had meanwhile observed him attentively. "He is doubtless the owner of the tent, who has returned this morning with the other caziques.—Allumapu?"

Meyer turned inquiringly to the Indian, who had heard his own name. The latter seemed to understand what he meant, for he nodded again smilingly, and Reiwald exclaimed in dismay:

"Dear me, doctor, he can put us out! What are we to do? Shall we invite him to drink a cup of coffee?"

"Of course," replied the doctor; "but, above all things, give him a piece of tobacco. That is the customary coin hereabouts, and it will gladden his heart more than any thing else; see, how he smiles since he has heard the mere word?"

Reiwald acted immediately upon the suggestion, and the young Indian really seemed delighted with the gift; but he accepted it with so much grace, and such a noble, frank bearing, that he almost embarrassed the Germans. Nor did he refuse their invitation to partake of the coffee, though perhaps he never before had tasted any. But, as the Germans added sugar, he seemed to relish the beverage greatly, and, addressing his guests or hosts—for they were both—in tolerably good Spanish, he asked them if none of them spoke that language.

All difficulties were now overcome, and they could sustain a conversation with him. Allumapa told them that the caciques had assembled that morning to punish a white criminal, whom they had always treated with kindness, making him many presents, but who had infamously betrayed and defrauded them. The witnesses were at hand, and, if convicted of the charges preferred against him, he would have to expiate his crimes.

While he was speaking, a loud cry of pain suddenly rent the air, and Reiwald and the doctor started up from their seats. Allumapa beckoned them to keep their seats, but the piercing shriek was repeated, and they were unable to remain longer in the tent. It is true, Meyer attempted to detain them, for he was more familiar with the savage customs, and, kindly as he and his friends had always been treated by the Indians, he did not wish to meet them at a moment when their anger was aroused—especially against a white man. Besides, they could not render any assistance to the criminal, nor was there any reason why they should. But Reiwald and his friend did not allow themselves to be kept back, and at last even Allumapa followed them. Meyer, however, mindful of the warning which Cruzado had given him not to interfere with any thing that might transpire, and not to disturb the Indians, quietly remained reclining at the fire, and from time to time heard the shouts and shrieks which penetrated from without.

"Don Carlos!" suddenly exclaimed a soft voice, and Meyer started, for his attention was given to the drama outside, and he did not think of his wife. But the voice continued in a kind though slightly reproachful tone: "You have so long been away from me, and yet, on on your return, you do not vouchsafe me a single affectionate word! Is it not wrong in you to treat me thus? If you knew how profoundly I have repented of the injury I did you, and how grievously I was punished for it, you would certainly take compassion on your poor Mercedes, and no longer be angry with her."

Meyer groaned aloud, but he did not move. Mercedes approached: she felt that she must take the first step toward their reconciliation, and, putting her hand on his shoulder, kissed her husband's lips, which he suffered without resistance.

"Don Carlos," she whispered, "why do you not look at me? Have you entirely forgotten the time when you called me your dear, beautiful Mercedes—when you sat for hours by me and listened to the songs I sung and the airs I played on the guitar? Do you no longer recollect all that?"

"Señora," said Meyer, irritated at her not referring to her disappearance, and at alluding only to what he had said and done, "do not remind me of my weaknesses. I confess to you that I was a fool."

"Oh," sighed Mercedes, covering her face with her hands, "then I am lost— irretrievably wretched! Would you had left me to my fate! Death would soon have delivered me from my misery; but as it is, you have only appeared to make me feel the agony of my unfortunate position and behold the abyss on whose brink I am standing. Oh, I am very unhappy, and cannot even complain, for I know well that I myself have brought my sufferings on my own head by disdaining the happiness of which perhaps I never was worthy." And, as if overcome by her despair, she sat down near the fire and wept bitterly.

Meyer, it is true, had reason to be distrustful of his wife, for, aside from the indignities he had received at her hands during the last months of their wedded life, she had filled the measure of her iniquities by running away from him. But, soft-hearted as he was, he could not see any one weep, least of all a woman, much less his own wife. She had certainly grievously suffered after her separation from him; but what if she really repented? The cabin on the Maybne Lagoon rose again before his memory, and he saw there also a weeping, unhappy being.

"Oh, that I were dead!" said Mercedes at this moment, in a low, but mournful voice, "for what is in store for me but a life of endless wretchedness?"

"Mercedes!" exclaimed Meyer, in a low voice; but she made no reply, weeping and sobbing louder than before. "Mercedes!" repeated the German, after a brief pause, in a somewhat louder tone, "come — reassure yourself. You may perhaps become happy again."

"Oh, you do not love me any longer —you cannot love me," continued Mercedes, without raising herself. "I was a bad woman—I have treated you meanly and ungratefully, and you will never forgive me—you cannot."

"Oh, console yourself, Mercedes," replied her husband, who really began to take compassion on her. "The good God decreed that we should meet again, and all may yet be well."

"And can you ever forget the injury I did you?" cried the young wife, lifting her face and gazing at him with her large dark eyes.—She was still very pretty, and Meyer said, in deep emotion :

"I will try to do so, Mercedes. Dry your tears; your sufferings and hardships will soon be over, and we shall return as quickly as possible to Chili."

"My Carlos! my dear, dear Carlos!" exclaimed Mercedes, springing to her feet, folding him to her heart and covering his lips and forehead with kisses. But he returned her caresses less impetuously; disengaging himself from her embrace, and, casting a glance on her dress, he said:

"We must attend to your toilet. Your dress is almost in shreds."

"Ah, Carlos, I shall occasion you again much expense."

"Yes," sighed Don Carlos, in a low tone, "but that can no longer be helped. It is true, we shall not be able to get here many goods—but perhaps a shawl and a wrapper from one of the Indian women."

"My dear, dear Carlos!"

"Never mind," responded Meyer, lighting his cigarette; "it cannot be helped. The past is past, and—" He suddenly started and listened. A shot crashed without, accompanied with wild, piercing yells, as if from a thousand throats. At the same moment a horse passed the tent at a furious gallop, and the ground trembled, as if the whole camp were in uproar, or an enemy had suddenly taken it by surprise.

"What is the matter?" cried Meyer, arising from his couch in dismay. "A shot — heavens! my countrymen must have committed some folly—"

"But their rifles are here," exclaimed Mercedes, pointing to the two weapons.

"Well, something extraordinary must have happened, at all events," exclaimed Meyer, "and they are doubtless concerned with it. I know my countrymen."

"And you intend to leave me!" cried his wife, in great terror. "Oh, do not cross the path of the Indians while their anger is aroused. It is terrible."

"I cannot, indeed, help them now," replied Meyer, alarmed for the safety of his friends; "but I have least to fear from the savages. Let me go, Mercedes; I shall be back directly;" and, disengaging himself from her arms, he took his hat and rushed from the tent.

CHAPTER XXXIII.

MURDER.

The caziques, presided over by Jenkitruss, had assembled in the large council-tent to try a criminal not only charged with having stolen a large number of the horses, but also for murder. At that very time the old Indian ferry-man of the Nontue and Huetchun Lagoons had been slain on the northern shore of the narrow arm connecting the two lakes. When the Indians at the time pursued the horse-thief, on whom they were gaining rapidly, the ferry-boat or raft did not come over, despite their loud calls, and finally one of the chiefs was obliged to swim across on horseback—a dangerous attempt, which had already cost the life of many a bold man. The boat was fastened to the shore, but by its side lay the owner, dead and stiff in his gore, and, to all appearance, the arraigned criminal had assassinated him in cold blood, partly in order to get rid of a dangerous witness, and partly to prevent the Indians from crossing, and thereby to secure his flight.

His pursuers, in fact, were detained long enough for him to gain the other slope of the Cordilleras and reach the Chileno settlements; but the Penchuenches had not forgotten him and his crime, and it was the height of imprudence on the part of Don Pedro to venture again within reach of their lassos. Nevertheless, they treated the prisoner humanely until his guilt had been proved. He was allowed to go freely about the camp, but forbidden to mount a horse; and, if he had done so, whither could he have fled? At the ferry of the Ranco Pass there was encamped Tchaluak, to whom word had already been sent not to let any whites pass, unless accompanied by a messenger of Jenkitruss. Toward the north? How could he travel for many days across the Pampas without lasso or bola, and where were roaming hordes into whose hands he would inevitably fall? Flight was impossible, or nearly so, and Pedro Alfeirs knew the country too well to venture upon such an attempt at such a season. Besides, why should he do so? He enjoyed almost entire liberty among the Penchuenches—food in abundance had been given him, and all his wants provided for; in fact, for the time, his position was quite comfortable, and, by the ensuing summer, he would certainly meet with an opportunity to escape from the restraint so irksome to him.

Suddenly, in the midst of his supposed security, Pedro heard of the meeting of the caziques, and, almost before he had an inkling of the danger impending over him, he stood before his judges— a nearly-convicted criminal. He denied every thing, asserting that he had neither stolen horses, nor even taken the route by the ferry; that all the streams on the Pampas were dry, and, without being conscious of any crime whatever, he leisurely journeyed toward the Villa Rica Pass, and entered Chili by it. But these statements were refuted by Turcopan, who had seen him at the time south of the Nontue Lagoon, but did not suspect crime until Paillacan had called upon him to join in the pursuit of the fugitive. These two caziques afterward found the corpse of the ferry-man, and close by a white buckle such as no Indian wears, but it had been seen on a leathern strap fastened to Pedro's long boots.

As the Argentine still persisted in his denial, the indignation of the Indians surpassed all bounds. They knew that he had committed the crimes for which he was arrested, and hatred and resentment against the criminal drove them to extremities.

The Indians on guard outside were called in; the prisoner was seized and tied, and Saman whipped him with the heavy lower end of his lasso, so that he burst into wild shrieks of pain.

"Mercy! mercy!" cried the wretch. But his judges were ignorant of that word. As they themselves were able to bear with unflinching courage the greatest pain, so they despised the lamentations of others. Saman whipped him as long as he could move his arm, and Alfeira, writhing under the fearful punishment, cried out that he would make a full confession. It was not till then that he was unfettered, and, fixing his blood-shot eyes with a terrified expression on Saman, who remained standing with his uplifted lasso, he admitted having stolen the horses, and assassinated the ferry-man in order not to be betrayed by him.

A deathlike silence reigned in the tent, and the Indians listened with calmness to his account of the deed. They had no need of propounding additional questions to him.

"Take him out, Saman," said Jenkitrusa, in a dispassionate voice. "The caziques will meanwhile decide upon his fate. Take him out—we wish to be alone."

Saman seized Pedro, and said to him in an imperious tone:

"Come along, my boy! You have heard what the cazique said. I hope you will never again steal horses and assassinate Panohuenches. Come along!"

Alfeira stepped out of the tent. He was not fettered, which was deemed unnecessary, for he was in the middle of the camp, surrounded by the Pampas, having at that time no communication with the mountains, owing to the sudden rise of the Limai River. If he had run away into the plains, the Indians would soon have reached him, and even taken pleasure in the pursuit. He glanced around in dismay. Despite the danger, he thought that he might still make his escape: he foresaw the fate that awaited him if he submitted without resistance. Several years before he witnessed the exultation with which these Pehuenches dragged to death one of his countrymen whom they had convicted of a similar offence, and had then left his corpse on the Pampas a prey to the pumas and buzzards. But how was he to flee? No horse was near, save that of his executioner, who mounted it himself, and slowly rode down the street, bestowing little attention upon the prisoner. There were, however, groups of Indians everywhere casting on him glances of sullen hatred. Of course they would have attacked him the moment he made the slightest attempt to escape. Minute after minute elapsed, and his fate would presently be irrevocably decided.

What a time of suspense and expectation had the unfortunate old Chileno meanwhile passed through! How often had he asked and entreated the Indians to let him see his child! All was of no avail. The only reply was, that Jenkitrus was with his wives on the Pampas, where he would probably pass several weeks. On his return he would perhaps come to some decision. "Perhaps, come to some decision!" This was the only consolation—the only beam of hope illumining the darkness of his soul.

But Jenkitrus had now returned. José, who had been at the principal camp in order to fetch meat, which Mankelaw furnished him very liberally, informed the Chileno of the arrival of the cazique. He himself had seen Jenkitrus as he went to the council-tent, where, he was told, many chiefs had assembled.

In tremulous haste Don Enrique ordered his horse to be saddled, that he might speak with the cazique, and throw himself at his feet, if there were no other means of moving his iron heart. José entreated him urgently to desist from his purpose, as the chief had issued stringent orders that he must not be troubled until he sent for the Chileno. But was the latter to remain here in agony, merely because he was afraid of the cazique's anger? No; what could befall him? Jenkitrus might kill him; but he would rather die than bear any longer his misery.

José at last obeyed and caught his master's horse; but, owing to the long rest and good pasture, it had become so spirited that the peon was scarcely able to overtake it. But he was an excellent groom, and, like all his countrymen, well-versed in using the lasso. He led the animal to the tent, where Don Enrique was waiting, who, in his impatience, put on the saddle, strapped, and fastened it.

"The pistols are in the holsters, señor," said José, holding the bridle. "Had I better take them out?"

"No, compañero," replied the old man, "leave them where they are, but if they refuse to restore my daughter to me, I swear I will try to find out where she is; for I am determined to be no longer trifled with in this manner."

"Señor!" remonstrated the peon, beseechingly.

"No, no! pack up my travelling-bag and have it in readiness, lest I should afterward be detained. Get your own horse, too; the next hour must decide our fate."

"Oh, dearest señor," insisted José,

"beware of ruining yourself by your impetuosity—patience!"

"Begone!" cried the old man; "let me hear no more this word, which has made my blood boil for several months past. Begone—obey my order, and I will bear the consequences."

Without waiting for a reply, he vaulted with youthful agility into the saddle, and trotted to the other camp, where he knew the caziques and chiefs were assembled.

On his arrival, he stopped in surprise, for, while at a distance he heard piercing cries rending the air, a deathlike stillness prevailed in the camp. He listened; not a sound was to be heard, and, on coming near, he saw several Indians standing in front of their tents, or leisurely walking up the streets toward the council. He now rode slowly on, thinking he would meet with Cruzado, who was to lay his request before the cazique. At the place where he was halting, grew one of those small apple-trees, of which there were a good many throughout the camp, and which seemed to have been planted that the tents might be fastened to them. He dismounted, hung the bridle on one of the branches, and walked with a throbbing heart toward the place where his fate was to be decided.

The Argentine, Pedro, with whom Don Enrique was well acquainted, was passing out of the council-tent, looking livid and terrified. The old man quickly forgot his surroundings, for in the door of the council-tent appeared Jenkitruss, to whom he had so long vainly attempted to gain access. The bystanders shouted something to him, but he did not understand them. A few started back, others pointed to the road by which he had just arrived; did they refer to his child? He turned his head, bewildered and frightened, when suddenly the Argentine mounted on Don Enrique's white horse, and passed him at a full gallop.

"Stop the villain!" cried Jenkitruss, who saw at a glance how it had happened. "He intends to escape! seize him from the horse!"

The Indians hastened, and Jenkitruss threw himself in front to stop him—a flash!—a report!—and the swift-footed animal darted in another direction through the camp.

At this moment two Indians were driving a number of horses down the street, and a score of Penchuenches in a moment jumped upon their backs. Few of them had in the hurry taken lassos—to pursue the fugitive was their only thought.

Pfeifel and Reiwald were surprised at the whole scene, and at a loss to know what it all meant. The cavalcade pressed onward, without taking notice of them. The doctor was hurled aside; Reiwald, before he knew what had happened, fell to the ground, and the Indians rode over him, rending the air with demoniacal yells.

Jenkitruss stood in the middle of the street, with one arm uplifted, and the other pressed to his breast. No one particularly regarded him, for all eyes were fixed on the fugitive. The cazique made a step forward—reeled, turned, and fell heavily on his face."

---

* The supreme cazique of the Penchuenches, Jenkitruss, was really shot in this manner by an Argentine in his own camp, and in the midst of all his warriors. The murderer succeeded in making his escape. Mankelaw, the brother of the assassi-

The Indians, who had started in pursuit of Pedro, did not notice the event, and if they heard the shot, they scarcely knew who had fired it, much less at whom it had been discharged. The whole scene occurred with such rapidity that few minutes elapsed when all was over. Those who were able to lay their hands on a horse mounted it and galloped after the Argentine.

Meanwhile the wailing cry, "Jenkitrasa, the cazique, has been killed!" resounded through the camp. Some Indians, intending to raise him up, because they believed at first that he had been thrown down by one of the horses, beheld his wound and the life-blood issuing from it. Mankelaw knelt by his side—he held the upper part of his brother's body before him, spoke to him, and entreated him to reply. The cazique still breathed—he raised his eyes, but not a word fell from his lips—quivering convulsively, he lay a corpse in his brother's arms.

The Indians, men and women, now rushed out, and nothing was heard but howls and yells, which terrified the whites, who were not familiar with their customs on such occasions. Cruzado rushed past Meyer, who was just engaged in lifting the unconscious Reiwald from the ground and conveying him to the tent.

"Where is the doctor?" he exclaimed. "The cazique has been shot."

"Shot! Great heavens! by whom?"
"By the Argentine."
"Doctor! Yonder!" cried Meyer.

seated cazique, took his brother's place, and is still the supreme ruler of the Pampas.

Cruzado was soon at the side of Pfeifel, who, as soon as he understood what was the matter, at once accompanied the half-breed. But what availed science on this occasion? It could not resuscitate the dead. The cazique's poncho was removed, in order to discover where the bullet had struck him, but a glance at the wound convinced the doctor that human assistance would be of no avail. The bullet had struck the heart, and the pulse stood still.

Mankelaw remained motionless by the side of his brother. He covered his head, lest the Penobuenches should see his tears. The Indians now gathered in profound silence around the group. The fact that the white doctor still seemed to make efforts to revive Jenkitrusa, and applied his ear to the dead cazique's breast, caused them to hope that he might yet be saved. All eyes were fixed on Pfeifel in the utmost suspense, but as he shook his head mournfully, and covered again the cazique's pierced breast with the poncho, the Indians burst afresh into deafening lamentations, which lasted a long time. Mankelaw at length uncovered his head, and, looking around calmly, made a signal to lift up the cazique and carry him into the tent, which was done quickly and noiselessly.

Meanwhile Cruzado had approached Meyer, and, touching his shoulder, whispered to him:

"Get the whites out of the way; let them go to their dwelling and leave it no more on this day. The Indians are exasperated, else we may fear the worst. Make haste—I will remove the old man, and then request Mankelaw to take you under his protection. Go!"

The warning was too well meant not to be acted upon immediately, and, seizing the doctor's arm, Meyer led him over to the still half-paralyzed Reiwald, whom they assisted in reaching their tent. There they arranged his couch, and examined his injuries, which fortunately proved to be not very dangerous. The horses had all sprung over him; but, on being thrown down, his head was struck by the knee of one of the Indians, and a hoof had badly bruised the calf of his right leg; no bones, however, were broken, and ordinary remedies were likely to restore him.

There was the greatest commotion at the camp all day. A large concourse was surging up and down in front of the Germans' tent, and often were heard imprecations which might have made the hearts of the whites tremble if they had understood their meaning. But not an Indian entered; even Allamapu did not show himself there all day, and Pfeifel, almost frightened at their being left alone in this manner, finally intended to step out, but Meyer would not allow him.

It was not until late in the afternoon that Cruzalo made his appearance. The noise had ceased, and even the groans and lamentations of the women. The half-breed explained to them the cause of this stillness. The cazique's remains, according to custom, had immediately been conveyed to his camp on the Pampas, where he had left his wives, and where his funeral was to be celebrated with due solemnity. The ceremonies might last a week, and even longer.

For the rest, he told them that they need no more fear for their safety.— True, the Indians had been beside themselves with rage for a few hours, and had even demanded that the whites should expiate the crime committed by one of their race. But Mankelaw issued orders that no harm should befall them —not even the Chileno, on whose horse the assassin had fled.

And was the murderer overtaken? None of the pursuers had as yet returned. Pedro had taken the northern route toward the Cusu-Leufu, and they hoped to come up with him, at least on the banks, which, if he did not reach the only ford, would impede his flight, as they were precipitous; moreover, the river was very high, and he could not but fall into their hands.

For the next few days the camp seemed entirely deserted; only a small guard remained there, while all the others hastened to the Pampas to assist at the funeral ceremonies of a cazique. The hopes that the torture and execution of the murderer would add to the solemnity of these ceremonies were not to be supplied; for the pursuers, exhausted by hunger, and riding wearied horses, returned one after another to receive the tidings of the death of their beloved chief. The criminal had escaped!— Familiar with the ford of the Cusu-Leufu, and, fully alive to the fate that awaited him in case he should be captured by the Penehuenches, he plunged into the raging torrent and succeeded in swimming it. Although four or five followed, the horse of the Chileno soon distanced them. They lost sight of him; he was safe, unless fallen in with by the tribes on the other side of the river, before reaching the northern districts.

The unfortunate Chileno was meanwhile a prey to his anxiety, as he saw himself doomed once more to the same inactivity as before. It is true, he once took the rash resolution of repairing to the caziques, while they were engaged in those funeral rites, on the Pampas; but Cruzado prevented him from carrying it into effect. By such a step, he would have exposed his life to the greatest danger, without having any prospect of success. The Indians were encamped there in the paroxysm of their grief; for—while the rites of the Puelchuenches were observed, and the corpse dissected, until nothing was left but his skeleton, which was placed in an open grave with the ornaments and arms of the deceased, together with his horses, which were also killed—the loud lamentations of the women kept the whole tribe in a state of incessant and feverish excitement. They would have killed any stranger who attempted to disturb them, much more to carry off one of the women belonging to the cazique. The mourning-time had to be observed; it was not until it was over that Mankelaw would be able to decide concerning Don Enrique's application.

CHAPTER XXXIV.

THE CAZIQUE MANKELAW.

Two weeks had elapsed before messengers from the camp on the Pampas announced the return of Mankelaw and his companions, and their absence might perhaps have lasted even longer but for the fact that Tshaluak, who had meanwhile been waiting in impatience for the return of the strangers, had arrived on the banks of the Limai and demanded an interview with the caziques. For, the news of the death of Jonkitruss had been disseminated, and ambitious plans filled Tshaluak's mind, and urged the restless chief to take decisive steps. He had dispatched couriers in all directions, to the northern and southern tribes, and his own men, maddened as they were by the immoderate use of chicha, had been worked upon by his addresses and promises in such a manner that they would have blindly followed him wherever he led the way. He aspired to nothing short of the supreme sovereignty over all the tribes, from the settlements of the whites in the north to the regions where the Patagonians live under chieftains and rulers of their own. This dignity formerly belonged to his family, and whatever had deprived them of it—treason and rebellion against the rights of the Indians, as the old folks sometimes related to the children at the camp-fires—these family rights could never become extinct. Though one of the former caziques had been divested of them, his grandsons were justified in boldly claiming their restoration.

Tobaluak arrived with sixty of his men, having passed the now somewhat lower Limai without calling for the raft. The doctor was grieved on noticing that he wore his cloak; but he wore it inside out, so as to display the gay red lining, on which the brightly-burnished buttons had been sewed, and which, with his brown head, and wild, dishevelled hair, gave him a very singular and almost demoniacal appearance.

"Why, that must be Old Nick himself!" exclaimed Reiwald, as Tchaluak, dripping from his river-bath, galloped through the camp and halted in front of the council-tent, of which he and his men immediately took possession, without asking any one's leave. No sooner had he come than he inquired whether the Germans were yet on the Limai, and, on being answered in the affirmative, he immediately dispatched a messenger, and requested them to send him—some tobacco. He did not care to see them; but he sent for Cruzado, and, besides desiring of him information on many other points, he asked him whether the old Chileno had recovered his daughter, or what would become of her, now that the cacique was dead—a query which the half-breed could answer only by his usual "Quien sabe!"

On the same evening Cruzado saddled his horse, and rode out into the Pampas, to inform Mankelaw of Tchaluak's arrival, and of the claims he laid to the supreme dignity. At the same time he intended to advocate the cause of the Chileno, on whom he had taken compassion, and who seemed now to succumb to the grief and incertitude which had been gnawing so long at his heart. Hitherto hope had sustained him, made him indifferent to privations, and directed his eyes constantly toward the one longed-for goal. His mind now began to give way, and Cruzado feared the worst; he repeated incessantly that he was afraid lest Mankelaw, like his brother, would refuse to give up Irene, and keep her as his wife. Don Enrique's appearance for the last few days had undergone so marked a change, that it did not even escape the usually careless half-breed. His cheeks had become livid, his eyes lay deep in their sockets, and seemed incessantly in search of something; and, as he had formerly walked about restlessly, or packed and unpacked the presents which he had brought with him, so he sat now for hours motionless, a prey to the most distressing anxiety.

That his apprehensions were not altogether ill-grounded, Cruzado knew very well, though he took good care not to tell him so. He was too familiar with the Indians, and whatever Mankelaw might have thought of the course adopted by his brother, or might have said to him on this subject, who could tell what he was likely to do now, since the young woman was at his mercy? Cruzado could give the father but one consolation: that the wife of a cacique could not belong to another within one year after her husband's death, and that an infraction of this law, which was conscientiously observed by the Penchenches, was punished with death. He then promised to ride over to Mankelaw, and return as soon as possible with the cacique's answer; until then he encouraged him to hope that all would yet be well. Day after day passed by, but the messenger did not return. The Chileno sat waiting patiently in his tent, and when his throbbing heart threatened to burst, he murmured, in a low voice, "Paciencia!"

Cruzado meanwhile met the caciques at the camp on the Pampas, whither even Huitallan and Hucatchapan had hastened to mourn over the untimely death of their highest ruler, and render homage to the new one. Tchalnak's arrival, too, had not surprised any one; nay, it had been expected that he would come, as he was encamped at no great distance from the Limai. But the excitement ran very high when Cruzado informed the Indians of that chief's aspirations to the supreme power. At first the others intended to hasten back to the old camp to chastise him for his insolence, but Mankelaw quieted them. He said it was a subject that could not be fought out with lances and bolas, if they wished to maintain peace in their country, but must be discussed and decided in the council-tent; and there was no better opportunity than now, when most of the caziques of the Pampas were assembled. Only Huincaval and Jankin were absent. Messengers had been also dispatched to them with the mournful intelligence, but Huincaval happened to be at the fort of the whites, to receive the tribute of the Argentines, while Jankin had undertaken a journey to the southern district to keep up the friendly relations between the Penchoenches and Patagonians. Months must elapse before an answer could be received from either. Besides, the mourning-time was over, as the remains of the deceased cazique had been interred amid the usual ceremonies, and it remained only for the women to lament the premature death of their husband.

The signal to start was given, but Cruzado had not yet met with an opportunity to speak to Mankelaw in regard to the Oblieno's daughter, and it had, moreover, been decreed that the women, with a guard of honor, should stay for a short time longer at the place of sepulture.

The interpreter now approached the cazique, and, putting his hand on his arm, said, in a low voice:

"The waters of the Limai have fallen, the moon is in the heavens, the wind blows from the south, and the Cordilleras lie before us in the clear atmosphere. But on the Limai there sits an old man weeping over his lost daughter—his cheeks are hollow, and his eyes are dim—will Mankelaw restore the child to the father?"

The cazique made no reply, and looked down gloomily.

"Can you ask me," he said at last, "to do good to the whites, while my brother's blood reddens the ground?"

"The old man has suffered much; he will die," said Cruzado, quietly; "and the flower wither and perish. They are whites—but you are Mankelaw, the cazique of the Penchuenches."

Mankelaw looked him full in the face, but his prepossessing features had lost their stern and sombre expression. He did not reply, but walked slowly back to his tent, while two Indians galloped into the Pampas to catch a small chestnut horse.

"And the white woman will be allowed to accompany us?" exclaimed Cruzado, his eyes radiant with joy, when Mankelaw returned to him. "Oh, you take a generous and noble course, Mankelaw."

"To accompany us?" replied the cazique, evasively. "I had forgotten her; but I must not leave her here, as the Indian women hate her. I will for the present place her under the protection of my tent."

Cruzado looked up to him in dismay;

but the Indian's features did not betray his thoughts—his face was stern and impenetrable; and, walking to his horse, he sprung into the saddle. Some time elapsed before the other caziques assembled their respective parties, and in their midst appeared the young white woman, but disfigured by the mourning costume she was compelled to wear. She had been ordered to blacken her face, and, her head covered with a handkerchief, she complied with timid resignation.

"Poor child," sighed Cruzado, who had lived too long among the whites, and become too familiar with their habits, not to know what she suffered. He would gladly have whispered a word of consolation, but Mankelaw, as if afraid that he would do so, and wished to prevent it, did not allow the interpreter to leave his place, and, after she had mounted her horse, he invited her to ride on the other side.

The Indians conversed in a whisper. It was unusual that the widow of a cazique should be allowed to leave her tent so shortly after his death; but they did not wish to ask Mankelaw for the reason of this strange proceeding, for he looked gloomy and careworn. The cavalcade set out at last and galloped briskly across the Pampas until nightfall brought them to a halt. They did not once stop during the day, and now they erected only a single small tent, in which Irene was to pass the night. All the others encamped in the open air. At dawn the horses were already saddled and in readiness. As soon as the sun rose, the wild horsemen resumed their course across the plains, and Irene with them. They advanced until noon, when they reached a rivulet discharging its waters into the Limal. Here Mankelaw ordered a halt, and, turning to Cruzado, he said in a much kinder tone than usual:

"Tell the Chilian woman to wash her face in this stream."

Cruzado hesitated, and looked at him in surprise.

"Do you understand me?" added the cazique, quietly. "Until we arrived here, she was the widow of my brother Jenkitrusa, but she must not appear with a blackened face before her father."

"Mankelaw!" exclaimed the interpreter, profoundly moved.

"Do not speak another word to her," added the cazique, raising his hand warningly. "I know your language sufficiently to understand."

"Not a syllable, cazique," exclaimed Cruzado, joyfully. "You yourself must break to her the glad tidings;" and, turning to Irene, he said kindly:

"Señorita, the cazique desires you to wash away at this rivulet the black dye from your face."

"May I really do so?" asked the poor lady, timidly.

"You may, never fear."

"Come, Cruzado," said Mankelaw, who did not yet trust him; "we shall meanwhile ride over to the other side, that she may be undisturbed. She will follow as soon as she is ready." And he led the way at a slow trot until they reached a knoll where the camp on the Limal was plainly visible. They were also able to discern distinctly the tents to the left, where the old Chileno had taken up his abode.

Irene meanwhile finished her ablution, which was a great relief to her, for ever since her husband's death she had not been permitted to wash her face, while only food enough to sustain life had been allowed to the cazique's wives. Having washed the dye from her pale cheeks, she rose, mounted her horse, which was quietly standing by, and followed the cavalcade.

"*Huenta!*" exclaimed Tureopan, in surprise, on beholding again the beautiful widow, and seizing the arm of Paillacan, who was riding at his side. "How charming she is!- and how white her complexion!"

"Mankelaw did wrong in shortening the days of her mourning in this manner," replied Paillacan; "she is a dangerous legacy bequeathed him by his brother."

But Mankelaw did not heed their objections. Irene rejoined them, and they galloped until within four or five hundred yards from the next camp. Mankelaw stopped his horse; putting his hand on Cruzado's arm, he drew him aside, and said, smilingly:

"For the first time in my life I wish I could speak the language of the Chilenos. Help me—what do you say when you wish to tell any one, 'There is your father!'"

Cruzado, who could scarcely suppress his feelings, complied with the request. The cazique looked musingly, and nodded. He then turned and rode up to Irene.

"Irene," he said, and his noble features beamed with joy, as he stretched out his arm toward the camp. "There is your father."

"My father!" she exclaimed, almost petrified, and scarcely believing her ears. "My father?—Where?—Here?"

"You must speak to her, Cruzado," said the cazique; "I cannot. Tell her that she will meet her father in one of those tents."

The interpreter hurriedly informed her of the glad tidings, while a deep blush suffused her cheeks. But this lasted only a moment, and she then cried exultingly: "My father!—Santa Maria!" And her little horse sped with her as if he scarcely touched the ground.

"Ha! ha!" laughed the cazique, also spurring his horse. "How her chestnut pony runs!"

All followed at a gallop, the Indians being at a loss to know whether or not they were to overtake the fugitive Chilena. Some of them, in fact, unfastened their lassos, but Mankelaw, laughing, said to them:

"Never mind her, she is free, and will return to her family."

Nor would the swift hunters have been able to overtake Irene. Like an arrow, her horse darted across the Pampas, and, approaching the tents, she dropped the reins, and, stretching out her arms, cried:

"Father, father! where are you? Oh, come to your child!"

A wild cry issued from one of the tents—a wan, bent form, walked painfully forth. Irene scarcely succeeded in stopping her spirited steed, while she cried, "Father, come to me—como to me!" She dismounted. The old father was no longer able to advance—she was by his side, and embraced him. Overcome by the blessedness of the moment, he fainted in her arms.

At the same time the Indians approached, and one of them caught Irene's horse, took the saddle and bridle from it, and allowed it to graze.

Mankelaw halted in front of the group, while Cruzado hastened to attend to Don Enrique.

"Is he dead?" asked the cazique, in a low voice.

"He lives," exclaimed Cruzado; "his joy has overcome him."

"Go then and call your German doctor," said the cazique. "He will restore him to consciousness."

Giving the reins to the horses, the whole party now galloped over to the principal camp, and halted in front of the council-tent, which, to their astonishment, they found occupied by Tchaluak and his men. Tchaluak stood in front of the door, knitting his brow, with arms folded on his breast. He did not salute the new-comers, but seemed, on the contrary, to await their greetings. His face darkened as the others gathered around him in sullen silence.

"Ah!" exclaimed Mankelaw, casting a glance into the tent and noticing the busy scene in its interior. "Who permitted you to make a sleeping-place of the council-tent of the caziques? Leave it at once! Do you understand me? or shall I order my men to throw your saddles and blankets into the street?"

"Stop, Mankelaw," cried Tchaluak, menacingly, "I myself gave them permission."

"You, Tchaluak? And what right did you have to dispose of it?" exclaimed the cazique, whose eyes shot fire. "Allumapu, Saman,—this way, my men—expel the rabble."

The Indians hurried from all quarters, and Tchaluak's men probably did not deem it prudent to await the execution of Mankelaw's order, for many horsemen were galloping up, and it seemed to them as if they had somewhat overrated Tchaluak's influence, of which their cazique had boasted. At all events, Mankelaw treated Tchaluak most unceremoniously. Hence, they did not hesitate to comply with his order, and seized their saddles and bridles; and, as their baggage was piled up before the tent, they evacuated it speedily. Women were then ordered to sweep out and clean it, and Saman, who had kindled a fire in the centre, arranged around it seats, reserving for Mankelaw the place of honor at the upper end.

Tchaluak had gone down the street, his hands folded on his back, hatred and rage struggled in his breast, but he saw now that, in his drunken arrogance, on the shores of the lagoons, and surrounded by his own men, he had exaggerated his influence over the Penobuenobes. The Indians, reënforced as they had been by the attendants of the other chiefs, rendered it impossible for him to carry out his plan by main force, and his only hope henceforth was to move his peers by the power of his eloquence, and to win them over by means of promises; their people would of course follow. But his calculations proved futile, for he was to deliver his speech, which was destined only for the ears of the caziques, before a widely different audience.

No sooner had all arrangements in the council been completed, and the assembly taken their seats, than, at a signal given by Mankelaw, the furs covering the sides of the tent were removed, whereby permission was given to the Indians, generally, if not to participate in the deliberations, at least to listen to the speeches to be delivered. All were rendered curious by the previous events, and thronged around their leaders. Tchaluak's men had already declared openly that henceforth their cazique would be the only legitimate Apo of the Pampas, and that the supreme dignity must be conferred on him.

Tchaluak, on entering the council-tent and noticing the new arrangement, cast an angry glance at Mankelaw, and asked in a loud voice:

"Since when is it customary for chiefs, assembled in council, to admit the whole tribe? The old rule is that the leaders of the people shall exchange their views and opinions before the result of their deliberations is communicated."

The caziques were silent and looked at Mankelaw, who, rising from his seat, said calmly:

"Friends and allies, we did not meet to deliberate and decide upon peace or war, or on important domestic affairs of our people, but—"

"But who told you that?" interrupted Tchaluak. "I myself demand—"

"Silence—silence!" shouted the others, indignantly. "Mankelaw is speaking. You must wait until he is through."

"But I have summoned you," continued Mankelaw, "to place myself at the head of the tribes as heir of my family and of my murdered brother Jenkitruss, and to ask you if you will stand by me as faithfully and loyally as you did by the deceased apo."

"Listen to me, caziques!" exclaimed Tchaluak, almost beside himself, for no time remained for him to adapt his plans to the present circumstances. "Jenki-truss was our highest chief—he is dead, and we will honor his memory. He was brave and wise; he, however, obtained the supreme power, not, as our customs require, as the legitimate heir of the ruling family, but by election."

"His father held the same office, Tchaluak," exclaimed Tureopan.

"But his grandfather did not," cried Tchaluak. "He was elected cazique amidst strife and rebellion, owing to infamous slanders uttered against a family which time out of mind had held absolute authority on these Pampas. Cajapol, my great ancestor, was apo, and his descendants were reviled, because they desired to make peace with the whites, and put an end to war and massacre. By such means his kindred might be deprived of rank for a short time, but their rights did not become extinct. I, Tchaluak, stand here the last of that noble stock, and ask you, caziques, to honor the laws and customs of our confederacy, and not excite sedition in our native country. The people know what I have done," he added, proudly straightening himself; "the Molnches have felt my lance, and their young men have fallen under my bolas. I undertook three expeditions against the whites of the north; twice I penetrated to their fortified city of San Luis. On my return, their dwellings were in ashes, and the Pampas destitute of horses and cattle. I killed fifty prisoners during my last expedition; death preceded me, and bloody were the places I left behind me, while the pack-horses groaned under my booty."

"And where was Tchaluak," exclaimed Mankelaw, while a murmur of applause ran through the audience assembled outside, "at the time the whites built a fort at the only ford of the Casu-Leufu by which we could obtain our salt? Where was Tchaluak at the time my brother Jenkitruss called for him to assist in driving our enemies, with their rifles and cannon, from their fortified position? Tchaluak waged war against women and children—he surprised defenceless huts under cover of night, gave them to the flames, and drove away their cattle, but he did not venture to take part in an attack upon the armed and powerful. Tchaluak refused to join the expedition, and Jenkitruss and his men alone assaulted the fort, passed the pallisades, and reopened for us the path which no white man has since ventured to dispute with us."

"Yes, so it was!" shouted numerous voices, "that was what Jenkitruss did."

"And where was Tchaluak," continued Mankelaw, glancing angrily and disdainfully at the chief, "at the time the whites beyond the mountains carried destruction into the land of our red brethren, burned down their dwellings, and drove off their herds? Where was he at the time Jenkitruss again called to him to help his brethren against the common enemy and expel him from the red man's land? He refused to battle against armed men, but accepted it only against women and children."

"Because I wished to preserve our country from the horrors of war," cried Tchaluak, casting glances of hatred on the cazique.

"What!" exclaimed Mankelaw, contemptuously. "And for this purpose, I suppose, Tchaluak sent his messengers to the Poypus and Chanos, to the Dihuits and Teluchets, to excite them to rise against Jenkitruss. For this purpose, he held secret intercourse with the emissaries from Carmen, who appeared so stealthily at his tent, and whom he asked to pay no tribute, that they might become his allies against the Ponchuenches? Begone, false Tchuelche! Here stand the caziques of our country, and it is for them to say who is to be the ruler of these vast plains — Mankelaw, the brother of Jenkitruss, or Tchaluak, the traitor, who would have sold them to the whites?"

"Mankelaw shall be our cazique," shouted Paillacan, jumping up from his seat—"Mankelaw, the heir of Jenkitruss!" And the chiefs repeated with one accord, "Mankelaw!" while the hundreds of warriors who had listened outside with the utmost suspense to the speeches, burst into a shout for "Mankelaw! Long live the cazique Mankelaw! Down with his enemies!"

Mankelaw stood silent and motionless; not a muscle of his face betrayed the passions agitating his breast, and only when the crowd applauded him in deafening cheers, did a faint, triumphant smile play round his lips.

"And now, Tchaluak," continued Mankelaw, raising his voice, after the noise had ceased, "you see that your arrogant claims are rejected, and you know, besides, that I am not ignorant of your intrigues, of which my brother deemed you incapable. He ordered you already to leave the Noutue Lagoon and move southward to the Lieu-Leufu. I give you five days' time to change your place of encampment. Do you understand me?"

Tchaluak stood biting his lips, his right hand convulsively clutching his crimson cloak. It seemed as though he desired to address the assembly once more, but the searching look with which he scanned those around, convinced him that there was, in this vast concourse of people, probably not one who would have sided with him. He wrapped himself more closely in his cloak, and with a gloomy air said:

"Very well, the caziques have spoken; the laws of the Pehoehoenches have been trampled into the dust; they are no longer valid; brute force alone decides. Tchaluak withdraws." And, turning, he walked defiantly to the entrance, where the Indians quickly and willingly gave place to him.

Huentchapan, a powerful Indian, clad in a tiger's skin, with the claws crossed on his breast, started up on hearing Tchaluak's words, but Mankelaw beckoned him to calmness.

"Never mind him," said Mankelaw, kindly, when Tchaluak had left the tent, and was calling to his men. "On the Lien-Leufu, he is unable to injure us, and may vent his spite upon guanacoes and ostriches; white messengers will not reach him there."

"And what if he should join the southern tribes?" exclaimed Huitsallan.

"If they trusted him," replied Mankelaw, smiling, "they would not have sent to me that I might warn my brother of his schemes. He is powerless. And now, my friends, leave, that the chiefs may hold a secret council in regard to the steps to be taken at this crisis. The business of the Pehoehoenches is at an end; that of the caziques commences— have the side-walls put up again, Saman, lest we be disturbed."

CHAPTER XXXV.

PREPARATIONS FOR THE RETURN TO CHILI.

If Mankelaw had thus frustrated the schemes of an ambitious and arrogant heart, on the other hand he made happy two persons, who, in the joy of their meeting, forgot all that surrounded them. The father was indeed overcome by his feelings, and sunk into a long and deep swoon, and the doctor, whom Orozado quickly called to Don Enrique's assistance, had had a great deal of trouble in restoring him to consciousness; but joy does not kill a man so easily, and now that he sat on his couch in the tent, his arms encircling his beloved daughter, and his eyes gazing into hers, his heart overflowed with happiness.

How many sorrows had both of them endured within a few months!—how desperately had they struggled against the terrible calamities which had befallen them! But the time of adversity had passed, and they did not bestow a moment's thought upon the difficulties yet to be surmounted in the long and fatiguing journey back during the rainy season; they seemed to them of no consequence, for they would undergo them together, mutually relieving the hardships of the way by the love of parent and child.

Night came on rapidly, and the old man himself now prepared with trembling hands a resting-place for his daughter by his side, that he might hear her respiration, held her hand in his own, and not be disturbed again by maddening dreams, wherein she would be torn away from him afresh, and his search in vain.

The Indians were up and doing betimes in the morning. Tchaluak had already, after leaving the council-tent, called his men together, recrossed the Limai, and, without staying longer on the bank of the river, encamped at a place where his tents could not be seen; but no one took any notice of his movements. That the ambitious cazique was angry was a matter of course, but what could he do with his small force against the whole tribe of the Penchnenches, even though enthusiastically supported by his men? Nothing at all. That his own present neighbors, the Araucanians, would not assist him, was equally obvious, as they knew that it was owing to his artful designs that Jenkitruss's alliance with them had been prevented. His rage was powerless, and Mankelaw was strong enough to enforce obedience on his part, if he should ever refuse it.

But the preparations of the Penchuenches were not of a warlike character, and intended neither for defence nor pursuit. No one thought of such a thing, but only of celebrating the accession of the new cazique. The only celebration customary under such circumstances was a banquet.

At dawn two young mares were caught, and, at the time when the doctor and Relwald passed the Indians on their way to the old Chileno, to whom they intended to pay a visit in order to congratulate him on the success of his journey, and inquire of him when he purposed setting out for Obili, an operation similar to that which had filled Relwald with such dismay on the shore of the lagoon, was being performed on the unfortunate animals. Meyer stood quietly looking on, with his hands behind his back; but, seeing his two countrymen, he went with them.

"For mercy's sake, how could you look on so quietly while that horrible cruelty was practised?" said Relwald. "It wrings my heart to think of it."

"Well," laughed Meyer, "but really, you are right: it is abominable—about as bad as that method by which the geese whose livers are to be used for *pâtés de foie gras* are fattened. It is strange to what lengths man will go in order to gratify his palate for a moment. Talk to me of the tiger! there is no more ferocious creature on earth than a human being, whether civilized or not."

"But tell me what are the Indians doing there?" asked the doctor. "We really ought, at least once, assist them."

"You have already seen what it is," replied Meyer. "They remove the skin from the throat of the animal, and put a handful of powdered Spanish pepper into the gash. A lasso is then tied very firmly round the lower part of the neck, so that the warm blood streaming up mixes with the pepper. As soon as that is done they let the fluid run into a wooden bowl covered with a thin layer of fat, and then it looks like raspberry jelly, Mr. Relwald."

"Do not speak of it," exclaimed Relwald, with an air of disgust. "I can never again eat raspberry-jelly, for I shall always remember those disgusting blood-cakes.—Doctor, restore the old Chileno as speedily as possible, that we

PREPARATIONS FOR THE RETURN TO CHILI

may depart without delay to civilized society. Oh, the flesh-pots of Valdivia, how I long for them!"

"Yesterday he was quite unwell," said the doctor. "After fainting, he remained so feeble that he could not have mounted his horse; but I think his joy at having recovered his child must have restored his health."

"What a sweet creature she is!"

"By-the-way, did you notice the impudent manner in which that heathen Tchaluak strutted about yesterday in my red-lined cloak. I felt greatly tempted to cut his throat."

"I saw him," said Reiwald. "Shortly after his arrival he sent for tobacco; but, meeting us in the street, he did not salute us, nor even bestow a glance of recognition."

"I wish we had already passed through that part of the plains where he is encamped," said Meyer, thoughtfully; "he is a most infamous villain, and, if I were in the Chileno's place, I would rather take my daughter through Carmen and the whole Argentine Republic than pay Tchaluak another visit."

"But what can Tchaluak do after the supreme cazique has permitted us to leave his country?"

"What he can do? About all he wishes; for, as a matter of course, he would afterward not allow us to recross the lagoon to return to Mankelaw, and prefer charges against him."

"Suppose we should inform Mankelaw of our suspicion?"

"I have already spoken to Cruzado about it," said Meyer; "he also shook his head distrustfully, and said he would speak to Mankelaw. If the cazique give us an escort of several men, we might safely get back to Chili; but I am afraid he will not do so—we shall see. Ah, there is our old commander from 'Don Giovanni' all right again, to all appearance, and as fresh and blooming as a rose."

Meyer was not mistaken. Don Enrique had undergone an almost miraculous change: his eyes were radiant, his whole form was more erect and vigorous, and he came to meet them with almost youthful vivacity.

"Well, señor," said the doctor, in his broken Spanish, "no more medicine!"

"No more medicine!" replied the Chileno, smiling; "this medicine," he added, seizing his daughter's hand, "has cured me; and, now my friend, see to it that we set out very speedily. So long as I see the Pampas around me, I shall not feel entirely at ease."

"And are you able to mount your horse?"

"I can gallop anywhere, though we should remain day and night in the saddle. But tell me, Don Carlos, where is Cruzado?"

"He is just conferring with the cazique as to our departure."

"You may tell him, then, Don Carlos —but you must do so immediately, lest the cazique should take us for mean, niggardly men—that he has restored to me my only happiness on earth, and that at least I may be permitted to give him such goods as I have brought with me. I wish to present rich gifts to him; pray request Cruzado to beg, on my behalf, liberty to deliver them, and to thank him from the bottom of my heart."

"H'm, I believe those gifts will be

made in the right time to-day," said Moyer; "at all events, I will immediately go to Cruzado; for, if they enter upon the celebrations, you may have no opportunity for presenting them. Put up the goods, señor; I believe I shall soon return with a favorable reply."

So saying, he quickly went to the principal camp on the Limai in order to speak to the half-breed. He met him at the moment Cruzado was leaving the cazique's tent, and communicated the Chileno's message to him.

"Bueno," said Cruzado, inclining his head, "nothing could be more in season. The women happen to be with him. Pray wait for me here, Don Carlos; I shall bring you word presently."

Cruzado stepped back into the tent. Mankelaw lay on his couch, holding in his hand a short pipe, from which he slowly drew clouds of smoke, and blew them through his nose. His two young wives were seated at his side. They were sisters, and one of them held a chubby little boy on her knees, while the other was kneeling before her and playing with the little one.

"What brought you back to me, Cruzado?" asked the cazique. "Have you any further misgivings? I tell you, a single messenger from me could very effectually intimidate that man."

"No, cazique; but the Chileno, to whom you restored his daughter, requests you to permit him to thank you, and, as a proof of his esteem and love, to lay at your feet the presents which he has brought with him to the Pampas."

"I did not restore his child to him for the purpose of obtaining presents," said the cazique, frowning. "He could never have purchased her from me."

"But he does not want to purchase her; you have given her to him; and now he begs of you not to deprive him of the satisfaction of thanking you before returning to his native country."

"Oh, pray, cazique, let him come," said the two young women, caressing Mankelaw; "he has, perhaps, brought many pretty things with him, and he is so happy at having recovered his child."

"Let him go on his way," said the cazique, pushing them back gently.

"And take back with him all the presents he has brought along?" exclaimed the younger wife, in ludicrous anger. "So you can give away, then, something belonging to us? And do you know if you confer a favor on him by obliging him to reload his pack-horses with these goods? He has plenty of them in his native country; and the whites rarely come to us with such treasures."

"You will occasion even greater pleasure to him than to your wives, cazique, by granting his request."

"Well, then, let him come. We shall see if he has with him any thing that will please these foolish women."

"And tell him to bring his daughter with him," exclaimed the younger wife, "that we may take leave of her."

"May he do so, cazique?"

Mankelaw assented smilingly. "They will have their way in spite of me," he said. "Let her come."

Scarcely half an hour had elapsed, though the two 'young women often lifted the furs of the entrance, and looked out into the street, when they at length caught sight of the longed-for visitors, the old gentleman and his daughter; they also saw Cruzado, who led by the bridle a pack-horse carrying two large leathern sacks. The Chileno, they thought, could hardly intend to present them with so many gifts. But they were brought to the front of the tent, and two Indians carried them in and laid them on the floor close to the fire. The Chileno, followed by Irene, who kept timidly behind him, then entered the tent, and, with tearful eyes, approached the cacique. Don Enrique did not avail himself of the services of the interpreter. What he wished to say to the cacique must come from his heart, and, though the Indian should not understand his words, he could feel their meaning and intent.

The eyes of the two women filled with tears as the father stammered out his thanks, and, softly rising from their seats, they folded the young woman to their hearts, kissing her, playing with her soft silken hair, and embracing her again and again.

Mankelaw stood silent, but smiling, and listening to the words falling from the Chileno's lips, as though he understood them. When he concluded, and, in his gushing emotion, seized the young Indian's hand and pressed it to his lips, the latter, withdrawing his arm as if in dismay, said:

"Speak to him, Cruzado—It is good—he is an old man—I am glad that he is happy. I will have him safely conducted over the mountains. And now, if he has brought with him any presents for the women, let him unpack them."

Don Enrique commenced displaying with trembling hands the gifts he wished to present to them, and he was almost ashamed of their insignificance; for how gladly would he have given all that he owned on seeing his child seated between the two young wives, and knowing, as he did, that she was happy!

The Indians were overjoyed at the sight of the presents which were unpacked. In the first place, were rolls after rolls of tobacco, when the grave cacique burst into laughter; next, a package of silk handkerchiefs, which made the eyes of the young women beam with delight; then, a large piece of beautiful red calico, the favorite color of the Indians; glass beads, red, white, and blue, set in silver and gold; scissors, thimbles, needles, thread, indigo, Spanish pepper, candy, spoons, tin plates, knives and forks—in short, articles almost numerous enough to fill the tent. Whenever any thing new was produced, there were exclamations of great delight.

The cacique seemed highly pleased at the appearance, from the second sack, of splendid trappings and heavy silver spurs, for the Indians know very well how to distinguish genuine from plated goods.

"It is too much, Cruzado," said the cacique, deprecatingly. "Tell the old gentleman so. These gifts are twice as valuable as the tribute paid us by the Argentines."

"Do not depress his joy," replied Cruzado, smiling; "you see how gladly he gives all to you."

"We must share some of the tobacco with our men."

"He has requested one of the Germans to distribute twice as much among them."

"And the caciques?"

"He has presents ready for each of them. He is wealthy, and will return only the more easily and rapidly to his native country."

The sacks were now empty, Don Enrique having brought out last some gilded lance-points of excellent steel, and a drinking-horn beautifully wrought and inlaid with silver. Mankelaw was surprised at the large number of costly articles displayed before him.

"Our festival lasts three days; I cannot give you an escort before that time, but the sky is clear, and the wind blows from the south. Three days hence you will set out for your home. Until then you may leave your daughter with my own wives, who will take good care of her. When you wish to see her, come to my tent; you will be welcome.—And now let us go over to the caziques, who are waiting for me. The tobacco will please them," he said, smiling; and, wrapping a roll of it in his poncho, he left.

Don Enrique had not yet exhausted his stock. He made handsome presents to all the caziques, and lavished gifts on Allumapa, whom he recognized. Meanwhile the festival commenced outside. It was no carousal, such as they witnessed on the lagoon, for the intoxicating chicha was wanting, nor could the Indians, at this time of the year, obtain whiskey from the other side of the mountains; but they had enough to eat and to smoke, and that was all they cared for. Two mares had been killed, and the hunters had brought in three or four guanacos. Don Enrique, besides, surprised the wives of the cazique by causing Irene to boil for them a large kettleful of chocolate, to which they are very partial, and, as a matter of course, can obtain only very rarely.

Singularly-looking groups were soon formed outside. After appeasing their hunger, and lighting their cigarettes, the Indians lay down on their stomachs, in circles of twelve or sixteen, with their heads toward the centre, and chanted wild, monotonous airs; one of them first howled rather than sang the solo, when the others began the refrain, with their faces on the ground.

Reiwald had gathered about him a small private circle, apparently for his own pleasure, and seemed to amuse himself to his heart's content; at all events, he was in the best of spirits. He sat in the middle, holding on his knees a long roll of tobacco, from which he cut off pieces whenever any one desired them, and whistling Indian melodies which he knew by heart; but whenever the chorus was to be sung, he paused, and the Panchuenches began.

"Reiwald," said the doctor, on approaching him, "I believe you are giving a concert here!"

"I am rehearsing with the orchestra," replied the young man, laughing, "with whom I am going to Berlin. Don't you believe that we shall create a sensation there!"

"Half a dollar admission, and a crowded house every night," replied the doctor; "I am already deaf in my left ear, and I think I had better go to bed. Do not come home too late."

The festivities occupied three days, and the Indians displayed remarkable perseverance during this time. Old English sailors are able to sing a long time to the same melody ballads of naval battles, containing many stanzas; but only the South-American Indians, playing on the marimba, as in the north, or howling their ditties, as in the south, can continue for six or eight hours in succession.

CHAPTER XXXVI.

ON THE LAGOON.

At the festivities in honor of the new cazique's accession, an incredible quantity of food had been consumed, nearly all the tobacco smoked, and laughter, songs, cheers, and yells, resounded day and night throughout the camp; but no quarrels arose among these wild men, though, owing to the presence of the other caziques, large numbers of five or six tribes had assembled on the Limai.

The weather was exceedingly mild and favorable; the sky—a very rare occurrence at this unseasonable time of the year—remained clear, and the wind blew steadily from the south. Clouds sometimes enshrouded the summits of the Cordilleras, whose outlines, owing to the transparency of the atmosphere, were generally distinctly visible. It was obvious that the rivers in the mountain-districts had sufficiently fallen by this time to justify the travellers in venturing onward.

Don Enrique meanwhile was not idle, but prepared every thing so as to be ready to mount the moment the cazique, who treated him constantly with great kindness, would permit him to proceed. Pedro, indeed, had deprived him of his best horse, and probably killed it in his furious ride. The don's two pistols were also gone—but, no matter, he had no need of them, and he had now horses enough to spare for his own use as well as that of his daughter.

As the festival was drawing to a close, Mankelaw himself did not hesitate, well aware as he was of the inconstancy of the weather at this season, and of the possibility of an immediate change for the worst. In accordance with Cruzado's warning, he delayed the departure of his visitors, chiefly because of his desire that Tobaluak's men should leave the lagoon prior to the departure of the strangers. Now, or at least by the time they reached the shores of the lagoon, the five days allowed to Tobaluak would have expired, and the whites have nothing to fear from the avaricious and aspiring chief.

The cazique kept his promise of sending with them an escort to the frontier of the country. Possibly they would meet on the road roving bands of Panchuenches; perhaps some of the Araucanians expelled from Chili might be wandering about this part of the Pampas.

Allumapu offered of his own accord to be the leader of this escort, and, at an early hour on the fourth day, the horses were caught and saddled, so that the small accompanying party halted about eight o'clock in the morning, ready for immediate departure, in front of the cazique's tent.

Irene's little chestnut pony, which Jonkitrum had presented her, and which was, perhaps, the best horse of the kind in all that region, was led up to the door at the time she wished to go to her father's tent. Mankelaw had so ordered it. She was to take the noble animal with her to her home, in memory of her sojourn on the Pampas.

For the rest, in place of Cruzado, who, for reasons of his own, did not desire to return to Chili, and would accompany the travellers only as far as the lagoon, another interpreter offered them his services: it was Tymaco, Jonkitruss's escribano. As Cruzado was to remain with Mankelaw, and would be his interpreter in case a messenger of the Argentine Government should arrive in the mean time, Tymaco begged leave of absence of the cacique. He intended to embrace the opportunity to visit his friends on the other side of the Cordilleras, and to return with the first company of traders to the Otra Banda. At all events, he offered to be their interpreter for the time they might pass at the village of the Cacique Cajuante; thence they could reach in the course of a single day the settlements of the Chilenos, where the Indian language was no longer spoken.

As the time for their departure was drawing nigh, the two young wives of the cacique were profuse in their assurances of affection for Irene. They embraced and kissed her again and again, and told her how sorry they were that she would not stay with them; and yet, at heart, they were overjoyed at her refusal, for both of them had already been afraid lest their husband Mankelaw would retain the charming stranger, and their jealousy had occasioned them many pains. But the danger was over now, and the recovered daughter of the Chilian had really taken their hearts by storm, and awakened a sincere love for her during the short time of their intercourse.

The travellers halted at the chief's tent; what little baggage they had yet with them had already, at daybreak, by Allumapu's order, been conveyed to the opposite bank of the Limal, and the raft had been brought over again to take across Irene and Mercedes.

Mankelaw stood by the side of his horse in front of his tent; as a mark of respect he intended to accompany the party to the river-bank. Don Enrique thanked him once more, and the cacique embraced the old man cordially. He then seized Irene's hand and gazed long and intently into her face, which was suffused with a deep blush, bent over her in the most graceful manner, kissed her on the forehead, and said kindly in Spanish, "God be with you!" Cruzado had had a great deal of trouble in making him learn these words by heart. And then, as if the farewells were over, he leaped into the saddle. "Adios, Alemanos!" he exclaimed. "Tell them, Cruzado, if they wish to come over to us in the summer-time, they may hunt to their hearts' content, and," he added, laughingly, "I will have a young horse slaughtered for them every week."

"The cacique is very kind, indeed," exclaimed the doctor, when Cruzado had translated these words to him, "but if I ever cross the Cordilleras again, it must be at night, and by a very grievous mistake on my part. Intentionally, I shall certainly not return to the Pampas."

Meyer translated this as follows: "The doctor will probably avail himself next summer of the cacique's hospitality;" whereupon Mankelaw nodded kindly to the Germans. Mercedes, who now wore a decent Indian dress, was also present, but Mankelaw took no notice of her. He knew that Saman had sold her to the whites, and he did not concern himself in the transactions of his servants. He led the way to the ford.

The doctor wished to cross the river again on the raft, but Meyer assured him that if he did he would become the laughing-stock of the Indians; he therefore compressed his lips, and rode with the others into the water. This method of crossing was almost fatal, for his horse, as some animals occasionally have, had the bad habit of swimming on its side. No sooner did they get into the deep part of the river, than, regardless of its rider, the animal inclined to the right, and, of course, immersed the doctor. Fortunately, he succeeded in time in drawing his right foot from the stirrup; otherwise he would certainly have perished. Allumapu happened to swim at his side, and seizing conveyed him to the opposite shore.

The Indians noticed the doctor's mishap and laughed at it, but not so loud that the swimmer—whose ears were filled with water—could hear it. All of them had now safely crossed; the doctor dripping wet, and cursing in the midst of the warriors, with their long lances, who caught his horse again, lest he should he obliged to ascend the slippery bank in his wet boots. In a few minutes they reached the crest, and now arose tremendous cheers from the concourse of Penchucnches standing on the other side.

The travellers responded by giving three cheers—the men raised their arms —the women waved their handkerchiefs. The leader of the escort, seeing that Irene and Mercedes had mounted, uttered a yell—it was the signal to start. The Indians turned and galloped westward, in the direction of the mountains, which, lined by faint streaks of mist, lay in the blue distance.

"Well," said the doctor, angrily to Meyer, who was riding at his side, "I hope I am not to make the journey in these clothes?"

"But, my dear doctor, do you believe that we are all dry?" replied Meyer. "Our saddles were under water."

"But I am wet up to the throat," cried the doctor, indignantly, "and in this chilling breeze I shall certainly take cold."

"I will speak to Cruzado about it," said Meyer; "perhaps we shall halt somewhere, so that you may wring your clothes. Your rifle is wet, too."

"The deuce take the rifle," exclaimed Pfelfel, who was in an execrable humor; "I should like to know why I took it with me. But Relwald, whose head is always filled with vagaries, urged me incessantly not to go unarmed. It is worse than a useless burden, for, during our journey over the mountains, it rubbed my left leg so badly that it is quite sore. I wish I had given it to the cazique."

Meyer had not yet informed the interpreter of the doctor's wish when the company halted; for it seemed they had advanced only a slight distance, in order not to divest the parting scene of its due solemnity. But now the horses were unsaddled, and the blankets squeezed as much as possible in order to dry them, not only for the sake of the riders, but also for that of the horses, whose load was thereby considerably lessened. The Indians also kindly helped the doctor amid laughter and good-natured jokes. While the women, at Cruzado's request, slowly rode ahead, Pfeifel's clothes were taken off, and wrung until almost all the seams burst. Although he asserted he was still "moist," yet was he put in such a condition that the air in the course of a few hours would dry his clothes. They all then remounted, and sped again across the Pampas.

Pressing onward on their spirited and strong horses, the company presented a very fine appearance. It was headed by Allumapu, the leader of the escort, Cruzado, and the Chilian escribano. Behind them rode Don Enrique, with the two women, of whom Mercedes was the most talkative; she told the old Chileno so many things that he had to interrupt her repeatedly lest he should learn too many details of her adventures among the Penchacnchos. Then followed the Germans and forty armed Indian warriors, who did not ride in a very martial manner, but amused themselves in racing, catching each other with their lassos, and giving vent to their exuberant spirits.

Allumapu did not encamp until late in the evening, when the party in his charge halted for this purpose near a small lagoon. The weather was yet quite fair, but the wind commenced again to become variable, and it was evident that they could not count for any length of time on a cloudless sky and a south wind. Their movements no longer being impeded by pack-horses, the day's ride had brought them considerably nearer to the Cordilleras, and on the following noon they caught sight of the broad surface of the Huetchun Lagoon, with the darker green of the apple-grove; but nevertheless they did not slacken their speed, for Allumapu desired to cross the strait between the two lagoons before nightfall, so that the travellers might reach the summit of the mountains at the latest by the next evening.

Allumapu and his two companions were somewhat ahead of the rest, when, suddenly galloping up to Cruzado, he seized his arm and said:

"Look there, compañero! do you not see smoke rising above the trees?"

"It doubtless ascends from the ferryman's hut."

"It is farther to the left.—No, I see the smoke now in four or five places."

"One of the Germans," said Cruzado, "has a glass with which he can view distant objects."

"I have no need of it," replied the Indian, shaking his head; "my eyes do not deceive me; Tchalnak did not obey the cazique's order."

"It is likely," murmured Cruzado, "and we need not look for a very cordial reception at his hands."

Allumapu appeared very anxious, but made no reply, and quickened the movement of his horse, so that the others were scarcely able to follow him. But the nearer they came to the grove, the more distinctly they saw the smoke ascending into the air from many camp-fires, and there was no longer any doubt that the disobedient cazique had not yet removed his camp.

"Stop, Allumapu!" said Cruzado, "before we advance any farther and allow Tchalnak's men to see us, let me at least inform you of the danger to which we expose ourselves in entering his camp."

"Danger!" exclaimed the leader, defiantly. "What danger can menace us?"

"Not exactly us," replied the interpreter, "but the young woman just released by Mankelaw. Tchaluak is desirous of obtaining her, and who can tell what outrages he may commit in his defiant spirit?"

"Ha!" cried Allumapu, raising himself up, "are you sure of it?"

Cruzado now briefly related to him the conversation he had had with Tchaluak, or rather of the confession the chief had made to him in his maudlin drunkenness. The Indian knit his brow, and his eyes shot fire, but he did not for a moment slacken the speed of his horse. Onward they pressed toward their destination and were already able to discern the Noutne water, while a well-beaten road led to the narrows between the two lagoons, on which lay the ferry-man's raft. Concealed as they had been up to this time by the foliage, they had not yet been seen by any one on the other side; and, as the old Indian with his raft happened to be on this side in order to gather apples, the passage could be made without delay.

This time, however, by order of Allumapu, who meanwhile had secretly exchanged a few words with some of his brethren, the women and the white men were left until all the warriors had been ferried over. The ferryman, indeed, objected at first to the whole arrangement, asserting that the cazique had given him stringent orders not to take any one across without previously notifying him; but Allumapu communicated to him the orders issued by Mankelaw, the apo, and he could not but obey, even if any other choice had remained to him. But they were not to remain undisturbed, or at least not unperceived, for a long time. Just as the raft was making its second trip, and while Allumapu and his men were strapping their saddles to the backs of their horses, Tchaluak himself, followed by three or four of his men, was seen at a distance with his red cloak flashing through the branches. He galloped up and halted, apparently in a high state of excitement, in front of Allumapu.

"What!" he said to him, angrily. "Do you not know that it is customary for Indians of another tribe to announce their arrival to the cazique before setting foot in his camp and in his hunting-grounds? Whence do you come, and whither bound?"

"I did not know," said Allumapu, calmly, "that any cazique was encamped at this point, for Mankelaw assured me positively that Tchaluak would have removed his camp by this morning. I myself am commissioned to select here a place for our tents, as Mankelaw and his men will arrive to-morrow to prepare chicha."

"And what if the place selected for your tents is occupied?" asked Tchaluak, scornfully.

"I do not believe it," replied Allumapu; "for the apo's orders must be obeyed."

"And whom have you yonder on the other side?"

"The strangers who are returning over the mountains."

"There are women among them,"

exclaimed Tchaluak, hastily. "Did the cazique sell his brother's widow?"

"He released her," replied Allumapu, quietly, "and ordered us to escort her to her home."

"Very well," murmured the cazique, chuckling. "Mankelaw is a great cazique—the supreme ruler of a large country. Have them brought over—they are welcome.—But tell me where is that warrior galloping? Why does he not remain with his company? What is he about to do?"

"I have sent him back," said Allumapu, firmly, "to take word to Mankelaw that he will not find room for his camp."

Tchaluak looked wildly and defiantly at the young Indian, but Allumapu bore the look without flinching, and if there was any perceptible change in his features, it was a faint smile playing round his lips. But whatever Tchaluak thought, he did not speak another word. He gazed for a few minutes at the raft, which was now approaching the shore for the second time, and then, turning his horse and followed by his men, he galloped away, leaving the unwelcome guests at liberty to effect the passage of the river.

Scarcely an hour had elapsed when the travellers were transported to the other side. All mounted their horses again, for, though the distance between the landing-place and that for the tents was insignificant, no one thought of going afoot, much less of carrying his baggage. The pack-horses were reloaded, as though a long journey still lay before them.

Allumapu did not fail to notice the glance which Tchaluak had cast on him when he heard that the released white woman was among the travellers; and what with the cazique's suspicious bearing and the information Cruzado had previously given, he deemed it incumbent on him to proceed with the utmost caution. On the other hand, he did not wish to alarm the strangers needlessly. Tchaluak would not resort to violent steps when he knew that he had to deal with Mankelaw's messengers, and, having been forewarned in time of his evil designs, they were not afraid that he would accomplish much by any kind of strategy.

It is true, Allumapu would have preferred to continue the journey that very evening. But, in the first place, the horses were exhausted; and, next, the sun had gone down behind the Cordilleras, and night would overtake them at no great distance from Tchaluak's camp. It was, therefore, safer for them to remain under the protection of the friendly Peuchuenches, and the most important thing for them was to find an eligible place for erecting their tents.

On their arrival at the camp, the cazique met the strangers again, but he was as kind as he had before been morose.

"Allumapu," he said to the young man, "there was no necessity for your sending off that messenger, for, when Mankelaw comes to-morrow, he will probably meet some of us here, and have as much space as he wants. But, come; we are just engaged in finishing our last barrel of chicha, and your men will not object to a share."

Allumapu would have gladly declined this invitation, but he did not wish to irritate the cazique, and replied, "I thank you. My men will gladly avail themselves of your hospitality, but permit us to make our camp and shelter the women. I have been instructed to attend to their comfort."

"Oh, do not trouble yourself about that," replied Tchaluak. "You cannot shelter them in a more comfortable manner than by leaving them for the night with my wives. Our tent is large, and they will find there furs enough for soft and warm beds."

"I am much obliged to you, cazique," said Allumapu, quietly, "but I have been instructed not to separate Jenkitrum's widow from her father, but to have a special tent for them every night as long as they are under my protection."

Tchaluak bit his lips, but exclaimed, laughingly:

"Well, that may be arranged, too; you may bring the old man with her to my wives. He is welcome, and they will smoke with him."

"He will send presents to them," replied Allumapu, firmly; "but leave it to me to take care of Mankelaw's guests."

Tchaluak's horse reared, so violently and suddenly he had drawn back the reins under his cloak. The young Indian, however, feigned not to notice his agitation, and, glancing around cautiously, he now rode, followed by the party, through Tchaluak's camp, and selected a place on the Nontue Lagoon. Apple-trees were to be seen almost everywhere, which greatly aided the erection of the fur tents. Night had not yet set in when they had completed their work and were comfortably sheltered.

That Tchaluak really entertained insidious designs toward them, Allumapu considered certain, and, after a brief consultation with Cruzado, they agreed to set out before daybreak, and escort the strangers to a point whence they could safely reach the summit of the mountains. The half-breed deemed it prudent now to warn the Germans to be on their guard, and hold their arms in readiness; at all events, he thought it best for them to be prepared for any emergency.

"Well, this is too bad," said the doctor, after Meyer had communicated this advice to them; "you come after nightfall, and at a time when there is more water than powder in my rifle. I wonder how I am to get the bullet out of it."

"Have you no candle?"

"Only a very small piece; and, if I burn it up now, we shall be obliged to eat our supper every night in the dark."

"I think," said Meyer, "it will be better for you to be able to eat your supper than otherwise. Put your rifle in order without delay; it would be rather unpleasant if it should not go off when you really need it."

"And you think there is danger?"

"Well, I am afraid there is. Cruzado generally does not cry before he is in pain. It is certainly well for you to comply with my advice."

The doctor heaved a deep sigh, for he was tired, and would have preferred his bed, but Reiwald helped him, and they soon removed the wet powder from the barrel. After a short time, Reiwald succeeded in discharging the rifle.

The report must have been heard at Tchaluak's camp, but it could not be helped, and, besides, it did no harm. It was, perhaps, right to let him know that the whites were armed and prepared to defend themselves.

Don Enrique, who was not informed of the apprehensions entertained by the others, lest he should be unnecessarily alarmed, was now requested to send to Tchaluak such gifts as he intended for him, for the caziques always demand tribute on allowing strangers to pass through their camps.

The Germans also added such trifles as they could spare, lest Tchaluak should have any cause for dissatisfaction; and Allumapu himself took the presents over to him.

Meanwhile no precautions had been neglected to protect the small camp from a sudden attack. The tents of the whites were in the middle; the Indians (as their rear was covered by the lagoon), encamped in a semicircle; nor did they allow their horses to graze freely during the night, but fastened them to their lassos, tied to poles fixed in the ground. The moonlight was sufficiently bright to enable them to see their surroundings and quickly mount their horses in case they should suddenly need them.

Allumapu did not permit all his men to take part in the chicha carousal, though he could not forbid his whole detachment to comply with Tchaluak's invitation. One half of his men received permission to go over for an hour, when they were to return and relieve the other half. But it really seemed as though Tchaluak did not entertain any hostile designs toward them; besides, he would have hardly succeeded in prevailing upon his men to make an open attack upon Mankolaw's Penchuenches. At all events, he sat quietly in the chicha-tent, to all appearance highly relishing the beverage. He received the presents cheerfully, and complained only of the non-arrival of the Germans; he accepted, however, Allumapu's excuse that they were fatigued, and had gone to retire. The two barrels were empty by midnight, when Allumapu's warriors withdrew to their camp, and soon a profound stillness reigned around the lagoon —naught could be heard save the murmur of the waves driven ashore by the south wind.

CHAPTER XXXVII.

TREACHERY.

Allumapu, well aware of the danger to which Tchaluak exposed himself by bidding open defiance to Mankolaw's orders, now felt perfectly safe. Possibly the insidious cazique might attempt to deceive him, and in fact some of his suggestions seemed to indicate such a purpose; but the young Indian was firmly convinced that Tchaluak would never resort to force in order to attain his object. Nevertheless, Allumapu omitted no precaution, and posted sentinels all night around the camp. He himself slept calmly in the open air; he had stuck his lance in the ground at his side, and fastened his horse near a place on the shore where there was a great deal of long grass.

Cruzado acted otherwise; he had not yet forgotten his former conversation with Tchaluak, and for this reason he could not sleep. He rose at least ten times, and looked after the horses. The observation that thin patches of cloud passed from the south, covering the moon from time to time, did not reassure him. But his apprehensions were unfounded, and the morning-star shone above the fog of the Pampas before any thing whatever occurred to disturb the slumber of the party.

But did he not hear a noise at Tchalnak's camp? He listened—a dark form glided over the ground toward him—it was one of their own guards.

"What is the matter yonder, compañero?"

"The cazique strikes his tents," said the Indian; "I crept along the brake near his camp."

"Indeed!" said Cruzado, heaving a sigh of relief; "well, thank God, he seems to keep his promise, after all. Are their horses already saddled?"

"They are; they must have entered on their preparations an hour ago, but so softly that we did not hear any thing of it."

"I wonder why they are proceeding so cautiously," murmured Cruzado to himself; "well, in that event, it is certainly time for us also to get ready. Awaken your leader, my friend, and tell him what you have seen; I will meanwhile arouse the strangers."

Ten minutes had not elapsed when all the persons at the camp were awake, and engaged in their departure as noiselessly as Tchalnak's men. The horses were led up and loaded; but their precautions were needless, for they soon discovered that they were secretly watched. Among the trees there appeared now and then a form, which vanished as quickly as it had come. They were not, however, molested by any one, nor were any obstacles thrown in their way in completing their preparations. But Cruzado did not confide in this apparent quiet. Was it possible that the insidious Tchalnak had suddenly abandoned all his plans and wishes? At all events, it would be best to remove as speedily as possible out of his neighborhood, and, above all things, not to take formal leave of the cazique. If possible, he should be prevented in seeing again the young white woman.

Allmapu did not approve of this; it was, on the one hand, contrary to etiquette; and, on the other, it looked almost like fear. But, as they themselves were ordered not to leave the Pampas, but only to escort the strangers, he finally consented that this course should be adopted. The cazique might take umbrage at it, but then the whites were not his guests, and had passed only as Mankelaw's through the camp; hence, it was unnecessary for them to treat him so very ceremoniously.

Daylight dawned; the clouds, which seemed to have thickly gathered by this time, indicated an impending change of weather, for they reflected the red beams of the morning, and the mist floating over the Pampas prevented the sun from being seen.

The travellers were soon ready, and the women again in the saddle—Irene on her spirited little pony, and Mercedes on Reiwald's pack-horse, a somewhat heavy-looking animal, but gentle and easy to ride. The road was smooth and even, while it ran along the shore of the Nonine Lagoon, which lay on their left. On the right extended the wild plains which they could traverse for a long distance without meeting with any other obstacles than small streams, discharging their waters into the lagoon, or, farther above, into the Cusu-Leufu, but which, owing to the continued drought, did not contain much water. The route to the Villa-Rica Pass lay in that direction.

"Forward!" shouted Allumapu.—"Cruzado, send the señoras to the head of the column, and tell the Germans to remain near them—we will accompany the strangers as far as the first gorge in the mountains, and encamp there until nightfall. They will henceforth be safe. Forward!"

The order was issued. Irene, overjoyed on being allowed to leave this desolate region, gave the reins to her horse, and, turning to Cruzado, who rode at her side, she said:

"Ah, how glad I am, señor, that we are away from here, and shall no longer meet that repulsive cazique! Do you know that I was greatly afraid of him, and that my apprehensions prevented me nearly all night from shutting my eyes!"

"Afraid! Why, señora, should you be afraid?"

"You did not see the glance he cast on me yesterday," replied Irene, timidly; "nor was that the first time he met me. When we descended from the mountains he was encamped there with his men, and he persecuted me incessantly during our sojourn at his camp."

Cruzado made no reply; he raised himself in his saddle and turned back his head. The noise was heard of horses behind them, which could not belong to their party, and, as he glanced down the lagoon, Tchaluak's warriors emerged rapidly from the grove, and the red cloak was plainly visible in their midst.

"Caracho!" murmured Cruzado. "Are we, after all, still in danger? What do the rascals want of us?—Allumapu, Tchaluak's whole force is at our heels."

"I see them," said the Indian, calmly, but his eyes shot fire; "he will not not dare to obstruct our path." He added, defiantly, "he cannot."

"They are three to one."

"But he is unable to rely on all his men," replied Allumapu, laughing contemptuously. "Mankelaw's name strikes terror into their hearts."

"But what if he should attack us?"

"Tell your Germans to hold their fire-arms in readiness."

"But I suppose we cannot commence hostilities?"

"No, but the cazique is outlawed as soon as he lowers a lance against us."

"In that case I will also prepare for the conflict," murmured Cruzado, unfastening his bolas, which he wore, as the Indians did, around his body. "But look, there they are already!"

"Holy mother, señor," cried Irene, riding up in great terror, "is there any danger?"

"Quien sabe," said Cruzado, quietly; "please keep always in our midst. Don Carlos, have your friends their rifles in readiness? There is no telling what may happen."

"The rifles are ready and in good order; but, tell me, Cruzado, do you believe that—"

"Tell your friends, in case of an attack, to fire at no one but the fellow in the red cloak. He deserves it. Attention! Keep a sharp lookout."

"Ah! my friends," shouted Tchaluak, who headed his men, laughing, and waving his left hand toward them. "It was wrong in you, Allumapu, to depart without taking leave of me."

"We do not leave the Pampas, cazique," replied Allumapu, while Tchaluak's men came up and moved kindly among Mankelaw's Penchuenches; "only the strangers leave, and, as we could not know that you had risen so early this morning, we did not wish to disturb you."

"Not disturb us, my friend? How could you disturb us!"

"Keep back a little, men," said Allumapu to Tchaluak's warriors. "You will frighten our horses, and drive them into the lagoon."

"And where is my old friend the Chileno?" exclaimed the cazique, as if looking for him, though he had long before seen him between the two women; "Ah! yonder! Well, I must shake hands, and thank him for his numerous presents, especially the large quantity of tobacco he sent me yesterday.—Back, back, my boys, or you will press the women into the water. There!—lead their horses again into the road.—Ride to the head of the party, do you hear me!"

"Tchaluak, call your warriors back," said Allumapu, endeavoring to approach him; but ten or twelve of Tchaluak's men, laughing and chatting, brought their horses between him and the cazique, who had now ridden ahead, and forced his black horse between Irene and her father.

"Ah, Don Enrique," he exclaimed, holding out his hand to him, yet looking around to see who were near them, but there were scarcely any save his warriors, who had pushed aside the Germans also. "Don Enrique, I wish you a prosperous journey, my old fellow—a happy journey; and meanwhile we mean to keep your little daughter here—oh, my men!"

The old Chileno did not understand the words, but he was forced farther and farther away from Irene, and was unable to approach her again.

"Cruzado!" cried Don Enrique, in the utmost terror. "This way! Protect my child!"

"Bah, Cruzado!" laughed the wild cazique, at the same moment uttering a piercing cry. He then seized with his right hand the bridle of Irene's horse, which began to grow very restless. Another seized it on the right, and when those behind struck the animal with their lances it jumped forward, and would have speedily distanced the Indians but for their strenuous efforts to draw it back. In so doing they sped in a northern direction, Tchaluak and his confederate at a full gallop. Irene in the centre, and the Ponchnenches behind.

"This is base treachery," shouted Allumapu, in a thundering voice; and, passing an Indian who was tearing Doña Mercedes from her horse, to place her on his own, he pursued the cazique as fast as he could gallop. By his side, and almost outstripping him, was Relwald.

The doctor had already cocked and raised his rifle, but the movement of his horse disconcerted him. No sooner, however, did he see that the rest of

Tchaluak's men did not follow the cazique at the time the stratagem had succeeded, but turned to the north, than, accompanied by all the friendly Indians, he started in pursuit of them. At this moment he beheld the man who had Doña Mercedes before him on his saddle, and shouting, "Stop! you red-skinned villain," he dismounted and fired, apparently without aiming at all; but it was a lucky shot, for the bullet broke the horse's spine, and he fell in an instant, hurling the robber and the woman to the ground.

The friendly Indians, uttering triumphant shouts, rode up; one of them threw his lasso at the villain, who was soon writhing in its coil, while the doctor's horse, without waiting for its rider, continued meanwhile the pursuit on its own account.

Meyer who did not take part in the chase, because he was entirely unarmed, looked on with singular calmness while his wife was carried away. As he leisurely moved after the other men, he stopped in surprise, for he saw the Indian's horse falling simultaneously with the report of the rifle. But while one of Mankclaw's men was dragging her abductor along, Doña Mercedes sprang to her feet entirely uninjured—and Meyer groaned:

"I knew that the doctor would do mischief to-day."

Meanwhile the other Penchuenches passed them at a furious rate. They went by like swift shadows; clouds of dust rose behind them, and with the suppleness of serpents they avoided the protruding branches along the road. They seemed falling from their horses, but their hands clutching the mane they hung on the side, and, as soon as the obstruction had been passed, sat again erect in the saddle.

The young Indian, accompanied by ten or twelve of his best-mounted men, followed close on the treacherous cazique. Relwald galloped with him, but the trees which occasionally grew in the way, he was unable to avoid with the skill of the Indians, and had to turn and spur his horse to renewed efforts. Allumapu was so near Tchaluak that he might have thrown his bola at him, but here the use of this weapon was difficult, and then he could not have avoided hitting Irene by the cazique's side. They left their own men far behind, while Tchaluak's warriors, mounted as they were on fresh and good horses, were in this respect much superior to them.

If Allumapu had had to deal here with hostile Indians, the small force of bold pursuers would have perished, for the fugitives were too strong, but the latter themselves shrank from making an attack upon those who had hitherto been their allies. They were ready to abduct a woman, which was an affair of no consequence, but it would be far different if the blood of the Penohuenches were spilled, and all of them were afraid of Mankelaw's wrath. Allumapu was almost beside himself with rage, and often seized his bola to hurl it at the legs of Tchaluak's horse, but the distance between them was somewhat too great, and it was now widening every moment.

Tchaluak and his confederates made the utmost efforts to quicken the speed of Irene. Before them lay a narrow stream. The road led through it; on

TREACHERY.

the other side there were no trees, and on the open plains they would speedily distance the jaded horses of their pursuers.

"Stop!" shouted Tchaluak, "turn to the right—there is a break in the bank in front, and we cannot cross there; the other ford is near. Forward! Our friends yonder are unable to overtake us."

The warriors turned to the right, though some of the most daring passed the rivulet at the forbidden place, when suddenly a horseman came galloping to meet them. They could not avoid him; on the left was the precipitous bank, with a gap scarcely twelve yards in width, and groves of trees stood on the right. One of the Penchuenches lowered his lance, when Reiwald, who met them here, raised his rifle, and discharged it loaded with shot at the foremost Indian. The wounded man, uttering a piercing cry, fell from the saddle, and the dreaded rifle caused the Indians to fall back on both sides. Tchaluak was now in front of the young lawyer.

"Stand, villain!" shouted Reiwald. "I have you at last!"

"Kill the white dog," cried Tchaluak just as he heard the hoofs of a horse strike the ground behind him. It was Allumapu. The Indians did not know which they were to attack. The young Penchuenche's lance was lowered in an instant, and vibrated in such a manner that it was almost impossible to parry its thrusts. "Ha!" cried the cazique, seeing the danger, and dropping Irene's bridle, in order to gallop down the bank. The avenger pressed onward. "Help! help!" screamed Tchaluak, but it was too late—the keen iron entered his left side, and such was the impetuosity of Allumapu's onset that he hurled horse and rider into the rivulet, and he himself, unable to arrest the speed of his own animal, tumbled after them.

One of the Indians made a thrust at him with his lance, but at the same moment Reiwald's bullet hit him, and he fell lifeless from his saddle. Throwing away his rifle, and drawing his revolvers from the holster, the young German fired away at the Indians who were riding up; at a loss to know what sort of weapon was used against them, they fell back in dismay.

At this moment succor arrived. Amid deafening shouts of "Mankelaw! Mankelaw!" a few brave men came up on both sides of the rivulet, and while Tchaluak's warriors, bewildered and intimidated as they were, did not know whether to fight or flee, Allumapu's companions attacked them with the utmost vigor. "Mankelaw! Mankelaw!" Bolas whirled, lances flashed, and while the cry "Tchaluak is dead!" added to the discouragement of the enemies, they suddenly fled, leaving the battle-field and their fallen comrades in the hands of Mankelaw's victorious men.

Reiwald had jumped from his saddle and reloaded his rifle hurriedly, and Allumapu, without thinking of his horse, which he left to shift as well as it could, climbed the precipitous bank in the utmost haste. He beheld Irene, deadly pale, and trembling violently, but firmly holding the reins of her panting pony, and, on seeing that the young woman, who had been placed under his protection, was safe, the Indian uttered a cry of exultation.

The other Penchuenches, however, took good care not to continue the pursuit by themselves, for, in case their adversaries should return to the charge, even their united force would hardly be able to resist them. But such an attack was not likely to be made, as the rascal who had originated the outrage lay weltering in his blood in the bed of the stream.

Three or four of Allumapu's men had been wounded, but ten or twelve of his enemies lay on the ground, and others had received severe wounds, as they were seen reeling in their saddles. The riderless horses were caught, and among them the doctor's. Allumapu, mounting one, and beckoning to Irene to follow him, started back by the same route by which they had just arrived at such a break-neck speed. He disdained to notice the cazique.

The Penchuenches had meanwhile drawn the dead body out of the rivulet. They would not leave behind the silver stirrups and silver-mounted trappings. And what became of his remains? They were of no consequence—his own men might have come and taken them. He was a traitor, and did not deserve a cazique's grave. One of the Indians divested him of his red cloak and put it on with evident satisfaction and pride, which Reiwald, occupied as he was with his own horse, had not yet noticed. But while the warrior was strutting about, amid the jubilant cheers of his comrades, a heavy hand was suddenly laid on his shoulder, and the doctor, quietly taking the cloak from him, said:

"Pray permit me, señor. I suppose you would like to keep it, would you not? The scoundrels have almost worn it out already—there are holes in it, and it is bloody.—Come, young man, get me my horse yonder."

The Penchuenche laughed and did not resist the doctor, for his gesture was too eloquent to be misunderstood; and, moreover, the strangers had excited the admiration of the Indians, and filled them with respect, by the use they had made of their fire-arms. Now they prepared to rejoin their companions; a messenger had already come to call them back, and, after gathering the bolas and lassos lying about the scene of action, they galloped back to the lagoon.

But who can depict the transports of the old Chileno as he took to his heart his daughter, restored to him a second time, and the gushing emotion with which he thanked the friends who had so intrepidly risked their lives to avert the new calamity. Allumapu, indeed, protested that he had not contributed much to Tuhaluak's discomfiture, and assured Cruzado that, but for Reiwald's timely intervention, they would never have overtaken the enemy; still, he had given the death-blow, and Irene, blushing deeply, held out her hand to Reiwald, and thanked him with touching words.

Allumapu thereupon urged them to depart immediately. The sky was overcast, and the clouds had assumed a menacing appearance; the sooner they crossed the Witchi-Leufu on the other side of the mountains the better. The company formed again in great haste; all longed to get away from the wild country, the more so as only the Cordilleras lay between them and security. The young Indian, who seemed to be resolved not to leave the strangers until he knew they were safe beyond the Pampas, headed them again, and his warriors accompanied him until they arrived at a narrow gorge, where there was no fear of any renewed attacks on the part of Tchaluak's men.

Allumapu had hitherto kept timidly aloof from Irene, who was riding by her father's side at the head of the column, but now he approached her, and, holding out his hand, which she shook cordially, he said in a kind tone:

"Farewell, white woman!—your path is safe. We return to our plains. Allumapu never forgot the kindness with which you treated him when he lay a captive in your father's cabin. I could not avert the misfortunes which befell you, otherwise I would have done so. Farewell! May the sun shine upon your path, and when you remember the Pampas, let not all your thoughts be unkind. Believe me, you will have friends and well-wishers there. Farewell!"

Without waiting for a reply, he dropped her hand, turned his horse, and, followed by all his men, galloped back to the plains.

Cruzado meanwhile had taken leave of the old Chileno, who liberally rewarded him, and, besides, left him many horses. He was now halting by Meyer's side.

"Don Carlos," he said, shaking hands with him, "you are going back to Chili, but be cautious. If they should catch you—"

"Cruzado, good fellow! they have already caught me—present my respects to Saman. Farewell!"

So saying, Meyer nodded kindly to his friend, and followed the returning party up the slope.

CHAPTER XXXVIII.

CONCLUSION.

THE Indians were no longer dangerous to the travellers, for, though they had entertained hostile designs toward them, they would never have dared to follow the strangers, provided as they were with fire-arms, into these mountain fastnesses. The weather might still obstruct their path, if it should not continue fair for at least a day. They had to make haste, and, profiting by the favorable hours, they pressed onward with great rapidity. All were in good spirits; Meyer alone sat gloomy and taciturn in his saddle, and his ill-humor increased the nearer they came to the summit of the Cordilleras. He made no reply to the questions asked him, or at least evaded them, complaining of having a headache and rheumatism.

Next morning, at ten o'clock, Don Enrique and his friends reached the summit of the pass, but it seemed as if the rain had waited until they returned to a wooded country, for, from the moment they commenced descending the western slope, the sky became more and more overcast, and at dusk there was a heavy shower. It was, however, only the forerunner of what was to come, though during the night the rain ceased, and we need not say that they accelerated the speed of their horses. They pressed onward incessantly, and, by the time it commenced raining again next day, they had already performed the most arduous part of the journey. Before the waters could descend from the mountains, they would have crossed the Witchi-Leufu, by way of the Mayhue Lagoon. It was therefore resolved to pass the night again at the cabin of the Cazique Cajnante. Meyer also stayed there; he would have preferred to go elsewhere, but he dared not. Tymaco, the escribano, said that he had an old friend living close by, and that he would sleep at his house.

Cajnante was unfortunately intoxicated again on that evening, and did not even recognize his guests; but he was overjoyed next morning on seeing them, and learning the startling adventures they had passed through in the mean time. He told them, however, that he would not permit them to continue their journey for at least a day. His objections were not heeded, and the travellers resolved to start again in the forenoon, especially as messengers whom they had sent out informed them that both the Witchi-Leufu and the Pillan-Leufu were passable, but, as the rain continued, toward nightfall they would probably be so no longer.

Meyer had been on his feet all the morning, and ran out at least ten times into the rain, now under one pretence, and now under another. He cast melancholy glances to the small house on the hillside, whose outlines were to be seen through the foliage. What would poor Tadea think of him? Could he pass through the place and remain a night in her immediate neighborhood, without so much as calling upon her or informing her of the accident which had happened to him in the mean time, and which prevented him from keeping his word! It wrung his heart to think of the moment when he would meet her, and he would have preferred to sneak past her father's dwelling like a thief in the dark, but he was incapable of acting in that manner. He did not desire to have reason to reproach himself with his conduct toward her.

The horses were already being saddled in front of Cajnante's house; the old Chileno was as restless as ever, and as desirous of reaching his home at the earliest moment. But a few minutes remained to Meyer, and, with a heavy heart and a quick step he ascended the path leading to the cabin to which he had so intensely longed to return, and into which he was now almost afraid to enter. The door was ajar—perhaps he would not find any of the inmates at home—but yes, the Chileno was at work yonder in the field, and his wife was standing by his side, picking up potatoes. Tadea was not with them; she was probably alone at the house. He walked up to the dwelling and rapped softly. No one responded; he opened the door cautiously and put his head into the room.

"Ah, Don Carlos," said a well-known voice, "entra, Hombre."

"Pardon me," said Meyer, while he remained standing in surprise on the threshold. On the only chair to be found in the house, there sat the escribano, who had accompanied them from the Paropas, and in his arms he held Tadea, whom he kissed and caressed. Neither he nor Tadea seemed embarrassed at the presence of Don Carlos.

CONCLUSION.

"I hope I do not disturb you!" asked Meyer.

"By no means," replied the escribano, laughing. "The señor, Tadeo, is a fellow-traveller of mine—and, Don Carlos, I have the pleasure of introducing my betrothed to you."

"Your betrothed!"

"Yes, señor. I came over the mountains only for the purpose of paying a visit to her. But why did you not bring your wife along? Pray come in!"

Without speaking a single word, or setting his foot in the house, Meyer shut the door, put both his hands into his pockets, and went whistling on his way back to the cazique's cabin. He arrived at the right time. The women had already mounted their horses, and Mercedes told him she had some concern lest an accident had befallen him.— After shaking hands with the cazique, he galloped away with the others, accompanied by a few Indians who were to guide them across the two rivers.

The passage was difficult, and not entirely free from danger, the Pillan-Loufu having recently risen several inches; but they got safely over. The road thenceforth was better, and some of them could now and then ride abreast.

"Tell me, Meyer," said Reiwald to the German, who was trotting at his side, "what has been the matter with you for the last few days? This morning you are again in the best of spirits, but yesterday you looked as though you were meditating murder."

Meyer looked around to see if any one was riding behind them; then, bending over to Reiwald, he said:

"Let me tell you, my dear friend, whatever may be said of other women, the Chilenas are of little account. If you should ever take it into your head to marry, which I hope you never will, do not take a Chilena."

Reiwald laughed. "But what has turned you so suddenly against the fair Chilenas? You must have formerly thought otherwise in regard to them."

"Unfortunately I did," said Meyer, sighing, and casting another anxious glance over his shoulder; "but let us drop a subject which might prevent us from enjoying this fine morning. I hope we shall ford the Lifen without any trouble, and pass the Ranco Lagoon safely; there will then be no more water in our way, for we can turn aside from the Kinchilca River. I know the road. I have often travelled it over the mountains."

"But tell me confidentially, Meyer," said Reiwald, "what trouble did you have with the Chilian policemen? For it is my firm conviction that we are indebted to them for the pleasure of your agreeable company—and how comes it that you now venture again to enter the lion's mouth?"

"I had no trouble with the policemen, only with the custom-house officers, and nothing but my weak constitution was to blame for it; for cigars, on which the duty has been paid, do not agree with me—they are too strong. No one can prove any thing against me; they only suspect, and, as Cruzado has remained on the other side of the mountains, I believe they will have to let me alone. For the rest," he added slowly, "I do not intend to remain a long time at Valdivia, and—by-the-way, what day of the month is it?"

"I am sure I do not know," said Reiwald, "I lost the course of time on the Pampas; but the doctor knows all about it. He jots down every thing in his note-book.—Doctor, what day of the month is it?"

"Are you very particular about it?" inquired the doctor, drawing a small book from his pocket.

"I am."

"Saturday, June 16th, 12½ o'clock—about dinner-time."

"Bueno!" exclaimed Meyer, "that is all right."

"What is all right?"

"Oh, nothing of any consequence."

The conversation was interrupted, for the road ascended another acclivity, and became so narrow that they had to ride again in single file. Fortunately, they passed all the places made dangerous by high water, and reached Valdivia on the third day after nightfall. They would have arrived in the afternoon but for Meyer, who accidentally pushed a pack-horse from one of the numerous small bridges into the water, and then insisted that its baggage should be unloaded and examined.

Before the party entered Valdivia, Meyer had a long talk with his wife, whom he informed of his difficulty with the custom-house officers, and of the necessity not to show himself in public for a few days, in order to discover first if any of the custom-house men had been drowned or injured at the capsizing of the revenue-boat. Until then, he requested her to inform her friends, with whom she was to remain, that he had gone to the Rio Bueno, where he intended to rent a house—that he would return next day, and then take her to their new place of residence.

Meyer then disappeared in one of the lanes, and rode straight to the dwelling of Don Pasquale, with whom he conversed a considerable time. The first question was, "Is the steamer here, and will she sail at her usual time?"

"Of course," said the Chileno, who was glad of the German's return. "But you need not be afraid, Don Carlos; the affair has blown over."

"And no one was injured?"

"No, thank God, all were saved; but where have you been 'in the mean time?"

"It would take me a month to tell you the whole story. By-the-way, are you ready to settle with me?"

"Yes, sir."

"And do you wish to buy a horse?"

"Are you really going to leave Valdivia?"

"Yes, at least for a time. I am obliged to do so.—The steamer, then, will start to-morrow morning?"

"At ten o'clock."

"Bueno!" exclaimed Meyer. "By-the-way, have you a cigar, on which the duty was not paid? I long to smoke one."

Don Pasquale laughed. Their account was soon settled.

The same evening, a small boat, rowed only by two persons, glided down the Valdivia River, and, on reaching the bay, it steered straight toward the red signal-lights of the steamer. It was conveying a passenger. The boat went back with the tide to Valdivia.

CONCLUSION. 273

Our friends meanwhile had returned to their hotel, and visited in the course of the evening some of their fellow-passengers who had arrived by the emigrant-ship. The doctor had resolved to abandon all further "romantic" tours, and, at least for the present, seek his fortune in the city by practical attention to his profession. If he did not succeed, he could go to Valparaiso. But he thought he would do well here, for since his journey to the Pampas he had considerably abated his expectations.

Don Enrique and his daughter were to embark on board the steamer for Concepcion. Reiwald determined also to go north — whither? He did not know; perhaps to Valparaiso or Lima. He said he would leave it to chance to decide. The doctor was to sell his friend's horses as soon as he had an opportunity, and send him the money. The rest of his property Reiwald took with him.

At the appointed time next morning, the *Vapor* steamed down the beautiful bay to the open sea, and Irene, fondly leaning on her father's breast, fixed her eyes a long time with an expression of terror on the snow-clad cone of the Villa Rica. But her mournful thoughts yielded to a sense of security, and of the happiness restored to her, and she even tried on the same evening to chat with her fellow-traveller of the Pampas, young Reiwald, who had joined them, and who endeavored to recall all the Spanish words he had heard, in order to be as amiable and gallant as possible toward the young lady.

The steamer coaled at Lota and remained until nightfall. On the following day they were to reach Talcahuana,

whither both Don Enrique and Reiwald — who explained to the old gentleman that he wished to see as much as possible of Chili — had taken passage. On hearing this, Don Enrique of course cordially invited him to visit at their hacienda in the interior.

Talcahuana, where they intended to disembark, in order to continue their journey thence to Concepcion, came in sight, and Reiwald went to the bow of the vessel to obtain a better view of the scenery. While he was standing there and gazing upon the truly charming landscape, a voice at his side said:

"Well, how are you, Mr. Reiwald?"

"You are also on board the steamer!"

"Don Carlos!" exclaimed the young German, in surprise. "Where in Heaven's name do you come from! Have you been on board since we left Valdivia!"

"I hope you do not think that I fly!" said Meyer, laughing.

"And where is your wife!"

"My wife!—H'm," smiled Meyer, slightly embarrassed. "Well, we treat each other like children, and sometimes play hide-and-seek."

"You have run away from her!" exclaimed Reiwald, quickly.

"To tell you the truth," replied Meyer, "I did not know exactly if I should succeed in so doing, for I strongly suspected her of intending to take passage on the same steamer. But she must have missed it."

"And are you going to desert the poor woman!"

"Let me tell you, Mr. Reiwald," replied Meyer, "that she is a free woman, and I really wish that red rascal of an Indian who put her on his horse the other day had kept her. Unfortunately, the doctor's rifle did no damage, and the Indian escaped."

"But where are you going?"

"I am trying to get away from her as far and as fast as possible," said Meyer, emphatically. "At all events, I shall leave Chili, and, if possible, South America; but where I am going, I do not myself know exactly.—You are going to Concepcion?"

"For the present, perhaps only for a few days. I wish to see the city and its environs, which seem to be very beautiful."

"The scenery, eh?"

"Of course; you know I am a passionate admirer of the beauties of nature."

"You are," said Meyer, thoughtfully, while Reiwald, trying to look as unconcerned as possible, gazed upon the landscape. "Will you permit a well-wisher to give you some good advice—merely to aid your studies of natural history?"

"Certainly. What would you advise me?"

"Not to marry a Chilena."

"But, my dear Don Carlos—"

"Hush! you are in a fair way of doing so," said Meyer; "but a man's will is his hobby, and when—well, you are now forewarned," he interrupted himself. "If my example is not yet sufficient for you, you must not complain afterward."

"But I pledge you my word—"

Meyer looked him full in the face. At the same moment the engine stopped, and the anchor rattled overboard.

"You are lost!" he said. "Go ashore now, and, if you should ever cross the mountains again, present my compliments to the dear parientes.—Farewell." And, shaking hands with Reiwald, he turned and descended the staircase of the second-cabin.

Sixteen months had elapsed since the events related above had occurred, when Doctor Pfeifel at Valdivia received a letter and two large trunks. The letter read as follows:

"MY DEAR DOCTOR:

"You will be surprised on learning that I am still here at Concepcion; the reason of it is, that for three months past I have been the happiest man in all Chili, and—Irene's husband. I cannot describe to you how happy I am. By the next steamer I shall send you a detailed account of my adventures since we parted at Valdivia. For the present, let me inform you that Don Enrique, who has sold his hacienda on account of the mournful reminiscences connected with it, lives here at Concepcion. I have myself bought extensive vineyards, which I superintend in person, in the immediate environs of the city.

"Pray send the accompanying trunks in my name and that of Don Enrique, by a reliable messenger, to the Cazique Mankelaw. They contain presents for him, Allumapu, and Cruzado, and also a letter from us all.

"Pay the messenger with the money in your hands from the sale of my horses and saddles. I give you my address. Let me hear from you soon. With the most heartfelt wishes for your welfare,

"Your old friend and fellow-traveller,
"REIWALD."

THE END.

www.ingramcontent.com/pod-product-compliance
Lightning Source LLC
Chambersburg PA
CBHW032102220426
43664CB00008B/1100